Administering Informix Dynamic Server

Building the Foundation

Administering
Informix Dynamic Server

Building the Foundation

Carlton Doe

MC Press Online, LP

Lewisville, TX 75077

Administering Informix Dynamic Server: Building the Foundation
Carlton Doe

First Edition

First Printing—September 2008

MC Press offers excellent discounts on this book when ordered in quantity for bulk purchases or special sales, which may include custom covers and content particular to your business, training goals, marketing focus, and branding interest.

For information regarding permissions or special orders, please contact:
 MC Press
 Corporate Offices
 125 N. Woodland Trail
 Lewisville, TX 75077 USA

For information regarding sales and/or customer service, please contact:
 MC Press
 P.O. Box 4300
 Big Sandy, TX 75755-4300 USA

ISBN: 978-158347-076-3

To my wife, Catherine.
Words fail me. "Thank you"
can't even begin to describe my gratitude
for everything you have done
for me
and our family.
I love you.

To my children,
Whitney and her husband Tyler, Cameron, Mikhael, and Ethan.
I can't tell you how much joy you've brought me
as you've grown up and become who you are.
I am so proud of you.

I love you all (including "that boy") .

Acknowledgments

Wow! I can't believe I've finished another book. Each time I swear it will be the last, yet here's another one, and I've already committed to and started writing the follow-on to this book.

First of all, I want to thank you for purchasing this book. There are other books out there that you could have selected, but you chose this one. I realize you may even have bought it with money from your own pocket rather than a company expense account. In that case, I am especially grateful. In either case, however, I hope you'll find this book useful, a source for answers to questions you might have as well as content that will lead you to a better understanding of Informix Dynamic Server and how to use it in your environment.

As I look back from the very late 1990s to today, it's been an exciting few years to say the least. There was the internal coup at Informix, succeeded by the acquisition by IBM and all the fun and games that followed. But we, the Informix community, survived and are thriving today. Under the new thought leadership at IBM, IDS is blossoming everywhere.

Through it all, the IDS development team stayed focused on building a better data server for existing and future customers. It was the database equivalent of "if you build it, they will come." As I wrote in the dedication to my small IDS 11.10 book, I have never been more proud to be associated with and to represent the work of this development organization. They have produced incredible new features, such as MACH-11 and double-digit performance gains, while making the data server even easier to administer — if you need to do so at all! I am so excited about what is coming in the next releases and how much better the server is becoming.

It's because of the massive resurgence of IDS within IBM and the market in general that I decided to write this book and the one that will follow it. Existing and potential customers, as well as the competition, know IDS is back and back to stay. I wanted to do my part to help support and grow the IDS community.

Writing a book like this isn't easy, even if you've done it a couple of times before. There were seemingly unending late nights (along with countless deep sighs) when I had to force myself to look into the monitor and produce at least one page. Other times, the words seemed to flow from my fingers, and I had to force myself to stop in order to get some sleep before going to work later in the morning. In both cases, I ate a lot of Costco whole, dry blueberries. They are, in my opinion, the perfect writing snack food.

Thankfully, I didn't have to go it alone; many others made significant contributions or provided support. At the great risk of forgetting someone, I would like to acknowledge and pay tribute to those who made this book possible.

First, thank you to all the Informix engineers who answered my questions and kept me honest technically, especially John Miller, Jonathan Leffler, Jacques Roy, Scott Pickett, Mark Jamison, Guy Bowerman, Amit Dandekar, Charles Gonsalves, and Paul-John To. Thanks to Edgar Sanchez, Mark Jamison, Sudhir Katke, Randy House, Suma Vinod, and Sanjit Chakraborty for reviewing the manuscript for technical warts.

I am always indebted to Jacques Roy for his great work and expertise. He took my table sizing guidelines and created the Java methods you can download from the Web site supporting this book. He even put up with my massacring his code when I added a few tweaks because I'm a "bear of very little brain" and couldn't follow his logic.

Thank you to Jerry Keesee for taking time out of his insane schedule to write the Foreword, as well as for the career and other guidance he's given me.

Susan Visser in IBM Publishing has been a stalwart supporter and advocate for IDS books and my efforts to get this and my earlier IDS books published. Cathy Elliott is the high priestess/"wizardess" of the IBM Marketing world (yes, I know the female form of "wizard" is "witch," but she isn't one of those). The programs, initiatives, collateral, and support for IDS that Cathy can pull out of the hat just amazes me. She has always been one of my biggest supporters, and I appreciate her help. Finally, Michael Spano, my current manager, lets me run (almost) wild doing whatever I want to do, wherever I want to do it. Thanks for staying out of my way and shielding me from as much of the IBM garbage as possible.

In the greater International Informix Users Group (IIUG) community, a number of people have been very helpful and supportive, including Lester Knutsen, Walt Hultgen, Stuart Litel, Cindy Lichtenauer, Alexander Koerner, and many others. Thank you to Rob Partlow for the C program that ultimately didn't get used.

On the publication side — look, Merrikay, it's finally done! I was just a little late vis-à-vis my deadline. As publisher, you kept calling me in Argentina and other places during the last half of 2007 asking for a status report, and the news was never good. Thank you for your patience and for suffering through with me. The next one will be better, I promise.

If you find this book easy and fun to read, the kudos go to Katie Tipton. I have worked with several copy editors over the years but none as good as Katie. She refined my ramblings into a document I really enjoyed reading even though I've been living with it and reviewing it time and time again for months. She took a holistic approach (no, I'm not referring to a medicinal practice) rather than a chapter-by-chapter view and was able to correct a number of logical structural flaws in the manuscript. She even caught syntax and other errors that the technical reviewers and I missed. Finally, she was just nice to work with. Thank you for your amazing work and the liberal amounts of polish you applied so the work shines the way it does.

As I write this, the cover design process is just starting, and I've provided some cover ideas that are completely out of the norm for MC Press. Nevertheless, Jeff Phillips is excited to try and pull it together for me. Although it may appear to be vanity to some, a great-looking cover is important.

In closing, my family has never meant more to me than they do now. The kids are all well into the teenage years or young adulthood; one has even flown the coop to start her own family with a tremendous guy. Although there are occasions when I'd like to give one or more of those remaining a solid boot to the backside, I am amazed at how all of them have turned out and at what great young people they are. I am so proud of you and the wonderful things you are doing and achieving. My wife, Catherine, has played no small part in this process with the love, support, guidance, and protection she has given them. How she has managed to take care of them and suffer through twenty-something years with me defies all understanding and reason. Thank you for everything. My love to all of you. And, Daniel, that includes you, too.

—*Carlton Doe*
July 2008

Contents

Foreword

The fact that you're holding this book in your hands means you either are discovering or have already discovered the world's premier OLTP database. As the director of Informix development, I can't tell you I'm unbiased, but I can say that I'm uniquely qualified to testify to the incredible innovation and level of excellence that goes into every aspect of this product. For the last 15 years, I've had the good fortune to work with some of the most talented engineers, support staff, writers, and field specialists in the world. The evolution of technology and hardware over recent decades has been exponential. SOA, Web 2.0, and the 3-D Internet have all become a reality. At every turn, this amazing group of architects and engineers has anticipated and addressed your business challenges (as well as leveraged the opportunities that evolution provides!). This book is a portal into Informix innovation and functionality—including the most recent enhancements and updates—with a clear and relevant perspective that reflects Carlton Doe's many years of experience with IDS.

I've known Carlton 10 years. Over that time (and more), he's contributed multiple excellent books on Informix. He has a unique combination of extensive Informix knowledge and experience along with the capability to articulate his understanding in writing and as an educator. This book is a great resource for both new and existing users. Carlton's approach is informed by his personal experience and assumes the viewpoint of someone using the product in a typical end-to-end scenario: initialization and installation through administration, backup, and monitoring. The book also includes information about recently added Informix features—right up through the current IDS 11 releases.

From the beginning, Informix was built on a simple promise: to deliver industry-leading enterprise OLTP capabilities within an architecture that provides the absolute lowest total cost of ownership. Others may claim it—we deliver it! Our unique and proprietary architecture enables blazing performance, embeddability, and scalability, all with minimal administration overhead. Selecting the right database can give significant competitive advantage, and when the decision is based on technology, Informix is the choice of leaders. You may not realize how much of your world is already running on Informix. Informix runs your grocery or retail store, manages your online bank transactions, and processes your credit card authorizations. It handles lifesaving calls to 911. Catch a bus in Seattle, use your GPS to get around London, or book an airline flight—you're using Informix. Almost every telco router in the world relies on Informix, as does the Konkan Railway system in India, large financial institutions in China, and, in New Zealand, the largest dairy exporter in the world. There are many, many other applications I am not allowed to talk about. Because of its phenomenal availability and reliability, Informix is favored in mission-critical applications worldwide. Software vendors know that they can deploy their solutions on top of Informix without worrying who's going to administer it or how they'll keep the system up and running 24x7.

No one in the industry can match our breadth of solutions where customers achieve 99.999 percent availability and are able to easily scale out on low-cost commodity hardware. IDS 11 has elevated Informix to a new level of availability and scalability with active–active clusters sharing the same disk or managing workload on replicas located around the world. This functionality may sound complex, but it is designed and built into Informix from the ground up, with easy GUI administration, letting customers scale in minutes without complicated add-ons. It doesn't matter what platform you run your business on. Informix is available on all the leading hardware vendors: Linux, Unix, Windows, Linux for zSeries, and even Mac OS X. Here at IBM, we're leading the charge with Outside In Design and Agile Development, which expands our capability to respond on demand to business needs. Our incredible (and continually expanding) base of customers and business partners works directly with us on each release to help form the product direction. And a really cool thing: when you couple our visionary database technology and world-class developers with the powerhouse infrastructure, innovation, and momentum of a company like IBM, you're looking at an infinite horizon for Informix.

In this book, Carlton Doe has done an amazing job—yet again—of encapsulating Informix technology in a highly consumable format. He has a gift for clearly describing Informix Dynamic Server in a way that's accessible across the array of Informix enthusiasts. Enjoy this book. I hope the information within it will give you additional insight into the amazing work of the worldwide Informix community here at IBM.

Jerry Keesee
Director of Informix Development
IBM

About This Book

Because you are reading this book, I can assume you are either a Database Administrator (DBA) or someone responsible for maintaining one or more Informix Dynamic Server (IDS) database environments—what I call a Dynamic Server Administrator (DSA). What I don't know is whether you are new to IDS or, if you're not, how much experience you have with it. Perhaps you've worked with the Unix ports of less-capable data servers but now find yourself having to install and administer IDS. In doing so, you find that it's a whole new world. Or maybe this is the first time you've used an industrial-strength data server, having upgraded from some semi-featured, PC-oriented product. Now that you need some serious reliability, functionality, and speed, you're installing Informix Dynamic Server and wondering what to do next. For you, too, it will be a new world.

If you're like me, opening the box containing the IDS software distribution was both exciting and a little daunting. I was excited to get my hands on what is widely regarded as the fastest and best-architected data server on the market today. I wanted to try it out, kick the tires a little, see how well it performed. At the same time, I went to the Informix documentation site and was intimidated by the number and size of the manuals. A quick look revealed 32 books and nearly 9,000 pages—and that's just for the core data server, without factoring in the manuals for additional options, such as DataBlades. Was this data server so complicated that it required this much explanation?

The answer to that question is both a yes and a no. Yes, Informix Dynamic Server is more sophisticated than other data servers on the market today and, as a result, has more options you can use. You do not, on the other hand, have to ingest the entire documentation set to run or tune the data server. The documentation is there to explain, often down to the bits-and-bytes level, what IDS does and why so you can be a better DBA or DSA. To its credit, the IDS documentation is fairly complete, easy to understand, and extensive when it comes to explaining and illustrating the concepts involved in setting up and administering databases and the environments in which they exist.

Book Structure

In this book, I try to take the dry technical details in the documentation and put them into the context of daily life. I cover topics in what I think is their logical order of occurrence when working with a database environment. First, you design the environment; then you build and populate it. You create backups on a regular basis and monitor and tune as necessary. There are other responsibilities and functions, but these are the most important. I used this approach to build the subjects discussed in each chapter.

This book isn't intended to cover every single feature or mechanism of Informix Dynamic Server. Instead, it is designed to help you through the process of starting up and running database environments. You'll find it covers all the important and most commonly used features you will need on a regular basis. A future book, *Administering Informix Dynamic Server, Advanced Topics,* will address more advanced topics, including replication, high availability, distributed transactions, and other subjects that require a more extensive explanation. I think you should know about and be able to use those features, too, so I encourage you to get that book as well.

Intended Audience

This book is written at a high to medium level in terms of technical detail and is focused toward those who either are new to Informix Dynamic Server or are converting from earlier versions. I have purposely avoided the bits-and-bytes stuff as much as possible. For that level of understanding, consult the *IBM Informix Dynamic Server Administrator's Guide* and the other reference material in the IDS documentation library.

Even though much of what I cover here is explained somewhere in the manuals, do not assume this book is intended to replace the formal documentation. Nor should you think of this book as simply an overview of what the formal documentation provides. The recommendations and guidance given here are the result of years of personal experience with Informix Dynamic Server. You won't find this hands-on experience reflected in the formal documentation.

I do make one major assumption in writing this book: that you have a good understanding of the relational database model and the concepts of tables, columns, and other components of relational databases. To this foundation, you will be able to add the knowledge and experience you'll gain using the object-oriented features of IDS.

Book Summary

Chapter 1 – Introduction to Informix Dynamic Server

Chapter 1 covers the general design of the IDS data server. Terms and keywords used extensively throughout the rest of the book are also introduced and defined here.

Chapter 2 – An Introduction to Extensibility

This chapter explores the object-relational features and capabilities of Informix Dynamic Server.

Chapter 3 – Preparing for Initialization

In this chapter, I cover many of the topics you need to address from a design perspective when planning for the implementation of an IDS environment. For the most part, the discussion is general in scope because there are few hard and fast rules to follow when building a database environment. Where rules do exist, they are stated. At the close of the chapter, I explain the required environment variables, files, and other objects as well as how to set them up.

Chapter 4 – Installing and Initializing IDS

This chapter covers all the steps and configuration parameters for creating an IDS database environment or instance, with specific recommendations given for the most critical configuration parameters. At the end, I introduce the system-level databases that manage and control an IDS environment. This chapter is very detail-oriented, as opposed to the earlier, more concept-oriented chapters.

Chapter 5 – Basic Administrative Tasks

In this chapter, I explain most of the general day-to-day, or occasional, instance-oriented administrative tasks. These include adding or dropping disk space, starting up or shutting down the instance, and killing user sessions in the instance. The major graphical administration tools are introduced as an alternative to performing many of these tasks using the command line.

Chapter 6 – Building a Database Environment

In this chapter, I trade my DSA's hat for that of a DBA and cover building and populating databases in IDS instances. The chapter explains features such as table and index partitioning, constraints, logging, database and table population utilities, and a collection of IDS-specific SQL statements that are interesting to know about and use.

Chapter 7 – Backing Up and Restoring

One of the least glamorous, but still important, functions of operating a database environment is backing up what's on disk to tape. In this chapter, I cover a couple of backup strategies and their relative strengths and weaknesses. I explain how Informix Dynamic Server can execute moment-in-time backup and restore operations with the database environment online and fully functioning. The chapter also covers the process of executing backup and restore operations using the **ontape** utility, as well as the **ON-Bar** utility suite with the Informix Storage Manager (ISM), in great detail.

Chapter 8 – Monitoring the Instance

Throughout the book, discussions make reference to, and include illustrations of, output generated by the various IDS monitoring commands. In the final chapter, I focus exclusively on those commands and some of the more commonly monitored activities of a database environment. I concentrate primarily on IDS's command-line utilities as well as the functionality available in the new OpenAdmin Tool for IDS (OAT).

Conventions Used in This Book

In preparing this book, I used the following conventions:

- Each chapter begins with a general list of topics to be covered.
- Each chapter ends by briefly summarizing the most important points you should remember and then introducing the topics to be discussed in the next chapter.
- Reserved words in source code examples are not capitalized. I find that loading source code with capitalized words produces code that is more difficult to read and makes it hard to find important points of interest that the developer might have wanted me to easily see. Personally, I limit capitalized words to source code comments, when I want to call attention to an important word or instruction. This is an easier and less time-consuming way to highlight such information than building some sort of window box.
- You occasionally will see the slash (\) character used as a continuation marker in code examples that had to be broken into multiple lines to accommodate the width of the book page. In reality, you would execute these operations as one unbroken instruction string.

- Throughout the book, additional notes or points of special information are called out through the following notation:

- Warnings or other important messages are called out using this notation:

WARNING

1

Introduction to Informix Dynamic Server

In this Chapter

▸ Understanding the server's architecture

▸ Definition of key terms

By virtue of the fact that you're reading this book, either you are new to Informix Dynamic Server (IDS) or you're migrating from an earlier version of the data server and want to know how to use and manage the new functionality available to you. In either case, you're in for a good learning experience. There's a lot involved in understanding how this database server operates and how to make it perform in your particular environment.

The intent of this book is to make the learning process easier by distilling for you what you really need to know to configure, run, and tune a database environment using Informix Dynamic Server. Although at first glance IDS may seem similar to other data server products, this server is in fact unlike any other. It won't take you long to see that IDS is far more advanced technologically as well as more stable, easier to administer, and more robust than competing servers.

IDS 11, the focus of this book, is both very much like earlier versions of the product and also radically different. Version 11 incorporates significant new technology built on a completely modified server architecture introduced with IDS 9.1. Yet for all the changes, the server is still managed and operates as before—in many cases, it's even easier to administer!

Today's IDS is not a "regular" data server as many people might classify it; rather, it is an "object-relational" server. IDS includes high-performance core server technology developed in the early 1990s to take advantage of emerging symmetric multiprocessing (SMP) and massively parallel processing (MPP) technology, and it has been continually enhanced since then. The biggest enhancement was the addition of object-oriented database functionality throughout the server in 1995. This feature completely changed how DBAs and application developers can and should model and use data within their databases and applications. IDS now offers many more tools and options than the standard, relational-only data servers.

This chapter introduces the architecture of the data server and its three main components. We'll also go over some key terminology that is either unique to Informix Dynamic Server or has a new or different meaning when used with this product. By the end of the chapter, you should understand why the product has the name it does, what a thread is, and what the fundamental components of the data server are.

This book assumes you have some level of familiarity with the SQL language and with standard relational and object-oriented database concepts. However, we won't engage in a heavy bits-and-bytes discussion. If you need that level of detail, consult the documentation accompanying your distribution of the software or visit IBM's Informix Web site.

What Is Informix Dynamic Server?

Informix Dynamic Server is a data server—or, to use a marketing buzzword, an *object-relational database management system (ORDBMS)*. The server can work both with "standard" (or relational) data types, such as character and numeric values, and with object-oriented data types. This new technology is an extension to the ability the server has had for years to store nonnumeric or non-ASCII data in binary large objects (BLOBs). Today, IDS can do more than just write the binary stream to disk as it does with simple BLOBs. Using the appropriate functions, you can not only store the data "object" but also manipulate, search, alter, and correlate it; you can execute any operation against it that makes sense for the data and is provided by the function. This new functionality and associated data type support is commonly referred to as *extensibility* and *extensible* data types.

In general terms, though, the server's job is to provide an environment whereby data can be stored, retrieved, changed, and deleted in such a way that data itself is not lost, compromised, or modified outside the rules established by the data server or the database administrator. IDS contains both logical and physical mechanisms to accomplish these tasks.

From a logical point of view, IDS provides the ability to set rules and conditions governing not only the acceptable range of values for a column in a table but also where a row will be stored on disk. You can specify the conditions that must exist for data elements in the row to be modified or deleted. You can set up procedures to be invoked automatically and execute specific database actions to enforce still other rules when data in a table or column is added, modified, or deleted.

From a physical point of view, IDS keeps a series of logs that record changes made to data as they occur and provides a locking mechanism you can use to ensure that data requested by one user session can't be changed or deleted by another. The data server can create copies, in whole or in part, of database environments, either within the same physical server or on a separate server, to minimize the impact of a physical server failure, to distribute/collect data between database environments, to enable load balancing, or to provide continuous availability of data services. Last, IDS provides the ability to create backups of database environments that can be used to restore some or all of a database environment should a mechanical failure or user error occur. You can even configure the restore to stop at a specific point in time so the user error doesn't recur, permitting full data recovery up to the moment the operation took place. Other recently added functionality enables restoring a backup created on one physical server to another physical server even if the second server isn't using the same operating system (O/S).

Built on the widely heralded Dynamic Scalable Architecture (DSA), the IDS data server was designed to run on, and take advantage of, today's computer systems with multiple physical CPUs and larger memory stores. In fact, field studies have shown that as more physical resources (e.g., CPUs) are added to the system, IDS performance increases linearly.

Central to the design of DSA and its functionality is a concept called *process parallelization*, or the processing of compatible tasks in parallel. The general SQL-processing mechanism of the data server is built to work in smaller, discrete steps. These steps are allocated across the CPU resources so that they occur more or less simultaneously, or in parallel. Figure 1.1 shows how this process works from a conceptual point of view.

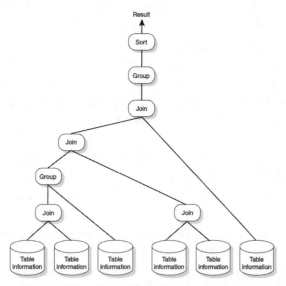

Figure 1.1: A conceptual illustration of parallel query processing

The figure illustrates how a query might be executed in parallel. At the beginning of the process, a series of disk reads occurs. The results from this step, and from every other in the process, are passed in real time up the processing ladder of functional operations. At each level of the process, there are fewer rows to work with, and the results generated by each operation are joined with the results of the other operations at the same level. Eventually, the data server returns the final result to the application in what amounts to significantly less time than if the query process executed the steps serially, waiting for each step to be completed before beginning the next step, and with larger amounts of data.

In addition to processing SQL operations more quickly, IDS executes most administrative functions—such as building indexes, updating database statistical information, and checking and potentially repairing the database system after a failure—in parallel as well. This type of functionality brings with it the responsibility to monitor and tune for it. As the data server administrator, you must set the resource limitations within which parallel processing of queries and other activities must occur. Look for coverage of this topic and other advanced tuning operations in the companion to this book, *Administering Informix Dynamic Server, Advanced Topics*.

Another key feature of IDS's architecture is the ability of the server to allocate and release physical server resources dynamically when necessary. For example, you might configure an IDS database environment to use x MB of system RAM, y data locks, and so on when the database environment starts. If the data processing load spikes, IDS will try to secure more system resources (e.g., memory) to handle the increased load rather than fail due to insufficient resources. Knowing that IDS's attempt to obtain additional system resources is not unbounded, you can set explicit boundaries to the resources that the database environment can take from the system.

Finally, you can adjust most IDS database environment configuration parameters while the database environment is online and processing user transactions. IBM continues to enhance this functionality with every release of the data server, and it is nearly complete now. IDS's ability to intelligently self-manage required resources and be administered without interruption accounts for the word "dynamic" in the product's name.

With the addition of object-oriented technology, IDS delivers proven functionality that efficiently integrates new and complex data types directly into the database. It handles time-series, spatial, geodetic, Extensible Markup Language (XML), video, image, and other user-defined data side by side with traditional legacy data to meet today's most rigorous data and business demands. IDS is also a development-neutral environment that supports a comprehensive array of application development tools for rapid deployment of applications under Linux, Unix, Apple Mac OS X, and Microsoft Windows operating environments.

The Informix Dynamic Server Model

Data server architecture is a significant differentiator and contributor to IDS's performance, scalability, and ability to support new data types and processing requirements. Nearly all data servers available today use an older technological design that requires each database operation for an individual user (e.g., read, sort, write, communications tasks) to invoke a separate operating system process. This architecture worked well when database sizes and user counts were relatively small. Today, these types of servers spawn many hundreds, even thousands, of individual processes that the operating system must create, queue, schedule, manage/control, and then terminate when they're no longer needed. Given that, generally speaking, any individual system CPU can work on only one thing at a time—and that the operating system must work on each process before returning to the top of the queue—this data server architecture creates an environment in which individual database operations must wait for one or more passes through the queue to complete their task. Scalability with this type of architecture has nothing to do with the software; it depends entirely on the speed of the processor—how fast it can work through the queue before it starts over again.

As I mentioned in the previous section, the Dynamic Scalable Architecture on which Informix Dynamic Server is built was designed to work with multiple physical CPUs and larger memory stores to create an operating environment with greater data server performance and improved stability. The DSA includes built-in multithreading and parallel-processing capabilities, dynamic and self-tuning shared memory components, and intelligent logical data storage capabilities, supporting the most efficient use of all available system resources. Three major functional components make up the architectural model for Informix Dynamic Server:

- The processor component
- The shared memory component
- The disk component

Let's look at each of these pieces individually.

The Processor Component

IDS provides the unique ability to scale the database environment by employing a dynamically configurable pool of data server processes called *virtual processors (VPs)*. (Look for a in-depth explanation of exactly how VPs work in *Administering Informix Dynamic Server, Advanced Topics.*) As you saw in Figure 1.1, IDS takes a database operation such as a sorted data query and segments it into task-oriented subtasks (data scan, join, group, sort) for rapid processing by virtual processors that specialize in each type of subtask. VPs mimic the functionality of the hardware CPUs in that they schedule and manage user requests using multiple, concurrent threads. Figure 1.2 illustrates how IDS's pool of virtual processors operate.

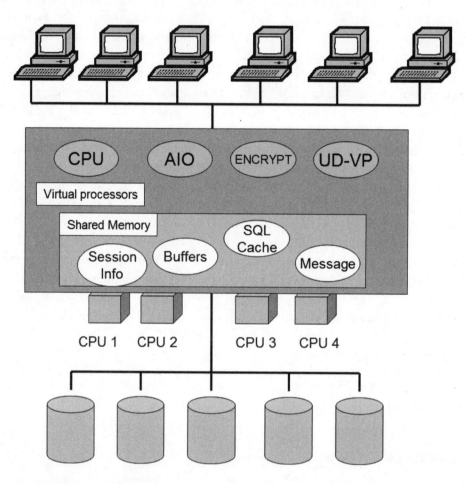

Figure 1.2: IDS virtual processor pool

A *thread* represents a discrete task within a data server process. Multiple threads can execute simultaneously, in parallel, across the pool of virtual processors. Unlike a CPU process-based (or single-threaded) engine, which leaves each task on the system CPU for its given unit of time (even if no work can be done, thus wasting processing time), IDS's virtual processors are multithreaded. As a consequence, when a thread either is waiting for a resource or has completed its task, a thread switch occurs and the virtual processor immediately begins work on another thread. As a result, precious CPU processing power is used to satisfy as many user requests as possible in the given amount of time. Figure 1.3 illustrates this capability, known as *fan-in parallelism*.

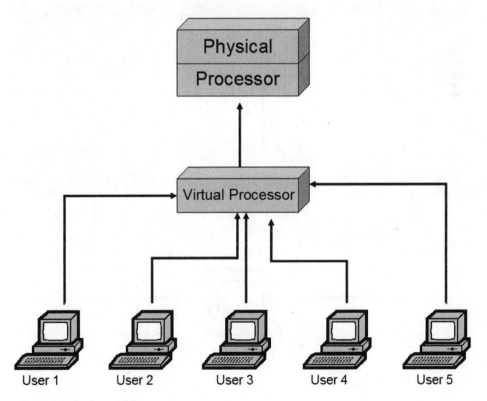

Figure 1.3: Fan-in parallelism

Not only can one virtual processor respond to multiple user requests in any given unit of time, as this figure illustrates, but one user request also can be distributed across multiple virtual processors. For example, with a processing-intensive request such as a multitable join, the data server divides the task into multiple subtasks and then spreads these subtasks across all available virtual processors. With the ability to distribute tasks, the request is completed more quickly. Figure 1.4 illustrates this capability, referred to as *fan-out parallelism*.

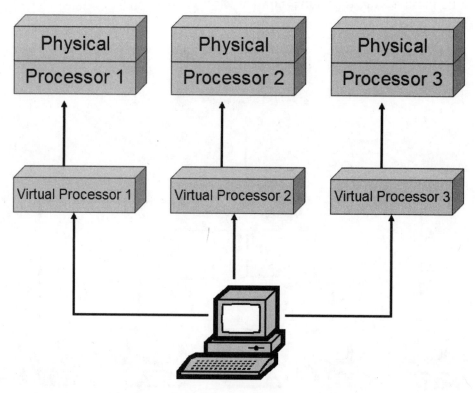

Figure 1.4: Fan-out parallelism

The net effect of IDS's two types of parallelism is more work being accomplished more quickly than with single-threaded architectures. In other words, the data server is faster.

Because threads aren't statically assigned to virtual processors, load balancing occurs dynamically within IDS. Outstanding requests are serviced by the first available virtual processor, balancing the workload across all available resources. For efficient execution and versatile tuning, you can group VPs into classes, each optimized for a particular function. Figure 1.5 illustrates this capability, showing VPs optimized for CPU operations, disk I/O, communications, administrative, and other tasks.

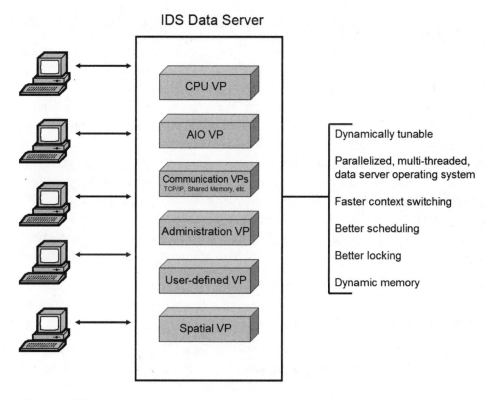

Figure 1.5: IDS virtual processors optimized for specific functions

The design of IDS's VPs also includes administrative access, resulting in the ability to easily look at and analyze the activities requested by users and the data server. With single-threaded servers, each operation is a separate and independent operating system process with its own data stack, instruction cache, and other O/S overhead, making it difficult to build a comprehensive view of what's happening inside the data server. In contrast, IDS's **onstat** and **oncheck** administrative utilities gather information from the database environment's shared resources and can easily display who is doing what and how much of an impact it's having on the system.

You can configure the database environment with the appropriate number of VPs in each class to handle the expected workload for that environment. You can even define custom VPs to be used only for specific functions. Called *user-defined virtual processors (UDVPs)*, these VPs have the same processing power as the database environment's core CPU VPs but are isolated from operating on core functionality. With this separation, if the user function that a UDVP is executing "misbehaves," the function can't intentionally or unintentionally cause an abnormal shutdown.

If necessary, you can also adjust the number and type of VPs while the database environment is online, without interrupting database operations—for example, to handle different load mixes or occasional periods of heavy activity. In Linux, Mac OS X, and Unix systems, the use of multithreaded virtual processors significantly reduces the number of O/S processes, requiring less context switching as a result. Windows systems implement VPs as threads to take advantage of the inherent multithreading capability of the operating system. Because IDS includes its own threading capability for servicing client requests, it requires fewer Windows threads, reducing the system thread-scheduling overhead and providing better throughput.

In making full use of the hardware processing cycles, IDS needs less hardware power to achieve performance comparable to or better than that of other database servers. In fact, real-world tests and customer experiences indicate IDS needs only 25 percent to 40 percent of the hardware resources to meet or exceed the performance characteristics of single-threaded or process-based data servers. This efficiency means your business can save money on hardware purchases as well as on ongoing maintenance.

The Shared Memory Component

With the consolidation of tasks and processes into VPs, all the memory used by the data server is consolidated as well. This large, single block of shared memory enables IDS to transfer data easily among the VPs. It also lets other user connections determine whether the data they need has already been queried by another user and can be used for their request, rather than having to go out to disk to get it. The memory inside this block is used and reused as needed to process user connections. When a user session terminates, the thread-specific memory for the session is freed and reused by another session.

If the database environment requires more memory to process its workload, the data server allocates additional blocks of memory dynamically from the operating system until it reaches the limit set during the database environment's configuration. When the need for the additional memory is gone, the additional segments of memory are released. You can make similar changes manually while the database environment is running. This ability to dynamically add and release memory helps eliminate down time to retune the environment as the workload increases and decreases. Released memory is returned to the general O/S pool for use by other processes, further enhancing the efficiency of the server's use of shared memory.

Four areas, or *portions*, make up Informix Dynamic Server's shared memory component:

- The resident portion
- The virtual portion
- The message portion
- The virtual-extension portion

When you start a database environment, at least two, and possibly all four, portions are allocated, according to the shared memory and connection configuration parameters set during the initialization process and the server functionality used. Chapter 4 provides more information about the shared memory configuration parameters. The following sections briefly describe the portions of the IDS shared memory component.

The Resident Portion

The *resident portion* of IDS's shared memory contains, among other things, general database environment information and the buffer pool that holds data operated on by user or database environment activities. Several system-wide structures are maintained in this part of shared memory. The logical and physical log buffer caches are here, as well as the system tables, which maintain information about chunks, dbspaces, locks, user connections, transactions, and mirrors. The system tables are accessible to queries through the System Monitoring Interface (which you'll learn about in Chapter 4). If you've enabled High-Availability Data Replication (HDR), the replication buffer is also stored in the resident portion of shared memory. You'll find more details on HDR as well as Enterprise Replication in *Administering Informix Dynamic Server, Advanced Topics*.

The biggest part of the resident portion consists of the data buffers used to store queried or modified data for user applications. Depending on the types of operations executed, these buffers can help eliminate a lot of disk I/O. When users request data, the data server first tries to locate the data in the buffer pool to avoid unnecessary disk I/Os. Depending on the characteristics of the database workload, increasing the buffer pool size can significantly reduce the number of disk accesses, which in turn can considerably improve performance, particularly for online transaction processing (OLTP) applications.

IDS holds frequently used table or index data in the buffer pool using a scorecard system. As each element is used, its score increases. Part of the buffer system holds the high-score elements, while the remainder holds less frequently used data. This segmentation of high- and low-use data is completely transparent to the application, which experiences in-memory response times regardless of which part of the buffer pool contains the requested element. As data elements are used less often, they are migrated from the high-use to the low-use portion. Data buffers in this area are flushed and reused through a first-in, first-out (FIFO) process.

Before IDS 10, all buffers were the same size: either 2 KB or 4 KB, depending on the operating system. The buffers were the same size as the "pages" on disk, permitting a buffer to cache one disk page. IDS 10 provided the ability to define regular data dbspaces with varying page sizes in multiples of the default page size up to 16 KB in size. To continue caching one page to a buffer, the data server will allocate a buffer pool for each page size in the resident portion of shared memory if you create dbspaces with different page sizes. Only one set of buffers will exist for each page size, though, so if you create three dbspaces using an 8 KB page size, they will share one 8 KB buffer pool.

The **BUFFERPOOL**, **BUFFERS**, **LRU** (Least Recently Used), and other configuration parameters determine the number of buffers and how they are allocated. With the addition of recovery time objectives, the data server itself can manage these parameters for you, eliminating work you used to do in earlier IDS versions.

Because the resident portion holds end-user data, it will always exist in every IDS database environment.

The Virtual Portion

The *virtual portion* of shared memory contains *thread stacks*, or thread-specific instructions, for the processing of each thread. Along with the thread stacks, IDS maintains pointers to the data that the thread is using in the buffer pool of the resident portion. The virtual portion of shared memory contains pools of memory for the following tasks and items:

- Sorting data
- Caching database dictionaries that hold information about the tables and indexes in the environment's databases
- Caches from user-defined routines
- The big buffer pools for the asynchronous I/O (AIO) VPs
- Storage of compiled versions of stored procedures

- The "global" pool to handle network protocol–based application communications
- Some memory-based tables used to monitor various aspects of the environment

The virtual portion also holds cached disk-access plans for the IDS cost-based optimizer. In most OLTP environments, the same SQL operations are executed throughout the processing day, albeit with slightly different variable conditions (e.g., customer number, invoice number). Each time an SQL operation is executed, the data server optimizer must determine the fastest way to access the data. Obviously, if the data is already cached in the buffer system, it is retrieved from there; if it is not, disk access is required. When this occurs, the optimizer has to decide on the quickest way to get the requested data. It needs to evaluate whether an index exists that points directly to the requested data or whether the data has been intelligently partitioned on disk, restricting the potential number of dbspaces to look through. When joining data from several tables, the optimizer evaluates which table will provide the data the others will join to, and so on. Although not really noticeable to users, these tasks take time to execute and affect response time.

Informix Dynamic Server provides a caching mechanism whereby data I/O plans can be stored for reuse by subsequent executions of the same operation. Called, appropriately enough, the SQL statement cache, this allocation of memory stores the SQL statement and the optimizer's determination of the fastest way to execute the operation. You can configure the size of this cache as well as when an individual SQL operation is cached (e.g., the first time, after two executions). To prevent filling the cache with single-use operations, most configurations cache an operation after it has been executed three or more times. You can also flush the cache so the query plans are refreshed if needed while processing continues. You would take this step after execution of the **update statistics** commands, for example.

Another interesting component of the virtual portion is the big buffer pool. Earlier versions of the data server had two types of buffers: regular and big. The regular buffers acted much as the buffers stored in the resident portion of IDS do now, but for every 100 regular buffers, earlier versions of the data server would allocate a single big buffer. The big buffer was eight data pages in size and was used to buffer large sequential reads or large writes, such as simple BLOB writes.

Today, a big buffer is allocated for each AIO VP. The buffer's size varies by operating system, but at 32 pages it is significantly larger than in earlier IDS versions. This larger size enables the big buffer to more efficiently service the sorting of writes during a checkpoint or the reading in of larger amounts of data for complicated analytical queries. Once data is read into the big buffer, it is reallocated to the regular buffer pool in the resident portion of shared memory for actual use. Because of the potential size of a simple BLOB, IDS handles the reading or writing of this type of object through the big buffer rather than through the regular buffer pool. (We'll review some of this terminology, including data page, checkpoint, and BLOB, later in the chapter.)

The virtual portion of shared memory expands and contracts as needed depending on the amount of memory required to accomplish its tasks—this is the dynamic portion of shared memory I spoke of earlier. You set the initial size of the virtual portion using the **SHMVIRTSIZE** configuration parameter. The **SHMADD** parameter controls the size of the additional segments added to this portion of shared memory. A third parameter, **SHMTOTAL**, controls the total amount of shared memory the database environment can allocate (which includes both portions).

The virtual portion of shared memory will always exist in every IDS database environment.

The Message Portion

Unlike the two portions of shared memory we've just covered, the *message portion* is created only if a co-resident application connection protocol is activated for the database environment. The message portion contains the buffers for exchanging information to and from local client applications running on the same physical server and connecting to the database environment via a shared memory connection.

You must define every connection protocol you want to use to connect to databases managed by IDS. If you've enabled a shared memory connection protocol, local applications connecting to the database server through this protocol leave messages requesting data or other actions and retrieve data or confirmation messages from previous requests in the message portion of IDS shared memory. This same type of communications process occurs for network protocol–based application connections, although not through this part of shared memory. (I'll explain this point further in conjunction with the **NETTYPE** configuration parameter in Chapter 4. Briefly, with connections based on network protocols, the listener thread passes messages and data to and from the global pool in the virtual portion of shared memory.)

The Virtual-Extension Portion

The *virtual-extension portion* of shared memory performs two functions. First, if a DataBlade or a user-defined routine (UDR) is executing against a UDVP, the data server isolates the data for these functions from the rest of the buffer pools. In doing so, it protects the main pools from potential corruption should the UDR misbehave and either execute a command detrimental to the health of the database environment or just die and corrupt the buffer structure. IDS creates and maintains the buffer pools to cache data for these functions in the virtual-extension portion of shared memory.

As I noted previously, if the virtual portion needs to expand, it tries to dynamically request additional memory from the operating system. Additional memory for the virtual-extension portion is created in and managed through the virtual portion, and it, too, dynamically expands and contracts as needed.

Depending on the current workload and functionality used, the virtual-extension portion may or may not exist in an IDS environment.

The Disk Component

In most installations of Informix Dynamic Server on Unix and similar operating systems, the data server itself, rather than the O/S, manages all interactions between the disks storing data and the database environment. The data storage elements are usually built using disk partitions devoid of a file system, known as *raw disk space*.

By their very nature, storage elements created in Unix raw space are guaranteed to be contiguous. The data server reads from and writes to these disks through Direct Memory Access (DMA) calls and Raw Sequential Access Method (RSAM) mechanisms. Because RSAM mechanisms are so much better suited to database-oriented disk activity than the Unix file system and its series of write buffers, significantly better performance has been achieved by letting the data server, rather than the operating system, manage database disk operations. Performance improves even more if the O/S supports kernel asynchronous I/O (KAIO), or the ability to process several I/O operations at the same time without having to wait for a response back from the I/O subsystem.

Database storage elements can also be created using regular O/S file system files, space referred to as *cooked space*. Using cooked space does not guarantee, however, that the disk blocks used to create the storage element(s) will be contiguous; in fact, you can be assured they will not be. This characteristic does have an impact on the overall performance of disk-oriented activities.

Some operating systems, such as Windows, use unbuffered and noncached I/O to communicate with cooked disk spaces. As a result, although you can use raw disk space in a Windows environment, doing so provides no significant performance benefit. With IDS 11, support for using O/S-based unbuffered I/O is expanding to other operating systems. For those environments that need the ability to manage all aspects of disk use with standard file system tools, this functionality (if supported on your port of the data server) may be able to provide near raw-disk speed with flat-file-based chunks and dbspaces.

Truth be told, this functionality is not exclusive to IDS. Although some data servers support only cooked storage elements created in file systems, others support both raw and cooked. Where IDS shines is in its ability to intelligently distribute data based on rules within the disk subsystem. IDS supports a number of partitioning schemes to improve the ability to quickly isolate and retrieve or modify data. This same functionality also permits much higher data availability, concurrency, and the easy management of older, less-used data (sometimes called *data life-cycle management*).

Several physical and logical divisions occur with disk drives to actually make up this component of the engine. To put these elements in their proper context, I need to introduce some additional terms. The next section covers these key words and some others you need to know to understand the data server's disk component. Chapter 3 provides an in-depth continuation of the discussion of this component.

Key Terminology

Throughout this book, I'll be using some key terms and phrases that either are unique to Informix Dynamic Server or have new or different meanings as far as this product is concerned. Before we go too much further, let me define some of the more common keywords I haven't used yet and describe how they apply to IDS. As you read the book, it might appear as though many of these keywords are, or could be, used interchangeably. This is not the case. To avoid ambiguity in terms of scope or precision, I will be careful to use the proper term in the proper context. I will also refrain from using computational slang that might be misleading, especially to those who are new to using this product.

Throughout the book, I'll be referring to "instances" and occasionally to a "data server." A *data server* is the compiled source code that you purchased a license for and which is loaded on your physical server; it is Informix Dynamic Server. This server contains all the utilities and programs to create, secure, administer, and connect database services to end-user applications. In terms of administration and tuning, you do very little, if anything, with the data server itself. With proper file system management and environmental variable handling, it is possible and quite common to have more than one version of the IDS data server installed on a physical server. You'll learn more about this topic in Chapter 3.

An *instance*, on the other hand, is a unique working or run-time environment that you create to host a collection of databases to which end users may or may not have access, depending on the instance rules or database-level security enabled. Up to this point in the book, I've been using the term "database environment" in place of the word "instance." Instances, and databases for that matter, are tuned for performance and throughput. Any changes you make to the general operating environment of a database are made at the instance level. The data server provides the operational code and maintains the general overhead as defined by the instance's configuration parameters.

A single physical server, with one version of the data server installed, can support multiple instances. Each instance has its own unique set of configuration parameters, memory space, and disk allocation; it does not share these things with other instances on the same physical server.

Physical Elements

To better understand how the physical elements combine to create logical structures, look at Figure 1.6. In this diagram, solid lines represent physical elements, while dashed lines portray logical structures.

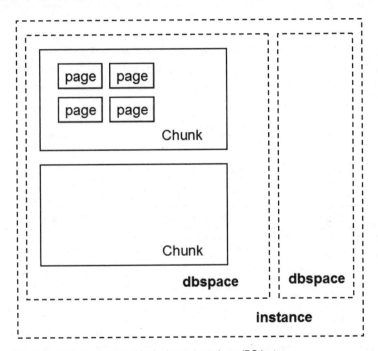

Figure 1.6: Physical and logical structures in an IDS instance

The basic physical element of an instance is called a *data page*, or simply a *page*. A data page has a fixed size called the *page size*; the page size is the smallest amount of data read or written from or to disk. As I mentioned previously, every port of IDS has an initial or default page size, which will be either 2 KB or 4 KB depending on the operating system. Most of IDS's monitoring and reporting utilities that display disk space usage list the space in pages rather than in kilobytes or megabytes. When converting to "real" numbers, you can simply multiply the number of pages by 2 (or 4, 6, 8, 12, or 16) to get an approximate size in megabytes.

While data is read and written in pages, the smallest piece of disk you can work with from an administrative point of view is called a *chunk*. From a physical standpoint, a chunk is usually an entire disk partition, although it can be a smaller but logically contiguous portion of a single disk partition (as I'll explain in Chapter 5). If you're using cooked space to create storage locations, a chunk is an individual flat file. From a logical point of view, a chunk is a collection of data pages and is the basic building block for creating, or adding to, dbspaces.

A *dbspace* is a logical collection of one or more chunks created on one or more physical disks. It is in a dbspace that databases and their data, arranged in tables and columns, are created and stored. You can also use dbspaces to stage or gather data for in-flight end-user operations. If you don't configure a couple of parameters that permit in-memory sorting or ordering of queried data, these operations will also occur on disk before the final query results are passed to the requesting application. Dbspaces cannot be shared between instances, although the physical disk from which a chunk was used to create, or add to ("expand"), a dbspace can be divided such that it contains chunks used by other dbspaces in the same or other instances on the same physical server. Figure 1.7 illustrates this scenario.

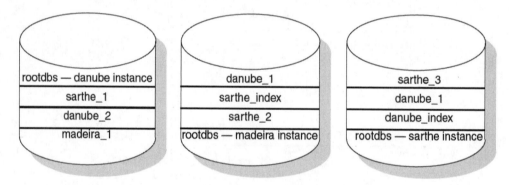

Figure 1.7: Interleaving dbspace chunks for multiple instances

The three disks shown in the figure have each been divided into four partitions. These partitions, or chunks, have been used to create a number of dbspaces for the three instances (**danube**, **madeira**, and **sarthe**) that exist on the physical server. In the case of the **danube_1** dbspace, two chunks from two different disks (Disk 2 and Disk 3) have been logically combined to create the dbspace.

When you initially create a dbspace, the first chunk of disk space allocated to it is addressed directly from within the dbspace creation process. Once created, if a dbspace needs more or less disk space, you accomplish this by adding or dropping additional chunks. You can never drop the initial chunk allocated to a dbspace; you must drop the dbspace itself and create a full backup to reuse the initial disk chunk of any dbspace.

So, an instance is a completely standalone data-processing environment with a collection of dbspaces containing databases that store data in a relational order of tables and columns, temporary work areas, and precompiled functions (called *stored procedures* or *user-defined routines*) that can be called either by an end user or by the instance itself to manipulate data. As you'll see in the chapters that follow, an instance has its own logical name by which it is known on the network and has its own configuration parameters that determine, to a certain degree, how the instance will operate.

Instance Elements

A couple of structures inside an instance are critical to the overall health and stability of the instance itself. The *rootdbs* is the core dbspace for the instance. This dbspace contains all the instance-wide overhead information and will be used as a last resort for some operations if sufficient space is not available in other instance dbspaces. Corruption in the rootdbs renders the entire instance inaccessible; the same is true for the physical and logical logs.

The *physical log* holds the "before image" of data prior to it's being changed. If the instance needs to reverse a change that an application has made to data, it uses the information stored in this log. The *logical log* holds some before images of the data, but it also records the changes made to the data and whether those changes were actually written to disk. Without these two types of logs, the instance cannot function.

Database Terms

You probably already have a good idea of what a *relational database* is and how one is structured from a conceptual point of view. You understand that data elements are stored in *columns* and that a series of one or more columns creates a *row*. Rows of data are grouped together in *tables*, and important, or key, columns can be used to create fast access paths into the data called *indexes*.

In addition to the character and numeric data types common to all relational databases, you also have the capability of using "nonstandard," or what in the IDS world are called *extensible*, data types. With these types, you can now create, manipulate, and analyze nonnumeric or non-ASCII data directly within the data server and its instances. You can create data types of your own design to meet your own unique applications or needs. With IDS's *object orientation*, elements from as small as a column to as large as a table can have various elements of inheritance and other functionality attached to them that are not possible in purely relational data servers. With this capability, you can analyze traditional data elements in new and exciting ways that are not easily accomplished under the restrictions of the relational database model.

IDS also has special, proprietary structures called *binary large objects*, or *BLOBs*. There are two types of BLOBs: simple and smart. *Simple BLOBs* are black-box data types as far as the data server is concerned. At a table level, references to where a BLOB is stored on disk exist, but there is no inherent definition of, or interface into, the BLOB other than the descriptive information you choose to add in regular character columns for a row of data. *Smart BLOBs*, on the other hand, consist of data types the data server can intelligently manipulate using functionality that has been added to the instance. This additional functionality could come from a DataBlade, a Bladelet, or your own UDRs. (We'll discuss DataBlades, Bladelets, and the object-oriented data types in much greater detail in the next chapter.)

The advantage of BLOBs is that a large amount of contiguous information or nonstandard data can be stored together rather than being broken up into fixed-length amounts, as required with standard data types. You can handle BLOBs differently than regular data types when storing them on disk as well. You can create one or more specially tuned dbspaces, called *BLOBspaces*, to store BLOBs. As with BLOBs, there are two kinds of BLOBspaces: *simple BLOBspaces* (usually just called BLOBspaces) and *smart BLOB-spaces*. BLOBspaces are not too different from standard dbspaces, particularly now that you can create standard dbspaces with varying page sizes. BLOBspaces were the first to have this page size variability so that BLOBs could be stored on a single *BLOB-page*. Smart BLOBspaces differ slightly in that while the smart BLOBs they contain are referenced from the base table, the actual storage and retrieval of smart BLOB data is managed through metadata created and stored within the smart BLOBspace. Chapter 5 provides more information about creating both types of BLOBspaces.

The BLOB data itself, whether simple or smart, generally falls into one of two orientations: text or true binary. *Text-oriented BLOBs*, as their name implies, are mainly character in nature and are represented as documents in some form. I've worked with instances where word-processing documents, with all their control codes, were stored as a single row in a table in a column defined as a simple BLOB data type. When a row was selected out of the table, the BLOB column was passed as a parameter to a shell script that invoked the word-processing program. To save the document inside the database, the user invoked a macro that passed the document back to the database for storage using an **insert** or **update** SQL command.

You can use the same type of interaction with BLOBs that are binary in nature. A *binary BLOB* is any other piece of nonstandard data to be stored in the database. This data could be a digitized sound sample, digitized images or video, or anything else digitally created outside the database environment that you need to store. As with the word-processing documents I stored as BLOBs, the application would be completely responsible for receiving and manipulating the binary BLOB data stream as it comes out of the table.

As I discussed earlier, tables to store data within an IDS instance reside in dbspaces created with chunks that can have two different disk formats: raw or cooked. *Raw space* refers to disk partitions that have no file system on them, while *cooked space* does have a standard file system in place.

A grouping of a table's rows is called a *table extent*, commonly referred to as an *extent*. Based on the number of rows you anticipate a table will need to hold, you can create an extent large enough to hold all those rows in a logically contiguous state. Due to the very nature of cooked file space, however, the rows won't be physically contiguous as happens when you create a table using raw space. If the table extent fills up with data and more disk space is required, the table will add another extent, although it may not be contiguous to the initial extent if there are other tables in the same dbspace. Figure 1.8 shows an example of creating additional extents that are not contiguous but are separated by extents of other tables, a process known as *interleaving*. (You'll learn more about table extents and interleaving in Chapter 3.)

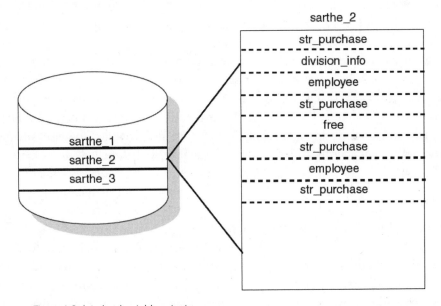

Figure 1.8: Interleaving table extents

Although you will never have truly contiguous extents with cooked space, too many interleaved extents will cause a thrashing condition to occur when reading data. In Chapter 8, you'll learn about a command you can run to show how much interleaving is occurring in a dbspace so you can take steps to reduce it if necessary.

When a table is created in Informix Dynamic Server, it can either reside completely in one dbspace or be split up into different dbspaces, depending on rules you set up. This process is called *fragmenting* or *partitioning* a table. Tables aren't the only objects that can be partitioned; indexes have partitioning options as well. Intelligently partitioning table and index data can result in tremendous performance increases as the data server's ability to parallelize operations is maximized. Chapter 5 explains the process of partitioning tables and indexes in much greater detail.

Types of Database Environments

Database environments themselves fall into two broad categories to which I will refer frequently in this book. *Online transaction processing*, or *OLTP*, environments are usually very disk read and write intensive. They typically serve many users executing limited and focused database actions and (depending on the processing environment) requiring almost instantaneous response times. Most general business workflow applications are OLTP oriented—such as order taking and processing, payroll modifications, and shipping and receiving functions. IDS is particularly well suited to the OLTP processing environment.

    Online analytical processing (OLAP) or *decision support systems (DSS)* environments are characterized by fewer total users but much larger data stores, more complex queries covering longer time periods, and less stringent response requirements. Another common term is a *data warehouse*, or in smaller, more focused data sets, a *data mart*. Transitional repositories, where data is staged and somewhat condensed, are called *operational data stores (ODSs)*. Although IDS's true strength lies in OLTP processing, many customers use IDS for data warehousing and other analytical repositories due to its storage scalability, extensive data typing, hardware efficiency, performance, and attractive administrative costs.

Transactions

Sometimes, several database actions have to occur as a matched set, or else all actions must be reversed. Such a group of actions is called a *transaction*. A commonly used example of a transaction is the transfer of money in a bank. Say you need to transfer money from your savings account to your checking account. For the transfer to be completed successfully, the sum of money to be transferred needs to be both debited from the balance of the savings account and credited to the checking account. These two actions balance the transaction financially. Should either the debit or the credit action fail, both actions must be reversed and the account balances restored to their original values.

    When I introduced the concept of the rootdbs, I noted that the IDS data server tracks changes made to data as part of a transaction using two components it saves to disk: the physical and logical logs. The physical log stores the original values of the data that is about to change. In transactions in which data is modified or deleted, the data server copies this information, along with the changes made, to the current logical log on a regular basis. Using our banking example, when both changes of the transaction are completed, the transaction is said to be *committed*. The original values and the changes made are written to the logical logs and marked as completed. If one part of the update process fails, the server *rolls back* the transaction and uses the original values stored in the physical log to return the data to its original state.

Checkpoints

Information stored in shared memory must periodically be written to disk. This activity helps ensure data persistence in the event of a failure that compromises the instance's ability to function. In some cases, data writes to disk occur automatically at the end of a task; in others, the writes occur as part of a *checkpoint*. During a checkpoint, data on disk is updated to reflect what is in shared memory. In earlier IDS versions, all other database activity was briefly suspended during a checkpoint in order to accurately capture some critical instance information and write the data to disk. With IDS 11, this suspension time has been significantly reduced, to almost nonexistence. In fact, it is now common for users not to notice any interruption to instance operations.

At the end of the checkpoint, the instance is said to be in a *logically consistent state*— that is, the data stored on disk accurately reflects what its true value should be. Look for a more detailed explanation of what a checkpoint is and what occurs during a checkpoint in *Administering Informix Dynamic Server, Advanced Topics*.

Summary

This chapter described the general architecture of Informix Dynamic Server and reviewed some basic terms in the context in which they are used with this data server. You should now understand what the three basic architectural components of IDS are, how the data server's shared memory operates, and the structures each portion contains. You should be familiar with the basic terminology, including the difference between a data server and an instance as well as what a chunk or dbspace is. You should know the basic differences between OLTP and OLAP environments, what BLOBs and a transaction are, and what a checkpoint does.

I've mentioned several times that IDS differs from other data servers on the market today from an architectural as well as a functional perspective. This chapter discussed some of the architectural differences. In Chapter 2, we focus on the functional enhancements available in Informix Dynamic Server through the integration of Illustra's object-oriented database technology with IDS's Dynamic Scalable Architecture.

2

An Introduction to Extensibility

In this Chapter

▸ What it is and why you should you care

▸ New database objects and how to use them

I n 1995, two things occurred that Informix hoped would propel the company to the pinnacle of the database market. First was the beginning of general-public access to and use of the Internet. CERN's World Wide Web technology was starting its global expansion, and with 14.4 Kbps and 28.8 Kbps modems, the general public began exploring new ways to obtain data. Second, Informix again led the market in releasing a significant upgrade to Informix Dynamic Server. The product, then called Universal Server, was touted as the birth of the next generation of data servers designed and optimized for the "Internet Generation." It was the result of a multiyear project to merge object-oriented database technology from Informix's acquisition of Michael Stonebraker's Illustra Server with IDS's Dynamic Scalable Architecture to create a new, hybrid, object-relational data server. Over the next year or two, competitors played catch-up, releasing products with similar monikers, but they were simply playing a name game, giving object-like names to functions that continued to manipulate data using standard relational operations.

Informix's demonstrations were exciting and eye-catching. Photos, video, and audio could be loaded into the database, and you could actually query the data objects themselves for matching properties such as color, shape, and tonal qualities instead of relying on descriptive metadata entered into character columns. There were ways to automatically generate Web pages out of the database itself instead of writing static Hypertext Markup Language (HTML) pages. The vision of the future was exciting and multimedia rich.

At the time, though, I worked for a wholesale grocery distribution company, and our critical business issues were tracking inbound and outbound foodstuffs, monitoring expiration dates, printing and processing pick tags on forklifts, producing inventory sheets for delivery drivers, getting paid by customers, and paying our suppliers. This was hardly the rich-media environment envisioned by Informix, and I suspected I wasn't alone. Few other customers I spoke with really needed all the whiz-bang stuff Informix was promoting. Some customers adopted the product, but most, like me, preferred to stick with our standard, relational data server.

Fast forward now more than a decade. The computing landscape has certainly changed. Web or graphical interfaces are now the norm and, where it makes sense, are media rich. From an Informix data server perspective, the default for new sales is the Universal Server's successor with all its bells and whistles. In fact, by the time this book is in your hands, IBM's official support for IDS 7 will be nearly over and you won't be able to buy the strictly relational version of the data server. For all intents and purposes, though, you wouldn't want to—IDS 11 is so much faster than IDS 7 that there's no reason to stay with the old version anymore. You might be tempted to say that even with this advantage the data server and its orientation are useless to you—most data generated and used by businesses continues to be the more standard character and numeric data types. I would counter, "Not so!" While IDS can do incredible things with audio, video, and other "complex" data types, its object-relational technology can also yield tremendous value when used with standard relational types. In fact, IDS lets you use these types in ways not possible with standard relational data servers.

This chapter explains what Informix Dynamic Server "extensibility" is, examines some of its components, and shows how you can use them in everyday applications to make those applications more efficient, easier to write and maintain, and more closely aligned with the way your business actually uses the data.

What Is Extensibility and Why Should You Care?

The current version of IDS grew out of the integration of two unique sets of technology, as I've mentioned, and was initially driven by a very large customer—a big government agency that performed sophisticated analysis and mapping of global geographic trends. The agency was entering all its standard data into an IDS environment while storing thermal, infrared, and other more complex data elements in an object-oriented database environment. This object-oriented environment was the Illustra Server, the product of research by Michael Stonebraker, a pioneer in the field of database technology.

Stonebraker was the first to create a commercially viable data server in which data elements were not static but had object-oriented properties such as *inheritance*, whereby you could define a new data type as having all the characteristics of an existing type and then add new characteristics unique to the new type. With the ability to define data as more than a simple character string or range of numbers, the data server could intelligently query and manipulate the data internally (provided it was given the routines) instead of having to transfer the entire object to an external application. This is what happened within the Illustra Server; data types that defined the characteristics of the various data streams from the agency's tests were created and stored in the data server along with programming routines that allowed a full range of data operations to occur. With these types and functions, it was possible to use standard SQL operators as well as "overloaded" operators against the data and to leverage the much more powerful physical server hardware to perform the operations rather than rely on a less powerful platform, such as an end-user PC.

From a workflow perspective, IDS lacked the ability to handle the more sophisticated data types and manipulation routines, but it was by far the fastest server for standard data operations. The Illustra data server was pretty slow handling standard data operations but provided the data and processing flexibility and speed needed for the customer to meet its objectives. As a result, the agency had to deal with data integration issues, combining data from both data server environments, on a daily basis. The customer wasn't shy in expressing its desire to have the best qualities of both servers in one product. To make a long story short, Informix purchased Illustra and embarked on a multiyear project to integrate its technology into the DSA.

No other mainstream data server on the market today offers object-relational technology such as IDS has. Some competitors claim in their marketing and sales materials to have the technology, but their manuals clearly state that they use standard relational stored procedures and views over regular relational types to make it appear as though a data element has object-like properties. Others have written separate servers that possess some capabilities, but these servers must be added to the base relational server and communicate through APIs to pass data back and forth first to the main data server and then to the application, resulting in decreased performance and compromised scalability.

So, what exactly is extensibility? As you can no doubt guess by now, *extensibility* is the ability to "extend" the functionality of the data server to manipulate data intelligently in its native format. This ability involves the creation of data types that reflect the attributes and characteristics of the data, routines to manipulate the data, casts to temporarily mask data characteristics, the ability to inherit characteristics, support for data and function overloading, polymorphism, and more. This functionality lets developers and DBAs build databases and applications that create and manage data according to *business* rules as opposed to mathematical modeling rules. Although the modeling rules have their place, they often make it much harder to create and maintain both the database environment and the applications.

With data created and stored the way the business uses it, applications can use that data more efficiently, resulting in faster development, fewer errors, better performance, longer business value, and reduced maintenance. With the ability to create your own data types, you can also solve problems that the standard modeling rules can't address or can address only in a very inefficient way.

Properly leveraging the technology requires developers and DBAs to think about data differently. They must be able to put aside the mathematical rules for representing data and see the data from a business perspective. As an example, although the rules might dictate that sales order information be divided into multiple tables, if the business always uses the combined data elements as a single object, the elements should be stored that way in the database. More important, developers and DBAs need to *use* the functionality and power in the data server and not treat the server simply as a "dumb" repository that cannot add value to the data.

It seems that in the name of "portability" the mantra today is to do all the work in the application; the database is seen as just a place to throw data while it's not being used. Under this philosophy, data servers have little value, so any one will do. Although this approach gives application developers job security, it is fraught with problems from a business perspective, including longer application development timelines, slower performance because applications are executed on lower-capacity hardware, exponential growth of network traffic with its associated expense of passing data back and forth, increased risk of data errors if multiple developers manipulate data differently in an attempt to create the same functionality in different applications, and so on. Proper use of IDS's functionality can significantly reduce or even eliminate these problems as well as bring new capabilities to the business.

Although extensibility is now standard in IDS, its use is optional; you don't have to use it in the creation or use of databases if you don't want to. Extensibility isn't just for flashy, media-rich applications, either; there are compelling business reasons to use it for "regular" applications. Let's look at one example.

Problem Solving with Extensibility: The Org Chart

Figure 2.1 illustrates a question common to all companies: Who works for whom? Represented outside the database world in this format, it's easy to see how each person relates to others in terms of the corporate structure. The organizational chart lets you quickly trace reporting lines to answer the question. Trying to represent and manipulate this data in a standard database, however, is very, very difficult.

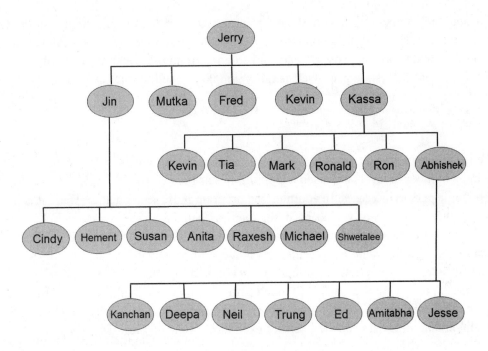

Figure 2.1: Analog representation of a department employee roster

Standard modeling rules permit only a master–detail relationship, which works fine for the company's president but fails from the vice-president's level on down. At this level and below, what should be the "master" element is part of the "detail" element for another master, but the data should, logically, be only one or the other. Modelers skirt this issue by having the data refer back to itself. For example, they define a table as follows

```
create table employee
   (employee_id serial unique,
    manager_id integer primary key,
    .
    .

   )
foreign key (employee_id) references manager_id
```

and then throw it to the application developers to have them try and create an efficient way of accessing the table's data. The developers have only two choices: either parse the data recursively, much like a puppy chasing its own tail, or use set processing.

Using the recursive approach, the program must be written to generate dynamic SQL statements that select all the people for a given manager, then recursively select all the employees under each of those people, and so on until no more employees exist. The individual SQL statement itself is fairly simple:

```
select employee_name, employee_id from employee
where manager_id = ?
```

The performance impact, however, is significant. Execution time increases exponentially with the number of levels traversed and multiplies as the number of employees managed by a single person increases. In addition, the program must keep track of where it is in the organizational tree as well as of all the interim results for each execution. While the results are part of the overall answer, parts of each result set need to be used for the next iteration, generating even more results sets that must be maintained, used for the next iteration, and then somehow consolidated and collated for return to the application.

The set processing approach isn't much better. With this method, the application has to figure out the manager's level in the corporate tree and then dynamically generate an SQL statement that joins data back to itself for each level of the organization. For example:

```
select count(*) from employee e1, employee e2,
  employee e3, employee e4, employee e5
where e5.manager_id = ?
  and e4.manager_id = e5.employee_id
  and e3.manager_id = e4.employee_id
  and e2.manager_id = e3.employee_id
  and e1.manager_id = e2.employee_id;
```

With each level, the join complexity increases and performance drops. In short, neither approach is very efficient or quick.

With the extensibility features built into IDS, we can represent and use the data in its native business format: a nested hierarchy. To do so, we simply register the Node DataBlade in the instance. Once we've done so, a new data type (the **node** type) and a small collection of routines to manipulate the type are available for database operations. The type and associated routines act like, and are treated as, native data processing elements.

With the **node** type and the server's ability to support longer object names, we can add a new column called **employee_reporting_structure** to the **employee** table. In this column, the employee's position in the company can be mapped using a hierarchical value and used as the key value to find relationships between employees:

```
create table employee
  (employee_id   serial,
   employee_reporting_structure node primary key,
    .
    .
    .
  );
```

Figure 2.2 illustrates how this data type represents an employee's position.

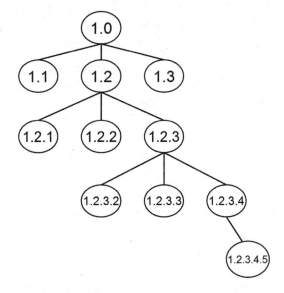

Figure 2.2: Using the Node DataBlade to model hierarchical data

As you can see from the figure, each level, as well as each member of the reporting structure, has a unique identifier. Adjacent levels represent an employee/manager relationship. A reporting structure value of 1.4.3.4 means that employee #4 reports to manager #3 who, in turn reports to manager #4, who reports to manager #1. With this data representation, interrogating any object becomes trivial—is it greater or less than another? Is it the ancestor, parent, child, or descendant of another object? Functions included with the Node Blade perform these calculations for you, so the SQL statement to find someone's manager, regardless of that person's place in the company, could look like this:

```
select ischild()
from employee
where employee_reporting_structure =
  (select employee_reporting_structure
    from employee
    where employee_id = input_value);
```

Other functions enable you to add, split, or graft levels together; to retrieve all the members of a particular level; and so on. Because the **node** type can be indexed, operations against columns of this type are executed with linear performance using either table or partial index scans just as with other indexed columns.

This is just one example of how you can use extensibility to solve a business problem that is impossible to handle efficiently in a strictly relational data server. I hope you can begin to see that *the data server really matters*. Distinct and significant differences exist between IDS and other data servers on the market today. With IDS's functionality and a little creative thinking, you can model data logically and physically to solve previously impossible or extremely difficult business problems, create a richer application environment, and make it easier to create and maintain applications.

With this background in mind, let's examine some of the unique aspects of IDS's object-relational technology, beginning with enhanced data types.

Extensible Data Types

Figure 2.3 shows the IDS data type tree. As you might expect, it has two main branches: built-in and extended types.

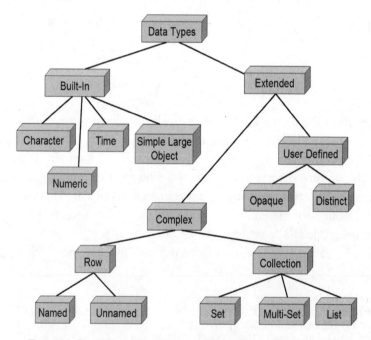

Figure 2.3: The IDS object-relational data type tree

The built-in branch encapsulates the standard relational data types that the rest of the data server market supports. The extended types break down into several subsets of unique data-handling functionality. We'll explore each of these types in greater detail in the following sections, with frequent reference back to this diagram.

I'll be using a number of code snippets and Data Definition Language (DDL) examples in the following discussions. You shouldn't necessarily consider this code optimal or representative of best coding practices. Its purpose here is to illustrate and explain the concepts and, I hope, spark some ideas about what you can do in your own environment.

The Relational Types

The upper-left part of Figure 2.3's diagram contains the relational types you're familiar with: **character**, **varchar**, **integer**, **float**, **decimal**, and so on. There's nothing unique here. The integer- and serial-oriented types are either 4 or 8 bytes in size; small integers are 2 bytes. With the increased byte count, you can now express a number in the range of –9,223,372,036,854,775,807 to 9,223,372,036,854,775,807. I hope this range is big enough to store your order numbers or customer identifiers! As with the 4-byte **serial** type, you must add a unique constraint to the 8-byte **bigserial** type to ensure uniqueness. Using one type in a table doesn't prevent you from using the other; you can have both a **serial** and a **bigserial** column in the same table.

There are two variable character types, with either a 255-character (**varchar**) or a 2 KB (**lvarchar**) limit, depending on the type. While the **varchar** type can be indexed, the **lvarchar** cannot. IDS also provides an extension to these basic variable-length character types. With the addition of a length parameter (**N**), the **lvarchar(N)** data type can store up to 32 KB of character data, depending on the operating system hosting the data server (check the release notes for your system's maximum length). Whether it's wise to store that much data in a character column is debatable; in my opinion, you should place such data in a smart BLOBspace type. That opinion notwithstanding, there is an interesting element to this larger data type: it can be indexed! Again, I would argue that putting an index on a 32 KB–wide character column isn't the smartest thing to do, but that's for you to decide.

You can express date and time values either with the **datetime** type, with precision from a year to thousandths of a second, or as an interval between two date and/or time values. The **decimal** and **float** types have precision before and after the decimal point, and so on.

The Extended Types

Now to the other part of the data type tree, and this is where it gets fun, especially for those who to this point have lived and died by the standard modeling rules. Some of these types will mess with your mind, particularly when you realize you can nest them inside each other. For example, you can have a column defined as a **multiset** of named **row** types that has one or more attributes defined using another **row** type or a **distinct** type. Confused? Don't worry. It will all make sense in a minute. Remember, though, that the objective is to show you how to model data the way your business uses it.

Complex Types

If I had to give someone an "elevator pitch" about the data types in the complex types branch, it would be that they give you the ability to store repeating sets of values in a single column and to condense a table into one column that could be available in as many tables as needed.

Row Data Type

The **row** type is similar to a **struct** (structure) in the C programming language. With this type, you can group logically related elements together into one column. In other words, it's like being able to collapse a table into a single column. There are two "kinds" of **row** types: named and unnamed.

Named **row** types are strongly typed and identified. As such, they exist at a database level, like the relational types you're more familiar with, and can be inherited into other objects. You can use a named **row** type to create a single-column table, or it can be one of many columns in a table. Listing 2.1 shows some sample named row types and how you might use them when creating a table.

```
create row type name_t
   (fname varchar(20),
    lname varchar(20));

create row type address_t
   (street_1 varchar(20),
    street_2 varchar(20),
    city varchar(20),
    state char(2),
    zip char(9));
```

Listing 2.1: Sample named row types (part 1 of 2)

```
create table student
  (student_id serial,
   name name_t,
   address address_t,
   company varchar(30));
```

Listing 2.1: Sample named row types (part 2 of 2)

In this example, two named **row** types have been created. You can use these types anywhere in the database design where it makes business sense to have this data grouped together. Imagine you need to create a module for a local night school with student and class information. You can create a table called **student** and use both of these types as shown in the sample **create table** statement.

Unnamed **row** types, on the other hand, are weakly typed and exist only within the table in which they've been defined; you can't use them anywhere else in the database. Because an unnamed **row** type is identified by its structure—in other words, by the attributes within the type—it can be used only as a columnar data type and not to create a single-column table. Listing 2.2 shows a couple of examples.

```
row(a int, b char (10))

row(x int, y char(10))

create table part
  (part_id serial,
   cost decimal,
   part_dimensions row
     (length decimal,
      width  decimal,
      height decimal,
      weight decimal (6,2))
  );
```

Listing 2.2: Sample unnamed row types

The two **row** types in this example, when used in a table definition such as that shown below them, are functionally identical even though their attribute names differ. The attribute names needn't differ, though, when you implement the same unnamed **row** type in more than one table; the table name is part of the structure's identity. Good design practice dictates that you formalize an unnamed **row** type to a named type if you're using it more than once in the same or different tables.

The last part of this example shows the creation of a table named **part** with some of the physical characteristics stored together in the **part-dimension** unnamed **row** column.

Row types can contain almost any other data type, including other extended types such as another **row** type. The exception is that serial-oriented types (4- and 8-byte) cannot be attributes of a **row** type.

From a design and application development perspective, several advantages and a few disadvantages apply when using **row** types. First, this type is intuitive from a business perspective. It makes sense that if you always use certain data elements together, you should model them logically and physically that way. Second, from an application development standpoint, it decreases the number of cross-table joins and other SQL operations to manage or manipulate the various disparate parts of a single logical element. On the other hand, although less code is required to access the data objects, the code is a bit more complex. Last, administering a named **row** type requires a little more foresight because you can't alter such types, as you can a character or numeric type; you have to drop and then re-create them. Another option is managing **row** type schema evolution to inherit a named **row** type into another named **row** type with the additional required attributes.

The sample code in Listing 2.3 shows two SQL operations executed from the **dbaccess** utility to manipulate data for the night school system table defined in Listing 2.1.

```
insert into student values (0,
   row ("John","Doe")::name_t,
   row ("1234 Main Street","","Anytown","TX",
        "75022")::address_t,"Big Co.");

select * from student where name.lname matches "Doe";
   student_id  1234
   name row('John','Doe')
   address row('1234 Main Street','','Anytown','TX','75022')
   company  Big Co.
```

Listing 2.3: SQL operations on named row types

The insert syntax is fairly straightforward, with two additions:

- The **row** keyword identifies that the data to follow will be inserted into a **row** data type.

- The name of the **row** type specified after the data elements (e.g., **::name_t**) converts, or "casts," the data into the required named **row** type so the data server can use the correct functions to manipulate the data. (We'll discuss casts and casting in greater detail later in the chapter.)

The second statement shows how you could write an SQL select statement and include a filter based on a value within one of the **row** types. Notice the "dot" notation used to identify the specific attribute in the predicate. If a **row** type was nested inside another type, there would be three "dotted" attribute names: the column name, followed by the column name in the nested type, followed by the attribute name of the nested type as shown in Listing 2.4.

```
create row type name_t
  (fname varchar(20),
   lname varchar(20));

create row type address_t
  (street_1 varchar(20),
   street_2 varchar(20),
   city varchar(20),
   state char(2),
   zip char(9));

create row type studentinfo_t
  (name name_t,
   address address_t);

create table student
  (student_id serial,
   name_address studentinfo_t,
   company varchar(30));

insert into student values (0,
  row (row ("John", "Doe")::name_t,
      row ("1234 Main Street","","Anytown","TX","75022")::address_t
    )::cust_t, "Big Co"
  );

select * from student where name_address.name.lname matches "Doe";
student_id  1234
name_address row(row('John','Doe'),
            row('1234 Main Street','','Anytown','TX','75022'))
company  Big Co
```

Listing 2.4: Accessing subelements of a named row type

As I mentioned earlier, you cannot modify the schema definitions of **row** types as you can for other objects in the data server; they must be dropped and re-created. To drop a named **row** type, you use the **restrict** keyword:

```
drop row type studentinfo_t restrict;
```

Collection Data Types

Moving to the other half of the complex type branch, we find three different *collection* types. A collection type, as the name implies, permits the storage of multiple occurrences of the same data type within one column. Think of an array, and you'll get the general idea. You can create a collection to store nearly any defined data type, including other collection types that can contain standard or extensible types such as a named **row** type. You cannot, however, store serial-oriented (4- or 8-byte), **byte**, or **text** types in a collection. There is a practical limit to their storage capacity, too; they can hold only 32 KB of data, which effectively limits their ability to store simple BLOB types as well.

Collection types are most useful when the data is meaningless without the context of the other elements in the collection, such as a list of golf hole scores, a to-do list, the line-item detail of an order, and so on. They are also particularly valuable when the individual data elements won't be queried by position, with the contents of the collection being returned to the application as a unit instead.

IDS provides three collection types: **set**, **multiset**, and **list**. Their functions differ only as to whether each type enforces uniqueness and order within the collection, as illustrated in Table 2.1.

Table 2.1: Collection types and their characteristic	
Type name	Description
set	Uniqueness is enforced, but order is not enforced. set {"apple", "orange", "grapefruit", "plum"}
multiset	Neither order nor uniqueness is enforced. multiset {"apple", "orange", "grapefruit", "apple", "plum", "grapefruit"}
list	Order is enforced, but uniqueness is not. list {"apple", "apple", "grapefruit", "grapefruit", "orange", "plum"} list {"apple", "grapefruit", "tangerine", "apple", "orange", "plum"}

As shown in the description of a list, the term "order" doesn't refer to an element's order according to its type (e.g., alphabetic, numeric); rather, it means that the order in which the elements exist in the list is important. You'd want to use a list to contain scores from a round of golf so you'd know the first element is for hole 1, the second is for hole 2, and so on.

Notice that the collection types use curly braces (**{}**) rather than parentheses to enclose the values of their elements. Collection types cannot contain null values, so make sure you add **not null** to any column definitions that use one of these types. Another interesting thing is that if you try to insert more than one element with the same value into a **set**, as in

```
insert into . .
values (set {"apple", "orange", "apple", "plum"});
```

the second occurrence of **apple** will be discarded without any error code being returned to the application.

Continuing with our night school example, let's use a collection type to build a table storing curriculum information. Listing 2.5 shows the necessary SQL statements.

```
create table class
    (class_id serial,
     class_name varchar(60),
     description lvarchar,
     prereqs set(varchar(20) not null));

insert into class values (300,
    "Performance and Tuning",
    "Covers advanced information on tuning Informix Dynamic Server",
    (set{"Relational Database Design", "Basic SQL Programming"}));

select * from class where ("Advanced SQL Programming") in prereqs;
```

Listing 2.5: SQL operations with a collection data type

The first SQL operation builds the table, and the second populates it with a row. This syntax is somewhat like the named **row** type in that you have to specify the collection type into which the elements that follow are being inserted. You can use collection elements as predicates in SQL operations if you specify the **in** keyword, as shown in the third operation of the sample code. You can retrieve collection types into array variables in programming languages that support array types. Using the IBM Informix 4GL, you can create a **set**, **multiset**, or **list** variable type to hold data queried from a collection type. Once retrieved into the array or 4GL collection type, elements can be parsed one at a time by moving up or down the list.

Returning to the sample code, imagine that a mistake was made when the prerequisites were defined. In addition to passing the listed courses, the student must have passed the advanced SQL programming class. To change the values of a collection type, you cannot modify just one (or more) elements in the collection; all must be rewritten. You can accomplish this either directly or through a variable, as shown in Listing 2.6.

```
update class set prereqs =
    (set{"Relational Database Design"
         "Advanced SQL Programming",
         "Basic SQL Programming"})
    where class_id = 300;

update class set prereqs = set_char where class_id = 300;
```

Listing 2.6: Modifying a collection data type

From a database design perspective, collection types enable you to collapse master-detail tables into one table. To date, most users of this functionality that I know of have been in the financial, scientific, or manufacturing space. One customer is a very large trading company that captures stock market transaction information for each trade by stock. Rather than create thousands of rows per stock per day in a detail table, the company uses a collection type to store all the trade information for the day in one column of a stock's trading day row. Manufacturers and scientists use collection types to capture temperature, velocity, heading, depth, and other readings from monitoring devices. It would certainly be possible to use a collection type to store line item details of an order as well.

User-Defined Types

Moving now to the far-right side of the extended data types tree, we come to the user-defined types. These types are a study in contrasts; one group is easy to implement, while the other requires more effort.

Distinct Data Types

A **distinct** type is modeled from an existing built-in type and is a prime example of the object-oriented principle of inheritance. Although a **distinct** type shares the same characteristics of the base type from which it is modeled, it has a unique name that distinguishes it from other, "similar" types. The data server segregates both the base and the **distinct** type from each other and prevents aggregation and other operations unless one type is cast as the other type. Because the **distinct** type is a different data type from a data server perspective, you can create user-defined routines or casts for it that do not apply to the base type. This is another object-oriented principle, known as *overloading*.

To illustrate how you can use **distinct** types, assume we need to build a module for a business that sells souvenirs in Europe. This business accepts only two currencies, U.S. dollars and euros, so we model the sales table as follows:

```
create distinct type dollar as decimal;
create distinct type euro as decimal;

create table sales
  (sku int,
   sales_date datetime year to second,
   us_sales dollar,
   euro_sales euro);
```

In this case, we've created two **distinct** types that inherit the characteristics of a **decimal** data type, namely precision before and after a decimal point. Sales are rung up and entered into the database:

```
        .
        .
   insert into sales
      values (1234, current, 15.0::dollar,0::euro);
   insert into sales
      values (5678, current, 0::dollar,75.0::euro);
   insert into sales
      values (1234, current, 83.75::dollar,0::euro);
        .
        .
```

Notice here that, as with **row** types, the "double colon" notation (::) is used to indicate that a **decimal**-looking data stream is being converted or cast into the target data type.

At the end of the day, though, the sales manager wants to know how much of each item was sold. Using an ad hoc reporting tool, she writes and executes the following SQL statement:

```
   select sku, (sum(us_sales) + sum(euro_sales))
      from sales
      where date(sales_date) = today
      group by 1;
```

Instead of retrieving sales totals by product ID, however, this query produces the following result:

```
   error: 674 - routine (plus) cannot be resolved
```

Why would this be so? From the manager's perspective, both sums should be able to be added together as if they were "regular" number columns, correct? Well, yes and no. While the columns share the same characteristics as a **decimal** data type, they are not a **decimal** type and, as a result, the data server doesn't know how to add a **euro** and **dollar** data type together.

This example highlights the value of **distinct** types: the prevention of logical computational errors as well as the ability to define a type that reflects the business value of the data it contains. Logically, it is incorrect to add U.S. dollar and euro monetary values together because their respective intrinsic values are not the same. A conversion or exchange factor must be applied to one or the other so it represents an equivalent real value with respect to the other currency value.

From a business value and modeling perspective, if the data reflects values in U.S. dollars, euros, or any other unit of measure, create a type of that measure so the data's value isn't defined by its column name alone. In a strictly relational server, once you get past the column name data loses its intrinsic value; it's either a number or a character because that's all a relational server can model. An example of this is a chicken processing company for which I once did some work. The company sold chickens based on weight, piece, and gallon, with multiple iterations of the three, yet it could define only decimal columns for all values. Application developers and ad hoc report writers had to check and double-check their work, as well as the results, to make sure they didn't add two decimal columns together that in fact represented a measure in pounds and gallons.

Returning to the earlier problem, it is reasonable to expect that the sales manager (or anyone else) should be able to get a report representing daily sales without having to jump through a lot of programming hoops or writing unnatural SQL. This is easily done in a couple of ways. I'll discuss one method here and explain the other later, in the section on data casting.

Because the base functionality of a **distinct** type is inheritance, when we define a **dollar** type using **decimal** as its base, the **dollar** type inherits built-in **decimal** functions that manipulate the type (**sum()**, **plus()**, and so on), so the server knows how to add two **dollar** or **euro** types together, for example. With that point in mind, to generate the sales report, we need to convert one of the types into the other. We could create a stored procedure or user-defined function that transforms the intrinsic value as well as the type of one data type into the desired target type. From there, we'd simply include the function call in the report operation to generate the report, as shown in Listing 2.7.

```
create function dlr_to_euro(parm1 dollar)
   returning euro
   specific usd_to_euro;
   return (parm1::decimal * .804)::euro;
end function;

create function euro_to_usdlr(parm1 euro)
   returning dollar
   specific euro_to_usd;
   return (parm1::decimal / 1.346)::dollar;
end function;

select sku, (sum(us_sales) + sum(euro_to_usdlr(euro_sales))::dollar)
   from sales where date(sales_date) = today
   group by 1;
```

Listing 2.7: Using user-defined functions to work with distinct data types

In a real-world module, you wouldn't hard code the exchange-rate value into the function; an additional function call would retrieve this factor in real time.

Opaque Data Types

An **opaque** type is the wildcard of data types. If no other type that exists in the data server is sufficient to model and store the data you need, you can create an **opaque** type to meet your needs. These types are similar to simple BLOBs in that they are encapsulated, or "black boxes," to Informix Dynamic Server. The data server has no idea what the data's structure is or how to manipulate it natively. From the server's perspective, it is a single "value" that cannot be subdivided into discrete component parts. As a result, you must define the characteristics of the type as well as all functions that operate on the type.

To define the type and to implement it, you use C or Java structures; manipulation of **opaque** types occurs through C or Java routines registered in the data server. The types can be fixed in size or can vary (with a specified maximum length) for each instantiation of the type. Regardless, they cannot exceed 32 KB in size. If you need more space, you'll need to store the data in one of the two smart BLOB types.

For the server to correctly pass the data out to the processing function, the data must be properly formatted as far as the host operating system is concerned. When you create an **opaque** type, you specify its alignment boundary in bytes, a step referred to as *aligning* the type. Table 2.2 lists the four possible boundaries.

Table 2.2: Opaque data type boundaries	
Alignment boundary	**Description**
1	1-byte structures such as characters
2	Structures that resemble an unsigned small integer
3	Structures that resemble an unsigned integer
4	Structures similar to the numeric double data type

If you don't specify a boundary, a default value of 4 bytes will be used for the type.

Unlike other data types, which are retrieved in whole or in part (e.g., smart BLOBs with byte range locking), for the most part when an **opaque** type is "retrieved" the user-defined routine (UDR) receives only a pointer to the type instantiation on disk. This is similar to receiving information only from the BLOB pointer column in a table whose BLOBs are stored in BLOBspaces. The exception to this behavior is if the type is going to be only 4 bytes in size and you use the **PASSEDBYVALUE** flag when creating the type.

In preparation for creating an **opaque** type, you must first create and register a number of UDRs, including routines for input and output, destruction (delete), operations (add, subtract, and others as appropriate), aggregates where appropriate, cost, selectivity (to satisfy **where** predicate conditions), indexes, statistical gathering for the IDS optimizer, and others. Listing 2.8 shows two examples of creating **opaque** types.

```
create function mytype_in(lvarchar)
returning my_type with (not variant);
external name "/funcs/my_type.so"
language C
end function;

create opaque type my_type(internallength=variable, maxlen=1024,
                    alignment=1, cannothash);
```

Listing 2.8: Examples of creating opaque types

Casting

By now, I hope you've realized that the expanded type capacity of Informix Dynamic Server provides a rich and useful modeling environment. It's one thing to build a model, but it's an entirely different story to actually use the types in applications. If the types cannot be used with each other easily, there's no value in having them. Usability and interoperability are partially solved through object-oriented functionality called *casting*.

A cast substitutes the value of one type into the value of another type so comparison and other operations can occur in a homogeneous manner. You've been using the relational server equivalent of casts, although you probably didn't know it. These functions enable inserting an **integer** value into a **decimal** column or a numeric value into a **character** column, for example. The fact that a comparable cast does not exist prevents storing a character in a numeric column—the server returns a character-to-numeric conversion error.

Casts in a database design are optional; they don't have to exist if all operations on a type will incorporate only identical types. This generally isn't the case, though, so you should create casts for any extensible type in your design. Casts, like functions, can be overloaded provided their source and target type combinations are unique. You can create casts for any data type except collections, BLOBs, and unnamed **row** types. Let's look at the two types of casts, implicit and explicit, and explore how you can use them.

Implicit Casts

An *implicit cast* is one whose actions are automatically invoked when one data type is used in conjunction with a dissimilar type—for example, an attempt to add a **euro** value with a **dollar** value.

You must use care when creating implicit casts because they can easily lead to incorrect results. Earlier in the chapter, in the souvenir seller example, we created a **dollar** and a **euro** type and used them in a table capturing sales data. The first attempt to obtain the sales totals for the day failed due to a data type mismatch; we worked around this issue by adding a function call to the **sum** operation. An alternative solution would have been be to cast the type, as shown in Listing 2.9, so that the operation would be executed successfully.

```
select sum(us_sales) + sum(euro_sales) from sales
where date(sales_date) = today;

    #  674: Routine (plus) cannot be resolved.

create implicit cast (euro as dollar);

select sum(us_sales) + sum(euro_sales) from sales
where date(sales_date) = today;

(expression)   120.00
```

Listing 2.9: Using casts to transform data types

The **create cast** syntax shown in this example instructs the server to treat the value of any column defined as a **euro** data type as though it were a **dollar** data type when the **euro** data type column is involved in a mathematical operation. When the second SQL addition statement is executed, the server can use the dollar **sum** and **plus** functions inherited from the **decimal** type functions and return a value. Problem solved, right? Not exactly. Although the result is accurate from a math perspective (e.g., 50 + 70 = 120), it is wrong from a business context.; 70 euros do not have the same intrinsic value as 70 U.S. dollars.

To fix the problem, we need to modify the cast to contain, as part of the casting process, a conversion not just of the data type but also of the intrinsic value of the data, using the exchange-rate function created earlier in the chapter:

```
drop cast (euro as dollar);

create implicit cast
  (euro as dollar with euro_to_usdlr);

select sum(us_sales) + sum(euro_sales) from sales
where date(sales_date) = today;

(expression)   80.00
```

Now when the sales total is generated, the sum of euro sales is first passed through the **euro_to_usdlr** function to perform the exchange-rate calculation. The returned result is then treated as though it were a **dollar** data type, so the overloaded **plus** function, which supports the **dollar** data type, can add the two values together. When properly created, implicit casts can mask redesigning database objects for future functionality now without requiring immediate application changes.

Explicit Casts

The strength of an implicit cast—the immediate and seamless conversion of values from one type to another—is also its greatest weakness. There may be situations when a source type might require more than one target type, necessitating the ability to dynamically choose which cast to execute when the source data type is involved in a calculation. IDS provides this functionality through *explicit* casts.

You've seen examples of explicit casts before in some of my syntax examples, although I haven't called them out until now. Both of the following casts explicitly state that the value of the **my_param** object should be treated as though it was a **new_type** data type.

```
 . . . my_param::new_type
 . . . my_param cast as new_type
```

At another iteration of the program or in a different part of the work flow, the value of the **my_param** object might need to be treated as though it were defined as a type called **really_new_type**. It is the ability to cast "on demand" that is the hallmark of the explicit cast.

As with implicit casts, you can predefine explicit casts within the instance so the casting logic doesn't have to be included in the application. For example, let's assume that the souvenir sales module requires modifications because the souvenir company has been purchased. The new owners want to see sales reports in U.S. dollars and need to perform other calculations with euros as though they were Japanese yen. To help satisfy the latter requirement, the original implicit casts are removed and a **yen** distinct type is created. Elsewhere in the database, a **yen_value** column is defined using the **yen** data type. With these changes in place, the series of operations shown in Listing 2.10 are attempted.

```
select sum(us_sales) + sum(euro) from sales
where date(sales_date) = today;
#  674: Routine (plus) cannot be resolved
```

Listing 2.10: Functional differences of an explicit cast (part 1 of 2)

```
execute my_function(in_1) returning yen
select sum(euro_sales) / yen_value from . . .
#  674: Routine (divide) cannot be resolved

create explicit cast (euro as dollar);
create explicit cast (euro as yen);

select sum(us_sales) + sum(euro) from sales
where date(sales_date) = today;
#  674: Routine (plus) cannot be resolved

execute my_function(in_1) returning yen
select sum(euro_sales) / yen value from . . .
#  674: Routine (divide) cannot be resolved
```

Listing 2.10: Functional differences of an explicit cast (part 2 of 2)

Why didn't this work? There was a cast to match the data type conditions; why wasn't it applied? Explicit casts, regardless of how they are defined, are never automatically applied by the data server. The specific cast must be called, as shown in Listing 2.11.

```
drop cast (euro as dollar);
drop cast (euro as yen);

select sum(us_sales) + sum(euro_sales)::dollar from sales
where date(sales_date) = today;

(expression)   120.00

create explicit cast (euro as dollar with euro_to_usdlr);
create explicit cast (euro as yen with euro_to_yen);

select sum(us_sales) + sum(euro_sales)::dollar from sales
where date(sales_date) = today;
(expression)   80.00

execute my_function(in_1) returning yen
select euro_sales cast as yen / yen_value from . . .

(expression)   2400.65
```

Listing 2.11: Successfully using explicit casts to transform data types

The first two statements drop any existing casts on the **euro** type. The next explicitly casts the **euro_sales** column to a **dollar** data type and then applies the math operation. Unfortunately, the result of that operation is worthless because no currency conversion occurred. The next set of statements creates explicit casts that include exchange-rate functionality. With these casts created, **euro_sales** data values are easily used with either a **yen** or **dollar** type as needed, with few application code changes required. When the **euro_sales cast as yen** syntax is encountered, the data server will recognize the external cast and the function to be applied, resulting in a "correct" answer from a mathematical as well as a business perspective.

User-Defined Routines and Aggregates

User-defined routines and user-defined aggregates (UDAs) are an expansion of existing server-side programming that has been available in Informix Dynamic Server for a number of years. In earlier versions of the data server, this programming was restricted to stored procedures written in Informix's Stored Procedure Language (SPL). The SPL continues to exist and be supported in IDS 11. Procedures written in that language function today as they always have; when created, the query optimizer parses them and stores the query plan in the instance's system tables for immediate execution. In fact, IBM added more procedural programming support to SPL in IDS 11, including loops, loop labeling, loop exit, and **goto** statements.

Starting with Informix Dynamic Server 9.1, you can write "external" routines, which are registered in the instance and executed like a stored procedure or any other function delivered as part of the data server binary. These external functions and procedures can be written in either C or Java and, as a result, can be far more sophisticated in terms of procedural processing than stored procedures written in SPL.

> The IBM Informix Dynamic Server documentation sometimes refers to user-defined procedures and user-defined functions as well as user-defined aggregates. From a mechanical perspective, user-defined aggregates and/ or functions differ from user-defined procedures in that their execution results in one or more parameters being returned to the calling statement, while a procedure's execution does not. We refer collectively to all of these as UDRs.

UDRs written in Java must be compiled into jar form. When you register a function in the instance, the contents of the jar file are copied into the server, stored in the default smart BLOBspace, and executed using the data server's HotSpot Java Virtual Machine (JVM). UDRs written in C must be compiled into object form (*filename.so*) and placed in a common directory defined with the **DB_LIBRARY_PATH** configuration parameter.

UDRs, more than application functions, should be as concise and precise as possible. An instance's performance can be degraded severely if too much time is spent processing verbose code. Although it is convenient to place business functionality in the server via

UDRs for common processing, it is even more important for the data returned from the routines to be relevant from a business perspective, be it data type, range, or any other business-oriented requirement.

When you create UDRs, it is critical to include error-handling capabilities using the **raise exception** and other built-in functions to signal the calling application if a mistake occurs and instruct it to ignore any data values returned. Because UDRs can overload other UDRs and/or built-in routines, good programming practice suggests you include a "specific" name or alias as an element when defining the UDR. For example, it's possible to create the following overloaded UDRs with different signatures:

```
create function
  comp_val (in_1 dollar, in_2 aus_dollar). . .
create function
  comp_val (in_1 aus_dollar, in_2 euro). . .
create function
  comp_val (in_1 euro, in_2 aus_dollar). . .
```

A UDR *signature* is the combination of the function/procedure name and the parameter list. When the UDR is called, the server uses the parameter data types to select which of the overloaded UDRs to execute. Administering UDRs requires using either the full signature or, if you're lazy like me, its alias as shown here:

```
create function comp_val (euro, aus_dollar)
  returning aus_dollar
  specific euro_to_ausdlr
  .
  .
```

To drop the function, you'd execute one of these commands:

```
drop function plus(euro, aus_dollar);
drop specific function euro_to_ausdlr;
```

Although there isn't much different in this example, using the alias can eliminate a lot of typing depending on the length of the signature.

Because UDRs are extensions of, and co-equal with, native data server functions, it's possible for a misbehaving UDR to interfere with normal processing or even cause an abnormal instance shutdown (i.e., a "crash"). To reduce the potential negative impact to an instance, IDS provides the ability to create user-defined virtual processors (UDVPs). Once you've created one or more UDVPs, a UDR's execution can be restricted to those VPs, significantly reducing the potential negative impact to the instance. Listing 2.12 shows an example.

```
VPCLASS    finance_vp ,num=2  # vps for finance UDRs
  or
onmode -p +2 finance_vp

create function comp_val (dollar, aus_dollar)
returning aus_dollar
specific dollar
with class ="finance_vp"
external name '/usr/Informix/shared_lib/comp_functions.so'
language C not variant
end function;
```

Listing 2.12: Using user-defined VPs to protect against an ill-behaved UDR

In this example, two different methods for creating a UDP are shown. The first occurs in the **$ONCONFIG** file, requiring an instance restart, while the second is executed while the instance is online and supporting end-user operations. Once the UDVPs are created, the C-based function is created and registered with the specific instruction that it is to use only the **finance_vp** virtual processor.

The **finance_vp** virtual processor, and any other UDVP, executes with the same priority as core CPU VPs. Because they are not CPU VPs, though, they exist and execute in their own thread and memory space and use no core processing space. If the UDR misbehaves, its impact is limited to the space the UDVP occupies, leaving core instance functionality unaffected.

By default, UDRs are single-threaded, although they can be parallelized if several conditions are met, including the following:

- Full parallelism is turned on with **PDQPRIORITY** > 1.
- The **parallelizable** keyword is added to the UDR registration statement.
- C- and Java-based routines use Parallel Database Query (PDQ) thread-safe API calls.
- Complex types are not used as input or output parameters.
- Data scans will search multiple table partitions.
- The UDRs are not iterator functions but execute once and then quit.

If you make a mistake when registering a UDR, you can modify its characteristics using the SQL **alter function** command:

```
alter function bigger (int,int)
  with (add parallelizable, add class="math_vps");
```

To monitor UDR processing, you can use **onstat** and other utilities.

User-Defined Aggregates

A user-defined aggregate is a special-purpose UDR whose function is to provide specialized value aggregation not furnished by the data server. As you are well aware, Informix Dynamic Server provides **sum()**, **divide()**, **mod()**, and other math functions for execution on built-in, relational types. These functions will not work with UDTs, may be insufficient if custom aggregations on built-in types are required, or you need to combine values stored in built-in and user-defined types.

An example of a UDA would be a customized Fibonacci sequence. A Fibonacci sequence adds two values together, creating a third; the third value is then added to the second, creating a fourth, which is added to the third, creating a fifth, and so on, yielding a value string such as

```
0,1,2,3,5,8,13,21,34,55,89,144 . . .
```

For whatever reason, a business need might exist to derive a Fibonacci total based on a seed value other than 0, potentially another first incremental value other than 1, and a specific number of iterations. The solution to this problem would best be accomplished using a UDA.

Creating a UDA is more involved than creating a regular UDR. Because UDAs are usually iterative in nature—creating a subtotal at each step of the aggregation to be passed to the next value retrieved—four subroutines are generally defined within the UDA. These subroutines handle the following functions:

- Initialization—Allocating and initializing data server resources for the function
- Iteration—Increasing the row count and performing the math for the iteration
- Combination—Adding the values of the iterator subfunction to the running subtotals that are returned
- Finalization—Returning the final value(s) and releasing allocated resources

The nature of UDAs usually dictates that they be created with C or Java, especially if the iteration subfunction requires scientific, statistical, monetary, or other processing logic or external subroutine calls to derive the new value. These types of operations are beyond the scope of SPL.

Functional Indexes

Indexes are pointers into the data where each occurrence of the indexed value (or values) exists. Like other data servers, Informix Dynamic Server can create an index using one or more data values. In a relational data server, indexes are created using the actual data values stored in the column(s). Not all data interactions are based on absolute column values, though; some might be best represented as a ratio, percentage, or some other representation of one or more data elements. IDS enables you to derive these relationships and use them to build a *functional index*.

Suppose, for example, that it was important to constantly operate on data identified through a weighted ratio of three columns. You could build an index of ratio results by first writing and compiling a function in either C or Java that creates the ratio. Next, you would register the UDR in the instance as shown earlier, using the appropriate UDVP and other parameters. Then, you'd create the index using a call to the UDR:

```
create index
    ix_w8ed_ratio(build_ratio(col3, col5, col10));
```

Functional indexes are also used to create additional *secondary access methods* or ways of comparing values. Most indexes resolve to one of two standard secondary access methods:

- B-tree—Data is equal to, less than, greater than, less than or equal to, greater than or equal to, and so on.

- R-tree—Data is composed of one of two elements:

  » Multidimensional—Data in several dimensions, such as geographic (latitude, longitude, altitude), either with or without a time component or the combination of several independent data elements into a multidimensional representation; for example, creating an index of cloth composed of its true color in dichromatic values, composition (e.g., cotton, silk, polyester), texture, manufacturer, designer and so on.

  » Range—Data with a component that spans a range of values as opposed to one discrete value; for example, the range of longitudinal values between two specific latitudes or the time span of an event or action.

If these methods are not sufficient or efficient to access data, you can create your own indexing scheme and register it in the instance through a series of functional indexes. This is what an IBM Informix partner company called Coppereye, Ltd., did; it developed a new way to index relational data that significantly reduces the time required to build and manipulate the index without sacrificing index performance. Coppereye built a DataBlade using its technology that, when installed, overloaded many of the built-in indexing functions. To use this new secondary access method, a DBA simply overrides the default (**with b-tree**) when creating the index:

```
create index
   ix_myindex on table_a (col2, col3) using coppereye;
```

DataBlades, Bladelets, and Other Add-ons

As I hope you've realized by now, the object orientation of IDS gives you the flexibility to store and manipulate data as best fits your business requirements. Several vendors have capitalized on this functionality to provide bundles of UDTs, UDRs, casts, error messages, and more to extend the processing capabilities of IDS. These bundles, called *DataBlades*, cover a wide range of activities, including the Coppereye index that I've already mentioned, biometric processing (e.g., voice, face recognition), audio and video processing, text search, and so on. The Enterprise Edition of IDS 11 includes the license to use several Blades at no charge to help customers with some of the most commonly requested functionality.

DataBlades and Blade-like functionality are not limited to large functional increases or companies that seek to sell and profit from their technology. Smaller functional additions, called *Bladelets*, can be freely downloaded from the Web sites of the International Informix User's Group (IIUG) and IBM developerWorks (*http://www.iiug.org* and *http:// www.ibm.com/developerworks*, respectively), and used to create point-specific solutions to a data manipulation or modeling issue. Regardless of the packaging, once a Blade is registered, its functionality is available through SQL, SPL, or API calls to external functions, and you can directly call or execute it as part of the functionality of another registered function.

The DataBlades and Bladelets binaries are installed at an instance level, typically in the **$INFORMIXDIR/extend** directory, but they must be registered in each database where their functionality is required. The definitions for the functions, data types, and other components that a Blade creates are stored in reserved tables of the database (e.g., **sysprocbody**) in which the Blade is registered. Unregistering a Blade from a database removes entries for the Blade from these tables.

Summary

For many years, data servers were regarded as critical entities in IT. Discussions about what to buy and when were driven by these servers, their speed of execution, and their functionality. Today, that attitude has changed. I don't mean to say data servers aren't important or have no impact in purchasing decisions; they are and do. But today, the focus is on the application and, specifically, on the development language. These elements capture people's attention with flashy graphics, cool-sounding names, and promises that they'll change the IT environment practically overnight. On the other hand, data servers are viewed as stodgy, boring, and good for nothing more than serving as bit buckets to dump data into and pull it back out of into the latest whiz-bang language. From the developers' perspective, only the lowest common denominator of data server functionality should be used because when they move on to another language (which promises to save the IT world again) in six months, its data access APIs might not support any data server–specific functionality other than basic query, update, delete, or insert operations.

In my opinion, nothing could be further from the truth. The data server matters, and it matters in a big way. It is precisely this turnover and flux in development methodologies that demands that business logic be executed in as business-native format as possible. IDS is uniquely positioned in the market as the only data server with the processing speed and extensibility features to create, store, and manipulate data in its business context. UDTs and UDRs, along with DataBlades and Bladelets, can be added to the server to enhance its native functionality in ways that are impossible with standard relational servers. With these enhanced features, you can significantly reduce development time while creating much richer and interesting applications.

Making a shift to and fully leveraging the IDS object-relational server requires changing how you think about modeling and using data, though. You need to be willing to forego standard relational rules in favor of what works best for your business and protects its data. For example, I feel every database should be designed with distinct types where appropriate. This practice prevents programmers and ad hoc SQL report writers from making serious data-calculation mistakes that could lead to poor business decisions.

With the background and information provided in this and the preceding chapter, you are ready to look in greater detail at what's involved in setting up and running an Informix Dynamic Server instance. We'll begin in Chapter 3 with the planning required for instance initialization. The discussion will be somewhat general in nature because very few solid rules apply; each Informix Dynamic Server instance will have its own unique conditions and requirements that will affect where and how the instance is created and managed.

3

Preparing for Initialization

In this Chapter

▸ General database design issues

▸ Disk drive configuration issues

▸ Introduction to backup strategies

▸ Setting the required environment variables

▸ Preparing for multiple residency

This chapter covers a broad range of topics related to general design considerations and decisions you need to make before initializing an Informix Dynamic Server instance and creating a database. We'll discuss database design issues, proper database table sizing, disk drive subsystem options, instance backup strategies, and the files and environment variables you need to create or set to begin creating an instance. By the end of the chapter, you should understand most of the important database and instance design issues and be ready to set up the environment necessary to create a new IDS instance.

Much of what we'll cover here is factual in nature, but certain areas are purely subjective. For some of the issues we'll discuss, there are no definitive rules to look to for guidance. Your application and data needs will be unique to your environment, and what might be appropriate for one environment will be inappropriate in another. It's up to you, the DBA, to decide what will work best in your situation.

Administering a data server such as IDS is as much an art as it is a science. With the flexibility and configurability of this product, performance can depend greatly on the administrator's ability to build and optimize the instance and databases correctly in response to the types of applications run against them. That said, IDS becomes more automated and self-managing with each release. Although data servers will likely never be completely hands-off, IDS is by far the closest to achieving this goal of all the major servers on the market.

One word of advice as we get started: Before you begin the process of installing and using Informix Dynamic Server, be sure to review the readme, release notes, and other documentation files on the installation media for late-breaking news or install information. Don't overlook the machine notes document, which contains O/S tuning recommendations.

In a shift from earlier releases, the documentation files on Linux, Macintosh, and Unix ports are available before you install the server. After you un-tar the distribution, you'll find these files in the **Server/doc** directory. You can also access the files through the **README.html** file in the top level of the un-tar'ed distribution.

After installation, a broader set of documents and other notes is available in the **$INFORMIXDIR/release/en_us/0333** directory for U.S.-based distributions. The path below the **release** subdirectory may vary for other geographies or languages.

Logical Database Design

In preparing for a new or additional IDS instance, you should spend as much time as possible in the design phase for both the instance and the database (or databases) that the instance will contain. Taking the time to identify factors such as overall performance requirements, general database and table sizes, table interdependencies, table and index partitioning (fragmentation) policies, frequency of access or update, required restore granularity, and other elements will help ensure that the implementation's performance, security, manageability, and cost will meet expectations.

Experience has taught me that you should never create a design simply for the stated overall length of the project. The instance and databases invariably exist significantly longer, and the ability, in terms of access and capacity, to manage and modify the instance, databases, and tables should reflect this longer-term thinking. That said, we all must work with the amount of money allocated for any given project. Depending on how your company works, you'll either have to limit your design to the allocated budget or help sell a budget to satisfy the design and ultimately work within the approved budget. In any case, when considering the factors that will affect the instance or its databases, you cannot ask too many questions or seek to understand too much about the application processes that will be run against the instance.

Let's consider the database portion for a moment. Here, you need to know not only how many tables there are but also how the data elements are interrelated. You also should have a pretty good idea of how much growth is anticipated in individual tables over a given period of time. Forecast the impact this growth will have in terms of disk space. Your calculations will determine how you'll create your tables and will affect their dbspace placement and partitioning. These factors, in turn, will influence the number and size of dbspaces you create, the disks that will hold them, and how you'll protect them against media failure.

Another factor affecting table design, placement, and partitioning is the types of applications that will be run against the database. Will they be update or read intensive? What are the types and scope of the common queries that will be run? Will end users have direct access into the instance via ad hoc SQL tools? If so, what protection do you need on tables or columns?

The best way to discover the various factors and conditions that will affect the database is to create a good functional design of the entire application process. This job involves analyzing general performance requirements and availability constraints. To begin, ask the following types of questions:

- What information do end users need to see, and how will it be displayed?
- What types of data are going to be stored to provide this information?
- How will the application query the data?
- How will data be entered, modified, or deleted? When and how will this occur?
- What is the acceptable length of time for completion of a database operation?
- How much data will be used to initially populate the tables?
- What is the anticipated growth pattern for each table? Under what conditions will this growth occur?

I've heard some people call this process "getting intimate with your data." As a DBA, you need this level of understanding to assist the application development process or to help manage the installation and then administer third-party applications.

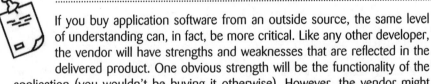

If you buy application software from an outside source, the same level of understanding can, in fact, be more critical. Like any other developer, the vendor will have strengths and weaknesses that are reflected in the delivered product. One obvious strength will be the functionality of the application (you wouldn't be buying it otherwise). However, the vendor might be less adept at creating (or at taking the time to properly create) the database environment that will best support the application. You can directly and positively impact the application's speed by obtaining as much information as possible about the vendor's database design and how the application works against it.

When the application is installed, examine the size, placement, and population of the dbspaces. Depending on your hardware resources, you might be able to use suggestions from this book and other sources regarding table placement and partitioning to alter the default installation and achieve better performance.

In addition, you should monitor the types and sizes of database operations performed and tune appropriately to enhance concurrency and performance. You might need to conduct this tuning at an instance level or an SQL level. IDS 10 and later releases let you register SQL optimizer directives for statements you can't directly access to modify; the data server applies these directives when the statements are executed. IDS 11 and later include functionality that captures the slowest and most expensive SQL operations so you can quickly see which ones you need to work on.

In short, don't simply take the vendor's word on how to set up or tune the instance. Remember, though, that you might be able to learn something from the application provider, so keep your eyes and ears open to the ideas and approaches the vendor uses for any given condition.

Based on performance requirements and an understanding of table relationships, sizes, and growth patterns, you can make decisions about the amount of disk space needed to implement the design. The logical design of the database should be the guide to building the database at the physical level. It will dictate whether to partition tables and indexes as well as how to write the partitioning expressions. Taking this instance design process one step further, once you know the type of data each table in a database will store and understand the expected usage pattern, the desired number, type, size, and placement of dbspaces within the disk drives will become obvious.

Last, understanding how the application works will enable you to determine the logging mode for the database(s) and will influence decisions about backing up the logical logs. Preliminary values for shared memory and other IDS tunable parameters may also be derived for use when initializing the instance.

Calculating Table Sizes

When you use unformatted disk partitions (i.e., raw space) on Linux/Unix platforms, Informix Dynamic Server allocates disk space for tables by creating contiguous reserved sections within dbspaces of a size set by the DBA. This is done to reduce disk head movement and seek time as the table is read. Rather than skip around all over the disk, the head can move through contiguous allocations of disk space. One benefit is a significant performance increase.

Whenever a table needs more space, the data server tries to allocate space for another section of the same table as close to the table as possible, joining the spaces together logically. In some cases, the table's next allocation is directly adjacent to another allocation of space for the same table, so the two allocations are joined physically as well, preserving the efficiency of the read process.

In dbspaces with more than one table continually expanding, the new addition of space for any table cannot always be attached to the end of the existing table's allocation. This circumstance creates a condition called interleaving that looks very much like it sounds. Figure 3.1 illustrates the logical concept of *interleaving* by showing an allocation for table A followed by an allocation for table B. The latter allocation, in turn, is followed by an allocation for table C and then by another allocation for table A.

As you can imagine, after a while you may have any number of allocations, known as *table extents*, scattered all over the dbspace. In such cases, the data server must create, store, and manage a series of pointers to link the tablespace sections together into a logical whole. Costs are incurred, first in lost CPU efficiency as the server spends time maintaining these lists. Reduced I/O throughput is another cost. Severe interleaving causes the disk head to fly all over the place to read the table. Disk rotation speed and positioning latency eventually constrain I/O operations.

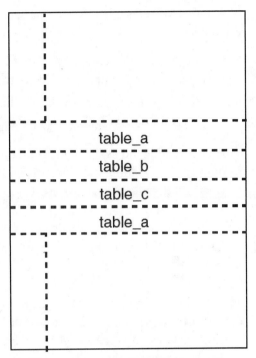

Figure 3.1: Table interleaving in a dbspace

On systems where dbspaces are created in formatted file systems (i.e., cooked files), some of the previous discussion doesn't apply because you have no control over where the operating system will write blocks of the flat file that makes up the chunk and/or dbspace. In fact, you can be certain the blocks will not be contiguously aligned and interleaving will occur. Disk speed and latency will constrain I/O efficiency, but that drawback presumably is offset by other advantages that dictated the creation of the chunks and dbspaces in cooked space. With cooked files, the operating system is responsible for maintaining the forward and backward pointers to all portions of the dbspace. This fact doesn't completely release the data server from internal maintenance problems, though. It may not have to maintain the physical links, but it still must maintain the logical links. This work can consume CPU time if the number of extents for any given table grows to a large number.

You can control interleaving by calculating, in advance, how much disk space a table will need at creation time and over a given amount of time. Years ago, when I worked with earlier versions of Informix data servers, I used the following general rules when calculating table sizes:

- Start with the original row count for the table, and add to it the anticipated number of new rows that will be added to the table over the next six months.

- Use the resulting number of rows to calculate the initial extent size.

- Use that same six-month growth number to calculate the next extent size.

When calculating the next extent size, I divided by 6 rather than by 7 as the manuals recommended. Dividing by 6 yields a slightly larger next extent size, but the end result is fewer additional table extents overall. I recommend using a six-month growth rate to allow sufficient time to roll out the application and see how the database actually grows. You can track usage and growth patterns more accurately over this longer period.

Another benefit of using a six-month window is that if some tables grow more rapidly than anticipated, you should have enough time to review and revise the database design because the original table extent size is larger. As a result, the table won't begin allocating additional extents as quickly. You can test and install the new design as part of the overall development process instead of just resorting to allocating more chunks to dbspaces or moving the table into other, larger dbspaces in a crisis situation.

The same general sizing philosophy still applies today, although it can become more complicated when you partition tables across or within dbspaces or partition indexes away from the table into different dbspaces. To calculate general table sizes for non-partitioned tables, use the worksheet provided in the Appendix (or the Adobe Acrobat version available on the Web site supporting this book). The worksheet uses the six-month anticipated growth figure, but you can adjust this window up or down depending on your confidence in understanding the growth that will take place in any given table. Should you decide to partition a table or to partition indexes away from a table, you'll need a different approach to table sizing.

Let me briefly introduce partitioning, also known as *fragmentation* (we'll get into the details in Chapter 6). *Table partitioning* is the ability to place parts of tables in any number of dbspaces based on logical conditions you create. You have two options for table partitioning. A *round-robin* partitioning strategy creates an even distribution of newly added rows across all the table partitions based on row count alone. *By expression* partitioning lets you explicitly state conditions that determine the specific dbspace in which a row will be stored.

With by expression partitioning, if the columnar data for any given row is modified and the column or columns are part of the partitioning expression, the row automatically will be moved into the appropriate dbspace. This is one reason why the "rowid" structure used in earlier versions of IDS is no longer of any value. Multiple rows could share the same rowid based on their placement within table extents partitioned across multiple dbspaces.

There is a way to mimic a rowid within a table; however, you incur a significant performance penalty for doing so. Adding the SQL phrase **with rowids** to the **create table** SQL command creates an additional column and an associated index in the table that together function somewhat like a **serial** data type. The combination guarantees uniqueness of values for that column within the table. You can query the column just like any other column, but the query won't be performed quickly even with the index in place. If the ability to query quickly for one unique row is required, you're better off creating a unique constraint and querying the table via the constraint. Chapter 6 provides more information about constraints.

One of the biggest performance benefits you can realize in your database environment can come from partitioning tables by expression. The data server's optimizer will, where possible, use the expression statement to determine which table partitions to include or exclude when processing a data operation. This optimization can eliminate a significant amount of I/O overhead during query or update statement processing.

The ability to partition indexes means an index can be left in the same dbspace (or dbspaces) as the table (i.e., be "attached"), be semidetached, or be completely detached and created in one or more dbspaces using a logical statement similar to that used to partition tables. A semidetached index would have a partitioning scheme that included the dbspace where the table (or a partition thereof) was created. A detached index would be partitioned into dbspaces other than where the table was created. In writing the index partitioning expression, you select combinations and values of the index keys. However, you cannot specify extent sizes for index partitions as you can for table partitions.

When trying to calculate extent sizes for partitioned tables, you must be aware that you can specify only one set of extent sizes for the entire table. The initial extent size for all the table's partitions will be the same size regardless of the logic in the partitioning expression that determines partition population.

Much like a non-partitioned table, when a partition needs more space, the data server tries to allocate to it the amount specified in the **next size** phrase of the extent sizing statement. If you partition a table using round-robin partitioning, all the table's partitions will take additional disk space at about the same time. This makes sense because all the partitions should be holding about the same amount of data at any given moment. In trying to calculate extent sizing for a table partitioned with round-robin partitioning, use the normal table sizing worksheet. When you've completed your calculations, take the initial and next extent sizes and divide them by the number of table partitions you plan to use.

If you partition a table using round-robin partitioning, be sure to detach any indexes into another dbspace. See Chapter 6 for a more detailed explanation of the reasons why this is so important.

If you're using by expression partitioning, a partition will take additional space only when it fills. In sizing tables that will be partitioned using this method, balance the amount of data you anticipate will be stored in the various partitions against the sizes of the dbspaces in which they'll be created. Try to load balance the disks as evenly as possible without sacrificing the advantages gained by partitioning. Be aware that unless the data can, from a logical point of view, be fairly evenly distributed, there will be wasted disk space because some partitions will have more rows than others.

In deciding on a next extent size, you might be tempted to use a fairly large value if all you're considering is the largest or most active partitions of the table. However, a large extent allocation could swamp a dbspace if a small, little-used partition of the table finally filled up and needed more space. This table partition would be allocated a large amount of disk space that would be wasted.

For this reason, it's preferable to place larger, more active table partitions in their own dbspaces and use a rather small next size value regardless of the initial extent size. The little-used partitions will allocate a small amount of disk space when they need it. The larger or more active partitions will allocate more extents, but these extents will be logically concatenated to form one large extent because there's nothing else in the dbspace to cause an interleaved condition.

So, how do you calculate extent sizes on partitioned tables? Place larger, more active partitions in dbspaces with no other tables; smaller partitions can go in dbspaces with other tables. Use the table sizing worksheet, and calculate the initial and next size values using the projected row count for one of the smaller partitions you expect to have based on the partitioning expression.

One final note on by expression partitioning: You need to balance the constraints of the total amount of available disk space against the business or system logic driving the decision to partition. The amount of disk available will determine whether you can justify the cost of the wasted disk from partitioning in relation to the benefit gained through faster performance.

The decision to partition indexes off from the table should be driven by the general operational environment of the database. OLAP queries are more sequential in nature and will see less of a performance gain than OLTP queries, which are heavily index-driven. (Chapter 1 provides a slightly expanded explanation of OLTP and OLAP environments.) Should you partition indexes across one or more dbspaces, the data server sizes the index extents for you automatically. The index extents are created based on the extent size given in the table creation statement as well as the size of the index keys. If disk space is at a premium in your environment, be aware that the total size of an index row grows by 4 bytes per key value if you partition the index.

Disk Drive Issues

Whenever I work with people to set up a new IDS system or to make changes to an existing system, one of the first questions I ask is how they're "running" their database drives. Are the drives mirrored (with copies driven by the operating system or the data server itself), in a Redundant Array of Independent Disks (RAID) array (which, depending on the level implemented, can be used to mirror disks, too), in some type of storage array, or just sitting on SCSI controllers and treated independently as JABOD, or Just a Bunch of Disks? The question isn't as pointless as it may appear. Storage arrays can be either direct-attached or network-based and can be configured with or without simple hardware-based mirroring, memory caches, and hardware-based RAID controllers. To further complicate the picture, you can implement software-based RAID functionality from within the operating system or through any number of add-on software products. Each of these options has implications for the IDS environment in terms of performance, reliability, and availability.

Depending on your performance requirements (or your level of paranoia), you'll probably have a mixture of disk drive environments to deal with. Although there is no one definitive answer for any given environment, there are some guidelines you should follow.

One statement can be made categorically about drives that will be used in an IDS instance: Regardless of what you do with the other drives supporting chunks and dbspaces in the instance, the drives on which the rootdbs, the logical logs, and the physical log reside *must* be protected against disk failure in some fashion. Whether you choose to use the data server's mirroring functionality, simple SCSI controller-based mirroring, or a full software/ hardware RAID implementation of one level or another, these structures are too important to the operation of the instance to be subject to mechanical disk failure without immediate failover protection. The following sections address the different disk drive options and the tradeoffs that apply with each alternative.

Mirroring

For software-based mirroring, your first choice is that provided within Informix Dynamic Server itself. You can set up mirrors of chunks—and, by extension, dbspaces within an instance—and have the data server handle the maintenance of the mirrors. The mirrors operate asynchronously, but the instance must wait for a completion signal to be returned from both the mirror and the primary disk before a disk write is considered complete (as explained in the next paragraph), thus potentially affecting performance.

Using Informix's mirroring has two disadvantages. The first is a potential impact to overall instance processing speed. The CPU and asynchronous I/O virtual processors (AIO VPs) control the mirror writes. These tasks must be coordinated with all the other service requests these VPs are processing. In earlier versions of the data server, AIO VPs were defined statically, and if all were busy, mirror writes had to wait their turn. IDS 11.10 and later releases mitigate this limitation somewhat because the data server dynamically allocates additional AIO VPs to manage the instance's I/O workload. This new functionality notwithstanding, disk contention can still affect mirror writes, causing the instance to wait for the write-complete acknowledgement. Although it may generally be true that hardware-based mirroring is faster than software-based mirroring, the performance benefit depends heavily on the controller that is managing the mirroring process.

The second disadvantage of Informix mirroring is that you must mirror whole dbspaces; there are no options for mirroring just one chunk of a dbspace. Not too many years ago, the price of disk storage made purchasing an extra complement of disk space to act as mirrors an expensive proposition. Nowadays, the cost of buying a second set of storage has decreased significantly. Although the price for a given unit of storage is now generally considered "cheap," data volume has exploded, so the overall cost of storage is just as high as, or even higher than, back in the "good old days" of open systems, when disks cost a dollar per megabyte.

On the flip side, one can make the argument that the data server itself should be monitoring the drives because it is the process directing the write operations. The logic within the data server evaluates the return codes from the disks and decides what constitutes a disk failure. These return codes might or might not constitute a failure condition to an outside layer of software or a hardware controller.

Another advantage of using IDS's mirroring is improved query performance. The data server will use the mirrors as well as the primary disks for data reads under certain conditions. This technology, called a *split read*, works as follows. When a row is requested from a table, its relative rowid determines which disk will be used to satisfy the query. The rowids are divided in half, with one half being supplied from the primary disk and the other half serviced from the mirror disk. As a result, those rows that are read from the mirror can allow the primary disk to satisfy other query operations or to accept and process write operations, further boosting throughput.

In a more OLAP-oriented environment, queries are generally more sequential in nature. With mirroring and split reads, a read request can be spawned for both halves of the data server–managed mirror set and execute in parallel. The query will be completed faster because twice as many disks are being used to scan for data. I should also note that although IDS mirroring may not be the fastest in terms of write I/O throughput, mirroring (either software- or hardware-based) is the best option to ensure data availability in the event of a mechanical disk failure.

RAID

The last few years have seen storage arrays become the de facto standard for data storage in companies large and small. These arrays range from the relatively simple (a small set of drives fronted by a drive controller directly attached to the physical server) to highly complex, network-based disk servers with internal mechanisms to back up and recover the drives, distribute data between storage arrays, and more. Because of the physical requirements and limitations of hard drives (each is x by y inches in size), there is a practical limit to the size of the storage arrays—they have to fit through the door! To compensate and increase their storage capacity, the arrays are generally populated with very high-capacity disk drives. Although this solution might be attractive from an executive perspective—"Great, we can store more stuff in the same space!"—it can hurt data server performance.

All storage arrays provide one or more levels of RAID technology to create logical units (LUNs) of storage for physical servers to use. Although this practice is attractive from a disk management perspective, when you couple it with very-large-capacity drives, it is not at all uncommon for multiple physical systems to contend for I/O access to their LUNs, all of which were created from sections of the same set of physical drives in the array. The end result is drive contention and reduced performance. Having multiple LUNs on the same drives isn't the only issue associated with RAID; each level has its own performance characteristics that need to be understood before building dbspaces.

Using RAID technology, groups of disks are organized into RAID "sets" that appear to the operating system as one large disk drive (LUN). Within a RAID set, you can divide data over the drives in a type of "divide and conquer" methodology, or you can protect against data loss due to drive failure by storing either an exact copy or an error-correcting code on other disks. In some cases, you can do both. In the event of either a physical device failure or corruption of the data due to component malfunction, the RAID set can, if properly configured, revert to the copy of data, ensuring higher availability and reliability to users. Once you've corrected the problem (by replacing a failed drive, for example), the data on the failed or corrupted drive is regenerated onto the new drive, which is then placed in service.

Achieving a true level of fault tolerance in the storage array requires you to provide redundancy throughout the entire array. This includes independent input power sources, disk adapters and controllers, backup power for controller cache stores if they exist, and so on. In general, though, depending on how you choose to implement RAID technology and allocate LUNs over the physical devices, you can accomplish some significant cost savings with respect to total disk space purchased while still achieving a measure of performance enhancement and failure protection.

RAID level specifications are slightly vague, so you'll find some differences in how any given RAID level is implemented from vendor to vendor. Although seven levels of RAID exist, most vendors offer products in levels 0, 1, 2, 3, 5, and 6. Some vendors also support a pseudo-level called *0+1* or *10*, which is a combination of levels 0 and 1. For more information about RAID and its design theory, read Paul Massiglia's *The RAIDbook* (St. Peter, MN: RAID Advisory Board, 1997), published by the coalition of vendors who defined the RAID specification.

For most database applications, levels 0 and 1 (and the hybrid) are the most appropriate to use because of their relative speed compared with the other RAID levels. If disk performance isn't an issue but total disk usage is, you should consider implementing RAID level 5. Level 5 is also commonly used for data mart and warehouse environments, where a significant amount of data must be stored yet protected against loss. Let's look at each of the more common RAID levels in greater detail.

Level 0

A level 0 RAID set (illustrated in Figure 3.2) *stripes* data across two or more drives, somewhat akin to IDS's round-robin partitioning.

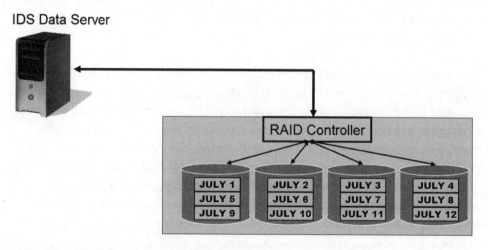

Figure 3.2: A RAID 0 stripe set with data distributed across all drives in the set

The primary advantage of using RAID level 0 is access speed when processing large blocks of data. When an operation calls for a row of data, all the drives on the RAID set initiate a search for the row or components thereof. Because each drive has a smaller subset of the rows to parse, the row in question should be found more quickly than by searching through one larger drive.

Unlike IDS's partitioning (whether round-robin or by expression), with RAID level 0 you can't be assured that a single row will be completely stored on any one disk volume. Its components might be spread across more than one disk, which could cause problems if a drive fails and no protection scheme, other than backups, is in place. You would have orphaned components of rows on the surviving disks that you could never clean up or completely restore short of dropping the table, re-creating it, and reloading the data.

Nor, unlike with IDS's partitioning by expression, can you apply logic to the way the data is distributed on the disks. A request activates all disks, not just those partitions determined to possibly contain the data based on the request. Because all drives are handled synchronously in a level 0 RAID set, performance could be affected significantly in high-volume OLTP environments. For any given query, all drives could be busy searching for a small number of rows that might not even exist on their media. Reads and writes for other sessions would be delayed while all disks report back to the controller the status of each individual read or write request.

In OLAP environments, you should see a general increase in performance using level 0 because larger blocks of data are usually being processed.

The decision whether to use RAID level 0 or round-robin partitioning must be based on real-world performance tests to see which runs faster in your environment. Don't let access speed be the sole criterion when deciding which technology to use. You must also consider the ability to manage the data at a logical level through the **alter partition** command rather than at the physical level. It is much easier to understand the distribution of data throughout the database or table by creating a **dbschema** report than by scrutinizing RAID configuration screens.

Also be aware that a disk environment based on RAID level 0, while potentially providing faster response time, has no failure protection incorporated into it. If any part of the RAID set fails, all data in the set is lost.

Level 1

A level 1 RAID set, illustrated in Figure 3.3, is simply disk mirroring. This level provides the highest level of data availability, but it is the most costly RAID level to implement because of the disk space requirements.

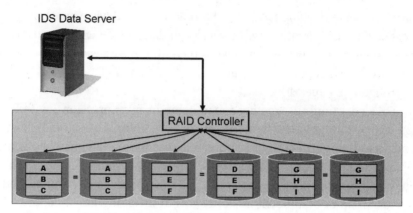

Figure 3.3: A RAID 1 set with data mirrored between disk pairs

In a hardware-based implementation, the RAID controllers monitor the result codes returning from the drives as well as any diagnostics the controller might run. If the controller detects what it determines to be a failure, the affected drive is removed from service while the remaining disk in the pair continues to operate.

In choosing a vendor for a level 1 RAID set, check to see whether the mirror drive is handled synchronously or asynchronously; the answer will influence performance. Some vendors have not only 1:1 mirroring but also a mirror *spare* that is part of their RAID set implementation. This spare becomes a surrogate mirror for any surviving disk in a disk pair that experiences a failure, providing comprehensive and continuous mirroring even in the event of a single-drive failure. In theory, and depending on the number of drives you've configured into level 1 RAID sets, you should be able to recognize that a failure occurred, replace the failed drive, and regenerate the data before another drive fails in a set, forcing the array to operate solely on the remaining disk in the pair. Some vendors let you create more than one spare disk in a RAID environment, further enhancing your ability to handle disk failures and recovery in a graceful and methodical manner.

Although you should see faster performance from a hardware-based level 1 RAID set, you'd have to test to see whether your vendor's implementation is faster or slower than IDS's mirroring utility. The one advantage most level 1 RAID sets (and other higher-level RAID sets) provide is the ability to "hot swap" drives—that is, to remove a failed drive and insert a replacement without having to shut down the server or the RAID array. Whether it works as advertised and won't crash the RAID array and your instance with it is another matter and should be tested in a controlled situation. If your level of paranoia is such that you'll shut down the instance as well as the RAID set to swap out a failed drive, save your money and use IDS's mirroring unless you experience a significant performance boost from using RAID mirroring.

Level 0+1/10

Quite a few vendors now have, within their products, a RAID pseudo-level called 0+1 or 10. As these names imply and Figure 3.4 illustrates, this level uses a mirrored stripe set.

Level 0+1/10 enables you to take advantage of the speed that RAID level 0 striping can offer in the correct environment along with the security and availability that RAID level 1 mirroring provides. Because 0+1/10 is not an official RAID level, vendors' implementations will vary more than other RAID levels. As a result, you should conduct a series of tests to ensure compatibility and performance within your environment and its requirements.

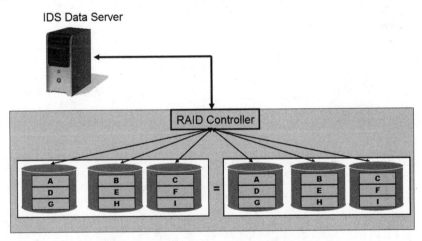

Figure 3.4: A RAID 0+1 set with data striped and mirrored across drives

Levels 5 and 6

Although they are very popular, RAID levels 5 and 6 are the slowest of all the RAID levels. You should implement these levels only if access speed is not an issue or if the majority of your disk actions are reads rather than writes.

Levels 5 and 6 are nearly identical in that data is stored in up to 75 percent of the disk space. The remaining 25 percent of the disk is used to store what are called *parity bits*. These code bits, the result of work done by a special Hamming Error Correction Code algorithm, allow for the reconstruction of data on other drives should the data become unavailable on the primary disk. Figures 3.5 and 3.6 illustrate these two RAID levels.

IDS Data Server

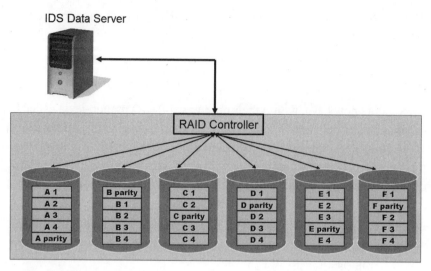

Figure 3.5: A RAID 5 set with parity bits distributed across all drives

IDS Data Server

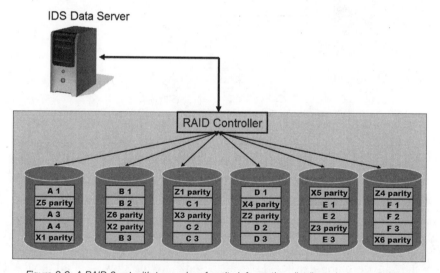

Figure 3.6: A RAID 6 set with two pairs of parity information distributed across all drives

In RAID level 5, the parity bits for an individual disk are written across other drives in the RAID set. RAID level 6 distributes not only parity information across other disks but also a second set of error-correction codes inversely to the first set. This second code set enables a RAID 6 set to survive a two-disk failure situation.

The I/O throughput for levels 5 and 6 is very low because of the disk contention involved in trying to write not only the original data to the target disk but also the parity information to the other disks. In the event of a disk failure, reading from parity information is pathetically slow.

The one advantage these two RAID levels have is that they provide a decent degree of data availability at about half the disk cost of implementing a RAID level 1 mirror set. The only way to successfully implement a level 5 or 6 RAID set is to have a large write memory cache on the controller. This requirement will impact hardware costs and, along with performance, should be considered when evaluating whether to use one of these RAID levels.

Software-Based RAID

Some of the functionality provided by hardware-based RAID sets can also be had through the use of RAID functionality built into the physical server's operating system. Raid levels 0, 1, and 5 are most likely supported natively.

Software-based RAID technology comes with a number of performance and systemic disadvantages. Primary among these is that the work involved in supporting the RAID set is borne by the system's CPUs rather than offloaded to dedicated I/O processors on a RAID controller. This means that the CPU cycles that could be used to support data server or application thread demands are instead spent calculating parity values or managing data distribution across drives. Unlike hardware-based solutions, software-based RAID generally does not provide the ability to hot swap failed drives, requiring you to shut down the system to deal with drive failures.

Which to Choose?

Which of all these possible disk solutions should you choose? The answer depends on the priorities for your site and on any budgetary constraints. If high availability is important, use IDS's mirroring or RAID level 1. For higher query performance with large block transfers, such as in an OLAP environment, use RAID level 0 if you're willing to sacrifice protection against disk failure. If you're a "want the cake and eat it too" type of person, choose a vendor that supplies mirrored stripe sets as part of its RAID implementation. If cost and convenience are more important factors than performance, use RAID level 5 or 6, depending on the level of availability you want to achieve. If cost is the be-all determining factor, use the software-based RAID functionality provided with the operating system.

The key, as I'll discuss in greater detail later, is to maximize the number of I/O devices that the data server can use while at the same time limiting disk contention because several very active LUNs are created using the same physical devices in the storage array.

Using Cooked Files or Raw Space for Dbspaces

As I alluded to in Chapter 1, with very few exceptions dbspaces have historically been created using "raw," or unformatted, disk space in Linux and Unix environments. More recently, the proliferation of storage arrays has led many customers to begin to use regular Linux/Unix file-system files, often referred to as "cooked" files, to support chunks and dbspaces. With Windows ports of the data server, the only supported option has been cooked space.

Historically, we've seen a performance difference between raw and cooked space on Linux/Unix ports of the data server. This performance difference was due to the loss of direct memory access (DMA) transfer of data directly out of shared memory to cooked files. IDS 11 adds a new **$ONCONFIG** parameter, **DIRECT_IO**, that enables the data server to bypass O/S buffers and write directly to the flat files used to create chunks and dbspaces. With this feature enabled, you can approach the same performance metrics using cooked space as you can with raw space.

The feature is O/S-dependent, so consult the release notes that accompany your distribution of the data server to see whether this enhancement is available for your port. Be aware, though, that even with this new functionality, you're still constrained by factors within the operating system regarding file sizes, file system limits, and so on. In addition, the actual flat file(s) supporting the chunk(s) will still be allocated all over the drive based on the O/S block size rather than being allocated contiguously as with raw space. Whether or not delays from disk seeks and latency are significant enough to make a difference in your environment is an exercise left to you. Generally speaking, I would assume not.

A few final thoughts on this topic: First, when creating flat files for chunks on a Windows port of the data server, you need to follow a precise file-naming convention (which we'll discuss more later). Second, although it's possible to use both raw and cooked space for devices in an instance, you should not mix raw and cooked chunks within a single dbspace or performance will be compromised. Third, you may be safer using raw space if your general application support team isn't terribly skilled. With raw space, an inexperienced tech with root-level access can't inadvertently delete your database files with a misplaced **rm** command. It also is highly unlikely a tech will try to reformat or mount the disk partitions. I'm not saying that using raw space is guaranteed safe, but it may reduce your risk of instance corruption or loss.

Using Symbolic Links

Regardless of whether you use raw or cooked space on Linux/Unix ports of the data server, when it comes time to enter device names for disk and tape drives—whether in the instance configuration file, as parameters to command-line utilities, or through the SQL administrative API—you should use symbolic links that point to these devices rather than actual device names. There are several reasons to use symbolic links; the two most important are disk/tape device management and the ability to migrate the environment to another server or to another set of disks on the same server. Let me illustrate, by way of personal experience, why using symbolic links is advisable.

I once worked in an environment where we referenced the chunks used to create the dbspaces using the actual device names returned from the disk partitioning process. One day, a drive failed and I replaced it with another. Even though the drives were the same model, the replacement disk ended up having less usable space after the disk analysis phase was completed.

Because the environment was using actual device names and no other replacement drive was available, I had no choice but to use that one physical disk. Luckily for me, even though the disk had less usable storage space, the last partition of the drive had not been used to create a chunk within the instance, so I was able to continue the disk swap. Had we used symbolic links to reference the disk partitions and I had needed that last partition, I could have grabbed the total amount of space I needed from another drive or created a logical drive with segments from two or more other drives; then I could have pointed the original symbolic link to wherever I created the new space. There would have been no impact on the instance.

Should you ever need to move your database system from one part of a disk array to another or change the underlying disk formats (e.g., nonstriped to striped), having symbolic links for device identifiers makes the process significantly easier, especially if you define mirroring using IDS's bundled technology. This process involves the following steps:

1. Configure the new physical disks as well as any new logical disks (array LUNs).

2. Take any mirrors offline.

3. Drop and re-create the mirror disk's symbolic links so they point to the new disks.

4. Bring the mirrors back up, and allow them to fully recover.

5. Once the mirrors have recovered, repeat the steps for the primary chunks.

If you need to move to a new machine, and the new machine and software are compatible enough for a database restore to work, the use of symbolic links for device identifiers (both disk and tape) will enable you to avoid nearly all the problems or issues related to disk media in the move. Simply create the new disk partitions or logical disks, re-create the symbolic links in the same directory structures as on the original machine, and execute a restore from archive. (As you'll see in Chapter 7, another option for changing the location of devices is to execute a "redirected restore" operation.)

Another advantage to using symbolic links is the ability to employ naming conventions that make sense for your environment. Symbolic links can also make it easier to trace the physical implementation of the logical design. Because the device name used to build the chunk is what the **onstat -d** command returns, you should use names that make sense to you and help you administer the system rather than names like **/dev/rdsk/c0b0t2d0s5**.

Creating symbolic links is fairly easy to do. As I'll explain later, when I set up a new physical server, I create a subdirectory called **devices**. Under this directory, I create another directory using the instance name for each instance that will be running on that machine. I create all the symbolic links to the chunks I'll be using for an instance in the appropriate subdirectory using the **link** command. Check your O/S manual for the correct syntax for this command. It generally is called **ln** (that's a lowercase letter "l" as in "link") and, for symbolic links, uses the following format:

```
ln -s pathed_device_name desired_symbolic_name
```

For example, to create a symbolic link called **styx_chnk_1** in the **/opt/IBM/informix/ devices/styx** directory that points to a raw device, you would execute:

```
ln -s /dev/rdsk/c3b0t4d0s3 styx_chnk_1
```

Although symbolic links have their own unchangeable permissions, you must correctly set the ownership and permissions of the original devices to which they point for the device to be usable by the instance. Use the **chown** and **chgrp** commands to set ownership and group membership of devices to be used by an IDS instance to **informix**; the file permissions should be **660** or **rw-rw----**.

Working with Cooked Files

The process of creating and then using cooked files in a Linux, Mac OS X, or Unix instance is not difficult. First, select a directory and file name to create. Second, use the **touch** command to create the file in the chosen directory. Last, set the permission, ownership, and group membership of the file as explained in the preceding paragraph.

Listing 3.1 illustrates the creation of a couple of cooked files that will be used for dbspaces in an instance, showing several options for the commands.

```
#
# cd /ifmx_data/tagus
# touch r_dbs chnk1
#
# chmod 660 r_dbs chnk1
# chown informix r_dbs
# chgrp informix r_dbs
#
# chown informix:informix chnk1
# ls -l
rw-rw--- informix informix 18:34 0 r_dbs
rw-rw--- informix informix 18:34 0 chnk1
#
```

Listing 3.1: Creating cooked files for use in an instance

When you actually use the cooked file to create the dbspace or chunk, the file created by the **touch** command will expand to whatever size you specified for the dbspace or chunk. Remember that the system **ulimit** and other file-oriented kernel parameters will have an impact on the successful expansion of the file. The machine notes I mentioned earlier in this chapter generally provide recommendations about how to tune the O/S to support the potentially large files created. Be sure to check those notes as well as the operating system documentation for other parameters you might need to tune.

Once you've created the cooked files, you will still want to reference them using symbolic links, as explained earlier.

With Windows ports of IDS, you must follow a strict location and naming convention when creating the files for chunks and dbspaces. This topic is covered in greater detail in Chapter 5.

Dbspace Design Issues

The process of taking disk drives or LUNs, dividing them into chunks, and then creating dbspaces populated with tables is two parts science and three parts trial and error. I touched on this topic at the beginning of the chapter when I noted the importance of knowing as much as possible about the logical design of your database. The types and frequency of Data Manipulation Language (DML) statements that will occur in the database, the number and size of the most active tables (whether they're reference tables or "active" tables receiving new data or updates and deletes), and the desired restore granularity will influence how many dbspaces you'll create and where, physically, you'll create them.

The overall goal in moving from the logical design to the physical installation through the placement and creation of dbspaces is to balance I/O across the drive spindles. At the same time, you want to set up your physical installation, or model, to maximize the effect of the mechanism you've selected to protect your data and enhance throughput, be it IDS mirroring, RAID level 0, or anything else. This is particularly difficult with today's storage arrays and their massive drives.

To maximize the money spent, array administrators are pressured to provide as much usable space as possible with the least amount of ongoing administration. For them, this means one or two RAID 5 or possibly RAID 6 sets, using all the drives in the array. Due to cost, both for the connections and for the massive amounts of memory that front the connections, you'll probably have only two or three connections to the array. The array sales team will constantly have reiterated that there's no need for finer levels of control and no need to worry about disk contention because "we take care of it with our controller/array cache!" Yeah, right. The design of RAID requires all devices to actively participate in every disk operation. If there are five, ten, or more LUNs created out of one massive RAID 5 set using all the drives, I/O access for all systems using these LUNs *will* be serialized.

The massive amounts of memory cache are, for the most part, useless from an IDS perspective. The data server will maintain the most frequently used data in its own memory buffer system, which is much quicker to access than the arrays. The data server will even pre-read data into the buffers if the query plan calls for sequential data scans. The only place where array cache is of value, from an IDS perspective, is for write operations. Instead of having to wait for serialized I/O to the device, the array can park the data in its cache and report back to the instance that the write was completed. It is absolutely critical in this case to ensure that the array cache has multiple redundant layers of protection so the data actually gets to disk. Otherwise, data inconsistency could occur, with some data supposedly committed but not actually written to disk. That would not be a good thing.

Although doing so can be very difficult, you must try to persuade your array administrators to segregate drives for data server use only. Once the drives are segregated, you must get as close to a 1:1 relationship of LUNs to physical devices as possible. You won't be able to fully leverage the I/O and other parallelism features of the data server if you're stuck with serialized I/O or disk contention because multiple chunks were created on a few very large drives. One approach you might try, particularly if you need to buy new storage, is to see whether you can purchase older models that use smaller drives. This option might be less expensive, saving the company money and making it easier to avoid disk contention.

For the rest of this discussion, we'll assume you live in a perfect world and can manage the storage space as you would like. I don't need to say how important it is in an OLTP environment to put the most active tables or table partitions into dbspaces either isolated to their own disks or with other dbspaces containing little-used reference tables. The same holds true for indexes. If you're using raw space, you'll want to create the most active dbspaces using chunks created as close to the center of the disk platter as possible to minimize actuator movement. If you use mirroring, be it IDS's or one of the other suggested approaches, not only should you create the mirror devices on different disks but you should attach the disks containing the mirrors to a different controller than the primary disk devices. That's the science part.

Once you have the instance, database, and application implemented and running, you'll be able to see how close the theory was to actual use and make any adjustments needed to improve performance or enhance security—the three parts trial and error. The flexibility designed into IDS makes this part of your job much easier to accomplish. Using table partitioning by expression, you can rather painlessly divide tables across dbspaces to balance I/O and maximize the efficiency of both the tables and the dbspaces in which they are built. Or, you can use the flexibility provided in IDS 10 and later to create multiple partitions of the same table in one or more dbspaces for administrative purposes.

IDS development recommends a 1:1 correspondence of disk chunks to dbspaces. Some engineers even go so far as to say that, rather than loading a dbspace with a bunch of tables or partitions of tables, you should put only a couple of smaller whole tables or a partition of one larger table in a dbspace. At first look, this suggestion might appear a bit absurd, but if you take into account the added flexibility of the backup/restore process as well as the **DATASKIP** parameter, this approach makes sense.

The **DATASKIP** parameter lets the instance continue operating even if dbspaces are completely offline, provided that any down dbspace does not contain the rootdbs, the physical log, or any of the logical logs. A table that might have some, but not all, of its partitions in offline dbspaces will still respond to queries, provided the required data is not on the down partitions. An error will be returned to the application, indicating that part of the table was unavailable to satisfy the query.

Because IDS provides the ability to execute a "warm restore" of noncritical dbspaces, you can restore any offline dbspace while the instance is up and running. Chapter 7 provides more information about the backup and restore options available to you.

If you follow the 1:1 chunk-to-dbspace recommendation, as well as guidelines for table population within a dbspace, and a dbspace fails completely, only one part of a table or a couple of small tables will be affected. You can restore these in a relatively short time.

A closing thought on dbspaces: Just as you should calculate your table sizes with an element of "fudge" for unexpected growth, don't skimp on the size of your dbspaces. As you begin to work in your new environment, you invariably will see unexpected growth in tables or encounter a sudden need to maintain new data elements. I've seen too many companies try to contain expenses by buying just enough disk space to keep the project going at what was perceived as current needs. It usually didn't take long before these sites were facing an expensive investment in time and material to either purge data they would rather have kept available or buy more hardware and bring in additional resources to meet new demands or relieve disk performance bottlenecks. It is always more expensive in the long run not to plan for growth.

Kernel Tuning

As I described in Chapter 1, with Informix Dynamic Server, all data server and end-user overhead is absorbed by the virtual processors—by the CPU and AIO VPs in particular. Each one of these virtual processors is, in fact, a separate Linux, Mac OS X, or Unix O/S process. Given that these processes are multithreaded, they will demand far more operating system resources than other processes. If your physical server will be supporting a number of IDS instances, you'll need to tune the server to support a power-user environment.

Specifically, you'll need to look at shared memory and process parameters. Each instance will need a semaphore for each VP and shared memory connection. You'll also need to tune for semaphore "sets" because you need a set for every 100 shared-memory user sessions. You need another set for each group of 100 or fewer VPs that initialize whenever you bring the instance from offline to online mode and another set whenever a VP is added dynamically while the instance is in operation.

On a physical server running just one instance of IDS, be sure to verify that the **SHMMAX** (or comparable) kernel parameter is set to a value large enough so that you can allocate in one block the amount of shared memory the instance will require. On a server supporting multiple instances of IDS, the **SHMMAX** value should be big enough to support the total amount of shared memory all the instances will require.

If you're using cooked files for dbspaces, you might need to look at the **ulimit** setting, I/O buffers, and other file system parameters.

As I mentioned earlier, a set of installation and other read-me-first type documents is available in the **SERVER/doc** directory of the un-tar'ed Linux, Mac OS X, and Unix distributions. Once you install the data server, you'll find a full set of documentation updates, errata, machine-specific notes, and other information in the **release** subdirectory under **$INFORMIXDIR**. Before installation, these documents are available in the **SERVER/ doc/** subdirectory where the IDS binary was un-tar'ed.

Pay particular attention to the document named **ids_machine_notes_*versionnum***, where ***versionnum*** is the version of your IDS binary. This file is available in plain text or HTML format, depending on your reading preference. It contains kernel tuning parameters for the particular operating system and port of the product as well as technical specifications for **$SQLHOSTS** and other configuration files, O/S patches used by development when creating the port of the product, new feature guidance, and related items.

You should evaluate the kernel tuning parameters as a baseline for proper operation of the data server on your physical server. IDS development makes these recommendations based on how they configured and tested during the development and quality control processes. The proper use of system-performance monitoring tools will permit you to see how well the baseline parameters are actually working in your system. You may find that you need to make adjustments to optimize performance on your physical server. This, too, is part of the learning process of using Informix Dynamic Server.

Backup Strategies

One of the more important decisions to make in the overall instance design process is how and when you will back up IDS instances (and the logical logs as well). These backups will protect you against the two types of failure situations from which no RAID set can recover: user error and the complete destruction of the RAID set due to malicious or natural events.

When you begin to consider your backup strategy, it's important to realize one important historical fact about IDS versus its major competitors. From the very beginning, all IDS and other Informix data server products have provided the ability to create full or incremental backups while the instance is online and fully functioning. There never has been a need to create mirror or snap copies, bring one to an inactive state, create the backup, and then resynchronize the two when the backup is completed. In Chapter 7, we'll discuss in greater detail exactly how this is accomplished. Needless to say, this feature makes your life as an administrator significantly easier and makes the job of establishing a backup strategy much simpler.

IDS provides two different backup and recovery tools, each with its unique strengths and weaknesses. The **ontape** utility dates back to the initial release of the data server and has long been the workhorse for customers large and small even though more sophisticated options are available. It was designed for use with up to two physically connected devices (one for the instance, the other for logical log operations). Before IDS 10, **ontape** required one or more responses to administrative prompts when creating a backup, making unattended operations difficult; that is no longer the case today. The utility executes serially, backing up the entire instance beginning at chunk 0 and proceeding through to the last chunk.

Recent versions of Informix Dynamic Server have expanded the functionality of **ontape**. The utility still backs up only an entire instance, but it can now restore to the dbspace level. Provided the dbspace does not contain critical elements such as the rootdbs, the physical log, or any of the logical logs, the restore can occur while the data server is online and functioning.

Only a couple of tape devices are supported by the **ontape** utility. These include 4mm and 8mm digital audio tape (DAT) and quarter-inch cartridge (QIC) devices directly connected to the physical server. Autochangers and jukeboxes are not supported. Although not originally designed to output to flat files, in IDS 10 and IDS 11 **ontape** provides a wealth of new functionality to enable hands-off operation to disk. We'll discuss these enhancements in Chapter 7.

> In a real emergency, you can use remote devices on other systems for backups, but I don't recommend this solution for general day-to-day activity. Messages about device closure at the end of a job are not passed back from the remote system, and, as a result, the backup job appears never to be completed. To force closure or completion, you have to manually interrupt the process.
>
> For example, an attempt to back up full logical logs to a remote device will stall after the first log is written. Because the **ontape -c** command never receives a confirmation of the log being written to tape, when the next logical log fills, the backup process will leave it on disk, assuming the other log has not yet been written to tape. Over time as more logs fill, this will cause the instance to stall in a log-full condition if you haven't enabled dynamic logical log creation. Even if you have, if this condition isn't caught the instance will, over time, run out of disk space as it eventually fills with not-backed-up logical logs.

The other tool backup and recovery tool available in IDS is the **ON-Bar** utility suite. This option actually consists of two components: the **ON-Bar** API and the Informix Server Manager (ISM), a basic tape management system that works with the API. Unlike **ontape**, **ON-Bar** expects the tape management system to handle all user interaction prompts, making it the preferred utility for integration into an existing enterprise backup and recovery plan. Before IDS 10, **ON-Bar** was the preferred tool for hands-free operations, but that may change with the new **ontape** functionality in IDS 11. You will need to balance the functionality of the **ON-Bar** utility suite (with or without the bundled storage management software) against that of **ontape** to see which suits your needs best. Both are excellent choices.

With either **ON-Bar**'s ISM or a third-party storage management solution, you have the ability to do partial (warm) or full instance backups and restores. You have, with a major caveat, the ability to perform moment-in-time restores to the second if necessary. Backups, and their associated restores, can be multithreaded and output to several backup devices to reduce the amount of time required to create a backup or perform a restore. IDS 11 adds additional functionality to the **On-Bar** utility suite. We'll discuss these features in Chapter 7.

Through the **ON-Bar** utility suite and the appropriate third-party tape management software, you can incorporate instance or logical log backups into the management software that handles all the other backups occurring across the enterprise. Using this management software, you can take advantage of the various tape devices and jukebox configurations that exist today (or may in the future) to store data on high-capacity tape devices or to create backups in parallel across multiple tape devices even if they're attached to different machines. You can automate the backup process because the tape management software handles the automated scheduling and the required communications between the data server's backup threads and the actual backup devices. The software also maintains, with the exception of one file written to in the **$INFORMIXDIR\etc** directory, the metadata of what was backed up and when. With this file and the metadata about both instance and logical log backups, you can execute restores as necessary.

Below are some general factors to take into consideration when putting together your backup strategy. Although I use the generic term "database" here, these points also apply to the instance level.

- How critical is the data? Granted, all the data in the database is important or you wouldn't be saving it, but how much can you afford to lose? How long could your business operate while you re-create the data?

- Can you re-create the data? What would the manpower, equipment, processing, and other costs be to recover and/or rebuild the lost data?

- What is an acceptable length of time to complete a full restore of the database? What is an acceptable length of time for a warm restore of a down dbspace containing part of a critical table or a collection of static reference tables?

- How important is it that you can recover to an approximate moment in time?

The answers to these questions will determine whether you back up the logical logs to tape, how often you back up the instance, and what backup level you use. These decisions also will affect the dbspace design as you consider the number, size, and placement of tables within dbspaces against the functionality of an **ontape** or **ON-Bar** restore. Chapter 7 provides a more in-depth discussion of these topics.

These factors should also be the driving force behind setting up a high-availability and disaster tolerance plan using IDS continuous availability and data replication technologies. Look for coverage of these topics in *Administering Informix Dynamic Server, Advanced Topics*.

Setting Up the Environment

In preparation for actually invoking the IDS installer, there are some files you need to create or modify and some global environment variables you need to set. For the purposes of this chapter, I will limit my scope to those items necessary for the data server and its instances to function or for a database application hosted on a physical server to run.

From a client perspective, there are too many possible logical and physical connection paths to a data server for more than a cursory comment. For non-Unix clients to connect to an IDS instance, a data-access driver such as ODBC or JDBC will need to be configured on the client. Correctly configuring this driver involves setting the instance name, host physical server, connection port number, and potentially other variables. The remaining portions of client-side connectivity are left to the reader as an exercise.

Preparing the Install Location

So far, this book has dealt with the ethereal—things to think about or concepts to incorporate into future work. Now it's time to start getting dirty, as it were. But first you must, as the King said to the White Rabbit in Lewis Carroll's *Alice's Adventures in Wonderland*, "begin at the beginning." The first step is deciding where to install the data server and, more important, how to set up the directory structures to easily enable future growth, upgrades, and administration. I have some very strong opinions in this area based on years of administering IDS instances and working with customers and their plans and/or problems. The advice given here applies, for the most part, to Linux, Mac OS X, and Unix ports of the data server. Windows has its own "interesting" administration characteristics.

The key to properly setting up the directory structure for all the reasons I've just given is to separate as many components as possible from the actual binary installation directory, referred to as **$INFORMIXDIR**. You should install only the data server and any other add-on binaries, such as DataBlades, in **$INFORMIXDIR**. Everything else should go in adjacent directories, as illustrated by the recommended directory configuration shown in Figure 3.7.

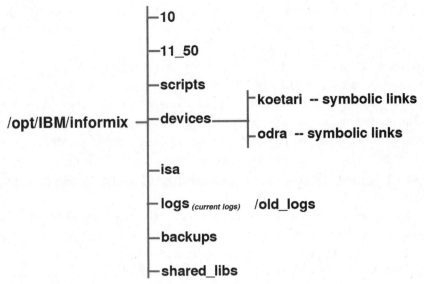

Figure 3.7: Recommended directory configuration for an IDS installation

In this example, the data server is installed according to general IBM standards in the **/opt/IBM/***product_name* directory. A separate directory exists for each major release of the data server (e.g., V10, V11.5) so that more than one version can be running at the same time. This structure also makes in-place migrations (and possibly revisions) extremely easy.

> On Mac OS X ports, the default installation directory somewhat follows the convention for that O/S: **/Applications/IBM/informix**. You can decide whether to follow this convention or to use **/opt**. If you're supporting IDS on additional operating systems besides Mac OS X, I recommend using /**opt** so that scripts, functions, and other utilities are completely portable across your environment. If you're new to IDS and using Mac OS X, follow the convention for the O/S: **/Applications/IBM/informix**.

The **scripts** directory contains all the administration scripts to execute tasks such as back-ups, managing the instance logs, external **ALARMPROGRAM** procedures, tasks, sensors, and so on.

The **devices** directory contains a subdirectory named for each instance configured on the physical server. In this example, there are two instances (named after rivers): **koetari** and **odra**. In each of these subdirectories are the symbolic links to each physical device (both disk and tape) configured in the instance.

If the Informix Server Administrator (ISA) or the OpenAdmin Tool for IDS is installed, I generally put it in a separate directory so it doesn't get erased if I delete an older version of the data server binaries.

I also concentrate all the instance logs into one directory so I, or anyone else looking at the installation, can quickly find all log information, including the **BAR_ACT_LOG**, **MSGPATH**, and other logs for each instance. I use a standardized naming convention that includes the instance name so I can easily distinguish between the logs if more than one instance is operational. I keep only the active logs in this subdirectory, storing a rolling two weeks' worth of logs in the **old_logs** subdirectory. The IDS scheduler or the system **crontab** executes a procedure in the **scripts** directory to manage the rolling of the log information.

I often move the next directory, **backups**, into its own file system because of size, but if instance or logical log backups are executed to disk, they are written into a single directory. Again, I use a unified naming convention, and the IDS scheduler or **crontab** invokes a procedure in the **scripts** directory to prune the backup files as mandated by the business rules.

The last directory shown in the figure, **shared_libs**, contains all the object files for user-defined routines (UDRs) written in C.

With this type of directory structure, almost nothing is tied to a specific version of IDS. In fact, I can easily change versions by resetting **$INFORMIXDIR** from **/opt/IBM/Informix/10** to **/opt/IBM/Informix/11_50**, or vice versa. Naturally, you'd want to shut down the instance before making this type of change! Even though **$INFORMIXDIR** may change, most of the critical configuration pieces, such as the log and device information, don't; you'd need to be sure to move the **$SQLHOSTS** and **$ONCONFIG** information between **$INFORMIXDIR**s. Someone who has never seen the environment can quickly locate the log records to see what's happened and then find and execute procedures out of the **scripts** directory as needed to fix any issue.

Although this approach works for Linux, Mac OS X, and Unix ports of the server, it's not so easy with the Windows ports due to restrictions imposed by the system registry. At this time, some locations are hard-coded into the installation procedures and cannot be changed. It is hoped that in a future release you'll have as much flexibility using Windows ports as you do with the other, open-systems ports.

Required Files

If we exclude the symbolic links created to point to disk chunks or tape devices as explained earlier in the chapter, there are three files you need to work with before trying to initialize an instance of Informix Dynamic Server. The first file is derived from the template **$INFORMIXDIR/etc/onconfig.std**. The other two, **$INFORMIXDIR/etc/sqlhosts** and **/etc/services**, require adding to or modifying what's already there. Let's look at each of these files in greater detail as well as at some environment variables you need to set.

The $ONCONFIG File

The file that acts as the **$ONCONFIG** file contains all the parameters the IDS process needs to create the shared memory structures for the instance. It also holds directions to, and information about, the most crucial physical devices that the data server process needs to contact to complete instance initialization or initiate a restore. Last, it contains all the additional parameters to manage optional functionality in the instance, such as data replication, SQL statement caching, administrative access, alarm processing, and much more. You must create a separate, unique **$ONCONFIG** file for each instance running on a physical server.

A template of this file called **onconfig.std** is installed in the **$INFORMIXDIR/etc** directory when IDS is properly installed. It needs to be copied using a unique name within the same directory for use by an instance of the data server. You can use almost any name you want for this file, but most IDS administrators keep "onconfig" in the file name. I generally name these copies **onconfig.***instance_name*, replacing ***instance_name*** with either the full name or an abbreviation of the instance for which the file holds configuration information. For example, the reference system I'm using to write this book has instances named after rivers: Amazon, Columbia, Kern, and Styx. The **$ONCONFIG** files supporting those instances are called **onconfig.ama**, **onconfig.col**, and so on. In Chapter 4, I'll explain some of the parameters in the **$ONCONFIG** file in much greater detail.

WARNING

It is crucial that you not alter the file permissions of the **$ONCONFIG** file copy from those of the **onconfig.std** template when you create or alter the copy. Also, do not delete or change the original **onconfig.std** file. If the file is writable by others and someone other than the DBA changes it, the instance could be destroyed the next time it is restarted from an offline mode. Beginning in IDS 10, the data server checks the permissions of this and several other critical files and generates an error if they are not set correctly.

The first time you start an instance, you'll need to hand-edit the **$ONCONFIG**. Rarely, you might also need to edit this file once the instance has been operational for a while. Caution and attention to detail are strongly encouraged. One small typo in this file can destroy the instance.

On Windows ports of the data server, you don't have an option when naming the **$ONCONFIG** file during instance initialization. The installation and initialization process makes a copy of the file, assigning a unique name that corresponds to the instance. The format for the file name is similar to mine but uses the full instance name: **onconfig.*instance_name*.** You can rename the file, but I recommend leaving the file name generated by the instance-creation process alone. If you want to override it, you'll need to edit the value in the **$ONCONFIG** entry of the **HKEY_LOCAL_MACHINE\SOFTWARE\Informix\OnLine*instance_name*\ Environment** registry hive once the instance is built. As with the other ports of IDS, before making a change you'll want to shut down the instance and copy/create the new file. Only then should you attempt to restart the instance.

The $SQLHOSTS File

The **$INFORMIXDIR/etc/sqlhosts** file acts as a connectivity guide to instances created on any physical server anywhere on the network. I liken this file to the IDS phone book; it points the way to the physical server on which any given instance is running and tells which communications protocol should be used to connect to it. All client applications use this phone book to connect to IDS instances. The instances also use it to connect to other instances when executing distributed operations requiring data to/from several sources.

A template called **sqlhosts.std** is provided when the data server is installed. Unlike the **onconfig.std** template, which must be preserved in its original form, I rename the template to **sqlhosts** and modify it as necessary to support the instances I need.

Table 3.1 shows the format of the file, which is quite simple. It is a five-field row, with each field separated by a tab or white space. One row is required for each instance or instance alias on the network to which you want to connect from the server on which you're modifying the **$SQLHOSTS** file; this includes instances on the same physical server.

Table 3.1: $SQLHOSTS file row format	
Field number	**Description**
1	The instance name or alias
2	The nettype "word" for the instance
3	The host name of the physical server on which the instance resides; 256 characters maximum
4	The network "service name" or port number to be used when connecting to the instance; 128 characters maximum
5	Options to be used when connecting to the instance

At this point in the book, we're just going to look at the basic configuration settings for this file. If you're using Enterprise Replication (ER), communications encryption, or other features, additional attributes will come into play for several of these fields. I cover these in the appropriate chapters of this book or *Administering Informix Dynamic Server, Advanced Topics.*

Field 1: Instance Name

The first field in the row contains the name entered in either the instance name (**DBSERVERNAME**) or the instance alias (**DBSERVERALIAS**) field. This name must be unique among all IDS instances across the network.

Field 2: Nettype "Word"

The second field describes the network protocol and type of interface required to connect to the instance. Its contents consist of an eight-character nettype "word" organized into the three components listed in Table 3.2.

Table 3.2: The three components of the nettype word	
Component number	**Description**
1	Type of data server
2	Network interface
3	Network protocol

Table 3.3 describes how the nettype word components (which are case-sensitive) are divided and lists their possible values.

Table 3.3: Possible values for each component of the nettype "word"		
Character positions	**Description**	**Possible values**
1–2	Data server	**on**—A holdover from when the data server was called Informix OnLine; the generally accepted default for IDS instances
		ol—An allowed alias for **on**; generally not used
		se—IBM Informix Standard Engine
		dr—DRDA-based connection
3–5	Network interface	**ipc**—Interprocess communications interface; used only for local shared memory connections
		tli—Transport-level interface
		soc—Socket interface

Table 3.3: Possible values for each component of the nettype "word" (Continued)		
Character positions	Description	Possible values
6–8	Network protocol	**tcp**—TCP/IP protocol
		str—Stream-pipe communications protocol
		imc—TCP/IP protocol used with the IBM Informix MaxConnect connection server
		nmp—Named-pipe communications protocol
		spx—IPX/SPX communications protocol
		shm—Shared memory communications
		ssl—Secure Sockets Layer, available in IDS 11.5 and later

In previous versions of IDS, the first two characters of the nettype word represented the data server. In IDS 11, the **dr** entry is changed from representing the IBM Informix Enterprise Gateway with DRDA product to that of a generic Distributed Relational Database Architecture (DRDA) client connection, enabling an IDS instance to interface seamlessly with other data servers in the IBM family.

Characters 3–5 indicate the network interface to use to establish a connection between the instance and the client application. Note that there is a separate entry for shared memory connections (**ipc**). This value is reserved for applications running on the same physical machine as the database engine. The fact that a separate interface exists for shared memory connections implies that all connections to the database engine operate from a client/server model regardless of where the application is running. All applications can, and should, be developed to take advantage of this model.

Characters 6–8 of the nettype word specify the network protocol to use to connect to the instance.

Only a few valid combinations of nettype words can be used on Linux, Mac OS X, and Unix ports. Table 3.4 lists these combinations, using an IDS instance as a sample server.

Table 3.4: A summary of the acceptable Linux, Mac OS X, and Unix nettype words	
Nettype word	Description
onipcshm	Shared memory connection
onipcstr	Stream-pipe connection
ontlitcp	TCP/IP protocol over the transport-level interface (TLI)
onsoctcp	TCP/IP protocol over the socket interface
ontlispx	IPX/SPX protocol over the TLI interface
onsocimc	TCP/IP over sockets to connect to the MaxConnect server
ontliimc	TCP/IP over TLI to connect to the MaxConnect server

Table 3.4: A summary of the acceptable Linux, Mac OS X, and Unix nettype words (Continued)	
Nettype word	**Description**
drsoctcp	DRDA communications over the TCP/IP socket interface
drtlitcp	DRDA communications over the TCP/IP TLI interface
onsocssl	Encrypted TCP/IP protocol over the socket interface
drsocssl	Encrypted DRDA communications over the TCP/IP socket interface

An additional nettype word for both Linux/Unix/Mac OS X and Windows ports, **onsqlmux**, supports applications that make multiple connections to the data server on behalf of each user—for example, a threaded application that establishes concurrent connections to several different databases within the same instance. This nettype option establishes a type of connection multiplexer for these sessions, helping to reduce the administrative and resource overhead associated with the connections.

> Activating Secure Sockets Layer (SSL) encryption requires more than setting a flag in the **$SQLHOSTS** file. The *IBM Informix Security Guide* provides detailed instructions on configuring and activating this protocol. You should also check your machine notes because this functionality is not supported on all operating systems.

Field 3: Hostname

Field 3 of the **$SQLHOSTS** file names the physical server hosting the instance. This name must be resolvable through either **/etc/hosts** or a Domain Name Service (DNS) lookup.

Field 4: Network Service Name

Field 4's value will vary based on the nettype word used for the instance. Depending on the interface and network protocol specified in the nettype word, this field may or may not have a real value in the connection process; however, in no case should you leave it empty.

If the nettype word defines a local shared memory connection (e.g., **onipcshm**), this field of the **$SQLHOSTS** row is not used; it functions simply as a placeholder—you can enter any character string in the field as long as the value is unique within the context of the file.

For all other connections, the value entered here usually corresponds to a "service name" entry in the **/etc/services** file. This service name is used as a cross-reference to the network port number and protocol through which the network-based instance connection will be established. The network service names for each instance on a physical server must be unique because the service name entries in the **/etc/services** file must be unique. Network service names needn't be unique across the network because their scope is specific to the physical server. Nevertheless, it's a good idea to assign unique names where possible.

If you don't want to use a specific alias name in this position, you can simply substitute the actual network port number. Regardless, this position cannot be left blank, and its values must be unique within the physical server. So, for example, if you're creating several instances with shared memory or stream-pipe connections, the first instance could have a value of **placeholder** in this field, the second could have **placeholder_2**, and so on.

To modify the **/etc/services** file to include the necessary services for an IDS instance, add an entry similar in format to those already in the file. Use the network service name from the **$SQLHOSTS** file as the service name in this file, choose a port number that hasn't already been used, and indicate the network protocol to use.

The port number chosen for an instance must be consistent and unique across the network for database access to occur from remote clients or servers. All other physical servers hosting instances that need to connect to this instance will need to use the same port number in their **/etc/services** file. The service names used in the **/etc/services** files associated with the port number don't have to match, but it's generally best if they do.

You are usually safe if you choose a port number above 5500; however, be sure to consult the documentation that came with your operating system for any restrictions or suggestions.

In Mac OS X 10.5.2 and higher, the **/etc/services** file contains a considerable number of pre-allocated port numbers. The numeric range of these numbers reaches into 40,000 to 50,000. If you plan to include Macintosh-based instances in your environment, you'd be wise to look there first for an open range of port numbers that all other instances will use. This way, you won't have a conflict with services on the Mac.

If a Mac-based instance arrives later and there is port number conflict, you'll either have to move the port number for the Mac service or change the port number for the IDS instance. If you decide to change the IDS port number, you can make the change on all the other servers provided there isn't an active connection to the instance in question and won't be until the change is made to the instance itself. On the server hosting the instance, you'll need to take an instance outage to change its port number.

Field 5: Connection Options

Unlike the previous four fields, you are not required to enter any values into field 5 of the **$SQLHOSTS** field. Its function is to let you set specific operational states for connections to the instance. As I'll explain in a moment, I feel it should be mandatory to set one of the states.

The syntax for setting values in this field is

```
option_letter=value
```

where **option_letter** is replaced by a letter denoting a particular option. You can define multiple options for each instance if necessary. Each option you define must have the **option_letter=value** format and be separated from other options by either a comma or a single white space. The total string length for this field cannot exceed 256 characters. Table 3.5 lists the valid options for this field.

Option letter	Description
Table 3.5: Available connection option identifiers	
b	Communications buffer size (in bytes) for the TCP/IP protocol
c	Connection redirection
csm	Communication Support Module; used for authentication
e	End of a server group definition
g	Beginning of a server group definition; used primarily with Enterprise Replication but can also be used for automatic client reconnection, high-availability service level agreement (SLA) definitions, and more
i	Used to assign a numerical ID to a server group
m	Used with the sqlmux protocol
r, s	Operating system security settings: **r** for client-side, **s** for server-side

The keep-alive option. Of the options you can set using field 5 in the **$SQLHOSTS** file, I strongly suggest leaving option **k**, the keep-alive option, enabled. Possible values are **k=0** (zero) for off/disabled and **k=1** (one) for on/enabled. Affecting only TCP/IP and IPX/SPX connections to the instance, this option periodically checks the connections between each user thread in the instance and the client application. If the client does not respond within a given amount of time, the user thread is terminated and all instance resources associated with it are released.

If you disable the keep-alive option, the detection of a broken network connection will cause the instance to immediately terminate the threads and resources associated with that connection. Be aware, however, that in the event of temporary network saturation, the server could interpret a blocked connection as a dropped connection and kill off threads that should be kept alive.

In the absence of the **k=0** parameter for an instance definition, the keep-alive option is enabled by default.

The security options. The two security options, **r** and **s**, let you control how a request for a connection to an instance and database is verified. When a request is made to connect to an instance for database services, the data server verifies that the user ID making the request as well as the computer from which the request is originating are "known and trusted" within the network. In the absence of a user ID, as can be the case in a PC-based client connection, the network identity of the remote machine must be known and trusted, and the user ID is verified by the **connect** SQL statement.

Unless you specify otherwise, the data server host uses the **/etc/hosts.equiv** or **$HOME/. rhosts** file on the client to determine whether the client/host relationship can be trusted. Table 3.6 lists the possible options for this parameter that can override this behavior.

Table 3.6: Possible values for the $SQLHOSTS security options	
Value	**Description**
s=3	Enables /etc/hosts.equiv and ~/.rhosts server-side lookup
s=2	Enables only ~/.rhosts server-side lookup
s=1	Enables only /etc/hosts.equiv server-side lookup
s=0	Disables /etc/hosts.equiv and ~/.rhosts server-side lookup
r=1	Enables ~/.netrc client-side lookup
r=0	Disables ~/.netrc client-side lookup

The verification process occurs in several steps:

1. The user ID is verified by checking in the server's **/etc/passwd** file. If the user ID making the request also exists on the server, the **user** ID is assumed to be known and trusted.

2. The client machine from which the request is originating is verified. The client's host name must be resolvable either through the server's **/etc/hosts** file or via a DNS lookup.

3. After resolving the client's host name, a check is made to see whether the client machine is to be trusted by the server. For the purposes of discussion here, suffice it to say that if a remote machine is trusted, services will be extended to the remote machine for user IDs existing on both machines without requiring a password.

4. If an entry exists for the remote machine in the **/etc/hosts.equiv** file, the instance and database connection is made. If no entry exists, the **~/.rhosts** file is checked to see whether an entry exists there for the user ID and remote machine name combination. If an entry is found, the connection is made; otherwise, the connection request is rejected.

The **~/.rhosts** file permits a user who has an account on both the server hosting the IDS instance and an untrusted client machine to establish an instance and database connection without having to enter a password. This file is created in the user's home directory on the server machine. Consult the documentation that came with your operating system for the format of this file. The general form is as follows:

```
user_id@remote_host_name
```

The **.netrc** file also exists in the user's home directory and permits connections from network-based clients where the user ID for the individual differs from that on the database server.

> When creating an **.rhosts** or **.netrc** file in an environment using DNS, be sure to create an entry with just the remote host name as well as an entry with the remote host name and the domain suffix.

The security option you can set as part of field 5 in the **$SQLHOSTS** file determines the level to which the server should search to verify that the connection is known and trusted. The **s=3** option is the default. The **s=0** option prevents any remote access to the server, while **s=2** permits only specific remote user ID connections. The **s=1** option prevents all access from nontrusted hosts by preventing **.rhosts** lookups from occurring.

The communications buffer size option. The buffer size (**b**) option lets you tune the TCP/IP communications buffer to more efficiently handle the amount of data commonly transmitted. The default buffer size for the TCP/IP protocol is 4,096 bytes. If you find that the server is consistently handling data transfers that are larger than the current buffer size (e.g., BLOBs), use this option to specify, in bytes, how large the buffer should be.

Be aware that each client connection allocates its own communications buffer. When setting the size of this buffer, make sure you have enough physical memory on the physical server to service all the concurrent users and their buffers, in addition to the IDS instances and any other applications running on the server. If you set this value too high for the number of connections to the instance, connection requests will be rejected.

The group, end-of-group, and group number options. A *server group* is a logical entity. Much like a dbspace is a set of one or more chunks, a server group is an alias for a set of one or more instances. Groups are most commonly used for Enterprise Replication to broadcast configuration, realization, synchronization, data, and other messages within the replication cluster. They can also be used for automatic client reconnection; if the first instance in the list doesn't respond, connection attempts will be made to the other instances listed in the group.

Each group has a unique numeric identifier set by the **i=number** parameter. When defining a group, you begin a full line in the **$SQLHOSTS** file with the group name in the first field (maximum length of 18 characters), the word **group** in the second (or **nettype**) field and a dash (–) in the third and fourth fields. You follow this with a list of instance entries as I've already described. The group will include all instance names that follow the initial group definition line until the end of the **$SQLHOSTS** file or the instance name identified by the **e=** parameter. The **$SQLHOSTS** entries shown in Table 3.7 provide examples of server group definition.

DBSERVERNAME	Nettype	Host name	Service name	Options
er_grp_1	group	—	—	e=tagus_net
cadmus_net	onsoctcp	host_1	net_1	g=er_grp_1
tagus_net	onsoctcp	host_2	net_2	g=er_grp_1
amazon	onipcshm	host_3	placeholder	
colorado_net	onsoctcp	host_4	net_3	k=1,s=2
rio_grande_net	ontlitcp	host_5	net_5	k=1,b=5124
er_grp_2	group	—	—	
red_net	ontlitcp	host_6	net_6	
green_net	onsoctcp	host_8	net_8	
yangzi_net	ontlitcp	host_7	net_7	
odra_net	onsoctcp	host_10	net_10	g=er_grp_1

Table 3.7: Sample server group definitions and an $SQLHOSTS file

In this table, there are two group definitions: **er_grp_1** includes the **cadmus_net** and **tagus_net** instances because of the **e=** option. The **odra_net** instance is also a member of this group because membership is specifically called out in the fifth field. As you can see, the instance definitions don't have to be sequentially ordered. The **er_grp_2** definition includes the last three instances because end-of-file is reached and **odra_net** belongs to another group. Although I specified group membership for each instance in **er_grp_1**, it is not required as shown in **er_grp_2**. Best practice (and enhanced readability) suggests using the **er_grp_1** approach rather than end-of-file. A less-skilled administrator might add an additional instance toward the bottom of the file and inadvertently make it part of a group, causing replication or connection problems.

   The connection redirection option. The benefits of server groups extend beyond replication. You can use them for automated client reconnection should an instance in the group fail. This capability is particularly useful when one or more nodes are defined as part of a fully meshed ER topology as illustrated in Table 3.8.

Table 3.8: Sample server group definitions with connection redirection options				
DBSERVERNAME	Nettype	Host name	Service name	Options
er_grp_1	group	—	—	e=tagus_net,c=1
cadmus_net	onsoctcp	host_1	net_1	
tagus_net	onsoctcp	host_2	net_2	
amazon	onipcshm	host_3	placeholder	
hdr_1	group	—	—	c=2
red_net	ontlitcp	host_6	net_6	
green_net	onsoctcp	host_8	net_8	
yangzi_net	ontlitcp	host_7	net_7	

There are two server groups defined in this table to which a client can connect. The ER cluster is fully meshed, update anywhere, so it doesn't matter which node the client connects to for service. With c=1, the client will randomly pick one of the instances in the group and try to connect if unsuccessful, it will cycle through the instances until successful. In IDS 11.10, it was important for an application to connect to the correct instance to execute write operations. As a result, with the c=2 parameter, the client would try to connect to the first instance in the group; if that instance was unavailable, the client would then try the others until successful. With IDS 11.50, this connection process becomes unnecessary because update operations can occur through any instance in the Multi-Active Cluster for High Availability (MACH-11) cluster. That release also introduced the Online Connection Manager and Server Monitor (ONCMSM) agent, which completely changes how remote connections can occur. Look for more detailed coverage of the configuration and use of MACH-11 technology in *Administering Informix Dynamic Server, Advanced Topics*.

The communications support module (CSM) option. With CSM enabled, you can encrypt communications between clients and the data servers. Supported ciphers include Data Encryption Standard (DES), Triple DES, Extended DES, Advanced Encryption Standard (AES) (128-, 192-, and 256-bit) in electronic Code Book, Cypher Block Chaining, Cipher Feedback, and Output Feedback modes. You'll find more information about using CSMs in *Administering Informix Dynamic Server, Advanced Topics*.

A closing note on the communications options set in the fifth position of the **$SQLHOSTS** file: IDS development recommends that you size the communications buffers identically on both the server and client machines for the most efficient network throughput and the least amount of network-related overhead on either machine. In fact, it might be to your advantage to increase the size of this buffer to the average size of the SQL statement and/or data set being returned. With a smaller size, the client and the instance must send more messages back and forth, consuming time and resources. A larger buffer size means fewer messages, each carrying more information, thereby completing the job more quickly.

Last, you can change at will those options that affect client connections, such as the keep-alive option and client-side **.netrc** lookups; these changes will take effect for client connections established after you make the change. Server-oriented parameters, such as the server-specific security options or communications buffer size, can also be set at will, but these changes require the instance to be shut down and restarted before they take effect.

Configuring $SQLHOSTS in Windows

Although the overall functionality of the **$SQLHOSTS** information is identical on Linux, MAC OS X, Unix, and Windows ports, the implementation on Windows is different. It can also become more complicated if you install using the services of a Windows domain server.

The **%SQLHOSTS%** (Windows syntax) information is located in a Windows registry hive under the **HKEY_LOCAL_MACHINE\SOFTWARE\Informix** tree, as shown in Figure 3.8.

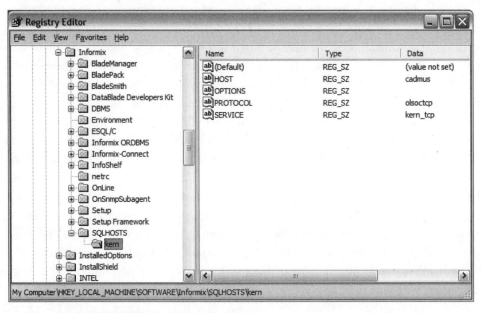

Figure 3.8: The SQLHOSTS Windows registry hive

During the data server installation process, you determine where this hive will be located. You can create one hive on each physical server or have each server reference one hive on the domain controller. If you choose to use a single, unified **%SQLHOSTS%** hive on the domain controller, you'll need to set an additional environment variable on the client machines when sourcing this hive.

The **%SQLHOSTS%** hives contain only four fields; the missing field is the instance name, but that is because each instance has its own entry in the hive as opposed to one hive entry for all instances. The layout of the fields in the hives differs as well. Table 3.9 describes their contents.

Table 3.9: %SQLHOSTS% hive fields	
Field name	**Description**
Host	The host name of the physical server on which the instance resides; 256 characters maximum
Options	Options to be used when connecting to the instance
Protocol	The nettype word for the instance
Service	The network service name to be used by the local machine to connect to the instance; 128 characters maximum

For the most part, the same parameters options are available on the Windows ports as on the Linux, Mac OS X, and Unix ports. Table 3.10 notes the exceptions.

Table 3.10: Differences in supported syntax and options for the Windows %SQLHOSTS% hive	
Exception	**Description**
Network protocols, nettype word	IDS Windows ports support only the **onipcnmp, onsoctcp, drsoctcp, onsocssl, drsocssl**, and **onsqlmux** network connectivity options.
Service name	• As on Linux, Mac OS X, and Unix ports, this name must match the entry in the **services** network port file. On Windows systems, this file is located in **%SYSTEMROOT%\windows\system32\drivers\etc**. • If you're using named pipe connections to access an instance, instead of entering a name in this field that corresponds to an entry in the **services** file, you need to enter the name of the pipe created to facilitate the communications. For example, suppose you create a pipe called **shrdmem_to_sarthe**. To define this pipe within the **%SQLHOSTS%** hive, enter **\\.PIPE\shrdmem_to_sarthe** in this field.
Security options	Only the following s= options are supported: **s=0** Disables both the **hosts.equiv** and ~**.rhosts** lookup. If set, all remote access to the instance is blocked. **s=1** Enables lookups only through the **hosts.equiv** file. **s=2** Not supported on Windows ports. **s=3** Lookups occur through either the **hosts.equiv** or ~/**.rhosts** file (default setting).
Communications buffer size option	On Windows ports, this option affects the buffer size only for named pipe connections.

As I mentioned, configuration of an IDS environment on Windows can change depending on whether you use domain services or not. This point is particularly true for client authorization, as Shailesh Gupta, a former IDS architect, explains in this excerpt from an e-mail exchange:

> First, if the user has supplied an account name as part of the connection, then the server will check whether the account name and the supplied password match. The authentication check is done as if the user was logging in on the physical server. As a result, if the server was configured to authenticate user accounts via [Network Information Services (NIS)] or some central Domain Controller, then the [data server] will do the same.
>
> There is a subtle issue of "how does [a data server] on Windows know whether to look up a user's account information locally or on a Domain Controller?" This is determined by how the [data server] was installed to begin with. If the [data server] was installed by the administrator while he or she was logged on locally to the physical server (non-domain), then it's called a "local install" and the [data server] would expect all user account information to exist on the physical server. If the [data server] was installed while the administrator was logged on to the Domain Controller, then the installation is called a "domain install." In this case, all user account information would be looked up via the Domain Controller(s).
>
> This is also true for tools such as the **onmode** utility. These utilities expect that you are either **domain\informix** or a member of the **domain\Informix-Admin** group.
>
> It is important to note that the client can send account name information even if the **connect as** SQL statement is not used. Having a **.netrc** file on the client side is enough. Similarly, on Windows clients, the **setnet** and **setnet32** utilities automatically set up the equivalent of a **.netrc** file on client machine. This means that the Windows clients would always send account name and password information to the instance when attempting to connect.
>
> Second, if the supplied account name and password combination do not match, then the [data server] checks to see if the client application is executing locally on the same physical server as the [data server]. If so, authentication is deemed to be successful. For this purpose, the client's hostname is matched against the [data server's] hostname.
>
> Third, if the first and second steps fail, the [data server] checks to see if the client is a trusted client. For this, the [data server] first looks to see if there is an entry in the **%SYSTEMROOT%\windows\system32\drivers\etc\hosts.equiv** file [and] then in the **.rhosts** file in the user's home directory. In Windows, since the existence of a home directory is optional, the **.rhosts** file is never consulted.
>
> Now when you set the **s=** parameters in [the] options field, the [data server] sets bits in a flag. As the [data server] proceeds through the authentication process and it reaches step 3, [it] will either check the **hosts.equiv** file, or both the **hosts.equiv** and **.rhosts** files, or either one of them depending on value of the flag. Since the .rhosts file is never looked at in the Windows ports, option **s=3** is the same as **s=1** and the **s=2** option will not work.

The **s=3** option is the default and is implied, so you do not need to set it explicitly. The **s=0** option, if set, prevents any remote access to the instance.

Environment Variables

Several environment variables can be set to influence how IDS functions. Some of them affect how the data server works; others impact how it processes SQL operations. A few environment variables are required; others are optional and should be set if the working environment differs from the IDS defaults. You can set the variables globally for all users in either the **/etc/profile** or the **$INFORMIXDIR/etc/informix.rc** file on the Linux, Mac OS X, and Unix physical server hosting the instance(s). These settings can be superseded at an individual user level or even a session level in several ways.

On Windows ports, you can view instance-wide settings in the registry under the **HKEY_LOCAL_MACHINE\SOFTWARE\Informix\OnLine\instance_name\Environment** hive. In this hive, you'll see that values for **%INFORMIXDIR%, %INFORMIXSERVER%, %SQLHOSTS%**, and other environmental settings are maintained. You can change these values at will and add new ones (of type **REG_SZ**) if necessary. Before you change any settings, though, I strongly recommend shutting down the instance.

These registry settings are not used by client applications that would execute on the same physical server, however. Setting up the proper environment would be highly dependent on the application and its database sophistication. You can change system-wide and/or individual environmental settings, such as **%INFORMIXDIR%**, on the **Environment** tab of the **System Properties** window (**Control Panel > System**) as necessary.

As you'll see following installation on a Windows server, a prompt in the **IBM Informix Dynamic Server 11.50** program group opens a command-line window, enabling you to execute any of the IDS command-line utilities. For commands in this window to be executed properly against the instance, a command file called **instance_name.cmd** located in **%INFORMIXDIR%** is run first to set the proper environmental variables.

On the client side, any number of environment variables may need to be set, depending on the application and how it is connecting to the instance. As I mentioned earlier, if you use a single, unified **%SQLHOSTS%** hive located on a domain controller, you'll need to set an additional environment variable called **%INFORMIXSQLHOSTS%** on each client machine. This variable should contain the physical host name in domain notation. For example, if the **%SQLHOSTS%** information were on a server named **hestia**, the value for **%INFORMIXSQLHOSTS%** in a Windows environment would be **hestia.**

The following paragraphs introduce the most important environment variables. I'll introduce and explain others as you progress through this book. For a comprehensive list of server and client-side environment variables, see the *IBM Informix Guide to SQL: Reference*.

Required Variables

The **$INFORMIXDIR**, **$ONCONFIG**, and **$INFORMIXSERVER** environment variables are required to be set for instance initialization or access. You must also modify the **$PATH** string. I recommend setting the **$DBEDIT** environment variable as well. As an aside, in IDS 11 it's now possible to use **$INFORMIXDIR** and other environmental variables in **$ONCONFIG** files, reducing the amount of redundant typing.

$INFORMIXDIR

$INFORMIXDIR represents the full path name to the directory where the IDS 11 binaries are installed. This variable must be set and exported into the user's environment before any of the variables that follow.

Although the practice is common, there is no rule that states that the IDS binaries have to be installed in any specific directory or that the directory itself is called **informix**. In fact, you can have multiple directories containing different release levels of the data server, as you saw earlier in the chapter (e.g., **informix_9_4, informix_10**). By simply resetting the **$INFORMIXDIR**, **$ONCONFIG**, **$INFORMIXSERVER**, and possibly the **$INFORMIXSQLHOSTS** environment variables, as well as **$PATH**, you can easily switch between release levels of the data server to test functionality or support third-party applications using different versions.

For users to be able to run Informix executables, you must add **$INFOR-MIXDIR/bin** to each user's **PATH** statement after exporting **$INFOR-MIXDIR** into the environment.

WARNING If you are developing applications to sell to others, never hard code a path for the IDS product directory or assume it will be called **informix**. Always read the **$INFORMIXDIR** environment variable from the working environment. Shell scripts should be written to read these environmental settings in as well.

$ONCONFIG

$ONCONFIG represents the name of the file, usually located in the **$INFORMIXDIR/etc** directory, that contains the active instance's configuration parameters. It is automatically pathed to **$INFORMIXDIR/etc**, so the correct syntax, in a Bourne or Korn shell environment, would look like this:

```
ONCONFIG=onconfig.sty;
export ONCONFIG
```

$INFORMIXSERVER

$INFORMIXSERVER is the name of the IDS instance to which connections will be made. The value you use here will be either the **DBSERVERNAME** or one of the **DBSERVERALIAS** entries from the **$ONCONFIG** file. Although you set this variable, applications are not forced to use this instance; you can override the connection by using the connect to *database_name@instance_name* SQL syntax or an equivalent connection string. With IDS 11.5 and the ONCMSM agent, clients can initially connect to a service level agreement (SLA) configured to look like a valid **DBSERVERNAME** or **DBSERVERALIAS** entry. From there, the agent will pass to the client all the required connection information for the target instance, including a real **$INFORMIXSERVER** value.

One note of caution: From a technical point of view, you do not need to set **$INFORMIXSERVER** before initializing the instance. However, if the variable is not set, the system catalog databases will not be created in the instance during the initialization process. These databases are critical for proper instance function. I therefore strongly recommend setting this variable before initializing an instance.

$INFORMIXSQLHOSTS

The **$INFORMIXSQLHOSTS** variable is not required unless you are going to use a file name other than **sqlhosts** to define database connectivity or if the file will be located somewhere other than in the **$INFORMIXDIR/etc** directory. The file specified by this variable must have the same format as the standard **sqlhosts** file provided as part of the IDS distribution. If you set this variable, the **$INFORMIXDIR/etc/sqlhosts** file is never used for database connectivity.

$DBEDIT

You are not required to set the **$DBEDIT** variable before initialization, but I recommend doing so to eliminate having to choose an editor every time you use **dbaccess** or **I-SQL**. I set **$DBEDIT** to **vi**, but you can set it to whatever your preferred text editor is.

Other Variables

You can set additional variables, such as **$DBDATE** or **$DBMONEY**, to affect the way IDS operates, manipulates data, or displays it to the user. For details about these environment variables, consult the *IBM Informix Guide to SQL: Reference.*

Multiple Residency Issues

Multiple residency is just a fancy way of saying "supporting more than one instance of IDS at a time on a physical server." You accomplish multiple residency not by reinstalling the IDS binaries into another directory but by creating unique copies of a couple of files and properly setting the required environment variables.

The **$INFORMIXDIR** environment variable stays the same unless you want to run a different version of the data server and have it installed in another directory. You can add all instance connection information for all the data server versions to one **$SQLHOSTS** file if you like. If you need to support different versions of IDS, installed in separate directories, setting the **$INFORMIXSQLHOSTS** environment variable will permit all instances of any version on the physical server to reference this single **$SQLHOSTS** file. Otherwise, all the instances can use the **sqlhosts** file in their **$INFORMIXDIR/etc** directory.

You'll need to create a unique **$ONCONFIG** file as well as a **MSGPATH** file for each instance. The instance name (**DBSERVERNAME**), instance alias or aliases (**DBSERVERALIAS**, if any), and instance number (**SERVERNUM**) must be unique for each instance on each physical server. As I noted previously, **DBSERVERNAME** and any aliases (**DBSERVERALIAS**) also must be unique throughout the network.

Obviously, the **$ONCONFIG** and **$INFORMIXSERVER** variables will differ for each instance. It also goes without saying that instances cannot share disk chunks unless you are using the Shared Disk Secondary (SDS) MACH-11 technology available in IDS 11 and later. I'll explain the **MSGPATH** file and server number in the next chapter, which presents a step-by-step process for initializing an IDS instance.

Beyond these changes, there's nothing very difficult about supporting several IDS instances on the same physical server. You simply need to ask and answer the same questions for each additional instance as for the first.

Of primary concern is the amount of CPU, memory, and I/O resources that will be available to support the operation of all the instances. You must carefully consider the varying demands each instance will make on the server so that one or more elements of the server's resources aren't overwhelmed. This point is particularly important for tuning shared memory within the kernel and setting the "memory forced resident" **$ONCONFIG** parameter. We'll discuss the **RESIDENT** configuration parameter in Chapter 4.

Last, depending on the number and type of backup devices used, the archiving of logical logs or the instances themselves may require some coordination.

Summary

Careful planning is necessary when creating any new system, and Informix Dynamic Server is no exception. When preparing to initialize your instance, remember that the decisions you make about certain issues will be influenced largely by your own specific situation; there are no hard-and-fast rules to steer you through this process. Your own skill, intuition, and previous experiences will be your only guides.

When planning for a new IDS instance, keep the following points in mind:

- During the design phase, identify as many performance requirements, general database sizes, table interdependencies, and other elements of the working environment as you can.

- Regarding disk drive options, regardless of what you do with the other drives in the instance, you *must* protect the drives that contain the rootdbs, the logical logs, and the physical log in some fashion against media failure. Know the pros and cons of each option before deciding which is best for you.

- When referring to disk and tape devices, use symbolic links rather than actual device names.

- When estimating table and dbspace sizes, don't skimp just to save a few bucks. It's always more expensive in the long run not to plan for growth.

- Shut down all unnecessary hardware and O/S services to free up resources for the instance processing.

- When considering running multiple instances on a server, carefully review the system's resource availability.

With the considerations involved in preparing for a new IDS instance safely behind us, we're ready to tackle the nuts and bolts of actually installing the product and initializing an instance. The next chapter introduces you to many of the instance configuration parameters and provides a basic idea of how you can tune the instance for better performance.

4

Installing and Initializing IDS

In this Chapter

▸ Installing and initializing the product

▸ Setting the major configuration parameters

▸ Understanding and querying the system-level databases

▸ Creating multiple instances on the server

The previous chapters may have seemed somewhat "light" to you in that the topics they covered received only a generalized discussion. This treatment was inevitable, given that each administrator and project has unique goals and requirements. The interrelationship of so many factors, and the differing degrees of importance they can have in the overall design of a database environment, makes few definitive statements possible. From here forward, though, I'll expose the nuts and bolts of initializing, administering, and tuning an Informix Dynamic Server instance.

Having worked through the logical design phase of the applications and the database environment you'll need, you're ready to begin configuring and initializing an IDS instance. This chapter walks you through the process of installing or upgrading the data server and initializing an instance. I'll explain what the most significant parameters of the **$ONCONFIG** file are in terms of creating a new instance and make some general recommendations about how to set these values. You'll also learn how to create more than one instance on the server. Last, I'll introduce you to the various system databases and their functions and explain how to query the IDS shared memory structures that the instance creates and uses to operate.

Installing or Upgrading the Server

One of the great things about IDS customers is the variety of ways in which they use the technology. These uses range from what some might consider "basic" OLTP applications except that they run against very, very large data sets to applications that push the data server's performance characteristics to the utmost. Some customers use replication to protect against failures; others just need to get data from server A to server B in a timely way. Still others need and use sophisticated data models with complex relationships between attributes in the database. The point is that no two customers are alike, and because each has different requirements, each should be able to tailor the data server's functionality and installed footprint to match those needs.

In IDS 11, IBM completely upgraded, and in my opinion improved, the installation process. One of the most important improvements is that the process is now standardized across all ports of the data server. By that I mean that regardless of the physical server's O/S, the installation process looks and feels identical. Now, that doesn't mean every installation mode is available on every O/S; for example, the Windows ports don't support console mode. That disclaimer aside, everything else works the same.

Regardless of whether this is the first time you've used IDS or you're upgrading from an earlier version, be sure to read the release and other notes for the software. In earlier IDS versions, these documents were available only after installation; now, you can read them before invoking the installer. They contain details about system prerequisites, O/S tuning advice, last-minute feature information, the installation guide for the O/S, and more.

On Linux, Mac OS X, and Unix ports, the documentation is available in the **$extract_location/SERVER/doc** directory. When opened, a **README.html** file in **$extract_location** also provides links to the documentation in case you prefer to use that option.

On Windows ports, you'll find the documentation in the **%extract_location%\IIF\doc** directory. A word of caution: There is also an **%extract_location%\doc** directory, but that location contains information only about the Java Runtime Environment (JRE) bundled in the data server.

Upgrading from an Earlier Version

Some readers of this book are undoubtedly moving from IDS 10 to IDS 11, but I suspect many, perhaps including you, are moving from an older version of IDS. If you look over the past several releases, you'll realize that IBM has added a considerable amount of new technology to the data server, making it a stronger and stronger product. IDS 9, for example, introduced "big" chunks, a new shared-memory buffer management system, dynamic logical logs, optimizer directives, raw tables, and a more efficient index management system. IDS 10 brought configurable page sizes, column-level encryption, point-in-time table-level restores, and massive Enterprise Replication (ER) improvements.

So, how do you get from where you are to IDS 11? Depending on which IDS version you're using, you'll either upgrade directly or perform an interim step first. Figure 4.1 summarizes the IDS migration pathway.

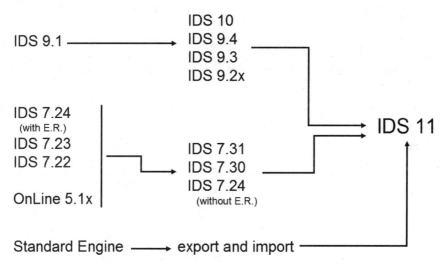

Figure 4.1: IDS migration pathway

As you can see, nearly all newer versions of IDS can be upgraded "in-place" to IDS 11. By in-place, I mean that you can load the new IDS 11 binary onto the physical server, shut down the instance while settings are pointed to the new binaries, and then restart the instance and begin using the new set of data server binaries. It's not a whole lot more complicated than that, as you'll see in a moment.

The IDS versions that can't be directly upgraded lack some significant systemic changes that occurred between those older versions and the more current interim versions. To keep the code base smaller and more manageable, IBM chose not to build these features into the IDS 11 conversion process. As a result, customers with those versions must go through a two-step process to get to IDS 11.

As you can see, it's also possible to move from IBM OnLine 5.1*x* or even IBM Standard Engine to IDS 11. For OnLine, you must first perform an in-place upgrade to (preferably) IDS 7.3*x* and then move to IDS 11. For Standard Engine, no direct path exists; the easiest and quickest method is to use the **dbexport** and **dbimport** utilities to extract the databases and then load them into the new IDS 11 instance.

In migrating from an earlier IDS version to IDS 11, I'm assuming you've already created a test environment and tested your applications and database environment as much as possible for problems. Having done so, all you need to do is migrate your production instances. Migration problems typically involve new instance reserved words that have been used as database object names or as variables in SQL operations. Table 4.1 lists some of the new reserved words for the latest releases of IDS. This list is not an exhaustive one; to see the full set of new reserved words for a particular version, consult the *IBM Migration Guide*.

Table 4.1: Recent IDS reserved words					
IDS 9		**IDS 10**		**IDS 11**	
avoid_execute	left	active	password	admin	updating
avoid_subqf	locks	directives	save	avoid_index_sj	uselastcommitted
cache	raw	encryption	table	idssecuritylabel	with
collation	retain	hint	template	index_sj	
costfunc	restart	inactive	test	inserting	
cross	right	inline	typeid	references	
full	selconst	inout	typename	sampling	
inner	standard	load	typeof	selecting	
instead	use_subqf	online	wait	sysdbclose	
item		optcompind	xadatasource	sysdbopen	
join		partition	xid	task	

Once you've completed testing and are ready to make the change, the process of performing an in-place migration to IDS 11 involves five major steps:

1. Prepare the source instance(s).
2. Install the new data server binaries.
3. Reset instance variables to point to the new binaries.
4. Restart the instance to begin conversion.
5. Verify data integrity, and create a baseline archive.

Let's look at each of these steps in a little greater detail.

Step 1: Instance Preparation

A couple of factors are critical in this step, and one of them, ensuring available room in the dbspaces, is highly variable.

In preparing to move to IDS 11, you need to make sure you have sufficient space in the dbspaces, particularly the rootdbs, for data and/or page conversion to occur when you move to the newer IDS version. How much space you need depends on the version from which you're moving. The earlier the version, the more space you'll need, especially if it's earlier than IDS 9.2.

With IDS 9.2, IBM changed the default storage mode for indexes from "attached" to "detached," or residing in a separate allocation of pages from those for table data even if the index was in the same dbspace as the table. When moving to or past IDS 9.2, many customers reported seeing their disk usage jump because the number of table pages previously allocated, which represented both data and index pages, became reserved for data use only and a new disk allocation was created for the index pages.

As a "belt and braces" DBA (in other words, I have backups of my backups!), I advise having at least 20 percent free space in your dbspaces before making this type of a significant version upgrade. This recommendation is particularly true for the rootdbs, where significant changes will occur in the existing system catalog databases and the new databases that are created. If you're upgrading from IDS 9.4 or later, the volume of available dbspace space isn't as critical, although I would hesitate if you have less than 20 MB in the rootdbs and less than 5 percent in the other dbspaces.

You also need to ensure you have plenty of available logical log space to record the transactions that will occur as part of the upgrade. I recommend 10 MB to 15 MB of available space. If your logical logs are in the rootdbs, the 10 MB to 15 MB for logical logs is in addition to the 20 MB of free space just mentioned.

You will want statistical information about current operations to compare against the new environment, so you'll need to collect optimizer plans for all frequently used operations, especially the more complex or time-consuming ones. To gather this information, you can use the **set explain on** SQL command and execute the statements through **dbaccess** or another utility. If you're on a more recent version, you can specify the **without execute** modifier, which stops execution of the statements after the plan is prepared. With this option, you can execute DML statements on your production databases without worrying about modifying data for your tests. In addition to capturing the optimizer plans, use O/S timing utilities to record time-to-execute information about the most critical SQL operations.

Collect statistical and configuration information by executing a **dbschema -d -hd** as well as an **onstat -pr** command. The **dbschema** command generates the data distribution information that the optimizer uses to form access plans. You can execute this command for the entire database or only for those tables you consider the most critical. The **onstat** command dumps the contents of the reserved pages in the rootdbs with all the pointers to physical and logical devices in the instance as well as backup and some checkpoint information. You'll also want to capture a copy of an **onstat -p/-P**, **onstat -g iof/iov**, and an **onstat -g glo** command. From an operating system standpoint, you might also consider capturing the output from **vmstat**, **iostat**, **sar**, or other utilities to measure the impact on physical server resources over time.

If you're using the **ON-Bar** utility suite to back up your instances, with or without the Informix Server Manager (ISM), make sure you create copies of all the bootstrap and other configuration files.

With these preparations completed, it's time to prepare the data and then create at least one full instance backup. This process involves the following steps:

1. Close all transactions. The easiest way to complete this step is to execute the commands listed in Table 4.2.

Table 4.2: Recommended process to close open transactions before upgrading the data server	
Command	**Description**
onmode –sy/–jy	Transitions the instance to quiescent (or single-user if supported) mode and disconnects all (or non-Informix) sessions.
onmode –c	Forces a full, sync checkpoint, clearing the memory of committed transactions.
onmode –ky	Shuts down the instance.
oninit –s/–j	Restarts the instance to quiescent (or single-user if supported) mode. Any open transactions are rolled back as part of the fast recovery process.
onmode –l	Closes the open logical log and begins to use the next.

2. Remove any outstanding in-place table alters. As we'll discuss in greater detail in Chapter 6, it is possible for a table to have multiple "versions" of its schema and data layout, depending on the types and frequency of changes that have been made to the table's structure. IDS gracefully handles schema variations behind the scenes during normal operations, but these variations could present a problem during an upgrade. To see whether any outstanding in-place table alters exist, execute the **oncheck –pT** command on all databases in the instances to be upgraded. Part of the output of this command for each table is a count of rows with different schema definitions:

```
Home Data Page Version Summary
Version          Count
0 (oldest)       43946
1 (current)      58920
```

In this sample output, the Version column lists the number of in-place alters that have occurred where all the data has not been fully changed. This number increases with each incompletely applied in-place alter. The Count column lists the number of rows in the table that have been changed to the various versions. In this example, just over half of the rows in the table have been updated to the latest version of the table's schema.

The easiest way to remove any in-place alters is to perform a pseudo-update by executing the following SQL operation, replacing **table_name** with the name of the table containing the existing in-place alters and replacing **column_name** with one of the table's column names.

```
update table_name set column_name to column_name
```

3. A cautious DBA would also check the integrity of the data and indexes in the databases by executing the **oncheck –cd and oncheck –ci** command (or the more thorough **oncheck –cD** and **oncheck –cl**—that's a capital "i"). Depending on the size of the databases, this check can take a lot of time. You could consider this step an optional one unless you've had data or index corruption problems or storage failures.

4. Stop any replication activities, be they ER, High-Availability Data Replication (HDR), or both.

5. Create at least one level 0 instance backup as part of your contingency plan. I usually create two, just in case I need the belt and the braces.

6. Shut down the instance(s).

Step 2: Install the New Version of the Data Server

We'll discuss the actual installation process in greater detail later in this chapter. I strongly recommend creating a separate directory for the new binaries as I described in Chapter 3. Obviously, you'll need enough file system space to store both the current IDS binaries and the IDS 11 installation.

Step 3: Reset the Environment Variables

As you learned in Chapter 3, three required environment variables must be set before you start an IDS instance: **$INFORMIXDIR** and its association into **$PATH, $ONCONFIG**, and **$INFORMIXSERVER**. If you move the **$SQLHOSTS** file or want to use a single **$SQLHOSTS** file for all versions of IDS on your server, you'll also need to set **$INFORMIXSQLHOSTS**.

Best practices recommendations are that you copy (not move!) the **$SQLHOSTS** and **$ONCONFIG** files from their original location to inside the directory structure of the new installation. In this way, you only need to reset **$INFORMIXDIR** and make sure **$PATH** reflects the new location of the data server **bin** directory.

Step 4: Restart the Instance

When you execute the **oninit** command to restart the instance with the IDS 11 binaries, the process of converting from the earlier version of IDS to IDS 11 will begin. I strongly recommend monitoring instance activities during this process, so before starting the instance, execute a **tail -f** command on the instance log file. For Windows ports, open the command window for that instance, and execute **onstat -m -r 2**.

With instance monitoring started, bring the instance into either quiescent (if executing the first step of a two-step upgrade) or single-user mode by executing an **oninit -sv** (quiescent mode) or **oninit -jv** command. You may see some messages in the logs about the conversion process. This is to be expected; the messages should indicate that the various operations are being completed successfully.

Step 5: Verify Data Integrity and Create a New Baseline Backup

Assuming no troubling messages appeared in the **MSGPATH** log file during the conversion process, prepare the instance for operations by completing the following steps:

1. Refresh optimizer statistics. To do so, execute an **update statistics high** operation on the **sysmaster** database, an **update statistics low drop distributions** on all end-user databases, followed by your normal **update statistics** commands so the optimizer has refreshed information with which to build access plans.

2. Again, a cautious DBA would check the integrity of the data and indexes in the databases by executing **oncheck -cd** and **oncheck -ci** (or the more thorough **oncheck -cD** and **oncheck -cI**). Unless you've had data or index corruption problems or storage failures, you can consider this an optional step.

3. Create at least one level 0 backup of the instance.

Should a critical error or failure occur and you need to roll back to the earlier version, you have two options. IDS has a reversion function you can execute to return to the earlier version. For a complete explanation of this function and any actions in the new environment that would prevent using it, see the *IBM Informix Dynamic Server Migration Guide*. My preferred method is to reset the environment variables to their original values and then execute a full restore. I recommend this approach not because the IDS reversion functionality doesn't work; it does. But with a restore, I know I have a known-good image of the data in its original and logically consistent format. This method may take longer than the reversion facilities, but I prefer the belt-and-braces approach to getting back to a known-good instance state.

A New Installation

With IDS's new deployment wizard and associated silent installer, you now have the ability to tailor which components of IDS are installed to satisfy your data server functionality requirements. With this capability, you can install just the base server functionality, with its 78 MB to 112 MB footprint (operating system and hardware dependent), or install all options, requiring close to 300 MB. With IDS 11, IBM has standardized the look and feel of the supported installation options, so the process is identical regardless of the platform on which you're installing.

You can invoke the Java-based installer in one of three modes:

- *Silent mode* runs completely unattended, without any administrative intervention. There is no ability to configure the installation as it occurs. You create and use a control **.ini** file to "replay" a desired installation footprint.

- *Console mode* provides a command-line–driven interface with multiple interactions, letting you configure the installation as it occurs. Figure 4.2 shows the console interface.

- *Graphical mode* uses a graphical interface to manage administrative interaction to configure the installation.

You can install IDS components using any of these three modes at two levels: bundle and product. In a bundle install, you can install all products—IDS data server, IConnect, Client Software Development Kit (CSDK), and so on—at once with a single command (**ids_install** for Linux/Unix, **setup.exe** for Windows, or the **.dmg** file for Mac OS X). This mode does give you the option to unselect products from the installation, but that typically isn't done; instead, the product install is used. At present, you can't "record" a bundle install to replay via the silent install mode. I'll discuss a workaround later.

On Linux and Unix ports where the product is distributed as a **tar** file, you can extract the file's contents and then execute a separate install procedure for each product—so you would execute **installserver** to install IDS, **installclientsdk** to install the CSDK, and so on. In the console or graphical mode of a product-level installation, an optional parameter triggers the "recording" of all actions taken into a separate configuration file for each product. Once you have these files, you can include them with the distribution

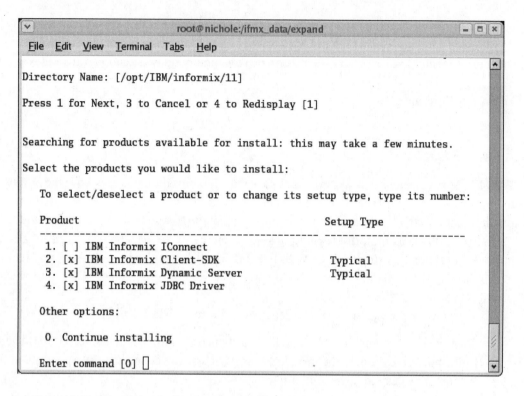

Figure 4.2: The console interface to the IDS installation process

of the data server and "replay" the install via the silent install mechanism on any number of servers to faithfully re-create the installation wherever necessary without any local interaction.

Going back to the bundle installer, although it's not possible to record the installation, you can create a bundle-level configuration file for use with the silent installer. Unfortunately, the process isn't automated at this time. You must copy the **bundle.ini** file found in the top level of the expanded IDS distribution and then modify the copied file, turning on or off product options as needed for your application or installation. On Mac OS X ports, you can copy this file from **$INFORMIXDIR** after you've installed the data server somewhere.

For the most part, a binary response controls each option. For example, the following two commands, respectively, turn off the installation of the CSDK and install the Eastern European language libraries for Global Language Support (GLS).

```
-P csdk.active=false
-SP SERVER/IIF.jar IDS-EASTEURO.active=true
```

I'll explain these "replay" files in greater detail later. For those considering this capability for the purposes of integrating IDS into an application, once you've installed all the products (whether via a bundle- or product-level installation), additional unattended configuration can occur using scripts provided as part of your application installation.

Installation Step-by-Step

The installation process itself is rather straightforward. The one catch is that system "super-user," or **sudo**, privileges are still required to execute the installation. On Mac OS X, you will need to enter the system's administration password if you're not logged in as **root**. For Mac OS X, this practice (installation by a non-root user ID) is the preferred method of installation. On Linux/Unix servers, after extracting the data server binaries and reviewing the release notes, get to super-user state and then execute the following command to complete a bundle installation in graphical mode:

```
ids_install -gui
```

Regardless of the operating system you're installing on, following a splash screen, the installation wizard starts, presenting a graphical interface (Figure 4.3) to the release notes and installation guide for your data server port so you can read the directions provided by IBM.

If you haven't done so already, it is critical that you review the release notes now, paying particular attention to the machine notes file. There, you'll find the recommended kernel modifications necessary for IDS to initialize and operate instances on the physical server. You must tune the kernel to these recommended settings for the data server to work properly. How you tune the kernel to include these values varies by operating system. In nearly all cases, you'll need to restart the physical server for these changes to take effect.

Two additional screens follow, the first welcoming you to the installation process and the second asking you to accept the licensing agreement.

Next, the wizard displays the screen shown in Figure 4.4, which prompts you to indicate where you want the data server to be installed. If you set the **$INFORMIXDIR** environment variable before invoking the installer, that setting will be read and populated into this field automatically. In the sample screen, the IBM standard path of **/opt/IBM/informix** is used as well as a version-specific directory for IDS 11.

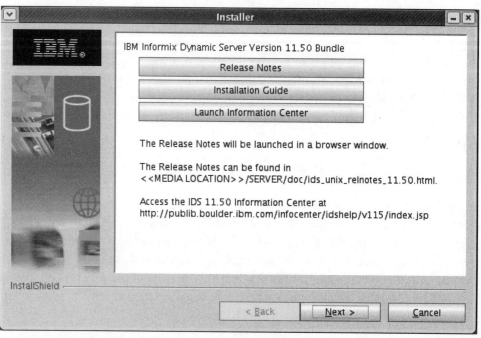

Figure 4.3: Opening information screen of the installation wizard

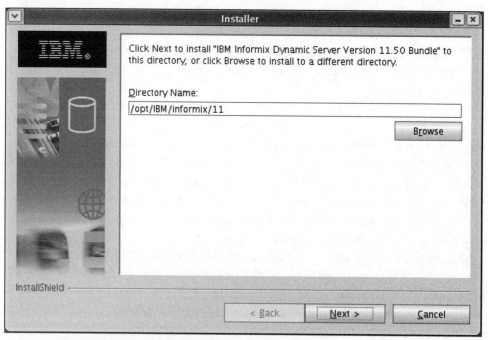

Figure 4.4: Specifying the installation location

When you install IDS on Mac OS X, the default installation location is in the **/Applications** directory consistent with the installation standard for that operating system; the exact location is **/Applications/IBM/informix**. Whether you choose to install there, in an IDS 11–specific subdirectory, or in the **/opt** directory structure recommended for other ports is up to you.

Each choice comes with advantages and disadvantages. On one hand, if you use the default location, you're following the O/S standard. On the other hand, as you saw in the previous chapter, I strongly recommend isolating a release level to a specific directory for easier upgrading and migration. If you install in the **/opt** directory structure, you aren't following the O/S standard, but if you're supporting multiple ports of the data server, you can create one set of instance and other administration scripts with paths to binaries and other utilities and use them across all platforms. The choice is ultimately yours and should be governed by what is most important to you and your organization.

From the next screen (Figure 4.5), you can choose to install all products and modules (the default) or execute a customized install. For this example, we'll assume you want to follow the default and install the Client SDK (which includes IConnect) as well as the IDS data server and the Informix JDBC driver. Selection of the **Custom** setup type option indicates that you want to specify which IDS modules are installed.

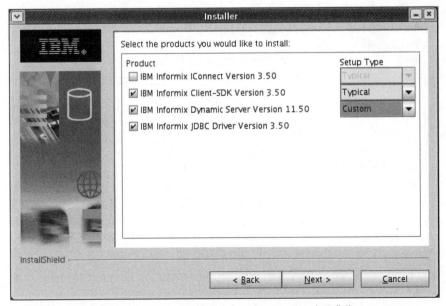

Figure 4.5: Specifying products to install and choosing a custom installation

Having invoked the custom option for the IDS data server, you next see a screen like the one shown in Figure 4.6. Here, you can select individual modules to include or exclude during installation. When you click on an option, the installation wizard displays a description of the option, along with the amount of disk space it requires, on the right side of the screen.

Most major modules have at least one or two levels of finer granularity of choices. For example, the **ON-Bar Utilities** option (not shown in the figure) expands to show another set of installation choices: the Informix interface for the Tivoli Storage Manager and the Informix Storage Manager. Choosing the custom option for the CSDK and IConnect products produces a set of module choices for those products in this hierarchy, too.

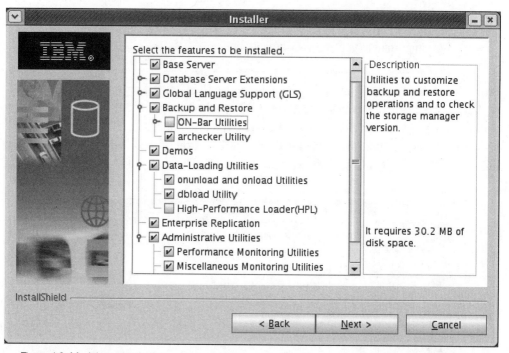

Figure 4.6: Module customization

The console version of the installer lets you choose from among the same options as those presented by the install wizard. Rather than click a twisty to expand the module hierarchy, you select a menu number for the module or module subcomponent.

After you make your selections and click **Next** to continue, the next screen asks whether you want to enable "role separation." Role separation is optional and is not required for the data server to work properly. If you choose to enable this functionality, the install process will exclusively assign separate, specific administrative functions related to auditing and Label Based Access Control (LBAC) to specific user accounts. Only individuals logging in as one of these users will be able to execute the specified functions. In an environment where data security requirements are very stringent, it would be wise to set up this feature. I must admit, however, that I have never used it. If you decide not to enable role separation and then later find out that you need to enforce it, you can add it on Linux, Mac OS X, and Unix ports of the data server. On Windows ports, you'll need to reinstall the product and reconfigure the instance.

If you choose to enable role separation, you'll be prompted through a screen similar to the one shown in Figure 4.7.

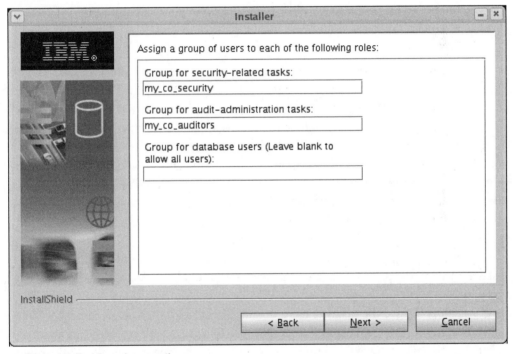

Figure 4.7: Enabling role separation

Here, you enter the group names of the users who will act as the Database System Security Officer (DBSSO) and the Auditing Analysis Officer (AAO). A third field lets you enter group names for a restricted set of users who can access instances. This field generally is left blank so that all users can access IDS data services. Table 4.3 describes the responsibilities of the two security roles.

Table 4.3: Role separation groups	
Role	Description
Auditing Analysis Officer (AAO)	User IDs in this group can enable or disable the auditing functionality of the server in instances and review the audit logs.
Database System Security Officer (DBSSO)	User IDs in this group serve as the general security administrators and should be considered the Master Security Administrator for the instance because they can control the access functionality of the other roles. For example, a DBSSO defines the audit masks that the AAO is able to use. As a result, it is the DBSSO who defines what is auditable and what is not; the AAO simply implements the design and monitors the auditing process.

Best practices specify that neither the **root** nor the **informix** ID be a member of either of these groups. Group names you enter here must also exist as operating system groups because logs and other utilities will have permissions set so that only those group members can read or use them. These O/S groups must exist (and should have at least one member) when you specify role separation; otherwise, the installation wizard will not let you proceed.

Regardless of whether you choose to enable role separation, the next screen gives you the option to create a "demonstration instance." This option is actually more powerful than you at first might think. If you say "yes" to this choice, another screen appears, giving you the option to use a default **$ONCONFIG** file, enter the path to an **$ONCONFIG** file you've already prepared, or let the installer determine how to configure and tune an instance based on your response to several questions.

Obviously, if you already have your own file, you can use that and initialize the instance with all the parameters (e.g., memory, buffer pools, locks, backup devices) as you'd like.

If you elect to have the installer use a default file or tailor the instance to your needs, a screen like the one shown in Figure 4.8 prompts you to enter the relevant basic information for instance initialization. One thing to be aware of is here that the default size of the rootdbs parameter (**ROOTSIZE**) will be several hundred megabytes. This value is much too large; you should reduce it to between 60 MB and 80 MB as illustrated in the figure.

If you choose to have the installer configure an instance for you based on an estimated workload, a screen like the one shown in Figure 4.9 appears, prompting you to specify the number of CPU virtual processors to create, your desired memory allocation, and the approximate number of transactional versus analytical uses the instance will need to support. The installer will use this information to create the instance.

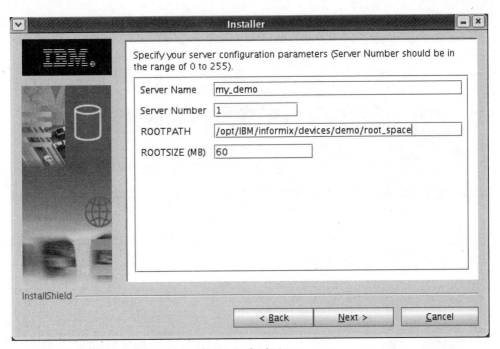

Figure 4.8: Parameters for initializing a demonstration instance

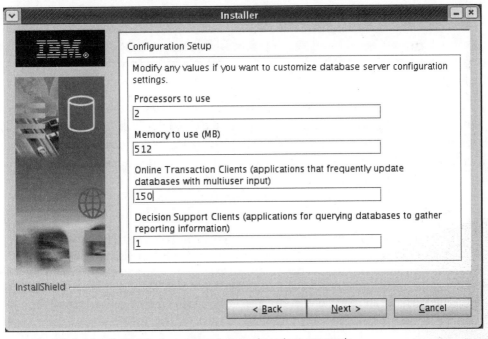

Figure 4.9: Guiding the installer to create an instance based on your needs

The next screen (Figure 4.10) displays a summary of the products to be installed and the expected disk footprint. The fact that the footprint for our sample installation is less than the maximum confirms that the choices made in Figure 4.6 have been carried forward as expected.

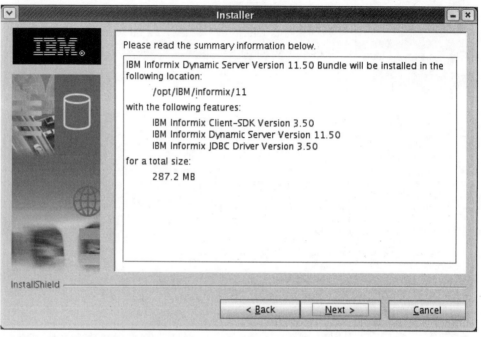

Figure 4.10: Installation summary screen

From here, the wizard displays the progress of the installation graphically on the screen. There is some log information output as well to the character-based window that invoked the installer. When the installation has been completed, a status screen is displayed that provides directions to the bundled documentation and recommendations for next steps in the configuration of an instance.

> If you ask the installer to create a demonstration instance for you, that instance may not initialize successfully. The main reason for this is that the kernel has not been modified to support the parameters required by IDS. This is particularly true for Mac OS X ports of the data server. Review the guidance and directions given earlier in the chapter (near Figure 4.3) about the file to review and actions to be taken.

Replicating the Installation on Multiple Physical Servers

Okay, so you've installed the data server once, but you need to do it *n* more times, and you want each additional installation to be exactly the same as your control installation. The best way to accomplish this goal is to use the silent installation mode with a "replay" file. Just like a "regular" installation, silent installation requires super-user access privileges.

If you're executing a product-level install in either graphical or console mode, you can "record" your choices by adding the **-record** *filename.***ini** option to the install command. The output file is identical in format to the template **.ini** file in the directory for the product; it just contains the **true** or **false** values for each module choice you made. Figure 4.11 shows an example.

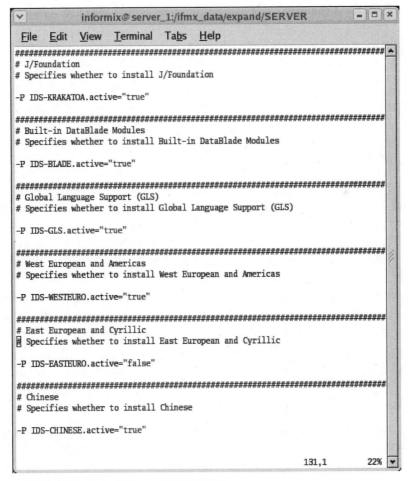

Figure 4.11: Replay file for a silent installation

To execute a silent bundle install, you must copy and then manually modify the **bundle.ini** file in the top directory level of the uncompressed installation media, or in **$INFORMIXDIR** for Mac OS X. The format of this file is identical to that shown in Figure 4.11; it just has all the options for all products in the IDS bundle.

Once you've created the file (or files, if you're going to do a series of product-level installs), you can replay the install by executing

> *Bundle install:*
>   `ids_install -silent -options` *filename*`.ini` *[other parms]*
> *Product install (IDS only):*
>   `installserver -silent -options` *filename*`.ini` *[other parms]*

and so on. If you don't indicate in the control file to accept the license, you must add that flag to the command string you execute for the installation to continue.

Once all the product(s) are installed (whether via a bundle- or product-level installation), additional unattended configuration (e.g., adding dbspaces, moving or resizing logs, creating databases and tables) can occur using scripts you provide as part of the installation process.

Modifying an Installation

Once you've completed an installation, you can always go back and make changes to the modules or products installed. To do so, simply re-execute the installation process as if you're executing a new install. As you make your new selections, the installation wizard will make the necessary changes by adding or deleting just the modules needed; it does not just reinstall the entire binary set. You may wonder how the wizard manages this process.

As a product or bundle installation is executed, the install process creates a set of control files of all installed modules and files. When you add or subtract modules, the wizard uses these control files to determine which modules and associated binary files need to be installed or removed, without affecting the rest of the installation. The control files are also used to validate package dependencies and verify that uninstallation occurs as it should. There are three control files for Linux, Mac OS X, and Unix ports, all located in **$INFORMIXDIR/etc: manifest.inf, IIFfiles**, and **IIFfiles.installed**. These files are *not* end-user modifiable; do not alter them! Windows ports maintain the same information in installer libraries.

The **manifest.inf** file, shown in Figure 4.12, contains information about the modules installed, their installation date and size, and basic meta data on the module's functionality.

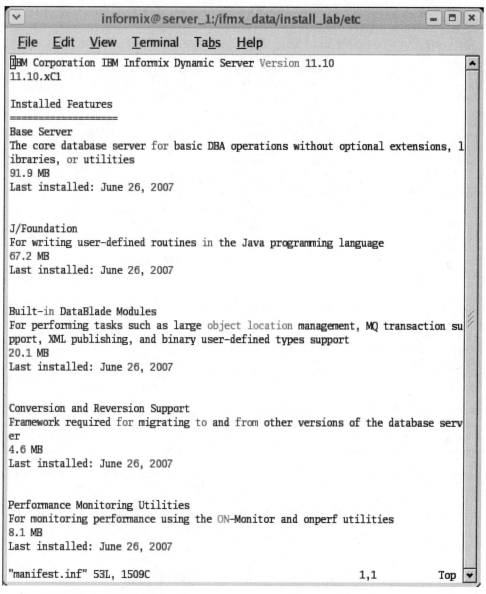

Figure 4.12: The installation manifest file

The **IIFfiles** and **IIFfiles.installed** files are identical in format but different in content. File **IIFfiles** contains a comprehensive list of all possible binary files for the IDS data server only. File **IIFfiles.installed** holds a list of the binary files actually installed. Figure 4.13 shows an edited example of what these files look like.

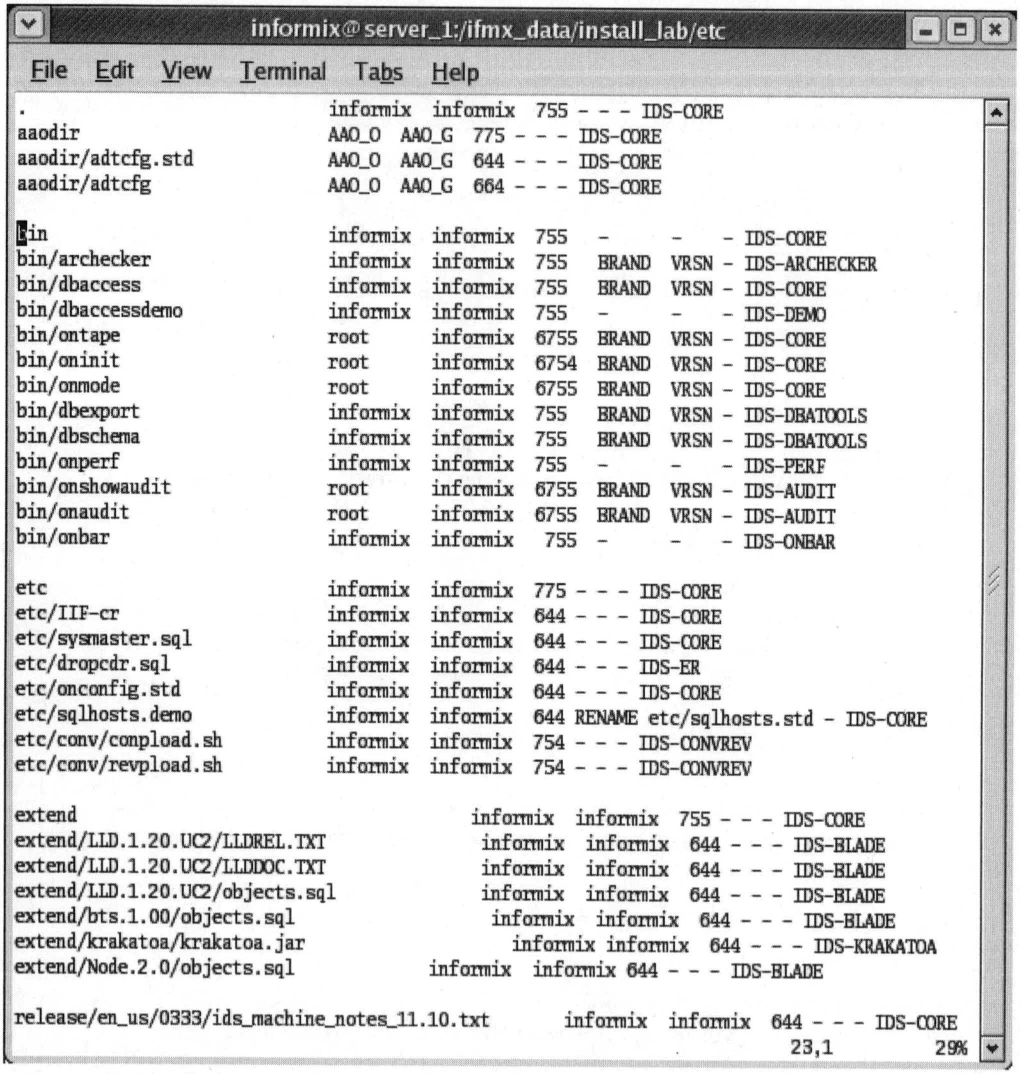

```
informix@server_1:/ifmx_data/install_lab/etc

File  Edit  View  Terminal  Tabs  Help
.                          informix  informix  755 - - - IDS-CORE
aaodir                     AAO_O  AAO_G  775 - - - IDS-CORE
aaodir/adtcfg.std          AAO_O  AAO_G  644 - - - IDS-CORE
aaodir/adtcfg              AAO_O  AAO_G  664 - - - IDS-CORE

bin                        informix  informix  755  -      -    - IDS-CORE
bin/archecker              informix  informix  755  BRAND  VRSN - IDS-ARCHECKER
bin/dbaccess               informix  informix  755  BRAND  VRSN - IDS-CORE
bin/dbaccessdemo           informix  informix  755  -      -    - IDS-DEMO
bin/ontape                 root      informix  6755 BRAND  VRSN - IDS-CORE
bin/oninit                 root      informix  6754 BRAND  VRSN - IDS-CORE
bin/onmode                 root      informix  6755 BRAND  VRSN - IDS-CORE
bin/dbexport               informix  informix  755  BRAND  VRSN - IDS-DBATOOLS
bin/dbschema               informix  informix  755  BRAND  VRSN - IDS-DBATOOLS
bin/onperf                 informix  informix  755  -      -    - IDS-PERF
bin/onshowaudit            root      informix  6755 BRAND  VRSN - IDS-AUDIT
bin/onaudit                root      informix  6755 BRAND  VRSN - IDS-AUDIT
bin/onbar                  informix  informix  755  -      -    - IDS-ONBAR

etc                        informix  informix  775 - - - IDS-CORE
etc/IIF-cr                 informix  informix  644 - - - IDS-CORE
etc/sysmaster.sql          informix  informix  644 - - - IDS-CORE
etc/dropcdr.sql            informix  informix  644 - - - IDS-ER
etc/onconfig.std           informix  informix  644 - - - IDS-CORE
etc/sqlhosts.demo          informix  informix  644 RENAME etc/sqlhosts.std - IDS-CORE
etc/conv/conpload.sh       informix  informix  754 - - - IDS-CONVREV
etc/conv/revpload.sh       informix  informix  754 - - - IDS-CONVREV

extend                              informix  informix  755 - - - IDS-CORE
extend/LLD.1.20.UC2/LLDREL.TXT       informix  informix  644 - - - IDS-BLADE
extend/LLD.1.20.UC2/LLDDOC.TXT       informix  informix  644 - - - IDS-BLADE
extend/LLD.1.20.UC2/objects.sql      informix  informix  644 - - - IDS-BLADE
extend/bts.1.00/objects.sql           informix  informix  644 - - - IDS-BLADE
extend/krakatoa/krakatoa.jar              informix informix  644 - - - IDS-KRAKATOA
extend/Node.2.0/objects.sql         informix  informix 644 - - - IDS-BLADE

release/en_us/0333/ids_machine_notes_11.10.txt    informix  informix  644 - - - IDS-CORE
                                                     23,1          29%
```

Figure 4.13: Extract of the IIFfiles file

As you can see from the figure, this is an alphabetical and pathed list of the files. The path is relative to **$INFORMIXDIR** and includes branding information such as file ownership and permission settings. The last column lists which module the binary belongs to, so if you want to know the specific files you're about to install (or remove) when you select a module, you can look in **IIFfiles**. Both the **IIFfiles.installed** and the **manifest.inf** files are updated every time you execute an install or uninstall operation.

Uninstalling

Unlike the installation process, in which you can choose whether to install at a bundle or a product level, you only have one choice when uninstalling: the product level. On Windows ports, you can use the uninstall option in the program group or use **Control Panel > Add/ Remove Software**. You can choose to remove everything, including dbspaces and chunks, or remove just IDS and related binaries.

On Linux, Mac OS X, and Unix ports, separate uninstall directories exist under **$INFORMIXDIR** for the CSDK, IDS data server, and JDBC driver products—called **uninstall_csdk**, **uninstall_ids*nnnn*** (where ***nnnn*** is the data server version number), and **jdbc/_uninst**, respectively. Each directory contains a Java **.jar** file that executes the uninstall of the product. The syntax for these files is

```
java -jar $INFORMIXDIR/uninstall_dir/uninstall.jar
```

where ***uninstall_dir*** is replaced with the product you want to remove. All three of these options support console- or character-based interaction by default; if you add the **-swing** flag, you can use a graphical interface.

An additional graphical interface is available for removing just the IDS data server. In **$INFORMIXDIR**, you'll find an executable called **uninstallserver**. Execute **uninstallserver** with the **-gui** flag appended to remove the data server graphically.

For all these options, you can also use the **-silent** flag to have the entire product uninstalled without any additional user interaction.

Understanding and Modifying Configuration Parameters

Part of the overall process of setting up an Informix Dynamic Server instance to run as efficiently as possible on any given machine is understanding what the various **$ONCONFIG** parameters are and the effect they have on the operation and maintenance of the instance. One of the great things about IDS is that over the years it has become almost a completely autonomic (to use IBM's term for self-managing software) data server. Of course, anyone familiar with data servers can tell you IDS has always led the market in ease of use and significantly reduced administrative requirements. It gets even better in IDS 11.

Today, you can change nearly all the parameters in the **$ONCONFIG** file without restarting the instance. Those that do require a restart are either not commonly used or need to be changed only once—generally to turn them "on" even if you don't use the functionality immediately. Many of the parameters that IDS administrators used to have to experiment with to manage operations, such as checkpoint durations, are now no longer relevant. In the case of checkpoints, the algorithm has changed completely. As a result, resources that used to be allocated to checkpoint-oriented processing can now be released back to SQL processing, providing a dramatic increase in performance. In other cases, the data server itself will monitor operations and automatically add and release resources or execute other housekeeping operations to meet an overall performance and recovery objective you set.

The *IBM Informix Dynamic Server Administrator's Reference* provides an excellent and comprehensive description of each **$ONCONFIG** parameter. That said, there are some you need to know about right now in trying to initialize your (perhaps first) instance. In this section, I explain the most important initial **$ONCONFIG** parameters. I've organized these parameters into logical and functional groupings that, in some cases, do not exactly match their location in the file. For the most part, the parameters are in alphabetical order within each grouping, except where a specific logical order is required to coordinate several parameters.

WARNING There are several parameters that use full paths to specific directories or files. The default paths used will most likely not match your environment, particularly if you use the best practices recommendation on creating the directory layout. Make sure you modify all parameter paths as appropriate.

When setting parameter paths, you used to have to use the full path name. In IDS 11, several parameters, including **ALARMPROGRAM**, **JVPCLASSPATH**, **JVPHOME**, **JVPJAVAHOME**, **JVPPROFILE**, and **SYSALARMPROGRAM** now support the ability to use relative paths from **$INFORMIXDIR**. For example, you can set **JVPHOME** using either of the following methods:

```
JVPHOME   /opt/IBM/Informix/11/extend/krakatoa
JVPHOME   $INFORMIXDIR/extend/krakatoa
```

In cases where a parameter might have more than one path statement, such as **JVPCLASSPATH**, the relative path works for only the *first path statement* in the string. So, for example, setting **JVPCLASSPATH** as follows

```
JVPCLASSPATH $INFORMIXDIR/extend/krakatoa/krakatoa.jar:
$INFORMIXDIR/extend/krakatoa/jdbc.jar
```

will resolve to the following, which won't work:

```
/opt/IBM/informix/11/extend/krakatoa/krakatoa.jar:
$INFORMIXDIR/extend/krakatoa/jdbc.jar
```

So make sure you're careful about using relative path strings in the file.

Before we discuss the various configuration parameters, you should know that IBM did a major overhaul of the **$ONCONFIG** file in IDS 11.5. Previously, there was little if any organization about where parameters were located within the file, what they controlled, and the range of values. With IDS 11.5, this has changed. All parameters for any given feature are grouped together. Preceding each group, a comment box provides a brief explanation of the parameter and the valid parameter options. In some cases, you'll see advice about how to set the parameters. This change is a long-overdue and very welcome update and should greatly help those new to IDS in understanding how to configure instance parameters.

When creating a configuration file for an instance, best practices dictate that you copy **$INFORMIXDIR/etc/onconfig.std** and rename it for the target instance. Typically, I put an abbreviation of the instance name after the period (.) in the file name; for example, **onconfig.sar, onconfig.tag,** and so on. From there, I edit the "new" file for the instance I want to start.

Initial Devices

The parameters in this group are the physical foundation of the instance. In most cases, if any of these values are inaccessible or corrupted, the fast recovery process will abort and the instance will not initialize or restart. (*Administering Informix Dynamic Server, Advanced Topics* provides more information about the fast recovery process.)

LOGFILES

The **LOGFILES** parameter determines how many logical logs are created during the initialization process. The logical logs created as part of this process are stored in the **ROOTNAME** dbspace, commonly referred to as the "rootdbs." As I explained in Chapter 1, IDS uses the logical logs to record changes to data (except for simple BLOBs stored in BLOBspaces) within logged databases. Depending on your application's needs and the number of users using the instance, you may need to tune both the size and number of logical logs.

Setting **LOGFILES** to 6 will provide more than enough logical log space for instance initialization if you use a **LOGSIZE** (covered next) value of 2,000 KB. Chapter 5 describes how to move logical logs to other dbspaces as well as how to tune their size once the instance is initialized.

LOGSIZE

Parameter **LOGSIZE** determines the default size of all logical logs created in the instance. Because the initialization process uses some log space and my sizing recommendation for the rootdbs parameter (**ROOTSIZE**) is only 60 MB to 80 MB, I would set **LOGSIZE** to 2,000 KB. Once the instance is functional, you can drop the original logical logs and create new logical logs at a size that best fits the activity level of the instance. If you'll be using BLOBs in the instance, the size of the newly created logs will need to be quite a bit larger.

MIRROR

The **MIRROR** parameter enables or disables the ability to use Informix Dynamic Server–based mirroring for the entire instance. You can set this parameter on (value **1**, or one) during initialization with no impact to the instance and then simply use the functionality when and where you need it. Or, you can leave it off (**0**, or zero) and then dynamically enable mirroring when needed without having to restart the instance.

MIRROROFFSET

I include this parameter in case you're considering using IDS mirroring. See the notes below on **ROOTOFFSET**.

MIRRORPATH

Again, this parameter applies only with IDS mirroring. The **MIRRORPATH** value specifies the fully pathed location of the rootdbs mirror. All other IDS-managed chunk/dbspace mirror information is stored in the reserved pages of the instance.

You can change the location of the mirror, but doing so isn't as simple as just changing the parameter value and restarting the instance. First, you need to disable mirroring on the rootdbs and then create the new mirror location. Shut down the instance, and change the parameter value to the new mirror location. Bring the instance up to quiescent mode, and then re-enable mirroring on the rootdbs. Once the mirror has synchronized, you can bring the instance all the way online. See Chapters 5 and 6 for a discussion about changing instance operating modes and using the **onspaces** utility or the SQL API to create or drop mirrors, respectively.

Notice that no sizing information is requested for this or any other mirror chunk you create. The instance assumes the mirror chunk will be at least the same size as the primary chunk it is mirroring.

PHYSDBS

The **PHYSDBS** parameter specifies the name of the dbspace containing the physical log. As previously mentioned, the rootdbs is the default location for this log and is the only choice when initializing an instance.

IDS 11 provides functionality that lets you change the location or size of the physical log without interrupting instance operations. This added functionality comes with some warnings and restrictions, though. We'll get into these and other details of working with the physical log in Chapter 5.

PHYSFILE

The **PHYSFILE** parameter specifies the size of the physical log. I advise an initial value between 10,000 KB and 15,000 KB, although you'll undoubtedly change the size once you have all the dbspaces created. Why? With the new checkpoint algorithm in IDS 11 as well as the recovery time objective (RTO), you'll need to set the physical log to as close to 110 percent of your buffer size as possible. Chapter 5 explains how to manage the size of the physical log and move it to another dbspace.

ROOTNAME

This parameter contains the name of the dbspace that will function as the rootdbs. Convention holds that the name of this dbspace is "rootdbs" but you can use any name. Allocation of disk space for this dbspace during instance initialization process occurs at a single-chunk level. After the instance is active, you can add chunks to the rootdbs if needed.

ROOTOFFSET

An *offset value* lets you create multiple dbspaces (or logical disk chunks to be added to dbspaces) within one physical disk partition if you're using raw disk space or even within one file name if you're using cooked space. Generally speaking, in today's world offsets are never used anymore because disks and LUNS are so easy to manage. Offsets inside a flat file are never used since it's easier to simply create another file. If you follow the naming and placement conventions suggested in Chapter 5's discussion about managing dbspaces and BLOBspaces, you should leave this parameter at **0** (zero) for this or any other dbspace created.

This particular parameter is for setting the offset value of the **ROOTNAME** dbspace. Because **ROOTNAME** is the first space created for an instance, it probably won't need to be offset by any amount into the raw disk partition, file, or LUN created for this dbspace.

In the Linux/Unix ports of the product, where raw space is most often used and disks/LUNs can be partitioned to match chunk size, the ability to use offsets is particularly helpful if ambiguity exists regarding what the proper size of a disk/LUN partition should be. If you cannot forecast how you need to partition each disk/LUN to meet future demands, you can use the offset value to create several smaller logical disk chunks from one larger physical disk partition. Using the offset value, you can mark the beginning point of a chunk within the larger disk partition. The chunk would then be expanded to the requested size and used to either create a new dbspace or add to an existing dbspace.

 The use of offsets requires meticulous documentation. The data server does not verify that device paths and offsets are exclusive. As a result, it's **WARNING** possible to enter offset values incorrectly and have two devices overlap each other, causing data corruption. In one environment where I used offsets, I never placed two chunks next to each other with respect to their size and offset values. I always inserted a 1 MB or greater buffer between the end of one device and the beginning of the other in case I made a math error in calculating the end point of a device as well as any system or IDS overhead that might cause the device to expand to just slightly more than its stated size.

ROOTPATH

The **ROOTPATH** parameter specifies the full path to the first chunk of the rootdbs. While it is customary to use an absolute path for rootdbs, and any other chunk/dbspace added to the instance, you can also use a relative path based on an environment parameter. For example, suppose I set the following in my environment setup script for this instance:

```
export DEVICES=/opt/IBM/Informix/devices/tagus
```

The following would be valid syntax for **ROOTPATH**:

```
ROOTPATH  $DEVICES/root_space
```

ROOTSIZE

The **ROOTSIZE** parameter defines the amount of disk space, in kilobytes, to allocate for the first chunk of the rootdbs. In a properly built instance, I recommend allocating between 60 MB and 80 MB. This setting will allow for the initial creation of the logical and physical logs as well as the system databases. As soon after instance initialization as possible, you should move the logs out of the rootdbs (as explained in Chapter 5).

With a rootdbs in this size range, some temporary table creation for sorting and order-by work can still occur in the rootdbs but not to any significant degree. You should create temporary dbspaces to serve that purpose. If you don't plan to create temporary dbspaces, you'll need to adjust the size of the rootdbs upward with additional chunks to permit this type of activity. We'll discuss temporary dbspaces in greater detail in Chapter 5.

System Configuration

You use the parameters in the system configuration group to set the instance's identity as well as most of the core instance overhead structures. These include the number of user connections that will be allowed and the protocols through which they can connect, the number of CPU VPs, and the maximum length of time that can pass between checkpoints.

When considering performance tuning, most people tend to think first of the parameters that affect shared memory. However, many of the parameters we'll cover in this section can significantly impact the overall performance of the instance. They should receive as much review during general tuning as those in the shared memory group.

ALARMPROGRAM

The **ALARMPROGRAM** parameter specifies the fully pathed name of a program or shell script the instance should execute if particular "events" occur. This program or script must be able to receive five input parameters, termed severity, class ID, class message, specific message, and a "see also" file reference. Each event can have its own notification scheme to alert the administrator or an automatic resolution procedure, depending on what is programmed into the **ALARMPROGRAM** program or script. A number of instance events have already been configured into the default shell script distributed with the data server.

You can set up this program to call other utilities to handle specific events. For example, there are a couple of template files that the default alarm program calls. These templates, in **$INFORMIXDIR/etc**, are called **logs_full.sh** or **logs_full.bat** and **no_logs.sh** or **no_logs.bat**, depending on your port's O/S. These script templates have only one event and action programmed. The first automatically backs up filled logical logs through the **ON-Bar** utility suite; the second does nothing at all.

I recommend leaving this parameter at its default value and working within the existing script as needed.

AUTO_AIOVPS

Parameter **AUTO_AIOVPS** permits the data server to automatically manage the number of asynchronous I/O virtual processors handling I/O to and from devices such as the logical and physical logs, flat-file–based chunks, and so on. Enabling this functionality imposes no performance penalty; in fact, it improves performance. Leave **AUTO_AIOVPS** at its default of 1 (one), or on.

AUTO_CKPTS

The **AUTO_CKPTS** setting permits the instance to execute a checkpoint when it needs to meet the recovery-time-objective time limit or mitigate against potential transaction blocks. Enabling this functionality imposes no performance penalty; in fact, it improves performance. Leave the parameter at its default of 1 (one), or on.

AUTO_LRU_TUNING

The **AUTO_LRU_TUNING** parameter permits the data server to automatically manage when and how the least recently used (LRU) queues are flushed. This capability represents another performance enhancement to the buffer management system introduced in IDS 9.4. When the instance detects it must flush parts of the queues to create space, the overall buffer flushing process receives a higher priority. Enabling this functionality imposes no performance penalty; in fact, it improves performance. Leave the parameter at its default of 1 (one), or on.

CKPTINTVL

Parameter **CKPTINTVL** sets the maximum number of seconds that can pass between checkpoints if the instance is handling active user threads. Writes that occur during checkpoints are the most efficient method of writing to disk because IDS sorts the data and organizes it by chunk before handing it off to the page cleaners (**CLEANERS**, covered next).

With the interval checkpoint algorithm and automatic checkpoints introduced in IDS 11, this parameter is now more of a worst-case trigger than a hard system limit to which you must manage. Leave it at its default of 300 seconds.

CLEANERS

The value you enter for the **CLEANERS** parameter represents the number of page cleaner threads started in the instance. IDS uses page cleaners to transfer data from the buffer pool to the disk write mechanism so the data can be written to disk. IDS development generally recommends you allocate one cleaner for each active disk in the instance, up to a maximum of 128.

CONSOLE

In the more recent versions of the IDS product, **CONSOLE** is pretty much a useless parameter. In years past, it wasn't much better; all the console messages told you was that the logical logs were full and needed backing up. This situation was already apparent because the instance had suspended operation while waiting for the logs to be backed up.

In the current versions of the product, the only message I've seen is that a particular logical log has filled. I usually set this parameter to **/dev/null** or **NUL**, although I suppose you could set it to a file (as is the default for Windows ports of the data server) and capture whatever is output there.

DBSERVERNAME

The **DBSERVERNAME** parameter assigns the instance a unique name among all IDS instances on the network. The parameter is limited to 128 characters and is case-sensitive. You cannot use uppercase letters, spaces, tabs, dashes, hyphens, or the at (@) character. This parameter's value is also used as the value for the **$INFORMIXSERVER** environment variable. The name is also entered in the first field of the **$SQLHOSTS** file.

In all cases, the name you use for the instance or its aliases (discussed next) should conform to the logical naming convention of your organization. In the examples in this book, you'll see that my convention is to use the names of major rivers located throughout the world. Why rivers? Why not!

DBSERVERALIASES

The **DBSERVERALIASES** parameter contains the secondary or alias name (or names) for the instance. Limited to 128 case-sensitive characters (like **DBSERVERNAME**) and to being unique across the network, these aliases are commonly used to define additional connection paths into the instance. The connection paths are usually network-related, so the alias names should reflect that. For example, to provide an additional TCP/IP-based connection alias to the **sarthe** instance using a second network interface card, I could enter **sarthe_tcp_2** in the **DBSERVERALIASES** field. For the connection aliases to work, they must also have valid entries in the **$SQLHOSTS** file and in the **/etc/services** file (or equivalent in Windows).

> While I say that the **DBSERVERALIASES** parameter is used mainly for network-based connection paths, this statement is not correct if you'll be using Enterprise Replication or the MACH-11 high-availability technologies. In these cases, the **DBSERVERNAME** parameter must be set to a network-based connection path, and you can use **DBSERVERALIASES** to define a shared memory connection path or another network-based connection path.
>
> In a note-within-a-note, IDS 11.5 provides the **HA_ALIAS** parameter as a workaround to requiring **DBSERVERNAME** to be a network-based connection path when configuring ER and MACH-11. Look for more information about configuring ER and MACH-11 in *Administering Informix Dynamic Server, Advanced Topics*.

DBSPACETEMP

The **DBSPACETEMP** parameter contains the names of the dbspaces to be used for sorting, order-bys, temporary tables, hash indexes, and so forth. The names entered here must be comma- or colon-separated, with no white space between them. The length of this parameter cannot exceed 254 characters, including separators.

Dbspaces listed in the **DBSPACETEMP** field can be explicitly created either as "temporary" dbspaces or as regular dbspaces, but they are used as though they were temporary dbspaces. I recommend using temporary dbspaces so that any instance-generated activity in the dbspaces isn't logged in the logical logs, as would be the case if the instance-generated activity occurred in regular dbspaces. Spaces created as temporary dbspaces can have any page size; however, all spaces must have the same page size. Most environments I've seen use the default instance page size when creating temporary dbspaces.

During the initialization process, you can enter temporary dbspace names that do not yet exist. A single-error message written to the **MSGPATH** file indicates an inability to find the dbspaces. This error will continue to be entered in **MSGPATH** each time the instance is started until you create the temporary dbspaces and use the names entered in **DBSPACETEMP** field.

Only those dbspace names entered in this field, or those explicitly set by an application or by the **$DBSPACETEMP** or **$PSORT_DBTEMP** environment variable, will be used by the instance as temporary space, regardless of their creation type.

IDS 10 provided functionality that can dramatically reduce use of the temporary space for operations. For a discussion of the **NON_PDQ_QUERY_MEM** parameter, which implements this functionality, see *Administering Informix Dynamic Server, Advanced Topics*.

DIRECT_IO

If you're on a Linux/Unix port of the data server *and* your O/S supports direct file I/O *and* you're using flat files (cooked space) for chunks, you should set this parameter to **1** (one) to enable faster I/O access to the chunks. If your operating system also supports kernel asynchronous I/O (KAIO) and it is enabled in the instance, you'll be able to reduce the number of AIO VPs you configure in the instance. Refer to the machine notes that came with your distribution of the data server for guidance about how to set this parameter if you're using cooked space.

MSGPATH

The **MSGPATH** parameter specifies the path to the one of the most important log files on the system, the instance log file, which holds all the routine and error messages the instance generates. Each instance on a physical server must have its own **MSGPATH** file. As I indicated in Chapter 3, I have a separate directory where all log files are written. For this and other logs, I generally include the instance name in the log file name; however, you can use any name. For example, the **MSGPATH** parameter for my **sarthe** instance would have the following value:

```
MSGPATH   /opt/IBM/Informix/logs/sarthe.log
```

The **MSGPATH** file will grow over time, so you should create a simple shell script or task that gets executed via the instance scheduler to manage this file through a rolling archive.

NETTYPE

How you set the **NETTYPE** parameter determines not only the number of users that can access the instance but also how they can connect to it.

There are two individual threads that make up the overall connection thread to the instance: a *poll thread* and a *listen thread*. The poll thread listens for messages from client connections through the network connection. The poll thread in turn passes these messages to the listen thread, which performs all the work of authenticating the user and establishing the connection to the instance by starting a "sqlexec" thread to process the SQL statement. The results of the SQL statement are returned in reverse order along the thread path. A poll thread is started for every unique combination of the **NETTYPE** parameters.

In the Linux, Mac OS X, and Unix ports of the data server, the **NETTYPE** parameter also lets you specify which VP class, CPU or NET, supports a particular poll thread for greater throughput and efficiency. Shared memory connections should be serviced only by a poll thread defined to use the CPU VP class, while all other connection combinations should use the NET VP class. When defining listen threads to run on CPU VPs, you cannot declare more than the total number of CPU VPs; otherwise, the instance will allocate additional NET VPs to handle the workload, reducing their efficiency.

Four fields, shown in Table 4.4, make up the **NETTYPE** parameter.

Table 4.4: The NETTYPE parameter fields		
Field number	Field name	Possible values (vary by port)
1	Connection protocol	**ipcshm, tlitcp, soctcp, tlispx, tlidr, socdr, sqlmux, tliimc, socimc, socssl**
2	Threads	The number of threads to start
3	Users	The number of concurrent user connections each of these threads will service
4	VP class	The VP class the thread(s) will run on; either **CPU** or **NET**

Regardless of which combination(s) you define, be careful to allocate only what is needed for instance connectivity. Over-allocating can burden the instance with additional unnecessary overhead, reducing its ability to execute other operations.

NUMAIOVPS

First, the **NUMAIOVPS** parameter, which sets the number of AIO VPs, may or may not be available in your IDS port. It was removed in IDS 11.5 and replaced by the **AUTO_AIOVPS** parameter value of 1 (one).

Older versions of IDS use AIO VPs for I/O to and from file-based chunks (if direct I/O is not available) and to and from the physical and logical logs. When initializing an instance on IDS 10 and earlier releases, follow the general recommendation of allocating three AIO VPs for general instance operations plus one AIO VP for each disk/LUN that contains one or more cooked file chunks. On IDS 11.10, set **NUMAIOVPS** to a much lower number and let **AUTO_AIOVPS** manage the number of VPs allocated based on instance operations.

On earlier IDS versions, you can use the optional but preferred **VPCLASS** parameter to define the number of AIO VPs to create. If you use this option, comment out the **NUMAIOVPS** parameter because it will be redundant.

VPCLASS

The **VPCLASS** parameter was introduced sometime in the IDS 9 release cycle and is intended as the emerging standard for defining VPs initialized in the instance. For backward compatibility, the original parameters for the CPU and AIO VPs still exist in the **$ONCONFIG** file in versions earlier than IDS 11.5. You'd be wise to adopt and learn the new format, though.

Using the **VPCLASS** parameter, you can define all user-configurable classes of VPs. You'll use it to define user-defined VPs such as those for column-level encryption, the integrated Java Virtual Machine, DataBlades, and more. The format of the parameter is

```
vpclass  class,num=number,options
```

For initialization purposes, you need concern yourself only with specifying VPs in the CPU and AIO classes as appropriate. As a result, you'll probably define them like this:

```
vpclass  CPU,num=3
vpclass  AIO,num=5
```

You won't use any of the additional options for instance initialization. For information about the options, consult the *IBM Informix Dynamic Server Administrator's Reference*.

When using **VPCLASS** to create the CPU VPs, you'll need to comment out the **AFF_NPROCS**, **AFF_SPROC**, **NOAGE**, **NUMCPUVPS**, and potentially the **MULTIPROCESSOR** and **SINGLE_CPU_VP** parameters. When using **VPCLASS** to define the number of AIO VPs for versions earlier than IDS 11.5, you'll comment out the **NUMAIOVPS** parameter. If you make a mistake and forget to comment out a parameter, instance initialization will fail, but the **MSGPATH** file will contain a clear diagnostic message indicating what you need to do.

Shared Memory

The configuration parameters in the next group affect the size and operation of the instance's shared memory.

BUFFERPOOL

BUFFERPOOL is a new parameter introduced with IDS 10 that combines several now-deprecated individual parameters. Previously, you had only one set of buffers for an instance. IDS 10 introduced the ability to create dbspaces using multiples of the default page size up to 16 KB. Each *set* of dbspaces created with a nonstandard page size requires a buffer pool of that page size to hold the pages read from or written to disk. As a result, IBM introduced this parameter to define buffer pools of differing page sizes.

An individual buffer pool is not allocated for each dbspace, regardless of its page size. Only one buffer pool of a given page size exists for any number of dbspaces defined with that page size.

As I explained previously, the data server uses the instance's buffers to buffer data for read and write requests. Such requests are the single largest consumer of the resident portion of shared memory, and they have the greatest impact on the instance's shared memory size. The more buffers you have in an instance (barring excessive flushing due to the **LRU_MIN** and **MAX_DIRTY** parameters), the greater the likelihood that commonly accessed information a user needs will be in the buffers, eliminating a call to disk. At the same time, too many buffers can lead to unnecessary bloat and overhead within the instance as well as the inefficient use of system resources. The system must maintain the extra buffers and check them during checkpoints for any impact they could have on the logical consistency of the data in the instance.

In the **$INFORMIXDIR/etc/onconfig.std** template file, you'll find two **BUFFERPOOL** entries. The first is the "default" entry, and the second is an entry for the default page size for your port of the data server. As you'll read in the next chapter, it's easy to add new db-spaces of varying page sizes. One of the methods automatically creates a buffer pool for a page size if one doesn't already exist. The **$ONCONFIG** file's default entry will be used to set those buffer pool parameters; more about this in the next chapter.

The second **BUFFERPOOL** entry is the one you need to modify now, before initializing the instance. The appropriate setting for this parameter depends greatly on the amount of physical server memory, the number of instances to be supported, the number of user connections, the types of operations executed (simple versus complex), and so on. A general IDS development rule of thumb says to allocate 20 percent to 25 percent of the physical server's memory to an IDS instance, but that doesn't take into account user load, multiple residency, and other operations the system needs to support.

To begin with, set the buffers portion of this parameter to 10,000 and set the **LRU_MIN_DIRTY** and **LRU_MAX_DIRTY** parameters to 70 and 80, respectively. Then monitor the cache read and write percentages as well as the size of the physical log size. Eventually, you'll want the buffers to approach 110 percent of the physical log size if the read and write percentages don't drop too much.

You can monitor these values by examining the output from the **onstat -p** command. During normal database operations, you want the **%cache read** value to be greater than 95 percent and the **%cache write** to be greater than 85 percent.

> Beginning in IDS 11, the data server will generate general tuning guidance for this and other parameters based on instance activity. The guidance is written to **MSGPATH**.

LOCKS

The **LOCKS** parameter has some, but not much, effect on the size of the instance's shared memory (each lock takes 44 bytes of resident portion memory), so the tendency has been to set it rather high—particularly in an OLTP environment where a lack of locks will cause applications to fail. Instance locks incur some overhead, so use good judgment when setting this parameter.

Because each lock needs to be monitored and accounted for, set this field to what appears to be a reasonable value and then monitor by executing the **onstat -p** and **onstat -k** commands. The minimum value you can enter for this parameter is 2,000; the maximum value is 8,000,000 for 32-bit ports of the data server or 500,000,000 for 64-bit ports. For a busy instance, I generally start at about 100,000 locks (requiring 2 MB or 4 MB of shared memory depending on the default page size for the port) and tune from there.

Unlike in earlier versions of the data server, the number of locks is no longer fixed. If the instance requires more locks than what you set here, it will dynamically add them using memory from the instance's virtual portion of memory to manage them. That point notwithstanding, the allocation and de-allocation of additional locks does take some time and effort, so try to size the **LOCKS** parameter as best you can once the instance enters test phase.

SERVERNUM

You use the **SERVERNUM** parameter to create an offset into the general shared memory structures of the operating system (**SHMBASE**) to allocate the shared memory the instance will use. Although you can specify a value of **0** (zero), I recommend choosing a value between 1 and 255 for this parameter. The value obviously needs to be unique if more than one instance of Informix Dynamic Server will be running on the same physical server. Sequentially numbering the instances is not required, nor must the number be unique across all instances on the network—it is specific to the physical server. That said, I recommend that you make **SERVERNUM** unique across the entire environment where possible; doing so lets you more easily move instances from system to system as needed without having to check for potential memory address conflicts. Obviously, if you have more than 255 instances, that won't be possible.

SHMTOTAL

The **SHMTOTAL** value sets the maximum amount of shared memory, in kilobytes, that the instance can allocate to support its activities. If the instance tries to allocate more memory than allowed by this parameter, the application whose database request caused the allocation attempt to occur receives an error message and the thread is dropped from the instance. A message is written to **MSGPATH** indicating that an additional allocation of shared memory was attempted but failed because of the limit placed here. Setting **SHMTOTAL** to **0** (zero) allows unrestricted shared memory allocation, but you should use this setting only with a great deal of caution and constant monitoring of the instance and the operating system.

SHMVIRTSIZE

Parameter **SHMVIRTSIZE** specifies the initial size of the instance's virtual portion of shared memory in kilobytes. This parameter may well require tuning over time as instance activity changes. I recommend starting around 250 MB (262,144 KB) and then monitoring the instance. If the instance needs additional virtual memory, it will dynamically allocate another segment of **SHMADD** size. You can monitor the addition of extra virtual memory segments via the **onstat -g seg** command.

The efficiency of the virtual shared memory portion decreases as additional segments are added. If one or more additional virtual memory segments have been allocated during normal database operations, you should tune this parameter to the sum of all the virtual segment allocations for the instance.

If an additional virtual memory segment is no longer needed by the instance, it should be automatically released by the instance. Sometimes this release is not executed properly. To force a release of an unused virtual memory segment, issue the **onmode -F** command.

SHMADD

The **SHMADD** parameter specifies the amount of additional memory, in KB, that will be added to the virtual portion of the instance's shared memory should the instance require more than what was allocated via the **SHMVIRTSIZE** parameter. I tend to be a little more aggressive with this parameter—I would set this to just over 120 MB (131,072 KB) but monitor to see how much additional memory is actually used if an additional segment is added.

The allocation of too many virtual shared memory segments can negatively affect instance performance. (I will discuss this subject more fully in *Administering Informix Dynamic Server, Advanced Topics*.) On the other hand, having one monolithic virtual memory segment that is barely used can be a waste of system resources. You can monitor the effectiveness of the virtual shared memory portion by periodically executing the **onstat -g seg** command.

EXTSHMADD

The **EXTSHMADD** parameter controls an extension to the virtual portion of shared memory. In this case, the portion holds the thread heaps of user-defined VPs and user-defined routines (UDRs) created in the instance. I would start with a 16 MB allocation (16,384 KB) and monitor from there. Obviously, if your applications rely on DataBlades or UDRs, you may need to increase this value.

SHMVIRT_ALLOCSEG

New in IDS 11, the **SHMVIRT_ALLOCSEG** parameter is intended to cause the instance to react proactively to out-of-memory situations and send you an alert if it can't add an additional segment of virtual shared memory.

The parameter has two components. The first specifies the threshold amount of memory below which the server will try to allocate an additional segment of virtual memory. This amount can be expressed in two forms, as either a value in kilobytes or a percentage of memory used. If you use a percentage value, you must specify a value in the range of .40 to .99.

The parameter's second component indicates the severity of the alarm that will be sent to **SYSALARMPROGRAM** if the instance cannot allocate another segment of **SHMADD** size. Table 4.5 lists the possible values.

Table 4.5: Possible values for the second component of the SHMVIRT_ALLOCSEG parameter	
Parameter value	Alarm level sent to SYSALARMPROGRAM
1	Not noteworthy
2	Information
3	Attention
4	Emergency
5	Fatal

Obviously, you'll need to make sure the alarm program or a sensor is configured to trap for the specified alarm event and deal with it appropriately.

To begin with, set **SHMVIRT_ALLOCSEG** a little aggressively so you are notified as the instance expands and runs into limits. For example, you could set it to

```
SHMVIRT_ALLOCSEG  50000, 3
```

which would send an "attention" event if the instance had less than 50 MB of virtual memory and couldn't allocate another segment either because of **SHMTOTAL** or O/S constraints. Once the system is up and running smoothly and you've tuned to actual usage, you might change the parameter to

```
SHMVIRT_ALLOCSEG  .91, 4
```

which would send an "emergency" event if the instance had less than 9 percent of virtual memory available and couldn't allocate another segment either because of **SHMTOTAL** or O/S constraints.

Backup and Restore

Next, let's look at several parameters that affect IDS's native backup and recovery process. Some relate to **ontape**, and others are used by the **ON-Bar** utility suite. For our purposes here, I'm only going to cover those required to get an instance up and operational — in other words, the parameters associated with the **ontape** utility. Chapter 7 provides guidance about setting parameters for **ON-Bar**.

IDS 11 brings several new and significant features to its backup and recovery technologies, one of which is worth briefly mentioning at this time. In earlier releases, the **LTAPEDEV** and **TAPEDEV** parameters supported writing only to either a tape device or standard I/O (**STDIO**), which in turn you had to capture through a pipe and shell script to redirect out to a file or other archive device. Although it was possible to set these parameters to a valid file name, there was no intelligent file handling; each successive backup overwrote the same file. That is no longer the case.

You can now set **LTAPEDEV** and **TAPEDEV** to a valid directory, such as **/opt/IBM/ informix/backups/** (notice the trailing "/"). When you do this, **ontape** backups, whether instance or logical logs, will be created in that directory with unique file names. We'll cover this topic in greater detail in Chapter 7.

LTAPEBLK and LTAPESIZE

For information about these two parameters, see the notes on **TAPEBLK** and **TAPESIZE** below.

LTAPEDEV

Parameter **LTAPEDEV** designates the tape device to be used for backing up the logical logs with the **ontape** utility. The default value for this parameter varies depending on the port. Linux, Mac OS X, and Unix ports are set to a generic file name; Windows ports are set to **NUL** so no backups occur. Regardless of the port, if you set this parameter to **/dev/null** or its equivalent, there are two serious side effects. The first is that a full recovery of the instance with the **ontape** utility could be impossible because each log is freed for immediate reuse once it fills and no longer contains the last checkpoint or an open transaction. Granted, the used log is not immediately erased and could be reread by a recovery operation if not overwritten, but this should be considered a high-risk assumption of availability. If enough instance activity has occurred that the logical logs created since the last backup are being overwritten, you will be able to restore only to the moment in time when the backup was created.

The second side effect is the inability to use the **ON-Bar** utility suite for backup operations. Of particular interest is that **ON-Bar** does not read the value of this parameter dynamically when a backup operation is executed; it uses the value as set at instance startup. So it's possible to change this parameter from a valid device to **/dev/null** while the instance is online and have **ON-Bar** continue to operate normally. I strongly discourage this type of modification, though.

I usually recommend that instance environments operating with logged databases always back up filled logical logs to disk or, even better, to tape so you can perform a more complete and/or granular restore in the event of a critical instance failure. As a result, set **LTAPEDEV** to a valid tape or disk device on your system and then use either the **ontape** or the **ON-Bar** functionality as explained in Chapter 7 to back up the logical logs on a regular basis.

If you're just looking to get the instance operational, it is perfectly acceptable to set this to **/dev/null** or the equivalent so that all the logged initial instance configuration changes are discarded. After the instance is fully configured, change the parameter to a valid device. I do this all the time.

TAPEBLK

This parameter sets the block size for the instance backup tape device (**TAPEDEV**) used with the **ontape** and **onunload** and **onload** utilities if they are processing I/O to or from a tape device. The default value for this parameter is a generic default that may or may not be appropriate for your device. In general, you'll want to use as big a block size as possible so your backup/restore operations can be completed as quickly as possible. Consult the device's documentation for guidance on setting this parameter.

TAPEDEV

Parameter **TAPEDEV** designates the device to be used when creating instance backups. This parameter's value can be a fully pathed directory, a fully pathed single file, **STDIO**, or a fully pathed symbolic link to a tape device or file name. If you use a file, directory, or **STDIO**, the server ignores the **TAPEBLK** parameter but the file size will be governed by the **TAPESIZE** parameter.

You can set **TAPEDEV** to **/dev/null** or its equivalent, but instance recoveries will not be possible if you do so. If you use any other valid option, including a file, the parameter's value will be ignored by **ON-Bar** operations with or without the ISM. Those operations will use the devices configured and administered by the storage manager.

TAPESIZE

The **TAPESIZE** parameter specifies either the total amount of data, in kilobytes, to be written to a tape or the largest size to which a backup file on disk can grow when you create a backup through the **ontape** utility.

In earlier versions of IDS, this setting was a hard limit and one that required a significant amount of guesswork on your part. Previously, when this amount of data was being written to tape, you were prompted to swap tapes so the backup could continue. Although on the face of it this does not appear to present a problem, if the parameter was set to the media maximum (e.g., 2 GB) and a particular tape in a backup sequence was mismanufactured so it was too short and couldn't hold that amount, the backup operation aborted. Similarly, if you were backing up to a disk file and reached the specified file size before the backup was completed, the backup was aborted. As a result, best practice was to use a value about 3 percent to 5 percent smaller than the labeled tape size or O/S file size limit.

Now, this parameter can and should be set to **0** (zero) when backing up to tape. As a result, **ontape** will send data to the tape device until it receives an end-of-medium message, at which point **ontape** will prompt you to mount another tape. This way, you can use media of the same format but with potentially different capacities. If you'll be creating backups to disk or directory, the value for this parameter cannot exceed the maximum file size limit imposed by the O/S as described in Chapter 7.

This parameter does not affect backups created via the **ON-Bar** utility suite to a third-party storage management product such as the ISM.

Starting the Instance for the First Time

With your environment variables set, the configuration and **$SQLHOSTS** files modified, and devices created, it's time to turn on the instance for the first time. I find it helpful to monitor not only the initialization command but **MSGPATH** as well. To that end, as user **informix**, I create the file as listed in **$ONCONFIG** using the **touch** command (or equivalent), make sure the permissions are set to permit read access for all, and then execute a **tail -f** command on the file to watch what spools out when I start the instance.

In another window, I execute an **oninit -ivy** command to start the instance. The -i flag tells the data server to initialize the rootdbs, erasing any previous structures that might have been there from a preexisting instance or a previous attempt to initialize the instance. You should therefore use this flag with *extreme caution* and only when you want to restart from the very beginning with an instance. The -v flag produces verbose output from the command so you can monitor the initialization process from the command's perspective. The -y flag acknowledges in advance that you realize you're about to initialize the instance and confirms you want to proceed.

As the instance starts for the first time, a significant amount of information is entered into **MSGPATH**. It includes status messages about allocating shared memory segments, verification of core physical devices, instantiation of virtual processors, establishing network connectivity (if defined for the instance), and so on. If all is going well, you eventually will see messages indicating that the system (**sys**) databases are being built and, depending on the size of your logical logs, that they are starting to fill up.

Four databases are built as part of instance initialization: **sysmaster**, **sysadmin**, **sysusers**, and **sysutils**. We'll explore these in greater detail in a moment. For now, simply know that it is *critical* that you *do not execute any command* against the instance, including trying to connect to it, until you see messages that all four of these databases have been built. This is why it's important to monitor **MSGPATH** as well as the output from the **oninit** command. The command output will indicate that the instance is operational well before it really is.

If you do execute a command or try to connect to the instance before these databases are built, there is a very high possibility you will corrupt their creation, rendering the instance unusable. I know; I've done it several times. It was no big loss because I was just playing around and didn't lose any data; I was reinitializing the instance, for heaven's sake! Still, you don't want it to happen to you, so wait until you see all four **sys** database build-complete messages. The build process doesn't take long—maybe a minute or two at most for all four.

The Sys Databases

When an Informix Dynamic Server instance is initialized, the **sysmaster**, **sysadmin**, **sysusers**, and **sysutils** databases are created as part of the initialization process. In this section, I explain the purpose of each database as well as what the System Monitoring Interface (SMI) is.

Several other system-level databases can exist in an instance, depending on functionality used. These include the **syscdr**, **sysha**, and **onpload** databases. I'll touch on two of these briefly here. You'll find an expanded discussion of each of these databases in *Administering Informix Dynamic Server, Advanced Topics*.

The sysmaster Database and the SMI

The **sysmaster** database and the SMI are two of the greatest features of Informix Dynamic Server from an administrative point of view. Through the SMI, an administrator can gain access to all information about instance operations. You can use this information for diagnostic and tuning purposes, forensic analysis, monitoring, or simple curiosity. IDS isn't a black box, with IDS development trying to tell you that you don't need to know what the data server is doing (just "trust us!") or that everything you need to know is in the graphical interface tool. There is literally little, if anything, hidden from you. That said, not all possible output from commands executed through this interface is documented. In some cases, you'd better be good at figuring out and following hexadecimal linkages.

The **sysmaster** database is a combination of real tables created in the rootdbs and a series of pseudo-tables maintained by the data server when an instance is started. The pseudo-tables created at instance startup are pointers into the shared memory for the specific IDS instance.

Through the SMI, you have the ability to gather information from both the real and pseudo-tables of the **sysmaster** database through a subset of the SQL language. Nearly all the information displayed by the **onstat** utility, and many things displayed by the **oncheck** utility, is created by commands parsed through the SMI.

You can find the full schema of the **sysmaster** database in the **$INFORMIXDIR\etc\ sysmaster.sql** file. This file contains a cursory description of what each table is and the purpose of each column. As I noted, the database is generated as part of the instance initialization sequence. There is, however, nothing to prevent the **sysmaster** database from being re-created at any time. I must say, however, that although it's possible to drop and re-create the **sysmaster** database at will, it would be a rather stupid idea to alter or remove structures so important to the overall health and welfare of the instance without reinitializing the instance itself.

The nature of the **sysmaster** database is such that a database schema cannot be created, nor can tables be unloaded once the database is built and operational. Because most of the tables are simply pointers redirected into shared memory, you can't change or delete the data in the tables, nor can you add new data to them. The **informix** user ID and other members of the DBSA group can, however, create stored procedures within the **sysmaster** database that can be executed when called either by the instance itself or by a user operation.

The **sysmaster** database is originally created using unbuffered logging, but you can change to a buffered log mode if desired. I don't recommend changing the logging mode, though, because little or no performance increase will result from the change. The tables themselves are, for the most part, in shared memory, so why buffer changes in shared memory again?

You can query the **sysmaster** database like any other database from within an application or through **dbaccess**. Unlike regular databases, selective user-based permissions cannot be enforced — "public" has **connect** privileges to all tables. Because the **sysmaster** database functions like a regular database, you can use data from it in joins or selects with data from other databases. Unlike regular databases, selects or joins to the **sysmaster** database can occur even if the other databases are using dissimilar logging modes.

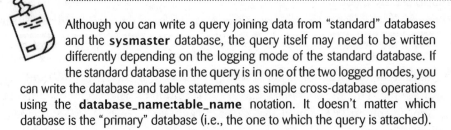

Although you can write a query joining data from "standard" databases and the **sysmaster** database, the query itself may need to be written differently depending on the logging mode of the standard database. If the standard database in the query is in one of the two logged modes, you can write the database and table statements as simple cross-database operations using the **database_name:table_name** notation. It doesn't matter which database is the "primary" database (i.e., the one to which the query is attached).

If the standard database is not logged, you must structure the query such that the standard database is the primary database, and the **sysmaster** database must be accessed as though it were part of a non-local, distributed transaction using the **database_name@instance_name:table_name** notation.

In becoming more familiar with the **sysmaster** database, you'll see that it contains quite a few actual tables and a large number of views. In many cases, these views represent earlier schema versions of tables for backward compatibility with customer and third-party applications. As with any other view, you should treat these with caution as to how long they might actually exist from release to release.

Check the information in the release notes directory as well as the documentation that accompanied your software distribution to see which tables and views are officially supported and will be found in future releases. The documentation will include the supported schema for these tables and views.

The sysadmin Database

New in IDS 11, the **sysadmin** database contains the new **task()** and **admin()** functions for the SQL-based administration interface. It also contains the command history table for these functions and is used by the database scheduler to store task functions to be invoked as scheduled. This database is also used to store performance and other historical data to enable DBAs to refine the efficiency of SQL operations.

The sysusers Database

The **sysusers** database is rather small in terms of tables. It contains user ID, role, and host information and indicates which user IDs, roles, and user groups can connect to which hosts and instances. This database is also used to manage the security grants by the **DBSECADM** officer.

The sysutils Database

The **sysutils** database is used by the **ON-Bar** utility suite. In it there are tables that track each instance, the storage spaces they contain, backup and recovery actions, the status of media and whether the backup objects they contain have expired, and so on. Information from this database can be used to re-create the **onbar** boot and other critical flat files.

The syscdr Database

The **syscdr** database is created when Enterprise Replication functionality is activated. Tables here contain the replicate definitions, replication rules, host definitions, and other administrative and maintenance objects associated with ER.

The sysha Database

Also new with IDS 11, the **sysha** database supports the high-availability functionality provided by Remote Standalone and Shared Disk secondaries. These instance types, and the MACH-11 technology, are covered in detail in *Administering Informix Dynamic Server, Advanced Topics*.

Summary

This chapter presented a lot of information for you to digest. You should now have a good understanding of how to upgrade IDS or install it for the first time along with the choices you'll need to make during the process. You should know the most important initial configuration parameters in the **$ONCONFIG** file and what they affect. You should understand the purpose of the various system management/administration databases. Although most of the **sysmaster** database is actually a pointer into shared memory, you can execute queries against it, as with any other database, to extract information about instance operations and performance.

When installing or initializing an Informix Dynamic Server instance, keep the following points in mind:

- Enable mirroring (**MIRROR** parameter) even if you plan to use hardware- or software-based products to protect the dbspaces containing the rootdbs, physical log, or logical logs against media failure. You aren't required to use mirroring, but once it is enabled, it's there if you need it. In an emergency situation, you can quickly create Informix-based mirrors without having to shut down and restart the instance.

- If you plan to use the **ontape** utility to back up the instance or its logical logs, you have several backup media options, so make sure you set the configuration parameters appropriately. Chapter 7 provides an in-depth discussion of all the backup and restore parameters.

- Set the size of the rootdbs to about 60 MB to 80 MB. The rootdbs needn't be very large because you should move the physical and logical logs into other dbspaces after instance creation. The ability to execute sort and order-by operations in memory with **NON_PDQ_QUERY_MEM** and to use "temporary" dbspaces to contain temporary tables further reduces the need for a large rootdbs.

- Make sure there is enough log space for the creation and population of the system databases during instance initialization. Back up the logical logs as soon as possible following instance initialization and configuration. In addition, because the physical and logical logs can be moved and resized at will, be prepared to move them almost immediately after bringing the instance up.

This chapter dealt with only one aspect of administering an Informix Dynamic Server instance that occurs very rarely. There are, however, a number of tasks you'll need to perform on a much more frequent basis, including changing database logging modes, administering dbspaces or BLOBspaces, and terminating user threads. The next chapter will cover these and other topics.

5

Basic Administrative Tasks

In this Chapter

- ▸ Changing the operating mode of the instance
- ▸ Changing database logging modes
- ▸ Creating and dropping chunks, dbspaces, or BLOBspaces
- ▸ Moving and resizing logs
- ▸ Safely terminating a user thread
- ▸ Starting and stopping an instance automatically

I f you were to use this book as a kind of operational textbook and perform the tasks in each chapter in order, by now you would have designed and initialized an active Informix Dynamic Server instance that you could use. In this chapter, I briefly introduce a couple of graphical tools that help you administer, tune, or diagnose IDS instances. I also cover the basic, day-to-day, server-oriented administrative tasks you'll encounter. You'll perform some of these tasks only once in an instance; others will occur with some frequency, depending on the level of activity and growth the instance experiences.

For the most part, you'll execute these operations at the command line or through the SQL API because it is the fastest and easiest to use. Depending on the graphical tool, though, there might be significant functionality overlap, so you can choose whichever method suits you best. By the end of the chapter, you should be able to add and drop dbspaces, understand and be able to change database logging modes, move and resize the physical and logical logs, and safely terminate a user thread.

Informix Administration Utilities

IDS comes with two graphical tools and one text-based utility you can use to administer and/or monitor IDS environments. I'm not a big fan of graphical tools, and everything you need to do in IDS can be handled easily via the command-line utilities, but I understand that some people have "grown up" in the computing world seeing only graphical tools. They believe such tools are the norm for almost anything, rather than crutches to help with systems that are so clumsy and cumbersome that graphical tools are the only way to try and mask their failings. With that editorial comment out of the way, let's have a look at what IDS offers.

OpenAdmin Tool for IDS

The OpenAdmin Tool for IDS (OAT) originated as a "skunk works" project inside IBM's Informix Advanced Technical Support organization. Its original design was twofold in nature: to give DBAs the information they need to analyze and manage SQL operations occurring in instances and to interface with the new monitoring capabilities provided by IDS's task, sensor, and database scheduler technologies. Written in PHP with the base source code available for download via an Open Source license, OAT replaces the Informix Server Administrator (ISA). Figure 5.1 shows the sign-on interface to the tool.

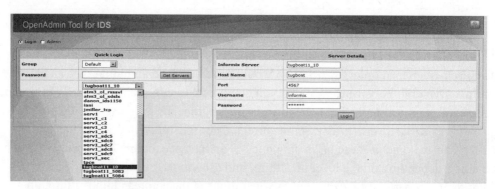

Figure 5.1: OpenAdmin Tool for IDS (OAT) sign-on screen

Early installation experiences with OAT were not very positive due to severe restrictions imposed on the product by the IBM legal department. For OAT to function, you had to do a significant amount of work to obtain, install, and configure a variety of disparate parts and pieces of software. Fortunately, IBM legal finally approved an integrated installer. You can now use the new installer, which contains all the required software, enabling a much smoother and easier install and configuration. I was involved in testing the new installer, and I like it very much. You can download the latest version of OAT with the single-click install for all platforms, including Mac OS X, from a new Web site maintained by the OAT development team, *http://www.openadmintool.org.*

From one instantiation of OAT with its associated Web services, you can administer as many IDS instances as you care to and have network access to. Once connected to an instance, OAT provides a variety of monitoring options, which you access through the menu on the left side of the display. You can see an example of this menu in Figure 5.2.

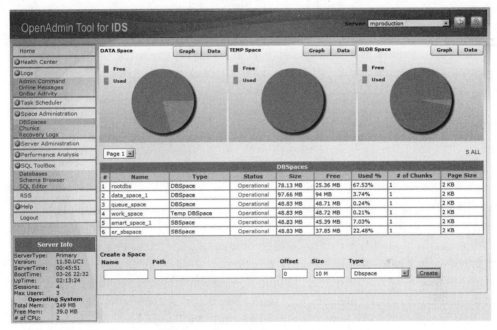

Figure 5.2: OAT's dbspace monitoring screen

The figure happens to show OAT's dbspace monitoring screen. Reached via an option under the OAT menu's **Space Administration** heading, this screen provides a graphical and/or text-based display of space usage and lets you add a dbspace. To add a chunk to an existing dbspace, select the menu's **Space Administration > Chunks** option.

Figure 5.3 illustrates some additional functionality available under the **Space Administration** section. In addition to regular and smart/simple LOB spaces, you can monitor the logical logs and the physical log. The various tabs on this screen let you add and drop logical logs, move or resize the physical log, or force a checkpoint. Last, you can set up a recovery time objective for the instance with time values measured in minutes.

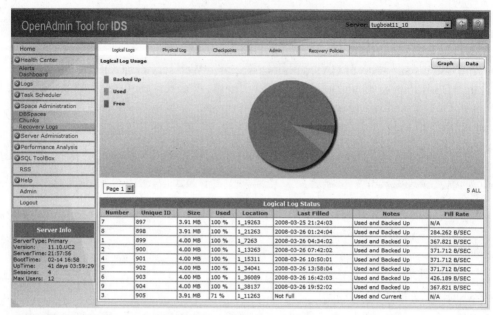

Figure 5.3: OAT reserved space monitoring screen

OAT's **Health Center** menu options provide access to alerts surfaced by the IDS monitoring utilities and sensors. The tool color-codes alerts from red (urgent) to yellow (warning) to green (notification) to catch your attention for the proper level of response. You can choose what you want to see (e.g., errors, warnings, general informational notices) as well as the severity level to tailor the display to your individual needs. A nice feature of this area is that in addition to indicating that x occurred (or didn't occur), the tool makes suggestions for how to rectify the condition. Future functionality promises that, where possible, you'll be able to resolve an issue by clicking an action button included in the alert message.

Also included under the Health Center is the ability to manage all tasks, sensors, and execution time(s) in the database scheduler. You can review each entry and modify its parameters and can see the number of times each task has been executed.

Options under the **Logs** menu heading let you view the last couple hundred of lines of the major instance logs.

Using options in the **Performance Analysis** section of the OAT menu, you can view information about the last 20 executed checkpoints, turn SQL tracing on or off, and set parameters for the traces. The **System Explorer** option starts off by displaying the equivalent of an **onstat -u** listing of user sessions. When you select a session, you can then view the equivalent of an **onstat -g ses** *session_id* command, with which you can monitor the session's SQL statements and resources. The **System Reports** option lets you select from a clickable list of basic instance- and system-level reports for immediate execution. Preconfigured reports include disk space usage, system backup information, memory usage, table-level activity statistics, most expensive SQL statements, slowest SQL statements, instance configuration information, and more. One of the more interesting report options displays maximum concurrent connections for the week, letting you monitor your license compliance if you purchased session or named-user licenses. You can choose more than one report at a time and execute the group as a unit of work to generate a single view of instance activity. Figure 5.4 shows a sample report from the OAT performance section that shows activity from the SQL administration API as well as user connections.

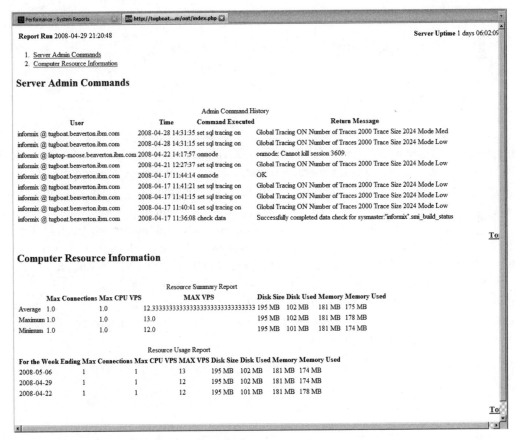

Figure 5.4: Sample OAT Performance Analysis report

The **SQL Toolbox** section of the OAT menu provides an interactive SQL editor, shown in Figure 5.5, as well as a database and table schema browser that is available once you select a specific database from the section's main screen. As you dive through the tables, you can reach a point where the data contained in the table is displayed.

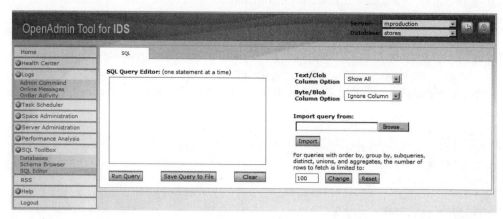

Figure 5.5: The SQL editor from the OAT utility

The menu's **RSS** choice gives you a selection of instance objects that, if changed, can trigger an alert sent to you via the RSS tool of your choice. Among the object choices are chunks, dbspaces, environment variables, physical log, virtual processors, and more. OAT comes preconfigured with the Bloglines, Google, Live Bookmarks, and My Yahoo! RSS services, but you can add the service of your choice if you want to use something else.

Last, as Figure 5.6 shows, OAT has the ability to sense and monitor MACH-11 clusters. As I write this chapter, you cannot administer all the cluster functionality through OAT, but I anticipate that functionality will be added in a future release.

OAT is a nice, easy-to-use, compact DBA tool that gives you the most critical information you need on a day-to-day basis. The ability to easily find the most resource-intensive SQL operations alone is of tremendous worth, without considering all the other things you can do with this tool.

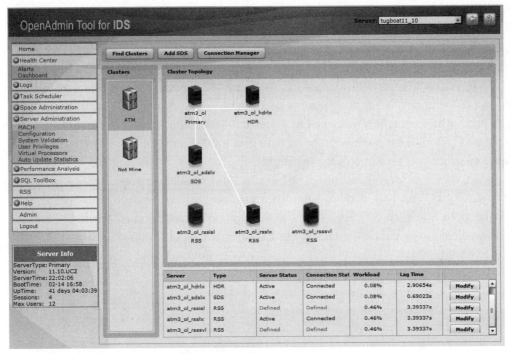

Figure 5.6: The MACH-11 monitoring screen from OAT

In between the time when I originally wrote this section and my review of it prior to publication, a significant number of enhancements were made to OAT. The ability to administer all aspects of MACH-11 clusters (including the new Connection Manager) has increased, and new functionality has been added to administer ER clusters. Another huge new feature is that OAT can now automatically maintain optimizer statistics according to general guidelines you set, such as percent of data change. Based on how you set up this functionality to execute, OAT will dynamically build and execute **update statistics** commands using the best practices guidelines developed by Informix Advanced Support. There are more new features, but I'll let you explore the tool and find them yourself!

Server Studio Java Edition

IDS's other graphical tool, Server Studio Java Edition (SSJE), has undergone a remarkable transformation over the years. Originally intended as a DBA tool to complement IDS's earlier graphical administration tools, SSJE is now an all-encompassing utility with reporting, monitoring, and full administrative capabilities for all objects and activities in an IDS system. AGS, Ltd., the tool's creator, recently added new monitoring functionality, called Sentinel, that provides a sophisticated and comprehensive performance monitoring, tracking, and forensic repository.

SSJE is nice to work with and easy to use even when executing complex instance or database operations. It has an appealing user interface that displays all the information you need, when and where you need it, to make informed decisions or take remedial actions. The tool is far too comprehensive to give a full review of all of its capabilities here, so let me just hit some of the highlights.

SSJE comes in several editions. The base version included with the IDS server provides basic DBA and instance administration capabilities. This edition includes the Connections Manager, which you can use to maintain instance connection definitions. The base edition also includes the Object Explorer, shown in Figure 5.7.

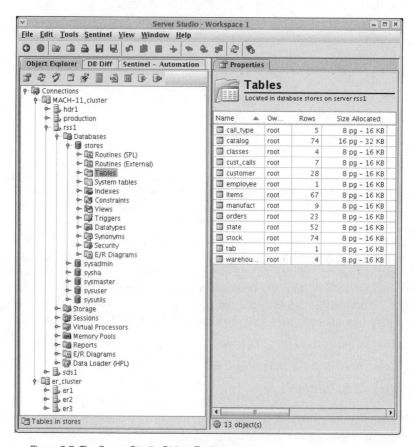

Figure 5.7: The Server Studio Object Explorer

As you can see in the figure, I have several clusters of instances built. Using the Object Explorer, I can drill down through the instances to see databases and all their objects as well as instance-level objects such as sessions and storage.

Also included in the base version is a Table Manager that lets you create, modify, or drop tables and an SQL Editor, shown in Figure 5.8.

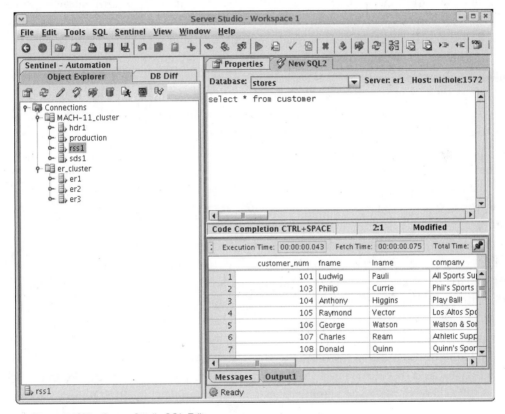

Figure 5.8: The Server Studio SQL Editor

You can use the SSJE SQL editor tool to execute the full range of SQL operations and browse results or return messages in separate windows. If you have a syntax error, the editor highlights the incorrect syntax word when the error is returned so you can find and repair the mistake quickly.

Additional functionality, such as test data generation, benchmarking tools, in-depth schema and dependency analysis, storage management, performance monitoring and analysis, and much more can be purchased and added on to the base SSJE configuration based on your needs.

The SQL Administration API

Embodying new functionality released in IDS 11, the SQL administration API lets you perform literally any instance administration command using an SQL function call instead of one of the command-line or graphical utilities. This functionality was created for several reasons. First, it enables an IDS administrator to standardize on a single set of administration tools that work across all IDS ports. This capability is particularly important when an environment contains a mixture of operating systems hosting IDS. Although it is trivial to create and execute shell scripts to perform operations in Linux, Unix, or Mac OS X, the same cannot be said for Windows. In such cases, administrators previously had to maintain two sets of tools.

The second reason behind the API's development was to make it easier for new administrators to transition to IDS. As I alluded to earlier, some new IDS administrators are uncomfortable moving to a server that is driven primarily from the command line. At the same time, they are quite comfortable writing and interacting with SQL. The SQL administration API provides a way to bridge the gap between what these administrators may be used to and the more robust and easier-to-use IDS data server. They can execute many operations using SQL instead of the more cryptic **onmode**, **onparams**, or other utility.

In addition, as businesses continue to focus more and more on data and data center security, they are restricting physical and virtual access to servers of all kinds, particularly data servers with business critical data. You can observe this trend in the restriction of using **root** or **informix** user IDs, the removal of **ftp** and other access protocols from operating system installations, and so on. Many companies are now starting to restrict **telnet** and other virtual connection utilities to the server. Up to this point, without the ability to log on to the physical server, it would be impossible to administer a data server such as IDS. But with the SQL API, you don't need **telnet** access; you can maintain and administer instances through any client SQL application.

The SQL administration API is a part of the **sysadmin** database introduced toward the end of the previous chapter. The API has three major components: two user-defined functions and a history table that tracks all activity through the API. The two functions, **task()** and **admin()**, are identical in terms of functionality and can be used interchangeably. Where they differ is in what they return after a command is executed. The **task()** function returns a text string describing what the function did; the **admin()** function returns an integer. Here are two examples showing the same command executed through both functions:

```
execute function
  task ('create dbspace', 'data_space_1',
        'opt/IBM/informix/devices/amazon/ama_chnk_20',
        '150mb', '0');
(expression)  created dbspace number 12
               named data_space_1

or

execute function
  admin ('create dbspace', 'data_space_1',
         'opt/IBM/informix/devices/amazon/ama_chnk_20',
         '150mb', '0');
(expression)  107
```

The integer value returned from the **admin()** function has significance. If the value is positive, it represents the serial number of the row in the history table tracking operations through the API. If the value is negative, the command failed. If the value is **0** (zero), the command executed successfully but there was no room to insert a new row in the tracking table. By default, the **sysadmin** database and its objects, such as the API tracking table, are created in the root dbspace. If you have a lot of activity through the API, the history table will grow, potentially filling the root dbspace if you have not adequately controlled what objects reside there.

There are two ways to control or manage the growth of the history table. First, you can move the database into another dbspace via the SQL API with the following command:

```
execute function
  task ("reset sysadmin", "destination_dbspace");
```

This operation can give you more room for this and other tables in the database to grow, depending on the size of the dbspace and other objects stored there. When you move the **sysadmin** database to another dbspace, that dbspace now becomes a "critical" dbspace from a data server perspective. If the dbspace becomes compromised, the instance will stop operations.

The second method involves using a monitoring and pruning facility that is registered in the new instance scheduling facility.

The history table is, in and of itself, not large. Table 5.1 describes its schema.

Table 5.1: Schema of the command_history table in the sysadmin database		
Column	Data type	Description
cmd_number	serial	A unique ID for the row
cmd_exec_time	datetime year-to-second	The time the command was executed
cmd_user	varchar(254)	The user ID that executed the command
cmd_hostname	varchar(254)	The host from which the command was executed
cmd_executed	varchar(254)	The command string executed
cmd_ret_status	integer	The status value from the command
cmd_ret_message	lvarchar(30000)	The return message from the command

The **sysadmin** database is much richer and provides more functionality than simply executing instance administration functions. We'll discuss its capabilities for scheduling tasks and other operations, as well as performance tracking and tuning, in other chapters of this book. Look for more coverage of these topics in *Administering Informix Dynamic Server, Advanced Topics*.

Changing Operating Modes

An Informix Dynamic Server instance can run in several different operating modes with different levels of end-user functionality. The instance can operate in some modes for an extended period, while other modes are transitional, but each mode has a specific function. It used to be that to execute some instance administrative functions, the instance had to be in a specific operating mode. For all intents and purposes, that is no longer true; with IDS 11, you can do almost everything you need to do without interrupting end-user processing. Nevertheless, it's important to understand what each operating mode is, what administrative or end-user access each mode allows, and how to change operating modes at will.

You can tell which mode the instance is operating in in a couple of different ways. The most laborious is to look through the **MSGPATH** file, either by executing an **onstat -m** command if a change occurred very recently or by directly browsing the log file for any messages indicating a change in mode.

The easiest way to check the instance's operating mode, though, is to execute the "**onstat -**" command. This command reports the mode and uptime status information, as illustrated in Figure 5.9.

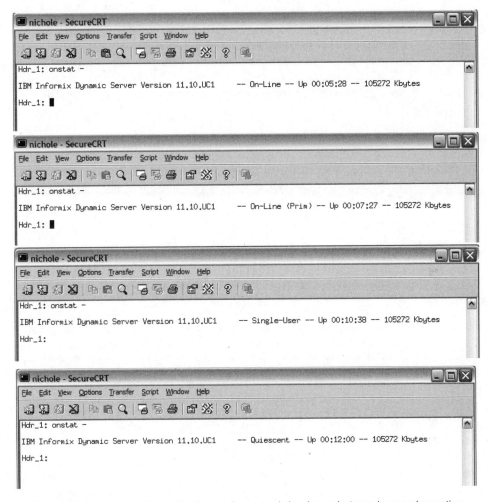

Figure 5.9: Output generated by the "onstat–"command showing an instance in several operating modes

The top line of output from any **onstat** command always lists the operating mode of the instance. In the figure, the instance is in several different modes, including normal multiuser, HDR primary, single-user, and quiescent mode. The only exception is if the instance is completely offline, in which case a "shared memory not initialized" message is returned.

WARNING

Only the **root** and **informix** user IDs should be able to change the operating mode of an instance. Be aware, however, that any user ID that is part of the DBSA group (typically members of the **informix** or **informix-admin** O/S groups), even if it is a secondary group, can change the operating mode of any instance on the server through any of the options—**oninit**, **onmode**, or the SQL API.

If possible, the **root** user ID shouldn't be used at all to change an instance operating mode. When this happens, the processes supporting the IDS virtual processors, including any UDRs, have root-level permissions. If these UDRs make external system calls, the calls will be executed with root-level permissions, which could be a "bad thing" if the UDR misbehaves.

Table 5.2 describes the seven instance operating modes.

Table 5.2 IDS operating modes	
Mode	**Description**
Administrative	An enhancement to the IDS 10 single-user mode. In this mode, the instance is fully online and functional, but only the user IDs identified through the **onmode -j -U, oninit -U,** or **ADMIN_MODE_USERS** configuration parameter are allowed to connect and use instance faculties. You can at any time update the list of user IDs that can connect to and use instance facilities; any changes take effect immediately. You should use administrative mode only for very specific tactical reasons, when you need to restrict end-user access while executing a specific administrative operation, rather than for day-to-day operations.
Offline	The instance is not running. Shared memory for the instance has not been allocated or initialized. No virtual processors are running.
Online	The instance is fully operational and available to all users with rights to access it.
Quiescent	The instance is fully active, but access to user-created databases and objects is suspended. This mode is somewhat equivalent to a maintenance mode in many other multiuser operating systems. Unlike operating system maintenance modes that permit some privileged user account access to the system, in quiescent mode all user accounts, including **informix**, are prevented from opening connections to any database structures other than those available through the SMI. When you shut down an instance, all user threads must be completely terminated for the instance to complete the transition to quiescent mode. In earlier versions of IDS, several administrative tasks, such as adding or dropping logical logs or manipulating the physical log, required an instance to be in quiescent mode before the task could be completed. These operations have been almost completely rewritten to execute without requiring a change in the instance's operating mode.
Read-only	In versions before IDS 11.5, this mode applies only to secondary servers in IDS's HDR or MACH-11 environments. In it, an application executing against databases on a secondary server can query the database tables directly, but **insert, update,** and **delete** SQL commands are not allowed.

Table 5.2 IDS operating modes (Continued)	
Mode	Description
Recovery	This mode is a transitional mode used as the data server initializes shared memory and starts the virtual processors for the instance. The fast recovery process executes in this mode. Even though shared memory is initialized in this mode, the SMI is not available for use.
Shutdown	Another transitional mode, this mode occurs as the instance moves from online mode to either quiescent or offline mode. Unless an immediate shutdown is being executed, all user threads are allowed to complete their tasks and terminate normally. However, new instance and database connections are refused.
Updatable	In IDS 11.5, instances configured to be HDR, Shared Disk Secondary (SDS), and/or Remote Standalone Secondary (RSS) can operate in this mode. When enabled, full end-user query and DML operations are supported. The new **UPDATABLE_ SECONDARY $ONCONFIG** parameter determines whether the secondaries support DML operations. At this time, DDL operations are not permitted.

WARNING

Once a command has been issued to change the instance to any operating mode, it cannot be reversed or canceled. Depending on the method you use to change the mode, if there are any active sessions, you will receive a prompt that lets you prevent sending the mode-change command to the instance. Depending on your response, either the mode-change command will be issued to the instance or the command will be aborted, leaving the instance in its original operating mode.

You can shut down, restart, or reinitialize an instance using two command-line utilities. You can also use the SQL administrative routines to transition the instance between operating modes, but not to start or initialize because the SQL administration functions exist only in the **sysadmin** database and the instance must be active to resolve and execute the functions. In IDS 11.5, OAT does provide functionality to start an instance that is offline. It requires an additional port and configuring an **xinetd** service to interact with the instance.

You use the **oninit** utility to bring an instance from offline to one of the operating modes as follows:

- **oninit −s** (lowercase "s") brings a configured instance from offline mode to quiescent mode.

- **oninit −S** (uppercase "S") brings a configured instance from offline mode to quiescent mode, but in this case if the instance was originally part of an HDR pair (either primary or secondary), the instance will be in standard mode and no longer part of the HDR pair.

- **oninit -j** brings a configured instance from offline mode to the new administrative mode. Be aware that the **-U** flag with the ability to specify user IDs that can connect to the instance in this mode is not supported. As a result, only the **informix** ID, members of the DBSA group, or IDs specified by the **ADMIN_MODE_USERS** configuration parameter will be able to connect to the instance.

- **oninit** with no flags brings a configured instance from offline mode all the way to online mode.

The **oninit** utility also has a **-p** flag, which I do not recommend using when restarting an instance. With this flag set, the instance will not remove temporary tables in the rootdbs or other dbspaces during instance startup. Using this option does slightly decrease the amount of time it takes for the instance to come online. However, because the disk space used by the temporary tables is not freed up, and these tables cannot be accessed by user sessions, it's a waste of disk space. I don't think the extra 10 seconds of waiting is worth the continual loss of disk space.

There is one other flag to the **oninit** command you should be aware of: the **-i** flag. As I mentioned in Chapter 2, using this flag initializes the rootdbs for the instance, effectively wiping out the instance. *Do not* use this flag unless you intend to rebuild the instance from scratch.

You can use the **onmode** command as follows to change the operating mode of an instance:

- **onmode -m** changes the instance from quiescent to online mode.

- **onmode -s [-y]** transitions the instance from online mode through shutdown mode to quiescent mode. Include the **-y** flag to eliminate a confirmation prompt. Once this command is executed, it prevents new user sessions from connecting to the instance. However, it will wait indefinitely until all connected user sessions have terminated before transitioning the instance to quiescent mode. To speed the shutdown process along, you would need to terminate the instance connections either using one of the graphical tools or by issuing the **onmode -z *session_id*** command.

- **onmode -k [-y]** shuts down the instance from either online or quiescent mode to offline mode in an orderly fashion. User threads are terminated immediately but gracefully, buffers are flushed through a checkpoint process, and transactions are rolled back if necessary.

- **onmode -u [-y]** immediately terminates all instance activity and takes the instance offline. This is the equivalent of pulling the plug on the instance. Transactions are marked for rollback in the logical logs, though. As with the **-k** option, using the **-y** flag eliminates the two confirmation prompts that otherwise would present themselves.

The **onmode** command includes other options, such as -**z** to terminate user sessions -**a** to increase the shared memory segment size, and -**c** to initiate a checkpoint. We'll consider these options later in this chapter or in other chapters as appropriate for the discussion.

Changing Database Logging Modes

As you'll learn in Chapter 6, when you create a database, you must select a *logging mode*. The logging mode of a database determines whether logical groups of database activity can be programmed to either succeed or fail as a complete unit. Such a group of related activities is called a *transaction*. In Chapter 1, we looked at a common example of a transaction, the transfer of money between bank accounts.

The logging mode of the database also determines whether records detailing the data changes that occur in the instance are created. If a database is in a logged mode, the data server tracks these changes by making entries in the physical and logical log structures. (In *Administering Informix Dynamic Server, Advanced Topics*, I'll explain how the fast recovery process uses the logical log records to ensure logical data integrity.)

In earlier versions of IDS, changes to the logging mode of a database occurred with some regularity, particularly during maintenance periods. If one or more tables required major data or structural changes, you ran the risk of triggering a lengthy transaction and experiencing a long, painful transaction rollback condition if the changes were attempted against the table(s) while the database was in logged mode. More recent versions of the data server enable you to alter a table to "raw," or unlogged, mode without affecting the other tables in the database. In this way, you can execute maintenance operations against the table(s) without generating logical log records while continuing to support other logged, end-user operations.

There are still occasions when you'll need to change the logging mode of the database, though. For example, if you're going to create a database using the **dbimport** utility, you should create the database in an unlogged mode unless there is absolutely no data to import. The reason is because the data server handles the entire **dbimport** operation as a single transaction. If an import occurs into a logged database, a long transaction could be triggered during the data load into the tables. Once the database is imported, you can change its logging mode to another mode.

Another reason to change the database logging mode is if you need to make major structural or data changes to a large number of tables within the database during a maintenance period.

Chapter 6 provides a full description of the logging modes available in Informix Dynamic Server. For the purposes of the discussion here, which focuses on changing database logging modes, we'll consider two types of logging modes: logged and nonlogged.

As IDS has developed over the years, the process of changing a database's logging mode has changed. In very early versions of IDS, changes to database logging modes had to be made while the instance was in quiescent mode using an instance administrative utility; a few changes could be made only via the **ontape** utility. This functionality eventually was expanded to include the **ON-Bar** utility suite. Then, IBM introduced the **ondblog** utility, used to mark databases for a logging mode change. With this tool, however, the change doesn't occur until a full instance backup is created. Last, it was possible for an application or individual user to make some limited logging mode changes that affected only their own particular application or user thread. Using the **set log** SQL syntax, a user or application could change the logging mode of an individual session from unbuffered logging to buffered logging, or vice versa. (The three buffered logging modes are *buffered*, *unbuffered*, and *mode ANSI*.)

The **ondblog** utility is a command-line utility that sets a flag to change a database's logging mode to whatever mode is requested when the next level 0 (zero) backup occurs, whether it be via the **ontape** utility or the **ON-Bar** utility suite. The flags for the **ondblog** utility are as follows:

- **ansi**—Specifies ANSI logging mode
- **cancel**—Cancels the previously requested logging mode changes
- **buf**—Specifies buffered logging
- **nolog**—Changes the database to a nonlogged environment
- **unbuf**—Specifies unbuffered logging

You can follow these options with one of two additional parameters. The first is simply a space-delimited list of databases that the logging mode change is to affect. The other option is an **-f** flag followed by the pathed name of a file containing a list of database names that the change is to affect; the databases are listed individually in the file, one to a row, without any additional punctuation. In the absence of a list of space-delimited database names or the **-f** flag and a file name, the **ondblog** utility changes all databases in the instance to the requested level at the next level 0 backup.

Changing a database from any logged mode to a nonlogged mode, or vice versa, requires a full instance backup either using **ontape** with or without the **ondblog** utility or using the **ON-Bar** utility suite with **ondblog**. With the **ON-Bar** utility suite or the SQL administration API, you can create a "fake" backup to trigger the logging mode change. As I explain in Chapter 7, creating a fake backup simply alters some flags in the instance to make it appear as though a backup occurred. Because this technique doesn't really create a backup, use it with care. I recommend creating a real backup whenever you change the logging mode of a database, so I avoid using the fake backup option.

Using the **ontape** utility to change logging modes is fairly straightforward. To change a database between any of the three logging modes, use the **-U** *dbname* (capital "u") flag for unbuffered logging, **-B** *dbname* for buffered logging, or **-A** *dbname* for mode ANSI. To completely change from a nonlogged or logged mode to the other, simply append one of the three flags just mentioned or **-N** *dbname* for a nonlogged mode change to an **ontape -s -L 0** (zero) command. If more than one database needs a logging mode change made, use the **ondblog** utility to record the changes that need to occur.

Whether you use the **ontape** utility alone or a combination of **ondblog** and **ontape/ ON-Bar** to change the logging mode of a database, the instance need not be in quiescent mode, but there must not be any active user threads attached to the instance at the time the logging mode change is attempted. Otherwise, you'll receive a rather cryptic −107 ISAM error.

If you issue an **ontape** or **onbar** command to change the logging mode on a database and the command is interrupted, the database will remain unavailable to user connectivity until a full instance backup is generated—with or without changing the logging mode.

In situations where you need to change the logging mode of a database to perform maintenance activities, you have several options for speeding up the process of creating a backup and changing the logging mode. The first is to use the **ondblog** utility to set the database names and logging modes, followed by an **onbar -b -F** command to create a fake backup. This is all that is required for the **ondblog** utility commands to execute and change the logging status of the database(s).

Another option is to edit the **$ONCONFIG** file, temporarily set the archive device (**TAPEDEV**) to **/dev/null**, and then execute the **ontape** command with or without using the **ondblog** utility. Like the **ON-Bar** fake backup, the backup operation is completed immediately, setting the archive flags and making the database logging mode changes.

A third approach is to use the SQL administration API and use the **archive fake** parameter to the **task()** or **admin()** routines.

Of course, before making maintenance mode changes, you should create a full backup of the instance in its native logging mode in case a restore is required. Upon completing the maintenance tasks, change the logging mode back to its original state by executing another fake backup using any of the three options just mentioned. Once you've made the change back to the desired logging mode, create a full "real" backup of the instance to tape or disk. Save it, along with the backup you created before beginning the maintenance period, so you have a before and after image of the instance available.

Managing Dbspaces and BLOBspaces

Like changing the logging mode of a database, creating or removing dbspaces or chunks is pretty straightforward using any of the graphical utilities, the **onspaces** command-line utility, or the new SQL administration API. As I noted in Chapter 3, the creation and population of dbspaces is a mixture of common sense, intuition, and guesswork. In creating and placing dbspaces within the available disk spindles, you need to know how the tables those dbspaces will contain will lie across the disks, how active they will be, and at what rate they're anticipated to grow. These anticipated growth rates and performance expectations should determine how and where tables get built.

In OLTP environments, highly volatile tables should be distributed (and possibly partitioned) across a number of smaller, high-performance drives. Other tables can be placed in larger dbspaces on larger drives where response is not so critical. In an OLAP environment, the volume of data to store will require either larger or more drives. The logical grouping and association of columnar elements, rather than performance, will drive the division of that data across the drives.

With the reduction in disk prices over the years and the uptake of storage arrays, whether network-based or direct-attached, being able to maximize I/O from a database perspective has become increasingly more difficult. It's almost impossible to find "smaller" disk drives, say in the range of less than 100 GB, in order to isolate high-use tables (or partitions thereof) to spindles without facing I/O contention from other data stored in different partitions on the same spindle. Storage array vendors and administrators generally take the path of least resistance when creating logical storage units that can be used to create cooked or raw chunk space. They typically will either throw most or all of the spindles into just a few RAID 1+0 (if you're lucky) or RAID 5 (if you're really unlucky) sets. Although such setups are simple to administer from the vendors' perspective, they make it extremely difficult to achieve the I/O throughput IDS is capable of giving you.

Let me make a couple of points of general interest, the first being that to achieve the best throughput when a checkpoint occurs, you should, whenever possible, allocate the chunks created to support spaces in a round-robin manner around the available disk devices. Although this was much more of an issue in releases before IDS 11 and its "interval checkpoints," on which trying to minimize user interruptions during a checkpoint was critical, managing chunks in this manner can still have a very positive impact on checkpoint execution time. Page cleaners (**CLEANERS**), which control the sorting and writing of data to disks during checkpoints, are allocated in chunk-creation order. If you create multiple chunks by using all the partitions on one disk before moving to another, when a checkpoint occurs, page cleaner contention will take place as multiple cleaners try to work on chunks all residing on the same disk. Distributing the created chunks between the various available disks permits a degree of disk write parallelism to occur during the checkpoint.

The second note concerns a functional difference among the administrative utilities. In the sections that follow, I will be showing how to use the **onspaces** utility, the SQL administration API, and some of the graphical tools to accomplish the same tasks. An important functional distinction exists between the options the various utilities provide that affects the creation of chunks to either support a dbspace or expand an existing dbspace.

When creating a chunk and setting its size, the **onspaces** utility allocates exactly the amount of space you request, in kilobytes, with the **-s** flag. The same *can* be true with the SQL API if you choose to specify the size in kilobytes, as in this example:

```
execute function
    task ('create dbspace', 'demo_space',
          '/opt/IBM/informix/devices/test/test_space',
          '50000KB', '0');
```

Figure 5.10 shows the output of the **onstat -d** command showing chunk-creation sizes. Here, the **demo_space** dbspace was created using the **onspaces** utility with its size specified in the only unit option available for the utility, kilobytes.

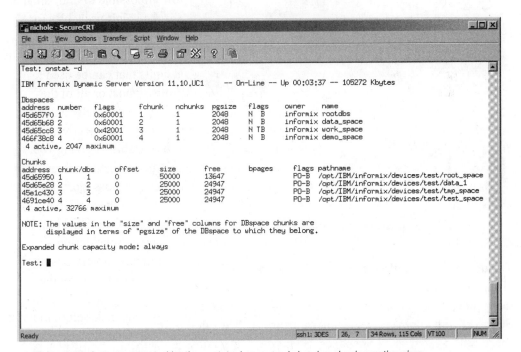

Figure 5.10: Output generated by the onstat -d command showing chunk-creation sizes

When using the SQL API to create a chunk or dbspace, you can specify its size using other units of measure, such as megabytes, gigabytes, or terabytes. For example:

```
execute function
    task ('create with_check dbspace', 'demo_space_2',
        '/opt/IBM/informix/devices/test/test_space_2',
        '50MB', '0');
```

When using OAT to crate spaces, you can specify sizes only in megabytes or in groups of 1,024 KB.

Thus, you can create several dbspaces, each with the same size yet with different disk allocations depending on how you create them. It is this difference in behavior that explains the discrepancy in the sizes displayed in Figure 5.11.

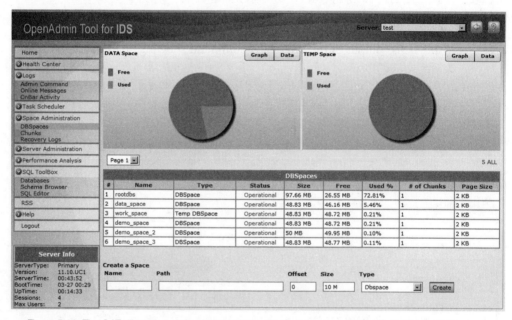

Figure 5.11: The OAT dbspace screen showing three dbspaces each created with the same size

The **demo_space_2** dbspace was created using OAT with a specified size of 50 MB. It was dropped and then re-created with the SQL API, also using 50 MB as a unit of measure; the results displayed were the same. The **demo_space_3** dbspace was created using the SQL API with kilobytes as the unit of measure. Space **demo_space**, the control/reference space, was created using **onspaces**. So if you create a dbspace with an initial 100 MB chunk using the **onspaces** command, the chunk size will be exactly 102,400,000 bytes, but OAT will display its size as 97..7 MB. Conversely, a dbspace created through OAT or the SQL API with MB units and having a 100 MB initial chunk size will actually create a 104,857,600-byte chunk although its size appears as 100 MB in OAT.

In any event, the output from an **onstat -d** command accurately reflects the true size of a dbspace in pages of **PAGESIZE** as illustrated in Figure 5.12.

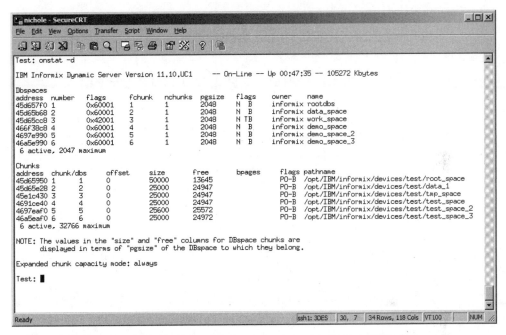

Figure 5.12: Output generated by the onstat -d command showing chunk-creation sizes

As you read the sections that follow, I would remind you that unless there are specific functional or syntactic differences in working with smart or simple BLOBspaces, I will use the term "dbspace" as a generic term to refer to both dbspaces and BLOBspaces.

Types of Logical Storage Spaces

Perhaps the biggest change to have occurred in the IDS data server in recent versions is the integration of object-oriented data server functionality into IDS's Dynamic Scalable Architecture (DSA) core. This development, which occurred back in 1995 with IDS 9.1, has given database and application designers a wealth of new data modeling and access functionality not possible with standard relational data servers. Some of the new data types require specialized storage spaces, so let's take a second to review the major physical and logical storage structures illustrated in Figure 5.13.

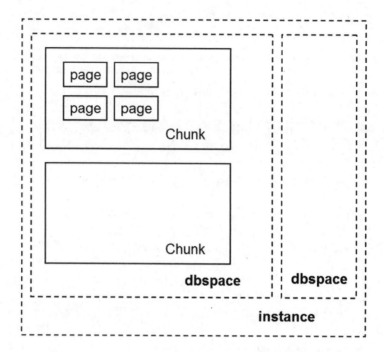

Figure 5.13: The basic physical (solid lines) and logical (dashed lines) storage
structures in an instance

The basic physical element of storage is called a *data page*, sometimes referred to simply
as a *page* and having a fixed size called the *page size*, which is the smallest amount of
data read or written from or to disk. Every IDS port has an initial or default page size,
which will be either 2 KB or 4 KB depending on the operating system.

Companion basic units of disk space are the *blobpage* and the *sbpage*. These elements
are the basic units of storage in simple and smart blobspaces discussed a bit later in this
section. The sbpages are similar to regular data pages in that they are either 2 KB or 4 KB
in size, depending on the port of IDS. On the other hand, blobpages can vary in size as a
multiple of the default page size, with the multiple ranging from 1 to whatever the limit is
for your port of IDS. There are performance and storage implications to how you set the
blobpage size. For example, only one BLOB can be stored on a blobpage, so if your average
BLOB size is 6 KB, you'd be wasting a lot of disk space if you used a 10 KB blobpage size.
Each simple blobspace can have its own blobpage size, so you can efficiently store simple
BLOBs in the space that best suits them.

Groups of pages (regular or BLOB-oriented) are called *chunks* and are the smallest
unit you can administer. You can create chunks on any disk device available to the physical
server hosting the IDS instance. When you create a chunk using raw space, the pages in the

chunk are contiguous, one following right after the other. This is part of what historically has generated a performance advantage to raw chunks. When you create a chunk using cooked space, the pages are linked together through file system inodes (a logical construct) because the pages themselves can be located anywhere within the file system. While you can "administer" a chunk, this ability is fairly limited; you can just add or drop one to/from an existing dbspace or blobspace.

> The maximum size of a chunk is 4 TB or whatever your operating system can support in terms of single allocation of raw or file system space. The current maximum storage capacity of a single IDS instance is just over 8 PB (petabytes), or 8 x10^{15} bytes! To put this number in perspective, this means you could store the contents of just over 1,000 U.S. Libraries of Congress in an instance. Wow!

A *dbspace* is a logical construct and is created using one or more chunks. Because a dbspace's chunks can come from any disk device available to the host system, a dbspace can be partitioned across any number of disk devices. This is the level at which you'll perform most of your administrative work because you'll create databases, tables, indexes, and other objects in dbspaces. You'll also back up and restore dbspaces (assuming we're not talking about the **archecker** table-level restore functionality). Every instance has at least one dbspace, the rootdbs, but most have more than one.

Dbspaces come in several varieties. Most administrators are familiar with the two most common: standard and temporary spaces. *Standard dbspaces*, usually referred to simply as dbspaces, are used to store databases, tables, indexes, and critical instance recovery objects—the physical and logical logs. Depending on the logging mode of the database as well as the individual table, data activity that occurs in these spaces may or may not be logged in the logical logs. Should you choose to, as explained in Chapter 1, you can mirror most dbspaces inside IDS, which gives you a disk-oriented failover option within the data server itself.

Temporary dbspaces (**DBSPACETEMP**) are similar to regular dbspaces in that they can contain tables and indexes; however, these objects cannot permanently exist within the database. More information about this type of dbspace is available a little later in this section.

There are two other types of commonly used dbspaces: the *blobspace* and the *sbspace*. Both can be used only to store binary large objects (BLOBs), which are then referenced by the balance of the row stored in a standard dbspace. Because blobspaces can store **text** and **byte**, or *simple blob* data types, they are often referred to as *simple* *blobspaces*. Sbspaces are used to store **clob** and **blob**, or *smart blob* data types and are commonly called *smart blobspaces*.

Because of the increased functionality inherent in smart blob data types, the physical architecture of an sbspace is different from that of a blobspace. Sbspaces have two storage areas: a "user" area where the smart large objects are stored and a large metadata allocation to manage the objects stored within the sbspace. This is part of what enables you to use byte-range locking on a **clob** or **blob** data type object and work on one part of the object while another user locks another portion of the same object and works on it. The space used for the metadata allocation is deducted from the total storage space of the sbspace and should be factored in to the calculation to determine the size of the sbspace. As we'll discuss a little bit later in the chapter, you can specify the size of the metadata allocation and even add additional metadata allocations to a sbspace. These abilities are important because it's possible for an sbspace to become "full" if it runs out of space in the metadata allocation even though plenty of room still exists in the user portion of the space.

Every instance must have at least one sbspace (**SYSSBSPACENAME**) to hold some instance statistical information. This space need not be very large—20 MB or so if you're not going to be using smart BLOBs in your database. However, certain instance functionality, such as Enterprise Replication, does require one or more sbspaces (configured to an appropriate size) for the feature to work.

You can create temporary sbspaces (**SBSPACETEMP**) just like temporary dbspaces. In this case, they only hold temporary **clob** and **blob** data type objects during an SQL operation. The advantage to temporary sbspaces is that they don't have a metadata area and operations on data they contain are not logged.

External dbspaces, or *extspaces*, are an extension to the dbspace concept. Whereas dbspaces are wholly managed by IDS, extspaces live outside the instance and are simply registered within the instance. Although external spaces can hold data or indexes, this information typically is/was not generated by IDS but by some other application or process. A programmer must create an *access method* to read from (or write to if allowed) the external data. IDS provides the Virtual Table Interface (VTI) and the Virtual Index Interface (VII) APIs as a framework in which these access methods can operate.

The most common use of external spaces is by DataBlades that must use data created by an external function or application or generate data for these external processes to use. Sometimes, though, the storage requirements for an object cannot be satisfied by the functionality provided through the IDS dbspace mechanisms, and the object must reside outside of the data server. The IDS 11 Basic Text Search (BTS) DataBlade is a perfect example of this case. The BTS indexes that drive this DataBlade's functionality require a flat-file format in order to be parsed. So, the BTS indexes are created in an external space and managed through the Virtual-Index Interface (VII) API.

With that background out of the way, let's look at the process of creating chunks and dbspaces. Assuming you are *not* using cooked space, you have two ways of dealing with disk chunks as well as dbspaces. The first is to make any individual chunk or dbspace a subset of a larger disk partition. With this approach, you use the O/S disk partitioning tool to create the largest possible hard partition the O/S can support on a disk. The second approach is to create a separate partition for each chunk or dbspace. We'll discuss this alternative in a moment.

If you're going to using cooked space, both options are moot because you'll be creating a separate file for each chunk or dbspace. Although you won't be using offsets in this case, you'll still need to set the offset value to **0** (zero) in the **onspaces** and/or SQL API space-creation commands.

Temporary Spaces

As I mentioned earlier, there are two types of dbspaces, regular and temporary. Regular dbspaces contain standard database table and index data structures. They can be mirrored, activity in them is logged to the logical logs if the database is in a logged mode, and they are included in backups created by the **ontape** utility or through the **ON-Bar** utility suite.

IDS uses temporary dbspaces to create temporary tables for hash joins as well as index, sort, and order-by operations. End-user applications can also use temporary dbspaces for creating explicit or implicit temporary objects. These tables and/or indexes exist only for the duration of an SQL operation and then are destroyed.

Temporary dbspaces are identified via the **DBSPACETEMP $ONCONFIG** parameter and cannot be mirrored, are not backed up, and are completely initialized at each restart of the instance. Activity caused by the data server in temporary dbspaces is not logged in the logical logs, regardless of the database logging mode.

Just because you have created one or more temporary dbspaces does not mean a user's temporary object(s) will be created there. IDS's default is *not* to use temporary space unless specifically directed to using a qualifier to the object creation statement. Without this qualifier, the object can be created in any dbspace, including the rootdbs if specified, and all activity for that object will be logged (assuming the database is in a logged mode) as though the object were permanently created in the instance. In a logged mode, all database activity is considered crucial unless explicitly identified otherwise; this includes the creation and use of user-generated temporary tables.

To create an unlogged temporary table, you append the **with no log** qualifier to the **create temp table** SQL statement:

```
create temp table ex_ample
(div_no integer,
 area_no smallint,
 tot_sales decimal(12,2)
)with no log;
```

IDS 11 introduces a new configuration parameter, **TEMPTABLE_NOLOG**, that causes all temporary objects to be created in temporary dbspaces even if the SQL qualifier is not used. This parameter is particularly helpful when you're dealing with application developers who don't care enough about SQL syntax to create their temporary objects properly.

In an instance environment where a number of temporary dbspaces are available and the application's design makes no special restrictions about which temporary dbspace(s) to use, they will be used in round-robin rotation. Statements that can be parallelized will spawn the creation of several temporary tables in several temporary dbspaces. These temporary tables will then be joined to create the desired result set. Joining the multiple temporary tables occurs quickly because each data set in a temporary table is already in sorted order. All that is necessary to join the tables is a comparison of the sort orders for each temporary table.

Another approach to maximizing temporary dbspace usage is the creative use of the **$DBSPACETEMP** environment variable for one or more individual user sessions to override which temporary dbspaces the sessions will use. This technique can result in greater instance performance when multiple data-manipulation–intensive applications are running simultaneously. You could direct one application that makes heavy use of, or causes the creation of, temporary tables to use different temporary dbspaces than another application. Doing so would reduce the amount of disk contention for the same temporary dbspaces from all the applications.

Offsets

An *offset* is, as you might surmise, a prescribed distance from a known starting point. As such, offsets are used to separate one chunk allocation from another when you create multiple chunks in the same raw partition. Figure 5.14 illustrates this concept.

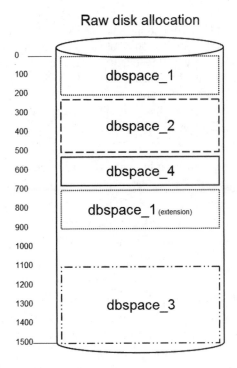

Raw disk allocation

Figure 5.14: Raw chunks allocated within a single raw partition with offsets

In the figure, a chunk for **dbspace_1** is created starting at the beginning of the raw partition (location 0). This chunk is 200 "units" in size. (What the units are in real life doesn't matter in this case.) An additional chunk is then allocated within the same raw partition. To prevent it from overwriting the first chunk's allocation, the administrator indicates via the **offset** flag of the **onspaces** utility or SQL API command that the chunk is to be offset 220 units into the raw partition. This gives the new chunk a 20-unit buffer from the end of the first chunk before its 300 units are allocated. This process continues for all the chunks allocated from within the same raw partition.

As you can tell from the figure, you are not required to create chunks from the top of the partition and then move down. As with the chunk for **dbspace_3**, you can set the offset value to whatever value you want before allocating space for that chunk. When creating multiple chunks within a single raw partition, I do recommend that you give the chunk allocations a couple units of space between each other as a safety mechanism.

WARNING IDS will not monitor your chunk and offset allocations to make sure they are mutually exclusive. You can create (and I have, by mistake) one chunk on top of another, which results in some interesting instance I/O and data consistency errors. For this reason, I strongly advise you to keep detailed and accurate records of start point and chunk size with the corresponding offset values if you allocate multiple chunks from within a single raw partition.

In an environment where design and implementation processes are happening "on the fly" throughout the life of a project, this approach can remove a measure of the guesswork and administrative headaches from disk partitioning and dbspace sizing tasks. Because there are fewer hard disk partitions to work around, you can increase the size of any given dbspace by as little or as much space as is left in the partition by adding more chunks at different offsets.

Another positive aspect of using offsets is that you have more control over where on a disk a chunk is located. You can create a chunk closer to or farther away from the center of the spindle, depending on performance needs, through the offset value itself.

On the other hand, offset-based space creation makes monitoring drive hotspots more difficult. Although you can monitor total dbspace and chunk activity through IDS monitoring utilities, O/S monitoring tools are of little value because they function at the hard drive partition level. Because there generally would be only one hard partition per drive, it would be difficult to monitor which chunk on a given drive was more active than another and be able to make whatever changes might be required to increase performance.

Partitions

The other approach to handling disk chunks and dbspaces in raw disk space is to create one or more physical partitions on the disk and use each partition as a single chunk. This approach requires more design work up front so that the disk partitions are sized correctly. I prefer this approach because it makes it easier to monitor disk bottlenecks using either IDS or O/S tools. The mapping of logical instance structures to the physical implementation is also cleaner and easier to follow.

Configurable Dbspace Page Sizes

Over the course of IDS's development, two major changes have been made to the creation and management of spaces. Both occurred recently, the first in IDS 9.4 with "big chunks" and the ability to create very large spaces. The second change occurred in IDS 10 and is referred to as *configurable page size (CPS)*, or the ability to create dbspaces with different page sizes.

Many people considered CPS a "me too" kind of enhancement because nearly all the other data servers on the market at the time had a similar feature. Unfortunately, this comment served only to highlight the ignorance of IDS's advanced capabilities on the part of those observers. The other data servers are constrained by the fact that they can store only a 3 KB fixed-length row on the equivalent of a page that is 3 KB or bigger. If the row contains variable-length character columns, the servers must store the row on a page size that reflects the fully expanded length of the row. With these data servers, the page boundary is fixed, the data server cannot "see" past it, and, as a result, a row must be wholly contained on one page.

IDS, on the other hand, has always used the equivalent of "forward pointers" to link portions of a row on one page with the rest of the row on another page or pages. This approach has given IDS administrators considerably more flexibility when designing their systems and has eliminated a tremendous amount of ongoing maintenance work. So why make the change now, and what's its impact to creating spaces?

The why is easy:

- Increased index key sizes, which are required for full UNICODE support with multibyte character sets
- Storage and I/O efficiency

CPS's impact on creating spaces is up to you and to whether you use it and the degree to which you do.

Looking at the first reason, increased index key sizes, it's important to remember that unlike data records that can span pages, index entries *must* be completely contained on a single page. With this restriction, some customers were running into error conditions when they created or modified indexes and the length of the index was bigger than the page size. Although you may question the efficiency of a 2 KB index, that limit can easily be reached in applications deployed globally with support for double-byte language sets through UNICODE. With CPS, you can now create index entries up to 3 KB in length.

The second reason behind CPS—more efficient storage and retrieval of the data element from disk—benefits both data and index pages. Looking at the I/O efficiency part first, as I mentioned earlier in this chapter, all I/O occurs at a page level. While IDS lets you store a 3 KB row across two pages, retrieving it requires two I/O operations. With DSA and the inherent parallelism, this increase in I/O calls was more than offset by other and greater efficiencies occurring in the instance. However, if you could cut session I/O in half, you could potentially double the instance's throughput for a given amount of time. Outstanding!

The next part of this feature deals with storage efficiency. Before getting too far into this aspect, let me briefly cover a bit of low-level IDS disk architecture. Although an IDS instance might have a default page size of 2 KB or 4 KB, not all the space is available for data or index storage. Approximately 28 bytes per page (for standard dbspaces) are reserved for page administration. These 28 bytes contain timestamp, identification, and other information the instance needs to identify and use the page in a dbspace. Some additional space is taken by each row, but we'll ignore that for the moment and just focus on the fixed allocation. Physically, some of this space is allocated from the top of the page; the remainder is allocated from the bottom.

With that background out of the way, IDS has always attempted to store data in such a way as to minimize I/O. If it could fit one or more complete rows on a page, it would. If one of the additional rows would not fit, it would be stored on a new page so only one I/O operation was required to retrieve it. Where a row length exceeded the page size—for example, a 3 KB row on a 2 KB page system—most of the row would be stored on a single page, called the *home page*, and the rest was stored on another page called a *remainder page*. If sufficient space existed, a remainder page would hold the trailing portion of more than one row, provided it didn't cause the trailing portion to be split onto yet another page. The whole idea was to minimize the amount of I/O operations to retrieve the row. With CPS, you can now manage page sizes for dbspaces holding your most critical tables to maximize the storage capacity of your spaces and, in the process, improve I/O rates and reduce "wasted" storage space, saving your company money.

Here's an example of how this works. Suppose you had a table with a fixed-length row size of 1,200 bytes. On an IDS port with a 2 KB default page size, you have only 2,020 bytes of usable space per page (2,048 minus 28 for overhead). When the first row is inserted, it goes on page 1. When the second row is inserted, it doesn't fit in the balance of the usable space on the first page, so it is stored on another page. Figure 5.15 illustrates this scenario, showing the impact of storing 30 rows. As you can see, there is a considerable amount of unused space on each page that in aggregate adds up to almost half of the allocated pages!

Now, suppose you could choose a different page size in which to store the rows. What would the impact be? Figure 5.16 illustrates the answer where the same 30 rows are stored in a dbspace with a 6 KB page. This scenario results in 6,116 bytes of usable storage per page.

Storage efficiency – 2 KB page

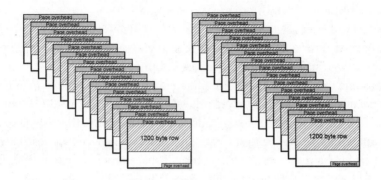

30 rows requires 30 pages = 60 KB of disk space

820 bytes wasted / page * 30 pages = 24,600 bytes or about 12 pages!

Figure 5.15: Storing a 1,200-byte row on a 2 KB page

Storage efficiency – 6 KB page

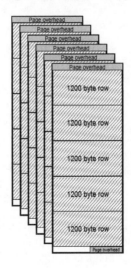

30 rows requires 6 pages = 36 KB of disk space

116 bytes wasted / page * 6 pages = 696 bytes

Figure 5.16: Storing a 1,200-byte row on a 6 KB page

As you can see, the results are pretty significant. We reduced total space used by 40 percent, and wasted space was virtually eliminated! Imagine the impact if the row count wasn't 30 but 3 million, 300 million, or even 3 billion.

With IDS 10 and later releases, you can use the **-k** flag (lower case) with **onspaces** to indicate the page size for a dbspace. The page size you select *must* be a multiple of the default instance page size, though, up to a maximum of 16 KB.

There are some caveats to using CPS. First and most important, the maximum number of rows per page has not changed, so regardless of the page size, you'll be able to store only up to 255 rows per page. As a result, don't create a table with a 4-byte row size in a dbspace built with a 16 KB page size. Second, critical dbspaces are restricted to the default page size. As a reminder, that's the root dbspace and any space with a logical log, the physical log, or the **sysadmin** database. Third, if you create one or more dbspaces with a page size other than the default, a new and separate buffer pool is created for that size of dbspace, as Figure 5.17 illustrates.

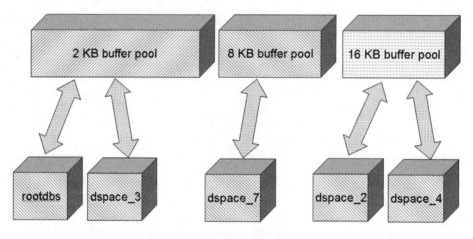

Figure 5.17: Separate buffer pools for each dbspace page size

The discussion of memory pool creation based on CPS parameters applies only to standard dbspaces, not simple or smart BLOBspaces, which we discuss later in the chapter.

If you look at the bottom of the **$ONCONFIG** file, you'll see the new syntax for configuring buffer pools. There is a "default" entry that **onspaces** or the other utilities use as a template if a new pool must be created as a result of a space-creation operation with an other-than-default page size. You can edit this entry as you see fit if you want all subsequent pools to use the same parameters. There is also an entry for the instance page size that is used by the root dbspace and other spaces using the port's default page size.

Here's how this works in practice. Suppose you're building an instance and you're going to create your first dbspace using CPS. If you create the space using **onspaces**, the SQL API, or one of the graphical utilities, the space-creation command will also create the buffer pool using the default entry parameters. If those parameters are not adequate for the space you created, you must shut down the instance, change the **$ONCONFIG** entry for that pool, and then restart the instance.

As an alternative, you can create the buffer pool first with the parameters you want. Then, when the space is created, it will use the existing buffer pool of that size. You accomplish this using either the **onparams** utility or the SQL API as shown here:

```
onparams -b -g pg_size -n num_buffs -r num_lrus
-x lru_max_dirty -m lru_min_dirty

or

execute function
  admin ('add bufferpool', 'pg_size', 'num_buffs',
         'num_lrus', 'lru_max_dirty', 'lru_min_dirty');
```

There is one more advantage you can leverage with CPS, although it is not one of the reasons behind the feature. Suppose you have a large concurrent user environment in which large amounts of data from several tables are constantly being reused and must persist in memory. Provided the rows sizes don't make disk storage overwhelmingly inefficient, you can create each of these tables in a dbspace of a different page size. Each table's data will thus be cached in a different buffer pool, increasing the instance's ability to execute in-memory operations and reducing buffer pool thrashing as well as I/O operations to re-read purged data. This approach should have a positive impact on instance performance.

Understanding Informix's Windows Naming Conventions

This section applies only to IDS instances deployed on physical servers running the Microsoft Windows operating system. If you're not using this port of IDS, you can skip this section.

When deploying on Windows, you must conform to the data server's naming conventions for your chunks to be recognized by the data server. Unlike the Linux, Mac OS X, and Unix ports of the data server, Windows environments do *not* use symbolic links when indicating the path of each device to the instance. The data server expects to see a nested set of subdirectories created on the drives supporting the rootdbs, the initial dbspace, and their mirrors if IDS mirroring is used.

Because of Windows registry issues, it is, for all intents and purposes, not possible to change where the root dbspace is created for an instance. The path structure is virtually hard-coded into the data server. If, during data server installation, you choose to create the demonstration instance, the chunks for that instance are created according to this default path. The path is **%ROOTPATH%\IFMXDATA***instance_name*, where ***instance_ name*** is the actual name of the instance. Likewise for other chunks in the instance; you can choose a different path through the **onspaces** utility and potentially some of the graphical utilities, but it is strongly recommended that you leave all the chunks in the same directory structure.

The files that an instance's directory contains have a three-part file name as described in Table 5.3.

Table 5.3: Naming convention used to identify chunks in a Windows instance	
File name part	**Description**
Space name	The actual name of the dbspace to which this chunk belongs. This part of the file name is limited to 18 characters and can use any alphanumeric character as long as the first character is not a number or a special character.
Space type	A pseudo-extension indicating what type of space the file is. Possible values are **dat** and **mirr** for primary and mirror chunk, respectively.
Chunk number	A three-character number indicating which chunk number the chunk/file is in the named space. The initial chunk of a dbspace is numbered 000 (three zeros). Additional chunks are numbered 001, 002, and so on.

You separate the space name and space type portions of the file name with an underscore and precede the chunk number with a dot. As a result, a directory listing of my **c:\IFMXDATA\sarthe** directory, which supports the **sarthe** instance on one of my test machines, lists the following file names:

```
rootdbs_dat.000
sarthe_1_dat.000
somebiglongnamefor_dat.000
sarthe_2_mirr.000
sarthe_3_dat.001
```

In this output sample, I have several primary chunks for dbspaces (**rootdbs, sarthe_1,** and **somebiglongnamefor**) as well as a mirror chunk (**sarthe_2**) and an additional data chunk added to the **sarthe_3** dbspace whose initial chunk is on another drive.

Creating Spaces

When you create a new instance, you create an initial dbspace, commonly called **rootdbs**. This space is created when you've entered valid values into the **ROOTNAME, ROOTSIZE, ROOTOFFSET,** and **ROOTPATH $ONCONFIG** parameters, as well as the **MIRRORPATH** parameter if used. Once the instance is up and running, you undoubtedly will need to add more dbspaces. You can do so rather easily using **onspaces**, OAT, Server Studio utilities, or the SQL API.

The creation of a new dbspace after instance initialization isn't much different or more difficult than creating the root dbspace. Let's look again at the screen you use to create a dbspace through OAT (Figure 5.18). The handful of required parameters appear at the bottom the screen.

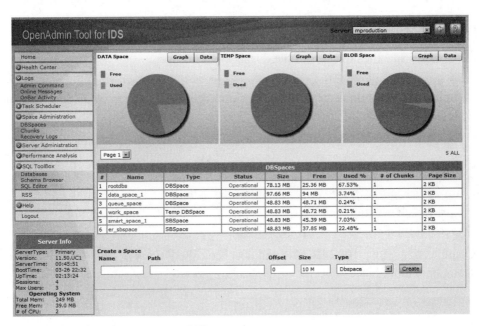

Figure 5.18: Creating a dbspace in OAT

 As I explained in Chapter 2, you should always use symbolic links instead of real device names to point to disk partitions or tape devices on Linux, Mac OS X, and Unix ports of the data server. I will follow that philosophy in the examples given here and in the rest of the chapters in the book.

Looking at the sample screen and how it operates, you can see that you simply enter the name of the space, the path of the chunk's symbolic link, and the offset value (if any) and size in "real" values to create a space. Use the drop-down box to select the type of space you are creating. After filling in the applicable fields, click the **Create** button to create the dbspace. If you create a temporary dbspace, including its name in either the **$DBSPACETEMP** environment variable or the **$ONCONFIG** file will activate its use within the instance.

To create a dbspace from the command line, use the **onspaces** utility with the following most commonly used flags:

- **–c**—Indicates that this is a create action.
- **–d** *dbspacename*—Specifies the name of the dbspace.
- **–p** *device_path*—Defines the path to the symbolic link pointing to the disk partition.
- **–o** *offsetvalue*—Provides the offset value, if any, into the disk partition; value **0** (zero) for none.
- **–s** *size*—Specifies the size of the dbspace in kilobytes.
- **–k** *pagesize*—Optional; specifies the page size of the dbspace in kilobytes and as a multiple of the default page size. If not used, the space is created using the instance default page size.
- **–t**—Indicates that the dbspace is to be a temporary dbspace; optional otherwise.

If the dbspace is to be mirrored, include the following flag:

- **–m** *device_path offsetvalue*—Specifies the path to the symbolic link pointing to the mirror disk partition and the offset value, if any, into the disk partition; offset value **0** (zero) for none.

For example, to create a 100 MB mirrored dbspace called **index_1**, you would execute the following operation:

```
onspaces –c –d index_1
  –p /opt/IBM/informix/devices/amazon/ama_chnk_1 \
  –o 0 –s 100000 \
  –m / opt/IBM/informix/devices/amazon/ama_chnk_12 0
```

The preceding **onspaces** operation has been broken into four separate lines to accommodate the width of the book page. In reality, it should be executed as one unbroken instruction string. I've attempted to convey this through the use of the slash (\) marker as a continuation character. You will see this notation used occasionally in other examples in the book.

If you didn't want to mirror the dbspace, you would simply eliminate the **-m /opt/IBM/ informix/devices/amazon/ama_chnk_12 0** portion of the command string.

To create a 150 MB temporary dbspace called **work_space_1** that is offset 200 MB into the disk partition, the command would be

```
onspaces -c -d work_space_1 \
-p / opt/IBM/informix/devices/amazon/ama_chnk_20 \
-s 150000 -o 200000 -t
```

Last, to create a 1 GB dbspace called **archive_space** with a 12 KB page size, the command would be

```
onspaces -c -d archive_space \
-p / opt/IBM/informix/devices/amazon/ama_chnk_2y \
-s 1000000 -o 0 -k 12
```

With the SQL-based administration functions introduced in IDS 11, you have another option to create spaces. As you learned earlier in this chapter, you can use the **task()** or **admin()** functions interchangeably; they do the same work, so don't worry that I'm only using one or the other in my examples.

The one caveat to using the SQL API is that you must make sure your input parameters are in the correct order for the command to do what you want. This order is driven by the original utility whose functionality is being matched. So, for example, when you're creating spaces, the size of the dbspace must precede the offset value. Otherwise, you'll create a 0 MB dbspace offset 200 GB into the raw partition! The IDS 11.5 and later documentation lists the required flags and the order they must be in for the command to execute properly and generate the result you expect.

To create the same 150 MB temporary dbspace called **work_space_1** offset 200 MB into the disk partition, the SQL API command would be

```
execute function
  task ('create tempdbspace', 'work_space_1',
        'opt/IBM/informix/devices/amazon/ama_chnk_20',
        '150mb', '200mb');
```

There are a couple of things to notice with this syntax. First, you execute a different command to create a temporary dbspace as opposed to a regular dbspace. Second, I've used "real" values to indicate the size and offset values. For more information about entering chunk and dbspace sizes, refer to the relevant discussion earlier in this chapter.

IDS 11.5 introduces additional syntax to the SQL API with respect to creating spaces of any type. The new **with_check** keyword verifies that the physical device specified by the device path actually exists.

Creating BLOBspaces, whether simple or smart, have their own set of flags and units of measure. Let's look at those items next.

Simple BLOBspaces

To create a simple BLOBspace, you eliminate the **-d dbspacename** flag from the **onspaces** command and use the following additional flags:

- **-b blob_name**—Specifies the name of the BLOBspace
- **-g page_size**—Specifies the size of the BLOBspace page *in pages*, not kilobytes

For example, the command to create a 1 GB, nonmirrored BLOBspace using three pages as a BLOBpage size would be

```
onspaces -c -b blob_world \
-p /opt/IBM/informix/devices/amazon/ama_chnk_3 \
-s 1000000 -o 0 -g 3
```

Using the SQL API, the command would look like this:

```
execute function
   task ('create with_check blobspace', 'blob_world',
         'opt/IBM/informix/devices/amazon/ama_chnk_3',
         '1gb', '0', '3');
```

You cannot create "temporary" simple BLOBspaces, but they can be mirrored. Simple BLOBspaces function almost like regular dbspaces, although there are a couple of differences. Unlike a regular dbspace, which is available for use immediately after creation (and for mirroring if done at an instance level), the logical log entries detailing the creation of a simple BLOBspace and its activation for use must occur in two separate logical logs. This means you'll probably have to force a switch in the active logical log via **onmode** or another utility using the -l (lowercase letter "l") option. This would be followed by forcing a checkpoint to occur by using the **onmode -c** command (or other utility equivalent) to completely activate the new logical log and complete the simple BLOBspace creation process.

While regular dbspaces *can* be created with a page size that is a multiple of the default page size, simple BLOBspaces *must* created using such a page size. The smallest value is 1 (one), but the size can be much larger than that. There are conditions you should be aware of, though, when deciding on the BLOBpage size. Although a BLOB could fill one or more BLOBpages, only one BLOB will be stored to a BLOBpage. To get the most efficient use of the BLOBspace pages, you should not make them too large or too small. Ideally, set the BLOBpage size as close as possible to the average size of the BLOB. This way, you're not wasting disk space when the BLOB is smaller than the simple BLOBspace page size or when the BLOB is larger than the simple BLOBspace page size and an additional BLOBpage is allocated within the simple BLOBspace to store the remainder of the BLOB.

I realize that using the term "average size" can be misleading. This phrase implies, in my mind anyway, a standard average. Sum up the individual sizes of each BLOB, divide by the number of BLOBs, and, voila!—the average size. The problem with this approach is that there could be a number of BLOBs significantly larger in size than the majority. These BLOBs could skew the calculation of the average. It is more appropriate to look at the average BLOB to be stored in terms of volume and size and calculate the BLOBpage size from that. Treat the occasional larger BLOB as an exception. Although these larger BLOBs will require more than one BLOBpage for storage, the amount of disk space wasted on the last BLOBpage allocated to store them should be relatively small compared with the total amount of space used.

If a table contains more than one BLOB column, or if several tables contain BLOB columns, build several simple BLOB spaces of varying BLOB page sizes if the average size of the BLOB columns varies significantly. To check how well you calculated the BLOBpage size, you can use the **onstat -pB** command to display the storage efficiency of the BLOBpages in each BLOBspace.

Smart BLOBspaces

Sbspaces have their own set of flags to control how they are created and operate. It starts with the flag to create the space: **-S** (capitalized). Most of the other flags from the **onspaces** syntax tree apply to smart BLOBspaces, including path, offset, size, mirror path and offset (if used), and so on. Because the objects in an sbspace will have different characteristics and permit multiuser access, there are additional flags to support this functionality.

The first two flags, **-Ms** *size_value* and **-Mo** *offset_value*, control the size of the metadata area inside the sbspace and what the offset into the space is before the metadata area is created. If you don't specify a value for either of these parameters, IDS will create the metadata area in the middle of the sbspace. When calculating the size of the metadata area, the data server will look at the total sbspace size and try to "guess" how many smart BLOBs could be stored in that amount of space. It will then allocate enough metadata area to store that number of objects. If the data server guesses incorrectly and you run out of metadata area to store information about a smart BLOB, you can add another chunk and make it contain nothing but metadata if you like (more about this technique in the next section). You can help the data server calculate the correct size for the metadata area if you indicate the expected size of the smart BLOBs you'll be storing in the sbspace. You can do that with a parameter we discuss next.

The additional parameters to control sbspace functionality follow the **-Df** flag. You specify these parameters in a single, double-quoted string, with each parameter comma-separated and no white space in the string. The string *is* case-sensitive, so make sure you type it correctly.

Table 5.4 lists the most commonly used parameters. Unless otherwise noted, any specification of size will always be in kilobytes.

Table 5.4: Additional parameters to control how sbspaces operate	
Flag	**Description**
ACCESSTIME	Determines whether the instance tracks when a smart BLOB is accessed. Can be either **OFF** (the default) or **ON**.
AVG_LO_SIZE	Used to indicate the expected average size of the smart BLOBs to be stored in the sbspace. If specified, the data server will use this value when calculating the size of the sbspace metadata area. In no case should this value be less than the default page size for the instance. Maximum value for this parameter is 232 KB.
BUFFERING	Determines how smart BLOBs are buffered. If **ON** (the default value), memory from the buffer pool in the resident portion of instance memory is used. If **OFF**, memory from the virtual portion of instance memory is used.
LOCK_MODE	Specifies how the smart BLOBs will be locked. If set to **BLOB** (the default), the first user operation on the smart BLOB will lock the entire BLOB, similar to simple BLOBs. If set to **RANGE**, the user operation will lock only those portions of the BLOB it's working on. To support **RANGE** locking, the **BUFFERING** parameter must be set to **ON**.
LOGGING	Determines whether changes to smart BLOBs are logged in the instance logical logs. Can be **OFF** (the default) or **ON**.
MIN_EXT_SIZE	Specifies the minimum amount of storage for each smart BLOB. You can set this parameter to an expected maximum size to accommodate anticipated smart BLOB growth. In no case should this value be less than the default page size for the instance. Maximum value for this parameter is 2^{32} KB.

The following example creates a 500 MB smart BLOBspace with functional parameters such as byte-range locking, logical logging of changes, and resident memory buffering turned on.

```
onspaces -c -S pics_sbspace \
-p /opt/IBM/informix/devices/tagus/sbspace_3 \
-s 500000 -o 0 \
-Df "AVG_LO_SIZE=2,LOGGING=ON,LOCK_MODE=RANGE,\
BUFFERING=ON"
```

While the **LOGGING** parameter controls whether changes to smart BLOBs are written to the logical logs, changes in the metadata area are always written to the logical logs. Make sure that you have sufficient logical logs and that they are sized correctly to accommodate data changes in the other data types as well as the metadata and the smart BLOB data.

Adding a Disk Chunk

Expanding a space by adding a disk chunk differs little from the original space-creation process. If, when you initially created the space, you selected Informix mirroring, all additional chunks added to that space must be mirrored as well. In these situations, you'll need to include the mirroring parameters as well as those for the main chunk itself. Once a mirrored chunk is added, you can disable the mirror as explained elsewhere in this chapter.

To add a chunk to a space from the command line, use the **onspaces** utility with the following flags:

- -a *dbspace*—Specifies the name of the space
- -p *device_path*—Gives the full path of the symbolic link pointing to the disk chunk
- -o *offset_value*—Provides the offset value, if any, into the file; value **0** (zero) for none
- -s *chunk_size*—Specifies the size of the chunk in kilobytes

To add Informix–based mirroring to the chunk as part of the addition process, include the following to the **onspaces** command:

- -m *path_name offset_value*—Provides the full path of the symbolic link pointing to the mirror chunk as well as the offset value in kilobytes, if any; **0** (zero) for none

Chunks can be added to spaces through the graphical utilities as illustrated in Figure 5.19.

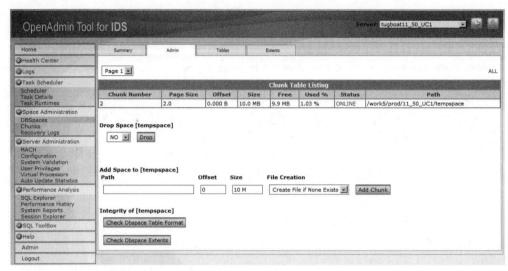

Figure 5.19: Adding a disk chunk through OAT

In this case, the dbspace already contains two chunks but a third could be added by entering the path of the symbolic link, offset and chunk size. Though best practices dictate always using symbolic links to point to chunks, you can choose to use actual device paths in the Path field. In this case, you use the last field in this form to have OAT create the flat file used as the chunk. Obviously, the user ID used to log into OAT will need to have the appropriate permissions on the directory where the file is being created.

When using the **onstat -d** command to display configured space, all chunks are listed in chunk creation order with their chunk and dbspace numbers in the bottom portion of the command output as illustrated in Figure 5.20. In this case, an additional chunk has been added to **data_space_1** dbspace. Notice that in the **nchunks** column of the top section of the command output, it indicates the dbspace contains two chunks while in the bottom section the last line shows that the seventh chunk created belongs to dbspace #2 as listed in the **number** column of the top section. There will be information for both the primary and the mirror chunk if Informix mirroring was used.

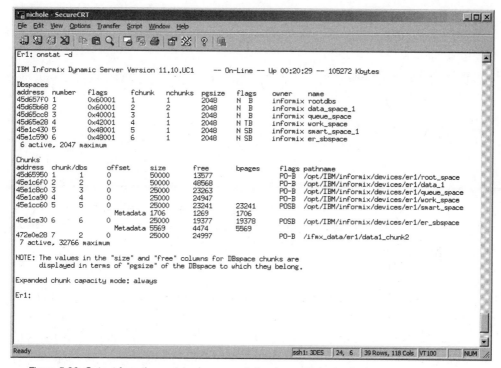

Figure 5.20: Output from the onstat –d command showing multiple chunks

In a Windows environment, when manually creating a file to support an additional chunk to be added to a space, remember to use the correct value in the chunk number field in the file name as explained in Table 5.3. For example, to add a 1 GB chunk to a simple BLOBspace called **my_blobs**, you would execute the following through the SQL API:

```
execute function task ("add chunk", "my_blobs",
    "f:f_sarthe_disks/myblobs_dat.001", "100MB", "0");
```

There is no **with_check** option when adding chunks.

As I mentioned in the previous section about smart BLOBspaces, when adding an additional chunk, you can indicate whether the chunk will hold both end-user (a.k.a. BLOB) data and metadata or just metadata. The latter is particularly valuable if your or the data server's initial calculation of metadata requirements is wrong. It is handled through two additional flags in the **onspaces** command:

- **-Ms** *size*—Specifies the amount of space in the chunk to be allocated to metadata
- **-Mo** *offset_value*—Provides, in kilobytes, the offset value (if any) into the chunk for the metadata area

I have not found a documented SQL API option to add a chunk to an sbspace and modify its metadata allocation.

Dropping a Disk Chunk

The ability to "reduce" the size of a space by dropping one or more chunks added after the space was created is not difficult. For the most part, you can execute this operation while the space is online. The exception is simple BLOBspaces. Unlike with regular dbspaces or smart BLOBspaces, dropping an additional chunk from a simple BLOBspace requires the instance to be in quiescent mode.

Before dropping the chunk, you need to make sure it is completely empty. From the command line, execute an **oncheck -pe** command, save the output to file, and review it. Each chunk of every dbspace will be listed individually, along with any table or index extents that may exist in the chunk.

If a table or index has extents in the chunk to be dropped, try to remove or move those extents to another chunk. You can concatenate tables somewhat by altering an index **to cluster**, which removes unnecessary extents; or you can unload, drop, and rebuild the tables in other dbspaces. Changing the partitioning strategy will cause the affected partitions to be rebuilt—possibly removing extents in the chunk to be dropped. See the "Altering Partitions" section of Chapter 6 to learn how to alter partitioning schemes.

Once the chunk is empty, you can use the **onspaces** utility with the following flags to drop the chunk:

- **-d space_name**—Specifies the name of the space containing the chunk to be dropped
- **-p** *device_path*—Gives the full path of the symbolic link pointing to the chunk to be dropped
- **-o** *offset_value*—Provides the offset value in kilobytes, if any, into the file; value **0** (zero) for none
- **-y**—Answers the confirmation prompt

You can also use the SQL API with the same parameters.

If for some reason the chunk is not completely empty, the drop process will abort and an error message will be returned. This situation can become an issue if the metadata area of an additional smart BLOBspace chunk is used to store information about end-user objects stored in other chunks. You won't be able to drop the additional chunk; the entire smart BLOBspace must be dropped. Conversely, if an additional smart BLOBspace chunk contains only end-user data, you can drop it even if the chunk is not empty. Doing so requires using the **-f** flag in the **onspaces** command string. I strongly recommend that you execute a full instance backup after making any changes such as adding or dropping a chunk to/from a space.

The initial chunk of a space cannot be dropped using any of the utilities even if other chunks in the space remain. You must drop the entire dbspace as explained in the next section.

Dropping a Space

Just as when you drop a disk chunk, you cannot drop a space if it contains any table or index extents. Follow the same **oncheck** utility procedure explained in the previous section to make sure no table or index extents exist in the space to be dropped.

You can drop smart BLOBspaces even though they contain end-user data. To do so, use the **-f** flag with the command string described next.

Dropping a space using the **onspaces** utility requires only two flags:

- **-d** *space_name*—Specifies the name of the dbspace to be dropped
- **-y**—Answers the confirmation prompt

The SQL API requires only the **drop dbspace** parameter and the dbspace name. Similar to the procedure for dropping a disk chunk, if the dbspace is not completely empty, the drop process is aborted and an error message is returned.

You can also drop spaces through OAT. Refer back to Figure 5.19, where, in the middle of the window listing the chunks for the space, you'll see an option to drop the space itself.

When you drop a space created using cooked files, the files themselves used as the chunks for the dbspace are not removed. You must remove these files manually to free the disk space they occupied.

Adding or Dropping a Mirror

If Informix mirroring was not enabled at the time the instance was created, you can enable the functionality at any time by making a small change in the **$ONCONFIG** file.

The **MIRROR** configuration parameter controls the mirroring function. If **MIRROR** is set to 1 (one), the functionality is active; otherwise, it is disabled. Unfortunately, the change requires restarting the instance. Once enabled, an Informix-based disk mirror can be added or dropped at will as needed.

You can now use the **onspaces** utility or the SQL API to add a mirror to a space on a chunk-by-chunk basis using the following flags:

- -m *space_name*—Specifies the name of the dbspace

- -p *device_path*—Gives the full path of the symbolic link pointing to the chunk to be mirrored

- -o *offset_value_of_primary_chunk*—Provides the offset value (if any) in kilobytes of the chunk to be mirrored; value **0** (zero) for none

- -m *mirror_device_path offset_value_of_mirror_chunk*—Specifies the full path of the symbolic link pointing to the mirror chunk and the offset value (if any) in kilobytes; offset value **0** (zero) for none

- -y—Answers the confirmation prompt

For example, to add an Informix mirror to the **dbs_1** dbspace, you would execute the following command:

```
onspaces -m dbs_1 \
-p /opt/IBM/informix/devices/tagus/dbs1 -o 0 \
-m /opt/IBM/informix/devices/tagus/dbs1_mirror1 0 -y
```

Dropping Informix mirroring from a space is a simple operation. Unlike adding mirrors, you can turn off or drop mirroring only on the entire space at once. The action is accomplished with two flags in the **onspaces** utility:

- -r *space_name*—Specifies the space name mirroring is to be removed from

- -y—Answers the confirmation prompt

You can drop mirroring with the SQL API using the **stop mirroring** parameter and the dbspace name.

It goes without saying that dropping mirrors does not remove the cooked files or raw partitions used as mirrors or the symbolic links that point to them. It simply removes their use in the instance. You must remove the physical objects manually.

Changing the Status of a Chunk

When Informix mirroring is active on a space and chunks are configured in mirrored pairs, you can bring either part of a pair offline or online at will, provided the other half of the pair is completely functional. One reason for doing this—particularly in Unix environments, where symbolic links should be used to point to disk space—is to be able to physically move data around within your disk environment without having to export, drop, and re-create tables.

This process involves disabling one side of the mirror pair, changing the disk partition to which the symbolic link points, and then re-enabling the "down" side of the pair. In bringing the disabled side back online, regardless of whether the physical location of the down side changed, IDS makes a bitwise copy to it from the side that remained active. This is not unlike what happened when the mirror was originally created. The end result, though, is that by virtue of changing the symbolic link, the newly activated side of the pair is physically relocated. You can reuse the old location for a chunk in any active instance on the server.

There is, unfortunately, no way to change a chunk's status using OAT, so you'll have to use either command-line or SQL utilities. When using **onspaces**, the -**D** flag takes a chunk down, while the -**O** (capital letter "O") flag brings the chunk back online. The complete syntax for changing the status of a chunk is as follows:

- -s *space_name*—Specifies the name of the dbspace to be affected
- -p *device_path*—Gives the full path of the symbolic link pointing to the chunk to be brought online or offline.
- -o *offset_value*—Provides the offset value (if any) in kilobytes; value **0** (zero) for none
- -D or -O—Specifies the action to be executed on the chunk: **D**own or **O**nline
- -y—Answers the confirmation prompt

For example, to take down the primary chunk of the **danube_1** dbspace, you would execute the following command:

```
onspaces —s danube_1 \
 -p /opt/IBM/informix/devices/danube/dan_1 —o 0 —D —y
```

When a chunk goes offline, messages will be logged in the **MSGPATH** file and alerts will be registered in OAT. The chunks status is also clearly visible in the output of an **onstat -d** command.

Setting or Modifying DATASKIP

The **DATASKIP** parameter determines how the instance handles queries that request data from spaces that are unavailable due to disk failure or another condition. If the parameter is turned **OFF**, the query fails; if turned **ON,** either for **ALL** or for a specific list of spaces, and the query needs to access one or more down spaces for data, the query is completed with the data it has access to but returns an error message to the application as well.

You can change the value of the **DATASKIP** configuration parameter by editing the **$ONCONFIG** file, executing the **onspaces** utility, or using the SQL API. An application can temporarily override the instance-level **DATASKIP** parameter by executing the **set dataskip** SQL command as part of a command block. To change the **DATASKIP** parameter value through the **onspaces** utility, you use one of two options for the **–f** flag. You can follow this flag with one or more optional qualifiers:

- **–f OFF** or **ON** [**ALL** | *list_of_space_names*]
- **–y** to answer the confirmation prompt

Using the **ON** or **OFF** option alone turns **DATASKIP** either on or off for all spaces in the instance, making the **ALL** keyword somewhat redundant. If you need to set **DATASKIP** functionality at a space level, you can list individual dbspaces in a comma-delimited list following the **ON** or **OFF** keyword.

The value for **DATASKIP** set via the **onspaces** utility or the SQL API lasts only for the length of time the instance is online. The original **DATASKIP** value from the **$ONCONFIG** file is used when the instance is restarted.

Setting the **DATASKIP** value so that it will survive an instance restart requires editing the **$ONCONFIG** file and inserting the appropriate value(s) for this configuration parameter. Keyword **OFF** or **ON**, followed either by the **ALL** keyword or a comma-delimited list of space names, is acceptable.

Creating, Moving, and Resizing Logs

One of the first tasks to be completed after initializing an instance that will contain databases in a logged mode is to create one or more dbspaces to hold the physical and logical logs, relocate the logs out of the rootdbs, and build new logical logs. Moving the logs out of the rootdbs eliminates a significant amount of I/O pointing at that one device and helps prevent a disk I/O bottleneck from occurring.

If all the databases in the instance will be unlogged, there is no pressing need, other than to free up space in the rootdbs, to move the logs to different dbspaces because little or no activity will occur in them. You should move them anyway just to remain consistent with the other instances containing logged databases. You probably won't need to increase the number of logical logs, either. The physical log will be okay as well if you simply move it into another dbspace if and when you move the logical logs.

In an instance with one or more databases in a logged mode, you'll need to manage the number and size of logical logs during the initial run-up of activity in the instance. Luckily, technological advances in the data server have made this process easier and have removed the penalty if you initially get it wrong. You can configure the instance to add additional logical logs automatically if necessary instead of suspending operations.

From a best practices perspective, when deciding where the logs will be stored, plan to store the physical log in a separate dbspace from the logical logs. The logs will be a focal point of considerable activity, so create the chunks for these dbspaces on some of the highest-performing disks in the drive subsystem. You can distribute the logical logs themselves in several dbspaces if you want, but you're not required to do so. The important thing to remember is that any dbspace containing logs, whether physical or logical, becomes a critical space from a data server perspective. If the log becomes unavailable, instance operations are immediately terminated. You would be wise to protect these spaces with Informix mirroring or a RAID 0 / 0+1 set.

The Physical Log

IDS 11 delivers a significant enhancement to the administration of the physical log. Before this release, any attempt to move or resize the physical log required the instance to be in quiescent mode, effectively forcing an instance outage. Granted, instance outages to administer this log were extremely few and far between, but outages are inconvenient whenever and for whatever reason they occur. They also can be quite costly if the instance supports one or more applications that must always be available.

With IDS 11, you can now change the size or location of the physical log without interrupting instance operations. Strict conditions must be observed, however. First, administration can occur only via the **onparams**, **onmonitor**, and, potentially, OAT and Server Studio utilities as well as the SQL API. In the past, administrators used to "cheat" the system by taking the instance offline, modifying the parameters for the physical log in the **$ONCONFIG** file, and then restarting the instance. If you try to do that now, you will seriously jeopardize the health of the instance and whether it will come online.

Second, it is important to realize that changing the physical log is *not* an in-place operation. As we'll discuss in the next chapter, some DDL operations occur gradually over time as individual rows are used (called *in-place table alters*), while others affect the entire table at once. In the latter case, the original table persists until a full and complete copy of the table is created and loaded with the new definitions. Once the new copy is activated, the original is deleted. I call this a "double disk space penalty" type of condition—you must have sufficient storage space to hold both the original and the new copy. This is how physical log administration occurs in IDS 11 and later as well. As a result, if you are resizing the log but leaving it in the same dbspace, you need to have sufficient space for the old and new physical logs, or the operation will fail.

Third, after administering the physical log, you should create a full instance backup. Although the data server does not require you to do so, it is a best practice that I cannot support strongly enough.

In OAT 2.21 and later, you have the ability to administer the physical log as well as the logical logs from this utility. To perform these tasks, use the **Admin** tab of the **Space Administration > Recovery Logs** option, shown in Figure 5.21.

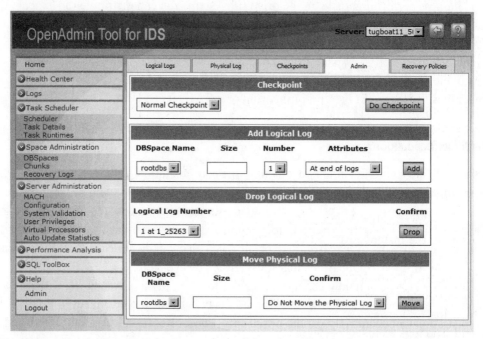

Figure 5.21: Administering the physical and logical logs through OAT

Changing the size or location of the physical log through the **onparams** utility uses the following flags:

- **-p -s** *size_in_kbytes*—Specifies either the new size of the physical log in kilobytes or the current log size, if you are not changing the size

- -d *dbspace_name*—Names the dbspace to contain the physical log
- -y—Answers the confirmation prompt

The size of the physical log is important for several reasons. First, the instance will trigger a full checkpoint whenever the physical log becomes 75 percent full. Second, with IDS 11 and later, the physical log is holding more data for longer amounts of time and so must be sized accordingly. With the new non-blocking checkpoint algorithm, instance activity is not suspended for the duration of a checkpoint. While modified data is being flushed from memory to disk and, as a result, the "before" image is being removed from the physical log, new transactions are starting, requiring new before data images to be stored in the physical log. With this increased duration and volume of data in the log, IDS development recommends the physical log size be approximately 110 percent of the instance memory buffer pool. Obviously, you need to evaluate this recommendation within the constraints of your business needs, budget, and system load. It is one of the few areas where the old adage "If some is good, more is better" actually applies.

You can monitor the physical log, as well as the physical log buffers, for usage efficiency using the **onstat -l** (lower case letter "l") and **oncheck -pr** commands. Using either command, look for the percentage of the log used at the time a checkpoint occurs. You can also use the **onstat -g ckp** command to obtain in-depth information about the most recent checkpoints.

The Logical Logs

Logical logs are just as easy to administer as the physical log. In earlier versions of the data server, the instance had to be in quiescent mode and logs were only appended to the end of the existing string of logs. These restrictions were removed early in IDS 9. Now, you can administer the logical logs at will with the instance online and supporting end-user operations.

New logical logs can be inserted either at the current location in the log string or at the end. The logs themselves can be different sizes rather than one fixed value for all logs. You can even configure the data server itself to add additional logical logs to the instance if it runs out of log space due to one or more large transactions or a transaction that isn't closed properly over time and remains open across logs. This does not eliminate events such as long transaction rollbacks, but it does give the instance more room in which to operate before declaring a rollback condition. Another nice feature introduced in IDS 9 is that once added, a logical log is immediately available for use. A system backup is not required to activate a logical log.

One thing that has not changed is the fact that at no time can there be less than three fully active logs in an instance. As a result, moving logical logs is a process of creating new logs (possibly in new dbspace(s)), and then dropping the original logs.

Changes to the logical logs require use of the **onparams** utility, the graphical utilities, or the SQL API. The syntax flags to add a logical log are as follows:

- -a -d *dbspace_name*—Specifies the name of the dbspace to contain the logical log
- -s *log_size* in kilobytes—Provides the new size of the logical log; necessary only if the new logical log is to be larger or smaller than the instance "default"
- -i (optional)—Indicates that the newly added log should be inserted immediately after the "current" logical log rather than at the end of the log string

If you don't specify the -s (lower case) option, the size of the new logical log will match the value of the **LOGSIZE** parameter in the **$ONCONFIG** file. This parameter establishes the default size for logical logs in the instance and is originally set by Informix at 10 MB in IDS 11.5. Earlier IDS versions had different default sizes, which sometimes varied by O/S port. The number of users the instance will support and the activity level they will generate will determine the best size for the logical logs.

If one or more tables contain simple BLOB columns, of either type **TEXT** or type **BINARY**, a "smaller" logical log size will most likely not be adequate. Simple BLOB writes bypass some of the normal instance-logging mechanisms and directly access the logical logs on disk. In fact, a simple BLOB "insert" is not considered committed until all the BLOB information has been written into the logical logs. A simple BLOB "delete" is not committed until the logical log that recorded the delete transaction has been backed up to disk. Depending on the amount of simple BLOB activity and the average size of the BLOBs, a tremendous amount of information will be written to the logs per unit of time. As a result, you will need to size the logical logs big enough to handle the volume without immediately filling.

As I indicated earlier in the chapter, smart BLOB activity logging in the logical logs is controlled with the **LOGGING** parameter to the sbspace creation or modification syntax.

Only logical logs that are not currently recording transactions, and that don't contain the last checkpoint, can be dropped from the instance. Dropping a logical log involves selecting it by its physical number, not its logical ID. Each logical log has a physical number that never changes as well as a logical number assigned to it when the log becomes the "current" log in the instance. The data server increments this logical number serially when the current logical log fills, and a "new" log begins to record transaction information.

To identify the physical number for each log, as well as that of the currently active log and the log containing the last checkpoint, you can use the output of an **onstat –l** command as shown in Figure 5.22.

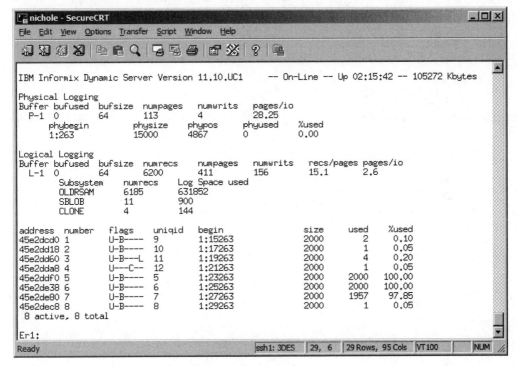

Figure 5.22: Output generated from the onstat –l command

In the lower part of the figure, you can see that the logical log with the physical number of 4 and the logical ID of 12 is the current log by virtue of its having the **C** status flag. It does not contain the last instance checkpoint record because the **L** flag is still listed for log ID 11. Because the instance from which this screen shot was taken is just a test instance, all the logical logs are the same size as listed in the **size** field of the output and are all stored in the same dbspace as indicated by the first part of the **begin** field. The integer value before the colon (:) in this field represents the number of the chunk in which the log is stored. As shown previously, the output from the **onstat –d** command (or equivalent from one of the graphical tools) will help you trace the chunk number to a specific dbspace. All the logical logs have been used at least once, as indicated by the **U** flag, and were backed up when activity moved to the next logical log, as indicated by the **B** flag. Compare this output with another screen shot from the same instance, shown in Figure 5.23. In this case, a new logical log was inserted after the current log but has not been used yet. This new log was also created in a different dbspace from the existing logical logs.

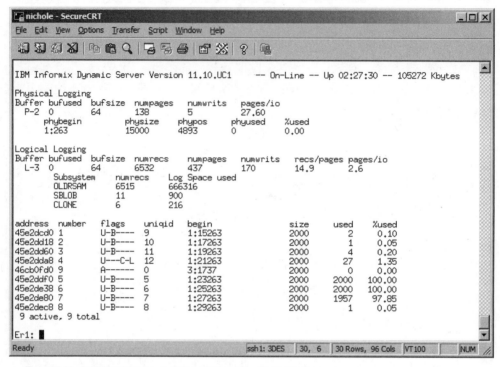

```
nichole - SecureCRT                                                    _ □ ×
File  Edit  View  Options  Transfer  Script  Window  Help

IBM Informix Dynamic Server Version 11.10.UC1    -- On-Line -- Up 02:27:30 -- 105272 Kbytes

Physical Logging
Buffer bufused  bufsize  numpages   numwrits    pages/io
  P-2   0        64       138        5           27.60
       phybegin         physize    phypos     phyused    %used
       1:263            15000      4893       0          0.00

Logical Logging
Buffer bufused  bufsize  numrecs    numpages   numwrits   recs/pages pages/io
  L-3   0        64       6532       437        170        14.9       2.6
        Subsystem      numrecs    Log Space used
        OLDRSAM        6515       666316
        SBLOB          11         900
        CLONE          6          216

address  number  flags    uniqid  begin       size   used  %used
45e2dcd0 1        U-B----  9       1:15263     2000   2     0.10
45e2dd18 2        U-B----  10      1:17263     2000   1     0.05
45e2dd60 3        U-B----  11      1:19263     2000   4     0.20
45e2dda8 4        U---C-L  12      1:21263     2000   27    1.35
46cb0fd0 9        A------  0       3:1737      2000   0     0.00
45e2ddf0 5        U-B----  5       1:23263     2000   2000  100.00
45e2de38 6        U-B----  6       1:25263     2000   2000  100.00
45e2de80 7        U-B----  7       1:27263     2000   1957  97.85
45e2dec8 8        U-B----  8       1:29263     2000   1     0.05
 9 active, 9 total

Er1: █
Ready                                    ssh1: 3DES  30, 6  30 Rows, 96 Cols  VT100    NUM
```

Figure 5.23: Additional onstat –l output after adding a logical log

Using the **onparams** utility to drop a logical log requires the following flags:

- **-d -l** *physical_log_number*—Specifies the physical number of the logical log to drop
- **-y**—Answers the confirmation prompt

> As with physical log administration, I strongly encourage creating a full instance backup after making logical log changes.

The size and number of the logical logs is as important as the size of the physical log. Rather than impacting the checkpoint process, the size of the logical logs affects transaction concurrency. The parameters **LTXHWM** and **LTXEHWM** identify, respectively, the percentage of the logical logs that can fill before forcing a rollback of an open transaction or before pausing other instance activity to allow a transaction to commit or finish rolling back. If the logical logs are too small, they will fill too quickly. While a smaller log size means the log information will be backed up quicker, there is a greater possibility of triggering a long transaction error condition depending on how much data a transaction is affecting.

On the flip side of the size issue, while a bigger logical log size generally reduces concern over long transaction conditions, the bigger logs take longer to fill. As a result, they are not backed up in as timely a manner. Should an absolutely catastrophic disk error occur, all you would have to restore from would be the instance backups and the logical logs that had been backed up. If you were filling only one logical log per day, your recovery options would be limited—particularly with the logical log on the failed disk.

Depending on your level of paranoia, you should size the logical logs to fill, and be backed up, about every 30 to 45 minutes of average instance activity. For information about configuring the automatic backing up of filled logical logs, see Chapter 7.

Starting and Stopping IDS Automatically

If you're lazy like me, shutting down each instance before rebooting the physical server hosting the instances, then restarting them once the server comes back up, is a task to delegate as quickly and as permanently as possible. I use the Linux, Mac OS X, or Unix system's own shutdown and initialization routine to handle these chores for me.

On Linux and Unix servers, I place two simple shell scripts, **start_ids** (Listing 5.1) and **stop_ids** (Listing 5.2), in the **rc2.d** and **rc0.d** directories, respectively, to automatically start and stop instances on a physical server during a server shutdown or reboot. You can usually find these directories under the **/etc** directory, but they are sometimes under the **/sbin** directory in some versions of Linux and Unix.

```
##
## start_ids
##
## Script to start the IDS instances when the server boots.
## This should be placed in the rc2.d directory and numbered
## appropriately.
##
## written by CARLTON DOE
##

export INFORMIXDIR=   ## include path to IDS binaries
export PATH=$INFORMIXDIR/bin:$PATH
echo "About to start IDS instances"
```

Listing 5.1: The start_ids script (part 1 of 2)

```
echo "Starting instance_name"    ## change instance_name to
   a valid instance
export ONCONFIG=    ## config file for instance
export INFORMIXSERVER=   ## DBSERVERNAME
oninit

## Repeat previous four lines as necessary for all
## instances on the machine. If necessary, also change
## the $INFORMIXDIR environment variable if multiple
## versions of IDS are installed.
```

Listing 5.1: The start_ids script (part 2 of 2)

```
##
## stop_ids
##
## Script to stop the IDS instances on shutdown of the server.
## This should be placed in the rc0.d directory and numbered
## appropriately for best results.
##
## written by CARLTON DOE

export INFORMIXDIR=    ## include path to IDS binaries
export PATH=$INFORMIXDIR/bin:$PATH
echo "Shutting down IDS instances"

echo "Stopping instance_name"
export ONCONFIG=    ## config file for instance
export INFORMIXSERVER=   ## DBSERVERNAME
onmode -ky

## Repeat previous four lines as necessary for all
## instances on the machine. If necessary, also change
## the $INFORMIXDIR environment variable if multiple
## versions of IDS are installed.
```

Listing 5.2: The stop_ids script

The number in the directory name refers to the run level of the operating system that will trigger the scripts in that directory to execute. Level 0 is server shutdown, and level 2 is the first multiuser level.

Scripts or programs in the **rc0.d** directory are executed in numerical order provided they are prefaced with a **K** (capitalized) rather than a **k** (lower case) as the machine is shut down. Likewise, in the **rc2.d** directory, scripts or programs prefaced with an **S** (upper case) rather than an **s** (lower case) are executed on system start and when the operating system on the physical server enters multiuser mode.

You can use any number-and-name combination (e.g., **S95_start_ids**) for these two instance-oriented scripts. I usually choose a rather low number for the **rc0.d** script to shut down the instances early in the server shutdown sequence. This gets the IDS processes cleaned up and out of the way before other subsystems on the server start shutting down. It also allows for a rollback of moderate length to occur before it is affected by other server actions.

I use a high number for the script in the **rc2.d** directory so that the instances are among the last services to be started. This lets almost all the other system daemons take their portion of shared memory and permits other processes started at boot to stabilize before IDS starts.

On Mac OS X systems, place the **ibm.informix.ids11.plist** script (Listing 5.3), written by Alexander Koerner of IBM Germany, in the **/Library/LaunchDaemons** directory to have instances started and stopped automatically during a server shutdown or reboot.

```xml
<?xml version="1.0" encoding="UTF-8"?>
<!DOCTYPE plist PUBLIC "-//Apple//DTD PLIST 1.0//EN" \
  "http://www.apple.com/DTDs/PropertyList-1.0.dtd">
<plist version="1.0">
<dict>
    <key>EnvironmentVariables</key>
    <dict>
        <key>DYLD_LIBRARY_PATH</key>
        <string>/Applications/IBM/informix/lib: \
                /Applications/IBM/informix/lib/cli: \
                /Applications/IBM/informix/lib/esql</string>
        <key>INFORMIXDIR</key>
        <string>/Applications/IBM/informix</string>
        <key>INFORMIXSERVER</key>
        <string>demo_on</string>
        <key>INFORMIXSQLHOSTS</key>
        <string>/Applications/IBM/informix/etc/sqlhosts.demo_on</string>
        <key>ONCONFIG</key>
        <string>onconfig.demo_on</string>
    </dict>
    <key>KeepAlive</key>
    <false/>
    <key>Label</key>
    <string>ibm.informix.ids11</string>
    <key>ProgramArguments</key>
    <array>
        <string>/Applications/IBM/informix/bin/oninit</string>
    </array>
    <key>RunAtLoad</key>
    <true/>
</dict>
</plist>
```

Listing 5.3: The ibm.informix.ids11.plist Mac OS X script

In formatting Listing 5.3 for publication, the library path specified by the **DYLD_LIBRARY_PATH** tag had to be broken into three separate lines. In reality, it should be one unbroken string of library locations. I have attempted to convey this through the use of the slash (\) marker as a continuation character.

This script assumes you use the Apple default install location for the data server. If you install IDS somewhere else, you'll need to modify some of the paths to reflect the correct installation location as well as point to the correct instance(s) on the physical server. You can change this existing template to execute shutdown operations as well.

On Windows systems, the easiest way to accomplish this is to allow instance services to be started or stopped along with the rest of the system's services whenever the server is rebooted. In the **Control Panel > Services** window, go to the **Startup** tab for the Informix Dynamic Server instance(s) hosted on the Windows server. Select the **Automatic** option to automatically start and stop the instances whenever the Windows server is restarted. Note that this option requires you to enter the proper password for the **informix** user account in the password box. If this password changes due to a system-level password expiration timer, you'll need to update the password in this field as well; Windows will not recognize the system-level change.

Basic Instance Access Control and Security

There are a couple of basic instance access and security controls you might consider implementing at the beginning of a new instance. First, think about whether you want all end users to have access to all tables in the database(s) or to just the subset necessary for their applications. Part of this decision hinges on whether end users have open access to the physical server and instances through query tools or open APIs or whether their access is restricted to just a set of specific applications. IDS supports "role" functionality you can use to restrict access to tables based on user ID.

Although roles existed in earlier versions of IDS, you had to specifically invoke them as part of the session initialization for their access privileges or restrictions to be active. In IDS 10, IBM enhanced this functionality with the ability to declare "default" roles for users and to have those roles automatically activated when a user connected. This capability involves use of the new **default** keyword in the role assignment command. Consider the following example:

```
create role hr;
create role it_dept;
revoke all on employee from public;
grant all on employee to hr;

grant default role hr to susan;
grant default role it_dept to melinda;
```

When these steps are completed, any access to the **employee** table is blocked except for those members of the **hr** group. Both Melinda and Susan are granted membership in a role that takes effect immediately when they connect, and, as a result, only Susan is able to read or otherwise modify the data in the **employee** table.

A second consideration is who should be allowed to create databases in the instance. You can effectively block all users except **informix** from creating databases within the instance by setting the **DBCREATE_PERMISSION** parameter in the **$ONCONFIG** file. By default, this parameter is left blank, giving all users the ability to create databases. You can restrict this ability by adding a comma-separated list of the user IDs that should have this permission.

A third consideration is whether you want to control the ability to create UDRs written in C and/or Java. Because routines created in these languages are considered external objects to the data server and can execute, to a degree, outside the control of the data server, they can pose a data and/or operational security risk to the instance or the physical server.

IDS has a mechanism you can use to control the creation of these external routines. It requires two steps. First, make sure the **IFX_EXTEND_ROLE $ONCONFIG** parameter is set to 1 (one) to enable the restriction functionality. Although turned on by default, this function can be disabled by setting the parameter to **0** (zero). Next, grant the **extend** role to those user IDs that need to create or otherwise administer the external UDRs.

This process also controls who can register DataBlades in the instance. Only the **informix** user ID and those granted **extend** role permissions can register a DataBlade.

The suggestions for instance access control and security provided in this section represent only the basics to consider in implementing a new instance. Look for much more detailed coverage of IDS instance and data security in *Administering Informix Dynamic Server, Advanced Topics*.

Terminating a User Session

Every so often, you'll find it necessary to terminate a user's connection to the instance. One of the greatest things about the multithreaded design of Informix Dynamic Server is that there are no individual system processes supporting each user connection that a brain-dead administrator (or user) must try to decipher before trying to kill the one supporting the target session. To be sure, an idiot with administrator or **su** privileges can still kill the **oninit** processes that run the entire instance, but that person had better be prepared to accept the ensuing wrath of users and DBAs.

As with all versions of IDS, if the user thread is listed as being in a "critical section," it should not be interrupted if at all possible. A *critical section* is defined as being that part of Informix Dynamic Server code that handles the completion of a transaction and ensures all disk updates have occurred as requested. Interrupting a thread in such a section will force a rollback of that particular transaction to occur. If the rollback cannot be assured, the instance will immediately shut down rather than allow an incomplete transaction to be marked as completed or rolled back.

You can use the **onstat -u** command to determine whether a thread is in a critical section. Figure 5.24 shows a portion of this command's output. In the sample output, the **X** in the fifth position of the **flags** column indicates that the thread for the **paf** user account is in a critical section of code.

```
IBM Informix Dynamic Server Version 11.10.UC1  -- On-Line -- Up 04:58:01 --
105272 Kbytes

Userthreads
address   flags    sessid   user     tty    wait      tout locks nreads    nwrites
45dee018  ---P--D 1         informix -      0         0    0     43        118
45dee5e0  ---P--F 0         informix -      0         0    0     0         245
45deeba8  ---P--- 5         informix -      0         0    0     0         0
45def170  ---P--B 6         informix -      0         0    0     0         0
45def738  Y--P--D 83        informix -      440a7e18 0    0     0         0
45df02c8  ---P--D 9         informix -      0         0    0     0         5
45df0890  ---P--- 19        informix -      0         0    1     169       2
45df0e58  ---P--- 14        informix -      0         0    0     0         0
45df19e8  ---PX-- 14942     paf      WHSE   1405098   0    1     13        0
```

Figure 5.24: Partial output from an onstat -u command showing a thread in a critical section

Upon instance restart, the fast recovery mechanism can usually clean up the problem, but the user or administrator should still verify that the data being worked on at the time of the involuntary instance shutdown was not lost or corrupted.

The output from the **onstat -u** command lists all the user sessions in an instance. You can obtain more information about a particular session by executing an **onstat -g ses** *session_id* command and querying through the SMI into the instance's shared memory. You can also get a good overview about a user session using OAT, as Figure 5.25 illustrates, as well as through Server Studio.

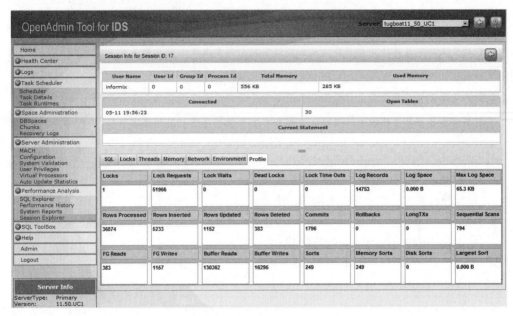

Figure 5.25: End-user thread information from OAT

Short of shutting down the instance, you can terminate a user session by executing an **onmode** -z *session_id* (lowercase "z") command, replacing *session_id* with the value listed in the **sessid** column of the output generated by the **onstat** -u command for the session to be terminated.

There is also a -Z (uppercase "Z") flag to the **onmode** utility that you can use if the session is coordinating a distributed transaction. The discussion of distributed transactions in *Administering Informix Dynamic Server, Advanced Topics* will provide more information about when, if ever, to use this flag.

Summary

In this chapter, we covered most of the more common Informix Dynamic Server administrative functions. Noticeably absent, of course, were the instance performance tuning and general monitoring tasks. I'll discuss tuning information throughout the book as we discuss the instance features or mechanisms that are affected by specific tunable procedures. We'll look at monitoring utilities in greater detail in Chapter 8.

You should now understand the different instance operating modes and be able to bring an instance online or offline at will. You should know the difference between a logged and an unlogged database mode. You should be able to create and drop dbspaces and simple/smart BLOBspaces and understand the differences between regular and temporary spaces. Last, you should know how to move and resize both the physical and the logical logs and be able to terminate a user session safely.

When executing these basic instance-oriented administrative functions, keep the following points in mind:

- Once an instance operating mode change command has been issued and is in progress, you cannot abort or reverse it.

- Changing the database logging mode to an unlogged mode enables major database modifications to occur without worrying about long transaction conditions. You can also convert the table to raw mode to make major data or structural changes to it while leaving the other tables available for end-user operations.

- Any time you make a major change to the instance or the databases it contains, be sure to create a level 0 (zero) backup.

- Create several temporary dbspaces in the instance for temporary tables created by order-by, sort, or user-directed **into temp/with no log** commands.

- Activity in user-created temporary tables will be logged if the database is in a logged mode. You can avoid this logging by creating the temporary table using the **with no log** SQL syntax or by setting the **TEMPTABLE_NOLOG** parameter.

- To help prevent I/O bottlenecks from occurring, move the physical and logical logs out of the rootdbs into different dbspaces.

- Before terminating a user session, use the **onstat -u** command to determine whether the session is in a critical section of code. To terminate a user session, use the **onmode -z** *session_id* command.

In the next chapter, we'll step away from being an Informix Dynamic Server Administrator and look at some of the basic tasks a database administrator would execute in a configured instance. Included in that discussion is the creation of databases, tables, and indexes. I'll cover table and index partitioning, the differences between indexes and constraints, and when indexes and constraints should be used. Last, several SQL commands of note will be briefly introduced.

6

Building a Database Environment

In this Chapter

▸ Database, table, and index creation

▸ Understanding and using partitioning

▸ Proper use of constraints and indexes

▸ Loading data

▸ Controlling and protecting multiuser access to data

▸ New and/or improved SQL commands

Most of the topics in this book relate to the administration of Informix Dynamic Server instances. This chapter departs from that focus a bit to discuss database administration issues and the impact the features and mechanisms of IDS have on administering a database. To that end, we'll look at database and table creation, partitioning, table population issues, and some SQL commands worth knowing about. By the end of the chapter, you should have a solid understanding of the basic tasks involved in creating and operating a database within an Informix Dynamic Server instance.

When performing DBA tasks, I've always preferred to create and execute database administrative commands (or DDL statements) using direct SQL commands executed via the **dbaccess** utility's query language option. You can also perform many of these tasks using the Server Studio graphical tool or other menus in the **dbaccess** utility. In my opinion, however, these alternatives represent a more cumbersome and less efficient way to work.

Even though using SQL commands might require more actual keystrokes to achieve the same result, I feel it gives me greater control and lets me get things done more quickly than the other options. Instead of wasting time moving to and from the mouse and scrolling through various drop-down menus, I can just type the commands I need to run and execute them. As a result, I focus here on using SQL commands.

Ultimately, the method you choose to use for your everyday work is a matter of taste and convenience. Even if you choose to use the graphical alternatives, however, you should become familiar with the command-line utilities. Although it's not as pretty as a graphical tool, I find **dbaccess** more efficient to use because the system incurs less application overhead repainting color-filled screens and managing mouse events. I can accomplish tasks more quickly because I can drive the whole process from the keyboard rather than moving my hands around, interrupting the work flow. Last, should you ever have to access a remote server via a very slow network connection, **dbaccess** will be all you have. For all these reasons, **dbaccess** is my default tool for managing databases regardless of the platform.

Let me begin by briefly introducing the **dbaccess** utility. Then we'll examine how to use this utility to perform the functions that are the subject of this chapter.

The dbaccess Utility

The primary tool that Informix Dynamic Server DBAs use to work with IDS is **dbaccess**. This keyboard-driven utility provides an environment where you, as a DBA, can perform nearly every important function of your job. With the addition of the SQL API in IDS 11, the **dbaccess** utility can serve as the primary tool for an IDS administrator as well.

For the most part, DBAs work using direct SQL commands to the databases residing within instances, although **dbaccess** also has a nested set of menus for database, table, and index creation tasks with some options for partitioning. In the Windows ports of the data server, you can use **dbaccess** from the console of the physical server supporting an instance or through a **telnet** connection to a server. Because **dbaccess** is a data server tool, it is not available in client-oriented tools and utilities such as IBM Informix SQL.

Invoking **dbaccess** from a command-line window, you can pass up to three sets of parameters to the utility. You typically will pass at most two parameters: the database name and possibly a menu and/or submenu choice, in that order. I usually pass a database name and the -**qn** flags to start the utility and have it automatically enter the SQL query option. As evidenced by some of the scripts you've seen thus far in this book, you can invoke **dbaccess** and have it execute SQL commands written in a file stored on the system. For a thorough explanation of all the **dbaccess** parameters, consult the first chapter of the *IBM Informix DB-Access User's Guide* that accompanied your distribution of the software.

The dbaccess utility provides six ring menu options:

- Querylanguage
- Connection

- Database
- Table
- Session
- Exit

Table 6.1 describes the function of each ring. The underlined capital letters represent the character shortcuts used to select the various options.

Primary ring option	Secondary ring options	Tertiary ring options	Description
Table 6.1: The ring menu options of the dbaccess utility			
Querylanguage	New Run Modify Use_editor Output Choose Save Info Drop Exit	Under the **Output** option: Printer New-file Append-file To-pipe	You use this ring to build and execute SQL statements. There are options to save the SQL statements in the current working directory and to change the output location for the results of the statement. The default (nonfile) output location is the window running the utility.
Connection	Connect Disconnect Exit		Use this ring to connect to or disconnect from a database in the current instance. When disconnecting, you must answer a yes/no confirmation prompt to complete the disconnection.
Database	Select Create Info Drop cLose Exit		Use this ring to obtain information about databases in the current instance and to create or drop databases. A series of submenus under the **Create** option are explained in greater detail elsewhere in this chapter.
Table	Create Alter Info Drop Exit		Use this option to obtain information about and to create, alter, or drop tables in the current database. A series of submenus under the **Create** option are explained in greater detail elsewhere in this chapter.
Session			This option displays basic information about the current **dbaccess** session and its connection to the instance.
Exit			This option exits the **dbaccess** utility.

Database Logging Modes

As I mentioned in Chapter 5, changes made to data within a database can be recorded to logs on disk to ensure data integrity in the event of a recovery operation. The creation (or lack thereof) of these records occurs by virtue of setting databases in the instance to use what is referred to as a *logging mode*.

If a database is *logged*, the data server uses the physical and logical log structures of the instance to record changes to instance data. Each database in an instance can operate in a different logging mode. The logging mode for a database is set at its creation, but you can change it at any time if necessary as explained in Chapter 5. An individual user or application can also make a minor logging mode change for their specific session within a logged database environment for the duration of the session by using the **set log** SQL command. Users with correct database/table access permissions can also change the logging mode of one or more individual tables so that changes are not recorded in the logical logs. This capability differs from what we discuss here and will be covered in greater detail later in the chapter.

IDS provides four different database logging modes. Two of them are very similar, differing only in when the logical log buffers are flushed to disk. The first mode, *no logging*, writes very little information to the logical logs. The only records written are DDL statements such as **create/drop table**, **create/drop index**, **create/drop procedure**, **rename table/column, alter table** statements, and so on. The changes to rows affected by these statements are not logged, just the fact that the command was given and the result code returned. An unlogged database environment has a comparatively very high throughput rate because no overhead is incurred for logging, but it has no ability to reconstruct database changes over time in the event of a critical instance failure. Only those changes written to the tables and indexes that survived would be available after restart. Recovery of unlogged databases in an instance is limited to restoring the last instance backup created.

> Earlier in the book, I referred to "catastrophic" failures, and in this section I make reference to "critical" failures. The former term refers to a failure condition that would require a restore from backup. The latter refers to a failure that would cause the instance to abort processing. After a critical failure, the instance can be restarted and successfully complete the fast recovery process.

Mode ANSI logging operates similarly to unbuffered logging (discussed next) but also enforces ANSI transaction-processing compliance. ANSI compliance includes such features and rules as unique owner naming for table references, different defaults for table-level privileges, differences in the update and read capability of cursors, and differences in how character and decimal data types react to data type overflows or definition statements.

Be aware that IDS does not strictly enforce all the ANSI standards in a mode ANSI database environment. If you issue non-ANSI SQL statements against a database in mode ANSI logging, the instance will generate a warning message but continue to process them. Unless your operating environment requires the use of ANSI standards, you stand to gain little from using mode ANSI.

Unbuffered logging and *buffered logging* operate in an identical fashion except for the moment in time when they write the logging records to disk. Both modes capture DDL statements. They also log all DML statements (e.g., **insert**, **update**, and **delete** SQL operations). However, **select** operations are not logged in the logical logs.

There is one exception regarding the logging of **select** statements: **select into temp** statements can be logged depending on instance conditions. The logging of **select into temp** statements can cause problems if an application or a query extracts a large subset of data to manipulate and then discard. The best way to avoid this problem is to create a temporary table in a temporary dbspace by using the keywords **with no log** or by setting the **TEMPTABLE_NOLOG $ONCONFIG** parameter. Chapter 5 provides more information about temporary dbspaces.

The difference between these two logging modes occurs in the writing of log data to the logs on disk. A database that uses unbuffered logging will flush the logical and physical log buffers containing transaction information whenever it commits a transaction. A buffered log database environment will hold transaction information in the logical and physical log buffers in shared memory until the buffer fills, a checkpoint occurs, or the user connection that generated transactions is closed and the transactions have not been written to the logs.

There is one other condition that will force a buffered log database to flush its transaction information. Because only one set of logical log buffers exists in an instance, if an unbuffered database in the instance commits a transaction, the buffered log information will be written out to disk along with the unbuffered log information.

Both of these logging modes have advantages and disadvantages. With unbuffered logging, data integrity and consistency can be guaranteed to the transaction level, even in the event of a critical instance failure. However, because every committed transaction causes a buffer flush to disk, there is increased disk I/O. In addition, because the flush writes information out of the buffer to the logical logs about transactions currently in process, the logical log pages will fill with redundant data over time. The logs fill faster, but they contain less "real" data than is written by a buffered logged database.

When a database uses buffered logging, significantly less disk I/O is involved with each transaction, so the instance will run faster. However, because the transaction information is held in shared memory, it is at risk should a critical instance failure occur. The transaction information not actually written to the logical logs on disk would be lost when the instance's shared memory was released.

As Malcolm Weallans, an IDS administrator and consultant with whom I've rubbed shoulders over far too many years to count, once told me, "What's the difference between using buffered and unbuffered logging? Your paranoia!" Few environments can tolerate the loss of committed transaction data, so I use unbuffered logging in all my environments except for large OLAP installations. These environments have very little transaction-oriented activity, so the need for logging is minimal.

When deciding on logging modes, be sure to take the following factors into consideration so you can choose the mode that's right for your particular environment:

- The volatility of the data
- The required overall database throughput
- The business impact of losing individual transactions
- The ability to re-create individual transactions

Creating the Database

There are two schools of thought regarding where to create databases. One recommends that databases always be created in the rootdbs, while the other advises creating them elsewhere. I subscribe to the second recommendation for several reasons. For one, the system tables for a database are constantly in use as arbitrators of where all the database objects are and what they contain. These tables hold statistical information that the optimizer requires to properly prepare and execute queries. Information in these tables is also used to validate data integrity and other constraints that might be placed anywhere in the database. In other words, these are busy tables.

The rootdbs contains all the overhead tables for the instance and can therefore be in high demand depending on what is happening in the instance. In addition, unless you create other temporary dbspaces, the rootdbs is the default dbspace for temporary tables as well as for tables created to facilitate order-by, sort, and hash join operations.

You'll suffer a performance penalty if you force all these actions to occur in one dbspace. Also, when a table is created, unless the creator includes syntax indicating where the table should be created, it will be created in the same dbspace as the database. As a result, unsupervised table creation in a database created in the rootdbs could fill the rootdbs and have a severe and negative impact on instance operations. My suggestion is that you create your databases on various high-speed drives located throughout your disk pool.

You can create a database in one of four ways: through the **dbaccess** ring menu options, the **dbimport** utility, an SQL statement run (e.g., from **dbaccess**), or the Server Studio graphical tool. When creating a database, you must specify the dbspace where you want to create it and the desired logging mode. Let's look at some of these creation methods in a little more detail.

Creating a Database with dbaccess

The **Database > Create** option in **dbaccess** prompts you through the process of creating a database. After you enter the name of the database, a ring menu appears with options for specifying the dbspace and logging mode.

The **Database > Create > Dbspace** option presents a list of dbspaces in the instance. The default selection is the rootdbs. Choose one of the listed dbspaces, and press the "enter" or "return" key. The **Database > Create > Log** option lets you select one of the four logging modes from a ring menu. The default is "None" (no logging). Exiting without making a selection in either of these screens invokes the database creation process using the defaults for both settings.

When exiting from the **Database > Create** option, you are given the option to either create the database (the default) or discard the information entered and abort the creation process entirely. If created, the new database becomes the "current" or "active" database for the **dbaccess** session.

Creating a Database with dbimport

The second method of creating a database, the **dbimport** utility, creates not only the database but also tables, indexes, and constraints. The utility continues, populating the database with data saved in ASCII format in files saved either on disk or on tape from a source database.

Be aware that Informix Dynamic Server treats a **dbimport** session as a single transaction. If you set the log mode flag to create a logged database within the session and there are a large number of data rows to load, a long transaction will most likely occur and the import will be rolled back. As a result, I strongly recommend not setting the log mode flag when using **dbimport**. Instead, change the logging mode afterward as explained in Chapter 5.

When you create a database using this utility, the selection of a creation dbspace and logging mode is handled via flags to the command. The syntax for these two options is as follows:

```
dbimport db_name -d creation_dbspace
[ -l | -l buffered | -ansi ]
```

The **-l** (lower case letter "l") option specifies that the database should use unbuffered logging, while the **-l buffered** option specifies buffered logging. If you don't use a log mode flag, the database is created in a nonlogged state. If you don't specify a creation dbspace, the database is created in the root dbspace.

Here's a more accurate syntax diagram that includes the most commonly used flags for the command:

```
dbimport db_name -d creation_dbspace
[ -l | -l buffered | -ansi ]
[ -i directory_name | -t tape_dev [ -b blksize
-s tapesize ] [ -f path_to_file ] ]
```

You have two choices when directing the command to find the SQL command file and data. They can be either on disk or on tape. If the files are on disk, you use the **-i** flag and enter the full path to the directory. Note that the actual directory must have the same name, with an **.exp** suffix, as the database you are importing.

If the information is on tape, you use the **-t** (lower case) option and enter the block size as well as the tape length if the export was created with parameters other than those for the **TAPEDEV** device. When exporting a database to tape, you have two choices as to where to store the SQL command file with all the table and index creation statements. It can be written to the tape as part of the export process, or it can be redirected to a file. I generally choose the latter option, for reasons I'll explain later.

For the **dbimport** utility to find the disk–based SQL command file when importing from tape, the **-f** flag and the fully pathed name for the command file is required. If the file was created in what is the current directory when you execute the **dbimport** command, simply enter the file name.

Creating a Database with SQL

Using a SQL statement in **dbaccess** is a quick way to create a database. If you invoke **dbaccess** without specifying a database name, selecting **Query > New** automatically invokes the **Database > Selection** screen because SQL statements must be directed toward a database. Pressing the "interrupt" key (usually **Ctrl-c**) bypasses this screen and brings up the **Query > New** screen. The SQL syntax is pretty straightforward:

```
create database db_name
[ in creation_dbspace ]
[ with log | with buffered log | log mode ansi ]
```

As with the **dbimport** utility, the database will be created in the rootdbs with no logging unless you specify otherwise. For example, the following operation creates a database called **chap6_db** in the **dbs_0** dbspace with an unbuffered logging mode.

```
create database chap6_db in dbs_0 with log;
```

Table and Index Creation and Partitioning

After you've created your database, it's time to create the tables that will actually hold the data. How you build these tables and what methods, if any, you use to preserve the integrity of, or speed access to, their data will affect the overall ability of the database to meet whatever design goals were established. In this section, I explain in detail how to build tables to balance disk I/O loads and enhance performance.

Creating Tables and Indexes

Tables and indexes can be created using the same four methods outlined in the previous section to create databases. Because the **dbimport** utility uses a database schema generated during the export process from a source database, tables and indexes are created using statements found in the **dbimport** command file. If you used the **-ss** (lowercase), or "server-specific," flag during the export process, dbspace placement, table extent sizing, and update statistics information was preserved for use during the import. If you need to make any changes to table placement or sizing before importing the database, you can easily do so by editing the command file (assuming you saved the file to disk rather than to tape if the export was created to tape). Don't modify columnar information (other than column name) in the command file, or you'll risk incurring data type mismatch problems as the data is read back into the table.

Default table-creation specifications call for the table to be created in the same dbspace in which the database was created, to use page-level locking, and to be either 16 KB (Linux/Unix) or 32 KB (Mac OS X/Windows) in size. Two settings, though, can affect the locking mode of tables created without a specific instruction: the **DEF_TABLE_LOCKMODE $ONCONFIG** parameter and its twin, the **IFX_DEF_TABLE_LOCKMODE** environment variable. Either can be set depending on your needs. If you want an instance-wide setting, use the **$ONCONFIG** parameter; otherwise, the environment variable value, set at a session-level, has precedence. The environment variable can also be set in the session that starts the instance, and its value will be in force until the instance is restarted. Setting either the parameter or the variable does not affect the locking mode of previously created tables, only that of standard tables created after you set the parameter or variable.

You can change the lock mode of the table even after it's been created, as I explain elsewhere in this chapter.

Using **dbaccess** ring menus to create and/or partition tables and/or indexes involves using menu options not unlike those used to create a database. The **Table > Create** and **Table > Alter** options bring up a screen where you enter or alter the column definitions through a series of ring menu options. When you create a table, additional options for creation dbspace, extent sizing, lock mode, and partitioning are presented as well.

You can also create constraints and indexes using **dbaccess** ring menu options, but the process is cumbersome in my opinion. Use SQL statements instead.

Figure 6.1 illustrates the process of creating tables through the Server Studio utility.

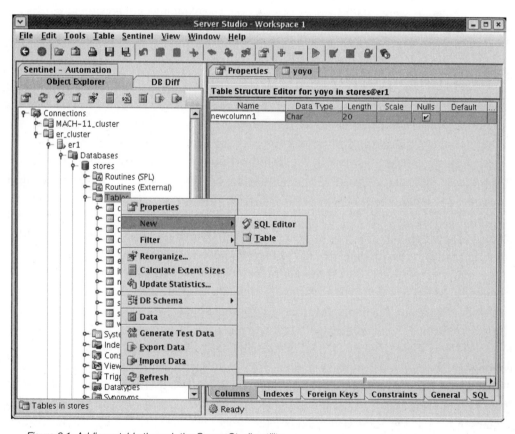

Figure 6.1: Adding a table through the Server Studio utility

In the **Object Explorer** interface, right-click the **Tables** option under the target database, and select **New > Table**. When creating a new table, you'll first be asked for its name and storage location. After specifying these entries, you'll be able to enter information for each column, as you can see on the right side of the window in the figure. Close the tab (or "document") to create the table.

Last, I find using SQL commands to create tables and indexes to be simple and elegant. It's also faster. You can find the syntax rules for these tasks in the *IBM Informix Guide to SQL: Syntax* that accompanied your distribution of the product. For the purposes of this discussion, rather than detailing all the syntax to create tables and indexes I'll focus on the application of the syntax. We won't cover in-depth schema design and normalization here; however, the correct application of partitioning depends on both. I'll use a test table and indexes created with statements such as those shown in Listing 6.1 as examples throughout the rest of the chapter.

```
create table store_sales
( division_no smallint,
  store_no smallint,
  category char(3),
  sales_date date,
  amt_sold decimal(8,2)
) in danube_1
extent size 550000 next size 5500
lock mode row;

create index ix_strsls_div on store_sales (division_no) in idx_space_1;
create index ix_strsls_cat on store_sales (category) in idx_space_2;
create index ix_strsls_dt on store_sales (sales_date);
```

Listing 6.1: Sample table store_sales and associated indexes

There are several things to notice about the syntax. Looking first at the table creation statement, notice the **in** clause that specifies the dbspace in which the table is to be created (**danube_1**). Next comes the table size information. The **extent size** parameter indicates how large the initial disk allocation should be in kilobytes. This is followed by a **next size** value (also in kilobytes) that indicates how much additional space should be allocated should the initial extent fill. As a last step, the **create table** statement sets the table lock mode.

As I mentioned in Chapter 3, correct table sizing is critical to a properly designed and implemented database. Without it, table extent interleaving will occur, causing a significant decrease in performance. The Appendix provides a sizing template you can use to create a reasonable approximation of your table's initial and next extent sizes based on the dbspace page size, row length, and estimated row count.

You cannot specify the size of the index allocation in the index creation portion of the operation, but you can allocate indexes to one or more dbspaces, as is done with the first two indexes in the figure. We'll delve further into the topic of index partitioning later in the chapter.

IDS 10 and 11 introduced new and fairly significant functionality to the index creation process that we ought to briefly discuss before moving on. Before these releases, creating and implementing an index usually required some sort of an outage, whether it was a formal maintenance window or an application outage. The process of creating (or deleting) an index required an exclusive lock on the table, meaning users had to be prevented from accessing the table until the command was competed. In addition, once the index was created, it was kind of a lame duck as far as the optimizer was concerned; the optimizer knew the index existed, but until **update statistics** was run on the columns in the index, it couldn't use the index in preparing an access plan. Executing **update statistics** required time and added to the table's outage.

In IDS 10, the process of adding or dropping an index became a background process in the instance, eliminating the need for a table outage. When an index is created, the rows are read and the index is created in "disabled" mode. Once the build is complete, the instance enables the index in a moment when no user sessions are updating the table. When the command to drop an index is received, the optimizer stops using the index for new access plans, and the index is dropped once all existing sessions have stopped using the index.

With the outage removed, IDS 11 adds functionality to generate optimizer statistics as part of the index build process so the query optimizer could immediately use the new index once created. This doesn't mean that once the index is built, an **update statistics** command is automatically invoked so it takes a while for the optimizer to use it; IDS development was much smarter about the process.

Development realized that as part of the index creation process, the data server has to execute the same operations as an **update statistics** command—it needs to know how many rows are in the table (i.e., **update statistics low**), and to create the bins and overflows, it must understand the distribution of the data in the requested columns (i.e., **update statistics medium/high**). This copy of this information is siphoned off during the static phase of the index build process and given to the optimizer. The net result: At the end of the index build, **update statistics low** information for the index as well as **update statistics high** information for the lead column are available for creating access plans.

Creation of the statistical information is triggered for you automatically; there is nothing you need to enable or set. This information is created when you create an index, alter a table that has an impact on an index, or alter the index's partitioning scheme.

In IDS 11, IBM has provided additional index-oriented functionality that significantly reduces application outages due to index or table creation and modification operations. In earlier IDS versions, if you changed a table or index, or changed a trigger executing on the table, and the table/index was part of a prepared statement or a user-defined routine (UDR) written in Stored Procedure Language (SPL), IDS would return a –710 SQL error when the table/index was accessed. The application would have to re-prepare the statement, or the SPL UDR would have to be re-optimized to reflect the "new" image of the object.

IDS 11 introduces the **AUTO_REPREPARE $ONCONFIG** parameter and its twin, the **IFX_AUTO_REPREPARE** environment variable. A setting of **1** (one), or "on," enables this functionality and causes IDS to check to see whether the table referenced in the statement or the index being requested by the optimizer access plan has changed. If it has, IDS automatically re-prepares the statement or re-optimizes the SPL UDR. Assuming the re-prepare/re-optimization is successful, the statement/SPL UDR will be executed.

Although this new functionality will reduce the number of application errors, a few use cases will still result in a –710 error. First, statements that are executing DDL operations (e.g., **alter table my_tab add col_34 smallint**) will not be re-prepared if the underlying table/index has already been changed once. The statement or SPL UDR will have to be explicitly re-prepared/re-optimized. Second, if multiple sessions are active against a table that a session is changing, it is possible for one or more of the other sessions to return an error, depending on when the shared locks are placed on the table to execute the modification. In this case, retry the statement.

It is important to understand that when IDS re-prepares/re-optimizes the statement, it will do so with the environment settings of the session that triggered the re-prepare/re-optimization. This means that if you've set session-specific parameters such as PDQ priority, **OPTCOMPIND**, and collation sequence, the statement/SPL UDR will be re-prepared/re-optimized using those values. This could have a negative impact on instance operations such as concurrency. The solution is simple: Control who can execute database schema changes and when those changes occur. You can then properly execute any re-optimization commands using the correct environmental settings.

Together, these new IDS features virtually eliminate any outage for administering tables, indexes and index-based constraints.

Additional Table-Creation Options

With IDS 9 and later, you have additional options when creating tables. Let's look at those for a moment.

In the examples so far (and in the rest of the chapter, for that matter), the syntax reflects the creation of tables in *standard mode*. This is by far the most common mode in which tables are created because it supports full transactional integrity, including constraints such as referential keys, data change logging and recovery, and so on. It is the default for all new tables. There is now, however, another mode tables can be created in: *raw mode*.

Raw mode tables function identically to standard mode tables but do *not* support transactional integrity such as logging of data changes, constraints, or keys. In earlier IDS versions, raw tables couldn't support indexes either, but that changed in the more recent releases so that indexes can not only exist but are used when the optimizer evaluates and prepares the access plan against the raw table.

Creating a table in raw mode requires adding the **raw** keyword to the table creation statement, as shown in Listing 6.2.

```
create raw table store_sales
( division_no smallint,
  store_no smallint,
  category char(3),
  sales_date date,
  amt_sold decimal(8,2)
) in danube_1
extent size 550000 next size 5500
lock mode row;
```

Listing 6.2: Table store_sales created as a raw table

You can use the **alter table** syntax to change existing tables to and from raw mode provided they don't have precluding conditions such as constraints.

As we discussed in Chapter 2, Informix Dynamic Server is now an object-relational data server and capable of representing and storing data in new constructs not available to less-capable data servers. One of these supported data types, the **row** type, is composed of multiple attributes, not unlike the way a table is composed of multiple columns. You can use **row** data types when creating a column within a standard (or raw) table, but you can also use them to create new tables or to create subtables that inherit properties of a specific master or *super-table*. For example, the example shown in Listing 6.3 creates two "named" **row** types and then uses those types to create a table containing information for students who might attend a class. Because the **row** types are explicitly defined as data types, they can be used anywhere in the database.

```
create row type name_t
 (fname char(20), lname char(20));

create row type address_t
  (street_1 char(20),
   street_2 char(20),
   city char(20),
   state char(2),
   zip char(9));

create table student
  (student_id serial,
    name name_t,
    address address_t,
    company char(30));
```

Listing 6.3: Using named row types to create a new table

Another way to create tables is as *typed* tables. Listing 6.4 illustrates this method. In this case, the output of a **dbschema** operation against the table will show the same column names and data types as the named **row** type.

```
create row type student_info_t
 (fname char(20),
  lname char(20),
  street_1 char(20),
  street_2 char(20),
  city char(20),
  state char(2),
  zip char(9));

create table student_info of type student_info_t;
```

Listing 6.4: Creating a typed table

The last option when creating tables is to create an additional **row** type that functions "under" the control of a super-type that was used to build one or more other tables. This new type is then used with one of the super-tables to create yet another table. An example will help illustrate this idea.

We begin with the **student_info_t** data type and the associated table created with it in the previous example. Next, we create a new data type with its unique attributes. In this case, though, the new type will operate under the **student_info_t** data type and inherit its attributes.

```
create row type class_enrollment_t
  (course_no int,
   course_date date) under student_info_t;
```

Next, we create the subtable using the new subtype, but in this case the table will operate under the table created with the **student_info_t** data type and inherit its attributes.

```
create table course_enrollment
  of type class_enrollment_t under student_info;
```

Interestingly enough, if you select the **dbaccess** utility's **Table > Info** option and choose either the **student_info** or **course_enrollment** table, you'll see the columns and individual data types. Yet, if you execute a **dbschema** operation against either table, all you'll get in terms of schema is the same syntax that created the tables in the first place, not a "standard" set of table/column definitions.

When one or more subtables are defined in this manner, they inherit all the properties of the super-table, including partitioning, triggers, indexes, constraints, and so on. If changes occur to these types of objects, including adding new columns to the super-table after the subtable is created, the subtable(s) will inherit them as well.

Partitioning Tables

One of the nice features of Informix Dynamic Server is the ability to *partition*, or fragment, tables and indexes. As the term implies, tables and indexes can be broken up and distributed across several dbspaces to achieve performance or design goals. Unlike RAID level 0 (striping), you can apply logical rules to the partitioning scheme, usually resulting in greater query performance and enhanced availability. The latter benefit stems from the fact that with IDS, you can set the **DATASKIP** parameter such that partitioned tables can still be accessible, even if one or more of the table's partitions are on dbspaces that are temporarily unavailable.

You can partition both tables and indexes. As you've already learned, there are two types of table partitioning schemes: round-robin and by expression. Indexes, however, cannot be partitioned by round-robin, only by expression. Using **by expression** commands, you can partition indexes into several dbspaces or into a single dbspace other than the one where the table resides. The other option when creating indexes, as illustrated in the last index creation statement in the previous script, is to leave the index *co-resident*, or in the same dbspace as the table.

Regardless of the partitioning method used, it's important to remember the impact that extent sizing will have on the partitions and their dbspaces. In the table sizing discussion in Chapter 3, I said that tables need to be correctly sized to prevent interleaving of extents and a decrease in performance as the disk heads move all over the place to read the data. In setting the initial and next extent sizes for a partitioned table, remember that all of a table's partitions (except those created using the information in the tip that follows) will be created and expanded with the same settings. As a result, you should set your extent sizes such that when a little-used table partition needs to expand, the amount of space it takes by virtue of the "next size" parameter in the table creation statement does not completely fill up the dbspace in which the partition was created.

Here's a quick tip: There is only one way to create partitions of different initial sizes. You must create two or more "rogue" tables with identical schemas. Create each table with different initial and next extent sizes. Then use the **alter fragment** SQL command (described later in this chapter) to create a new table by "attaching" the rogue tables together. Then use **alter fragment** again to modify the partitioning expressions to what you need. This technique will create a table partitioned into several dbspaces, with each partition having its own unique sizing parameters.

IDS 10 brought a significant change to the creation and administration of partitions: the ability to create several partitions in the same dbspace. In earlier versions, each partition had to reside in a unique dbspace, thus limiting the potential number of partitions. With the new **partition** keyword, it's possible to fully use larger dbspaces for table storage yet still reap the administrative benefits of table partitioning. Using this technique, we could partition the table in the earlier example shown in Listing 6.5.

```
create table store_sales
( division_no smallint,
  store_no smallint,
  category char(3),
  sales_date date,
  amt_sold decimal(8,2)
) fragment by expression
  partition part_1 (division_no =1) in danube_1,
  partition part_2 (division_no > 7) in danube_1,
  partition part_3 (division_no >= 5 and division_no <= 6) in danube_2,
  partition part_4 (division_no >= 2 and division_no <= 4) in danube_3
extent size 5500 next size 250
lock mode row;
```

Listing 6.5: Table store_sales created to use multiple partitions in the same dbspace

Understand, though, that if you create all of a table's partitions in a single dbspace, you'll suffer performance degradation if users are accessing data from all the partitions as I/O is serialized to that single device. On the other hand, if used to remove older data no longer accessed as frequently, you can more easily manage the process.

Round-Robin Partitioning

Rows of data loaded into a table after round-robin partitioning has been applied will be evenly distributed to all the dbspaces specified by the partitioning command in a sequential manner. If the table already contains data when you apply round-robin partitioning to it, that data will not be redistributed. It will remain in place unless unloaded, deleted, and reloaded, at which point the data stream will be treated as new rows being inserted.

Round-robin partitioning has all the weaknesses and strengths of RAID striping. Even with an index to assist queries, the instance must still search all the dbspaces containing partitions of the table for the requested data. That said, depending on the size of the table, partitioning a table by round-robin can still provide an increase in performance over leaving a table in a single dbspace.

WARNING If you partition a table using round-robin, any indexes created on the table must not be created as co-resident. If left co-resident, the indexes will be partitioned like the table, causing the index pages to be distributed sequentially through the dbspaces containing the table's partitions.

The result is a significant performance penalty because the instance must search all the index fragments in all the dbspaces to find the necessary information. At the very least, indexes of round-robin fragmented tables should be left whole but be "detached" and created in another dbspace.

Listing 6.6 shows the SQL syntax to create the test table using round-robin partitioning. Even though the extent sizes used are completely fictitious, I've changed the initial and next extent sizes to take into account data being spread across four dbspaces as well as the relocation of indexes into another dbspace.

```
create table store_sales
( division_no smallint,
store_no smallint,
category char(3),
sales_date date,
amt_sold decimal(8,2)
) fragment by round robin in
danube_1, danube_2, danube_3, danube_4
extent size 95000 next size 9500
lock mode row;
```

Listing 6.6: Table store_sales created with round-robin partitioning

By Expression Partitioning

By expression partitioning occurs when you divide table or index data into multiple dbspaces and/or dbspace partitions based on logical rules. You create the rules using simple SQL statements and can apply them at table creation or any time thereafter.

You can use almost any column in the table in the partitioning expression (I'll note some exceptions in the next section of this chapter). Unlike round-robin partitioning, adding by expression partitioning to a table or index that contains data causes rows to be redistributed according to the partitioning rules. Depending on the logging mode of the database and the number of rows to be moved, this redistribution could cause a long transaction to occur. A row will be moved between dbspaces as well if the row's value(s) in the column(s) making up the partitioning expression change and the row no longer qualifies to be stored in the same dbspace as before the change.

One of the best things about partitioning by expression is that you can leverage it to reduce the number of indexes created on a table and still provide equivalent, if not better, query response. The query optimizer will use the table's partitioning expression when processing queries to eliminate dbspaces and/or dbspace partitions from the read request. If the partitioning expression precludes one or more dbspaces or dbspace partitions from having the requested data, they will not be searched.

Using the schema for our test table, suppose there are six store divisions that might have data. Of these divisions, let's assume only four are really active. We could build a partitioning expression to put each of the four active divisions in separate dbspaces and to put the two less active divisions together in another dbspace. Doing so could eliminate the index on division because the data would already be segregated by division. Listing 6.7 shows what the syntax for this action might look like.

```
create table store_sales
( division_no smallint,
store_no smallint,
category char(3),
sales_date date,
amt_sold decimal(8,2)
) fragment by expression
division_no = 1 in danube_1,
division_no = 2 in danube_2,
division_no = 4 in danube_3,
division_no = 5 in danube_4,
(division_no = 3) or (division_no = 6) in danube_5
extent size 950 next size 95
lock mode rMow;
```

Listing 6.7: Table store_sales created with by expression partitioning

In this case, I set the extent sizes to accommodate the partition containing divisions 3 and 6. The smaller extent sizes will help prevent this partition from overwhelming the **danube_5** dbspace in the event another table extent is required. In the fictitious dbspace design we're using here, the other divisions' partitions are the only table structures in their respective dbspaces, so table extent interleaving caused by small extent sizes is not a concern; the additional extents will simply logically concatenate.

The partition expressions in the examples shown so far have been fairly simple and have used columns of the tables. You can create much more complex partitioning rules by using user-defined routines (UDRs) or secondary access method operator classes.

The first technique is particularly advantageous if your rules need to be more complex than "equals," "greater/less than," and so on. Using UDRs also permits you to declare a partitioning scheme on columns created with user-defined data types. The UDRs used for the partitioning statements can be written in any of the supported UDR languages but must evaluate to a Boolean result and cannot be of a "variant" type or generate output.

Using secondary operator classes in the partitioning scheme is no different from using UDRs from an implementation perspective. The rules differ slightly, though, as you might expect: The operator class must resolve to a B-tree index format. From there, you simply select which options from the operator class you want to use in the partitioning statement.

When you create a partitioning scheme using expressions, it is critical to create the statements correctly to enable IDS to quickly decide where it should store or find data. I discuss this consideration next.

Evaluating the Expression

The data server evaluates partitioning expressions from the top down and from left to right. Needless to say, the expressions should be mutually exclusive, but if they are not, a row will be placed according to the first condition satisfied.

Expression statements can use any column of a table other than BLOB columns. With one exception that I'll explain later (when we discuss dropping partitions), I advise against using **serial** (and related), **date**, and **datetime** data types in expressions because the distribution of rows of these types becomes lopsided very quickly, particularly if the table is not static but is constantly being updated. If you use these data types in partitioning expressions, you'll need to rewrite the expressions on a regular basis to redistribute the rows in the table. In addition, using a **date** or **datetime** data type in an expression slows down expression parsing because the data type must be converted to an integer to be evaluated.

For those cases when you must partition by date, IDS 11 provides new functionality that lets you use all the date-related functions, such as **month()**, **year()**, and **day()**, in your partitioning statement. Thus, it is possible to create a scheme such as the following, which never needs changing over time.

```
fragment by expression month(sales_date) = 1 in tagus_1,
month(sales_date) = 2 in tagus_2,
month(sales_date) = 3 in tagus_3,
month(sales_date) = 4 in tagus_4,
month(sales_date) = 5 in tagus_5,
month(sales_date) = 6 in tagus_6,
month(sales_date) = 7 in tagus_7,
month(sales_date) = 8 in tagus_8,
month(sales_date) = 9 in tagus_9,
month(sales_date) = 10 in tagus_10,
month(sales_date) = 11 in tagus_11,
month(sales_date) = 12 in tagus_12;
```

Using date-related functions eliminates the performance problems I mentioned in the previous paragraph (conversion of standalone **date** or **datetime** data types to integers) because these functions evaluate the date-oriented data types in their native mode.

You can use any of the SQL relational operators to create expression statements, including the **mod()** and **pow()** operator. Using **mod()** in expressions—commonly called creating a *hash* expression—results in an even distribution of rows in a newly partitioned table that already had data stored in it. This technique would, to a degree, simulate robin-robin fragmentation, but there would be some logic that the optimizer could use to locate the desired row(s) within the even distribution of data. A hash expression in a table creation statement would look something like this:

```
      .
    .,
cust_id integer
) fragment by expression
mod(cust_id, 3) = 2 in danube_1,
mod(cust_id, 3) = 1 in danube_2,
mod(cust_id, 3) = 0 in danube_3
lock mode row;
```

You should make your partitioning expression as simple as possible because the query optimizer will evaluate it every time a row is added to or modified in the table. In expressions where you use data ranges to define the partitioning conditions, list the ranges in order of restrictiveness, giving the most restrictive one first. This practice prevents rows from bunching up in the first dbspace. For example:

```
        .
        .,
    region_code smallint
    ) fragment by expression
    (region_code >= 200) in danube_3,
    (region_code >= 150) in danube_1,
    (region_code >= 100) in danube_4,
    remainder in danube_5
```

If we reversed the order of these partition statements and the first range of **region_code** was 100 or larger, practically every row would reside in the **danube_4** dbspace because every row would satisfy the first test. There might be a few exceptions where the **region_code** was less than 100, in which case the row would be stored in the **danube_5** dbspace.

The same logic applies when you use ranges inside individual expression statements. You should put the most restrictive segment of each range statement first since each segment in the range statement is evaluated individually to see if the overall condition is met. For example:

```
        .
        .,
    trans_code smallint
    ) fragment by expression
    (trans_code >= 50 and trans_code < 100) in danube_2,
    (trans_code >= 25 and trans_code < 50) in danube_3,
    (trans_code >= 1 and trans_code < 25) in danube_5,
    remainder in danube_1;
```

Note that both this example and the preceding one use the **remainder** clause in the partition definition. The examples provided by Informix make liberal use of **remainder**, but you should in fact avoid it whenever possible. The reason behind this advice is that the query optimizer always searches **remainder** partitions for each query into the table. Even if the rest of the partitioning expression appears to indicate the dbspace(s) that should have the requested data, the **remainder** clause implies variability in what that partition might contain. As a result, the optimizer always searches remainder partitions sequentially in case a row might be there that matches the query parameters. Depending on the size of the remainder partition, this behavior could hurt query performance.

Rather than use a **remainder** clause, write your partitioning expression so those rows with conditions outside the other defined attributes fall into another dbspace. For example, we could rewrite the earlier sample partition expression as follows to eliminate the **remainder** clause and make the expression more efficient.

```
    .,
    region_code smallint
    ) fragment by expression
    (region_code >= 200) in dbs_4,
    (region_code >= 150) in dbs_3,
    (region_code >= 100) in dbs_2,
    (region_code < 100) in dbs_5;
```

In this case, if there is a row whose **region_code** value is outside of the established range, it will be captured and stored in such a way that the query optimizer won't scan that space unless specifically instructed to do so by the operation parameters.

Partitioning Indexes

In the strictly relational releases of Informix Dynamic Server (i.e., IDS 7 and earlier), index and table pages were intermixed in the table's extent(s). This changed with the release of IDS 9 and later versions, where all indexes are automatically partitioned into their own extent space even if created in the same dbspace as the table. If you want to, you can use an expression statement to partition indexes into one or more dbspaces just as you partition tables. Indexes cannot be explicitly partitioned by round-robin, though.

The simplest expression statement simply creates the index in a dbspace other than where the table was created. For example:

```
    create index ix_strsls_cat on store_sales (category)
    in idx_space_1;
    create index ix_strsls_dt on store_sales
    (sales_date) in idx_space_2;
```

Partitioning indexes away from the tables they reference can significantly improve performance. I always try to put indexes in dbspaces on disks where the other dbspaces contain rarely referenced tables or table partitions. With this type of design, index-based queries are completed much faster because there is no contention in the dbspace containing the table for reads or writes to be completed on both the table and the index.

Just as you need to distribute the busiest tables in a database around the available disk spindles, so also should you distribute the busiest indexes among the available disks.

When moving to a more sophisticated partitioning scheme for an index, you can use any column listed in the index (with the same data-type exceptions mentioned in the previous section) to create the expression. Evaluation of the partition scheme for indexes is exactly the same as it is for tables, so the same best practices from the previous section apply. For example, here's a truly awful, although perfectly legal in terms of syntax, index fragmentation expression:

```
create index major_idx on store_sales
   (division_no, store_no, category)
fragment by expression
division_no > 4 in danube_index_1,
category = "A" or category = "F " in danube_index_2,
division_no <= 4 in danube_index_3;
```

In contrast to the process of partitioning tables, you cannot set extent sizes for indexes when they are partitioned. IDS allocates an initial extent proportional to the size of the initial table extent and that of the data types in the index.

Altering Partitions

You can alter table or index partitions at any time by executing the **alter fragment** SQL command. Using this command, you can completely reinitialize, add, drop, modify, or completely eliminate partitions. You can also use **alter fragment** to join two tables with identical schemas to form a single, partitioned table. In addition, this command lets you detach a table partition to create a new table. This section of the chapter focuses mainly on altering table partitions. Although it is possible to apply the same general principles discussed here to alter an index's partition scheme, I've found it's easier just to delete the index and then re-create it with whatever partition scheme I want.

Chapter 11 of the *IBM Informix Dynamic Server Administrator's Guide* lists the SQL commands whose actions are always logged in the instance's logical logs regardless of the logging mode of the database against which the action was executed. The **alter fragment** command is on this list. The implication is that when altering a table's partitioning scheme, you must make sure you have sufficient logical log space to support the alter command as well as any other transactions occurring in logged databases within the instance. It goes without saying that the values set for the **LTXHWM** and **LTXEHWM** configuration parameters will affect the actual amount of the instance's logical log space that can be used before a long transaction condition is declared. Keep this point in mind when trying to decide whether sufficient logical log space is available for the alter command to be completed successfully. This consideration can be mitigated by turning on the dynamic addition of logical logs. Just be sure to delete any additional logs added once the operation has completed.

In addition, you shouldn't execute the **alter fragment** command against an active table. Because the alter will be executed as a single transaction, it will lock the table in exclusive mode. If any sessions are using the table, the command will abort. Likewise, new connections to the table will fail while the alter command is being processed.

While fragments are being altered, the "double disk space" condition will exist. When you execute an **alter fragment** command, the old fragment(s) will continue to exist in their original state(s) on disk until the new fragments are created. Only after the new fragments are completely built, and any indexes resynchronized, will the original fragments be deleted. This behavior ensures data integrity for the **alter fragment** transaction. In the event of a rollback, the new fragments are deleted and the old fragments reactivated. Before altering a fragment, make sure there is sufficient room in the affected dbspaces to contain the old and new fragments.

Initializing, Adding, or Modifying Partitions

To illustrate the **alter fragment** command, let's use the **store_sales** table created at the very beginning of the chapter. To change it from its original state to a partitioned table, you would use one of the following commands, depending on the desired partitioning scheme.

```
alter fragment on table store_sales
init fragment by round robin
  in danube_2, danube_3, danube_4;

alter fragment on table store_sales
init fragment by expression
division_no = 1 in danube_1,
division_no = 2 in danube_2,
division_no = 4 in danube_3,
division_no = 5 in danube_4,
(division_no = 3) or (division_no = 6) in danube_5;
```

These examples illustrate the use of the **init** keyword to completely reinitialize a multiclause partitioning scheme. You can also use **init** to remove a partitioning scheme. As an example, to change the table back to being non-partitioned, the command would look like this:

```
alter fragment on table store_sales init in danube_7;
```

Unlike the **alter table** SQL command, you cannot mix actions in an **alter fragment** statement. As a result, adding a partition to a table and changing another partition's expression on the same table requires two separate statements to be executed unless you use the **init** keyword to reinitialize the entire partitioning scheme.

For example, to modify a partitioning scheme:

```
alter fragment on table store_sales
modify danube_3 to ((division_no = 4) or
(division_no = 3)) in danube_3,
modify danube_5 to division_no = 6 in danube_12;
```

As shown in this example, you can use this syntax to move a partition's data to another dbspace. The syntax rules are such that you must state the original dbspace for the partitioning expression as well as the new dbspace location for the rows that satisfy that condition. In this case, the first partitioning clause leaves the partition's data in the same dbspace, but the second clause moves the data in the **danube_5** dbspace to the **danube_12** dbspace.

To add additional partitions to an existing partitioning scheme, the commands would look similar to the following. The first command adds partitions to a by expression partitioning scheme; the second to round-robin.

```
alter fragment on table store_sales
  add store_no > 400 in danube_4;
alter fragment on table store_sales
  add danube_6;
```

Adding another dbspace to a table's round-robin partitioning expression will not cause a redistribution of rows already stored. The new dbspace will simply be added to the rotation to receive new rows as they are added.

Similar to manually adding a logical log while the instance is operational, when altering partitioning schemes, you can control where the new partitioning clause resides within the existing statement. You can use the **before** and **after** keywords to add the new partitioning clause anywhere in the partition statement. The one exception is that you cannot add partitioning clauses after a **remainder** clause if it exists. For example:

```
alter fragment on table store_sales
  add store_no > 400 in danube_4 before danube_7;
```

Dropping Partitions

You can drop partitions, but when you do so you must pay attention to where the data that the partition contained will go. By default, the data is placed in the **remainder** partition if one was created. As I mentioned earlier, it's best to avoid **remainder** partitions if possible because of the impact they have on query processing.

This creates a situation where dropping a table partition is not much different from moving the logical logs out of the rootdbs after the instance is originally created. Either you must alter the existing partitioning expressions or add new partitions with conditions that will let them receive rows from the partition to be dropped. After completing this action, you can drop the target partition.

If the new or modified partition conditions prevent a row from the dropped fragment from being stored elsewhere, a –776 SQL error and a –772 ISAM error will result, and the **drop fragment** transaction will be rolled back. Here's an example of a drop fragment command:

```
alter fragment on table store_sales
  drop danube_3;
```

If the table was created with multiple table partitions in the same dbspace, the syntax to drop one of the partitions contains the **partition** keyword as well as the partition name:

```
alter fragment on table store_sales
  drop partition part_3;
```

I like to create a **dbschema** of the table after altering its partitioning scheme to make sure the clauses are in the correct order to properly distribute the data. If they are not, I can execute a series of **add**, **modify**, or **drop fragment** commands to get the fragmentation scheme in the proper order. I can also use the **init** keyword to reinitialize the entire fragmentation scheme. Doing so could lead to a long transaction condition, however, so I avoid executing this type of command except during a maintenance period.

 Another option when trying to make large partitioning changes is to convert the table into raw mode, provided no precluding conditions, such as constraints, exist. This technique eliminates the transaction overhead but does have a recovery implication. After making the changes to the table and changing it back to standard mode, execute a level 0 backup.

Attaching Tables

You can join together two or more tables having identical schemas to create a single table by using the **attach** keyword of the **alter fragment** command. You can create the "new" table using round-robin fragmentation, where each table keeps its own rows or, by using the **as** keyword, you can create a by expression partitioning scheme and execute it as part of the **attach** operation. Creating an "attached" table using by expression partitioning will have an impact on creating additional attachments, as explained in the notes that follow.

Each table that gets attached to another table retains its original extent size parameters. Review these values before attaching to make sure there won't be any space problems in the dbspaces as the fragments grow.

The syntax for attaching tables looks like this:

```
alter fragment on table store_sales
  attach store_sales, midwest_sales;
```

In this syntax, the second (and any subsequent) table listed (**midwest_sales** in this case) becomes the "consumed" table and loses its identity, while **store_sales** is the "surviving" table and keeps its name.

A few notes on attaching tables:

- When attaching tables, remove any constraints that have been created. Trying to attach tables with constraints will generate either an –868 or a –888 SQL error, depending on which table has the constraint.

- Tables with **serial** and **serial8** columns cannot be attached.

- Only non-partitioned tables can be attached (or consumed) to an existing partitioned (or surviving) table.

- Although both tables can have indexes, even on different columns, as part of the attachment process all indexes on the consumed table(s) are dropped before the tables are attached. Only those indexes on the surviving table in a logged database will remain and be applied to the newly expanded table. If the database is not logged, the surviving index(es) are not applied to the newly created table. You'll need to drop and re-create them.

- Triggers, along with views, are dropped on consumed tables as part of the attachment operation. Triggers and views on the surviving table are preserved, but during the attachment process any triggers are disabled.

- You can use the **before** and **after** keywords when attaching tables to create the partitioning scheme in the order you need.

- Tables with named or unnamed **row** data types cannot be attached.

- Partitions of attached tables must all reside in dbspaces of the same page size.

Detaching Partitions

You can separate partitions from a "primary" table to create new, "detached" tables. Provided the primary table was partitioned by expression and, as a result, the ranges of rows in any given partition can be determined, detaching a partition can allow for more focused manipulation of the data in that specific partition.

Depending on how the partitioning scheme was written, detaching partitions into new tables can be an easy way to create historical tables. In this case, using **date** or **serial** data types in the partitioning expression would be of value. You could create a partitioning expression using a date-oriented column from the table. When the data stream is about to include rows with date values greater than a specific date, or when the table grows to a predetermined size, you could add a new partition with a more current date range for its expression. You could then detach the newly inactivated partition from the primary table to create a new table containing "historical" data.

Detached tables inherit any extent size and lock mode parameters given to the primary table. Nothing else is inherited from the primary table. You'll need to create indexes, keys, and constraints on the newly detached table.

The syntax for detaching tables simply requires the name of the dbspace containing the partition to be detached and the new table name. For example:

```
alter fragment on table store_sales
   detach danube_5 div3_sales;
```

If the table contains multiple partitions in the same dbspace, you must include the **partition** keyword along with the partition name as shown:

```
alter fragment on table store_sales
   detach partition part_5 div5_sales;
```

Altering Tables

So far, our discussion of table and index creation and modification has focused on the physical storage of the table or index, looking at partitioning schemes and how to implement them. There is another, bigger aspect to table modification, though: the table schema itself. This topic involves column definitions and order as well as constraints and referential integrity. We'll get to the creation of constraints and referential integrity in a moment. For now, let's look at the other aspect of table manipulation.

You can use the **alter table** SQL command to alter a table's schema and logging mode. Unlike altering a table's partitioning scheme, an operation that must be executed one step at a time, you can make any number of table changes through a single **alter table** command. Excluding constraints, these changes include changing the locking mode; adding, deleting, or modifying a column; changing the data type of a column; adding or removing security such as Label-Based Access Control; adding or removing row IDs or control columns for Enterprise Replication and/or MACH-11, and much more.

Depending on the actions to be taken, in some cases the alter will occur "in-place," while other changes require a complete rebuild of the table. In-place alter operations are completed almost immediately, impose very little in terms of a storage penalty, but can require ongoing monitoring depending on the number of alter operations executed against the table. Non–in-place alters have no monitoring requirement but come with a significant storage and time-to-execute penalty. Most of the non–in-place operations are those that modify a column's data type from one format to an incompatible format—for example, from an integer to a character. Other non–in-place alters include adding or dropping row IDs, dropping a simple BLOB column, or modifying a column that is part of a partitioning clause in such a way that the data the column contains would need to change storage location.

With non–in-place alters, a new version of the table in the target form is created, and data is transferred from the original table into the new table. This occurs with the original table locked in exclusive mode, preventing any end-user access. Once the new table has been fully populated, the original table is dropped. When you invoke this kind of operation, sufficient free space must exist in the dbspace(s) for both copies of the table or the operation will fail.

Most table alterations can occur using the in-place algorithm. When you execute an in-place alter, a new "version" of the table's schema is created, but data at rest is not immediately updated to the new version. When a row is updated as part of a subsequent operation, the schema of that row is updated to reflect the latest version of the table's schema. Figure 6.2 illustrates an in-place alter with schema versioning.

my_table

Row 1	col_1	col_2	col_3	col_4	col_5
Row 2	col_1	col_2	col_3	col_4	col_5
Row 3	col_1	col_2	col_3	col_4	col_5

```
alter table my_table add (col_6 int) before col_3;
insert into my_table values (.....);
insert into my_table values (.....);
```

Row 1	col_1	col_2	col_3	col_4	col_5	
Row 2	col_1	col_2	col_3	col_4	col_5	
Row 3	col_1	col_2	col_3	col_4	col_5	
Row 4	col_1	col_2	col_6	col_3	col_4	col_5
Row 5	col_1	col_2	col_6	col_3	col_4	col_5

```
select col_2 from my_table where conditions = row 2;
update my_table set col_1 = "xyz" where conditions = row 1
```

Row 1	col_1	col_2	col_6	col_3	col_4	col_5
Row 2	col_1	col_2	col_3	col_4	col_5	
Row 3	col_1	col_2	col_3	col_4	col_5	
Row 4	col_1	col_2	col_6	col_3	col_4	col_5
Row 5	col_1	col_2	col_6	col_3	col_4	col_5

Figure 6.2: In-place table alters and schema versioning

The **my_table** table had existing data in it when the **alter table** operation was executed to add a new column. After this operation, two new rows were inserted. The new rows were inserted using the new format, but the existing rows remained in their original form. In the next set of operations, one of the rows was selected, and another had one of its columns updated. The **select** operation didn't cause a refresh of the row's schema, but the **update** operation did, causing the table's data to look as depicted at the bottom of the figure.

If you executed a **dbschema** command against this table, it would return with all six of the columns per the latest "version" of the table. So, how can you tell whether a table has rows that haven't been updated to the latest version, and what can you do to fix that situation if it occurs? The **oncheck -pT** command answers the first part of this question, while "You don't really need to unless you really want to" answers the second. Listing 6.8 shows extracts from two **oncheck** commands. The top part of the listing is from the **my_table** table, and the bottom part is from another table.

```
Home Data Page Version Summary
Version          Count
0 (oldest)          2
1 (current)         3

Home Data Page Version Summary
Version          Count
0 (oldest)          2
1                   3
2                   0
3                  26
4 (current)         3
```

Listing 6.8: Partial output from the oncheck –pT command showing row versioning

As you can see, it is possible for a table to have data stored in different versions, and, for the most part, this state doesn't affect performance at all. When a row in an older version is selected, it will be returned in the most current format, with the instance inserting null values in those columns that haven't yet been added to the row. Although you don't need to worry about refreshing a table's rows to reflect the most current version of the schema, if a large number of schema changes have occurred over time and your applications are constantly querying "older" data, the process of modifying the row's contents before being returned could eventually slow query performance. Fixing this problem is easy; simply update one of the table's columns to itself for all rows, and all rows will be updated to the latest version. For example:

```
update my_table set col_1 = col_1;
```

Before executing this type of operation, you should evaluate the net change to the storage space required to store the table's rows in the latest version to make sure you have sufficient disk space.

Because altering a table executes as a single transaction, you should also ensure you have sufficient logical log space to prevent a long transaction from occurring. With in-place operations, this consideration isn't an issue because no data is immediately affected. Non–in-place operations may more problematic, depending on the amount of data the table contains. The easiest resolution is to execute a different **alter table** command first and change the logging mode of the table to type **raw**.

Raw tables and their functionality were introduced earlier. Changes made to data in raw tables are not logged in the logical logs, so it's possible to make substantial changes without risking long transactions. The disadvantage is that there is no ability to roll back changes or gracefully recover from aborted operations. For a non–in-place **alter table** operation, you can change the table to raw mode, make the required changes, and then return the table to standard mode. Because indexes survive the transition from standard to raw mode (and vice versa), if indexed data is affected, the indexes will change as part of the operation.

The fact that the indexes survive table logging mode changes and will change if needed during an **alter table** operation might or might not be a good thing, depending on the amount of reorganization the index must incur as a result of the table/data changes. If there are substantial indexed data changes, the index updates might significantly slow down the **alter table** operation. My preference when performing major **alter table** operations is to drop the indexes and then re-create them after the operation is completed. In this way, the index is rebuilt once, not multiple times, and is balanced based on the final set of data values.

Constraints, Referential Integrity, and Indexes

Next to the actual creation of databases and tables, maintaining the integrity of the data in the database is the most important responsibility of any DBA. Data integrity can be defined as the correct and accurate storage of data that maintains any interdependent relationships and/or semantic rules defined for the data. Stored procedures, user-defined routines, triggers, and the various types of constraints play a key role in achieving and maintaining this type of integrity from a data architecture and database design perspective as well as in enhancing the performance of database operations. Because they are part of your job, let's look briefly at what constraints and indexes are and how they function. While stored procedures, UDRs, and triggers can play a significant role in ensuring data integrity and enhancing performance, those topics are too broad to receive more than a cursory mention in this book. For more information about using stored procedures, refer to the *IBM Informix Guide to SQL: Tutorial* accompanying your distribution of the software. For more information about writing UDRs, see the *IBM Informix User-Defined Routines and Data Types Developer's Guide* accompanying your distribution of the software.

Stored Procedures, UDRs, and Triggers

Stored procedures are functions written in a combination of SQL and Stored Procedure Language (SPL). Procedures are stored in compiled form within the data server for an individual instance and can be used to maintain security, log actions to tables, manipulate data, or enhance database performance.

Although the general syntax of a stored procedure looks very much like C, the syntax has been fairly limited to basic program control statements such as **if-then-else, while**, and **for** structures. The rest of the functionality in a stored procedure is derived from SQL statements. IDS 11 introduces some major enhancements, with the addition of **loop, while loop, for loop,** labeled loops, **exit when**, and **goto** statements, helping to boost the procedural nature of SPL, although is still is not a full-fledged programming language in the truest sense.

User-defined routines are extensions of the embedded procedures written in SPL. They also encapsulate stored procedures because the procedures were user-created. Generally speaking, though, UDRs refer to procedures written in either C or Java. If written in Java, the UDRs are compiled into a class and then a **.jar** file. When registered in the instance, the **.jar** file is stored in one of the instance's sbspaces. The data server's integrated Java Virtual Machine is used to execute the UDR when it's called.

If the UDR is written in C, you must compile it to create a shared object library and then store it in a directory owned by the **informix** user ID and having **755** permissions. Best practices indicate this would be **$INFORMIXDIR/extend**, but you can put the file(s) anywhere on the system. All C-based UDRs must reside in a single location, though, as specified by the **DB_LIBRARY_PATH $ONCONFIG** parameter.

Stored procedures and UDRs can be called and executed by end-user applications or activity-based triggers also written and stored in the instance. While true for stored procedures, too, it is particularly important that UDRs be written in as concise and precise manner as possible. With the extra functionality those languages provide, you don't want to waste instance processing resources plowing though verbose code. Best programming practices dictate that you include proper error handling and security in the code so functionality or data errors are gracefully handled. Last, any data values returned from the UDRs should be relevant from a business perspective. In other words, the data should conform to the proper domain in terms of data type(s) returned and data ranges.

Because UDRs are treated as objects within the data server, you can use object-oriented programming and administration practices with them. For example, you can create *overloaded* functions. An overloaded function is a function created with the same name as an existing function but with a different data type signature. For example, consider this set of overloaded functions:

```
create function
  convrt_val (in_1 dollar, in_2 aus_dollar) . . .
create function
  convrt_val (in_1 aus_dollar, in_2 euro) . . .
create function
  convrt_val (in_1 euro, in_2 aus_dollar) . . .
```

Each function has the same name, **convrt_val** but has a different signature because it operates on unique combinations of data types. When the functions are registered and require execution, the data server will choose the correct instantiation of the function based on the data types passed as parameters to the function.

One other major difference exists between UDRs and stored procedures: The latter are executed by the CPU virtual processors, while the former can, and should, be configured to run on a specific class of user-defined VP. One enhancement resulting from the object-relational architecture of IDS is the ability to define your own set of user-defined VPs (UDVPs) and link specific data-manipulation operations to them. UDVPs are aliased CPU VPs, so they have the broadest range of functional powers in the instance. But as user-defined rather than instance-defined, they exist within the operating system as **informix** processes, not **root** processes. Even though you invoke the instance as user **informix**, during the process of turning on the data server, a **setuid** to root is executed and the instance processes spawned are owned by **root**.

It would be problematic if UDRs were registered to, or used, the instance's CPU VPs to support their execution. Because of the functionality provided in the C or Java language, nothing prevents a UDR from executing a shell-out to the operating system and performing O/S operations. If a CPU VP supported the UDR, the O/S operations would execute with full **root** authority—a major security concern, particularly if the function wasn't tested carefully enough and misbehaves.

The process of tying a UDR to a specific UDVP is simple. First, you create the UDVP, using either the **VPCLASS $ONCONFIG** parameter or an **onmode** command. Then, in the UDR registration command, include the **class** keyword as follows:

```
create function
  convrt_val (in_1 dollar, in_2 aus_dollar)
class="convrt_vp"
external name
  "/opt/IBM/Informix/11_5/extend/cnvrt_funcs.so"
language C not variant
  .
  .
```

Triggers are written in the same SQL and SPL hybrid language as stored procedures and can have some of the same type of functionality as stored procedures. Users, however, cannot call triggers; instead, the instance activates a trigger when its *triggering action* is executed. For example, you could create a trigger to be executed whenever a row in a table is modified. Or, you could write a trigger to be executed if only a specific column of a row within a table is modified. When the specific action for a trigger occurs in the database, the trigger will execute its logic. Often, a trigger calls a stored procedure or a UDR that can have a more robust set of programming statements.

In earlier versions of IDS, you were limited to one insert and one delete trigger on a table, but you could have multiple update triggers provided the triggering columns were mutually exclusive. That has changed in IDS 11, where you can now have multiple triggers for a single triggering action on a table. Given that you can have two or more insert triggers on a table, you may wonder how you control which one fires first. The obvious first thought is creation order, but you'd be mistaken to draw that conclusion.

Typically, triggers are composed of at least one but potentially as many as three separate components: **before**, **for each row**, and **after**. Certain actions can occur before the triggering operation executes, other actions can occur for each row in the triggering operation, followed by still more actions after the data changes occur. When there are multiple triggers for a single operation on a table, the instance will execute the **before** actions of all the triggers, then the **for each row** actions, followed by the **after** actions. In this way, there is no need to worry about the execution priority of one trigger over another.

Another major change to trigger functionality occurred in IDS 10. Previously, triggers were black-box objects; the triggering action occurred, and you had to wait for the trigger to complete its actions with no insight as to what was occurring. With IDS 10, IBM introduced functionality called *trigger introspection* that lets you use the DataBlade API and specific functions to see inside the trigger as it executes. With this access, it is possible to change trigger data values, capture a value (e.g., the creation of unique identifier for the row to be used elsewhere in the application), or cause other actions to occur that weren't written in the trigger. For more information about trigger introspection, consult the *IBM Informix DataBlade API Programmer's Guide* that accompanied your distribution of the software.

With the amount of functionality that triggers, UDRs, and stored procedures can have, you can enforce business rules at the database level rather than in applications. For example, the specific query statements to determine the gross margin of sales could be coded into a stored procedure or UDR and kept in the instance rather than coded into various user applications, ensuring consistency of results and simplified application code. You could use a combination of an insert trigger and UDRs to ensure that appropriate cross-reference information exists in a number of tables before a row is inserted into a particular table. Or you could use a modify trigger and stored procedures to automatically recalculate the totals of open orders whenever a price is changed on products in a sellable goods table. I trust you get the picture as to what these elements of IDS can do for your application or data.

Constraints and Indexes

You can also use constraints and indexes to enhance query performance, maintain relationships between data elements, and define ranges of values for data. IDS has supported constraints for quite a while, but there still seems to be a bit of confusion regarding them. Some of the confusion no doubt stems from the fact that constraints can appear to be just an index with a funny name in a **dbschema** output. Let's review the differences between indexes and constraints and discuss when each should be used from a design, performance, and data integrity perspective.

The Logical Differences Between Constraints and Indexes

An often-asked question is, "What's the difference between a unique constraint, a primary key, and a unique index?" The answer has two components. First, from a logical database design perspective, each of these items performs a different function. Second, while all three are enforced through an index, there are differences in how Informix Dynamic Server handles and administers indexes as opposed to keys or constraints. From a design perspective, I view constraints, keys, and indexes as follows.

Constraints are used to enforce *business rules* in a table. They fall into two categories. First, constraints can enforce uniqueness of rows. For example, customer name must be unique in the **customer** table, or a combination of customer ID and shipping address must be unique in the **address** table. Such constraints are enforced through the creation of indexes and are referred to as *index-based* constraints. The second type of constraint, commonly called a *check constraint*, is used to specify a range of values for a column or to derive values for columns. For example, the value in the **price** field must be greater than or equal to 50.00 to ensure minimum order cost; or, the value in the **maintenance cost** field must be equal to product cost times 18 percent. These types of constraints are not enforced by indexes; they are enforced by rules embedded in the table's schema.

Keys, both primary and foreign, are another type of constraint. Keys are used to define referential integrity, or data relationships, between tables—also referred to as *parent-child* data relationships. The keys prevent the addition of data to child tables where a valid cross-reference to the parent table does not exist. Keys can also prevent the deletion of data from a parent table when child rows exist in other tables.

Figure 6.3 shows an example of this type of design relationship in an order processing system. A unique customer ID—a primary key—identifies a customer within the system. A row in the **order** table must contain a valid customer ID (a foreign key to the **customer** table) as well as a unique order number—a primary key. The order detail table must have a valid order number (a foreign key to the **order** table) for the order line items the table contains. As this example shows, a table can have both primary and foreign keys. If you were to delete a row from any of these three tables without deleting the related rows, the entire order system would collapse.

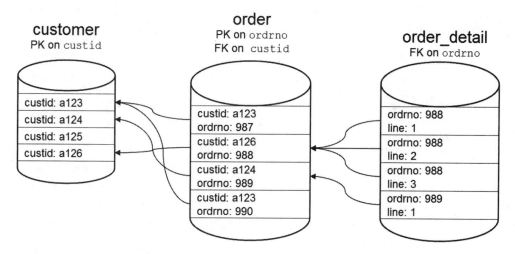

Figure 6.3: Referential keys applied to three tables

Preventing the deletion of a row from a parent table assumes that **on delete cascade** has not been enabled on any child table(s) in the key relationship. By default, IDS will not allow rows from a parent table to be deleted if rows exist in child tables that refer to the parent rows about to be deleted. If the **on delete cascade** SQL statement is added to the foreign key creation command, when a row is deleted from the parent table all the associated rows in that child table will be deleted automatically. You can use this technique to reduce coding overhead in applications.

All child rows must be deleted before the parent row will be deleted. Thus, if you issue a **delete** operation for a row in a parent table and most of the child tables have **on cascade delete** enabled but one does not, the continued existence of child rows in that one table will cause the entire transaction to be rolled back, and no rows will be deleted.

Indexes, as an entity, should be used only to enhance query performance. With this point in mind, I feel that a DBA should *never* allow the creation of a unique index as a standalone entity on a table. If uniqueness is required, it is a business rule and should be coded as a constraint. As I mentioned in defining constraints, some constraints are enforced through index structures. The query optimizer can use the indexes supporting these constraints to enhance performance. This benefit should be viewed as a secondary advantage of constraints rather than the primary reason for their existence. If you need additional query performance outside the business rules, create indexes.

Differences in Enforcement

Informix Dynamic Server enforces constraints differently from indexes. This difference affects how SQL operations operate and, as a result, how applications should be written. As an IDS administrator, part of your job is to help application developers with these kinds of nuances. The functional differences between indexes and constraints are as follows:

- Indexes are enforced immediately, regardless of the transaction state or database logging mode.

- Constraints are enforced at the end of a transaction.

For example, let's assume we have a customer information table with a customer ID column of type **integer** populated with rows numbered 1 through some number. Suppose you decide to keep the first 10 customer ID numbers unused. To make this change, you would execute a SQL statement such as

```
begin work;
lock table customer in exclusive mode;
update customer set cust_id = (cust_id + 10);
```

If a unique index existed on the **cust_id** column, the **update** operation would fail when attempting to update the first row. The **cust_id** of the first row would be changed to 11, but because a **cust_id** of 11 already exists in the index structures, the index would prevent the row from being changed.

If a unique constraint existed on the **cust_id** column, the transaction would be completed because all rows would be updated to their new value before uniqueness was checked. If the **cust_id** column were a parent column to other tables, the child tables would need to be updated first, followed by an update to the **cust_id** column. This would require setting constraints to deferred mode to complete the transaction.

By default, IDS enforces constraints at the end of a transaction. This is not a problem for single-statement transactions such as the **cust_id** update you've just seen. Constraint enforcement changes slightly when multiple statements are executed in one transaction. In that case, constraints are enforced at the conclusion of each **add**, **update**, or **delete** statement in the transaction.

In the case where parent and child tables need to be updated, enforcing the constraint after each statement causes a rollback of the transaction because the data has not been updated in all the tables. You can avoid this problem by using the **set constraints deferred** SQL command at the beginning of the transaction. With constraints deferred, constraint enforcement reverts to the end of the transaction for a multistatement transaction. Setting constraints to deferred mode lasts only for the transaction in which the statement is made. At commitment or rollback of the transaction, the affected constraints are reset to **immediate** mode.

How to Create Constraints

As I noted at the beginning of this discussion, there are two types of constraints: check constraints and index-based constraints. Each type of constraint is created differently.

Check Constraints

Check constraints ensure that data in one or more columns is within a specific range of values. Ranges can be "equal to," "greater than," "less than," or "between" in nature. A check constraint differs from a default value for a column in that the default value condition is triggered only if, during the insertion of a new row into the table, no value is supplied for that column. Naturally, you would want any column's default value to be in the acceptable range of values for any check constraint on the same column.

Using SQL commands, you can create a check constraint in several ways. For example, you could execute a statement such as

```
create table division
(division_no smallint,
  division_name char(16),
check (division_no > 5) constraint chk_div_divno);
```

Or, you can alter an existing table to add a check constraint on a column by executing the following:

```
alter table category add constraint
  check (category_no < 25) constraint chk_cat_catno;
```

Notice that in both examples I explicitly gave the check constraint a "name"—**chk_div_divno** in the first and **chk_cat_catno** in the second. Naming the constraint is not required but is highly recommended. If you don't explicitly name your constraints and referential keys, the data server creates names for the constraints that aren't terribly user-friendly, to say the least. For example, here's a snippet of database schema containing a check constraint created without a name:

```
create table "db_a".division
(division_no smallint,
 division_name char(20),
   check (division_no > 5 )
     constraint "db_a"._110_crom1);
```

By naming your constraints, you can also continue to enforce your own set of naming standards to coordinate the logical and physical models of the database environment.

Index-Based Constraints

As the name implies, index-based constraints require an index of some sort to function. There are two types of index-based constraints: referential integrity keys (both primary and foreign) and unique constraints. A foreign key uses a duplicate index, while a primary key and a unique constraint each use a unique index to support the constraint.

Best practice when creating index-based constraints involves a two-step process. First, build an index that mimics what the constraint's index should resemble; then create the constraint. For example, to create a referential relationship between two tables, execute the following types of commands:

```
create unique index ix_divsn_1 on division
(division_no) in danube_index_1;

alter table division add constraint primary key
(division_no) constraint pk_divsn_1;

create index ix_strsls_2 on store_sales
(division_no) in danube_index_2;

alter table store_sales add constraint foreign key
(division_no) references division constraint
fk_strsls_1;
```

To create a unique constraint on a table, execute the following types of commands:

```
create unique index ix_cust_2
  on customer (customer_name)in danube_index_3;

alter table customer add constraint unique
  (customer_name) constraint uc_cust;
```

When you've finished creating constraints and keys in this fashion, only one index will be created (as explained in the next section). A **dbschema** of the table will show both objects, however. You can also verify this from the **Indexes** and **cOnstraints** options of the **Table** ring menu in the **dbaccess** utility. The utility's **cOnstraints** option will display the different types of constraints that exist on the table and, for referential keys, the table and columns to which a foreign key refers. The **dbaccess** utility goes one step further when displaying information about primary keys; it also displays which table(s) and column(s) refer to the primary key that exists on the table.

WARNING When experimenting with constraints, never delete the index created or used by a constraint, or the information about a constraint from the **sysconstraints** table, in an attempt to remove the constraint. Always use the **alter table** command and the constraint name you entered or the instance created for you when the constraint was created. Trying to delete constraints by any other method will ultimately require restoring the instance from a backup. I know; I tried it. Once.

Partitioning Constraints

Looking at the syntax for creating constraints directly, you'll quickly see that there aren't any provisions for partitioning constraints the way you can indexes. This omission would appear to limit the usefulness of index-based constraints on partitioned tables because the indexes created to enforce a constraint would be created in the same dbspace as the table. For a table created with round-robin partitioning, such a constraint would have a significant negative impact on performance. For check constraints, this is not a problem; there aren't any indexes to worry about.

There is a way around the problem. The only way I can explain it is to say that indexes are "upgradeable" in terms of functionality. An index can be turned into a constraint, but the opposite is not true. This means you can, for example, create a unique index for a table with some sort of partitioning scheme. Then, you can execute an **alter table** statement and add a unique constraint on the same columns used to create the unique index. The instance will take the existing unique index and upgrade (or promote) it to act as a constraint.

This is why I use the two-step process to create index-based constraints as shown in the previous section.

As illustrated in that section, the name of a constraint created in this manner will not be the name of the index. You'll need to name the constraint or let the instance generate a name for you. After upgrading a unique index to a unique constraint or a primary key, if you look at the table information from **dbaccess**, only the original index with its original name will be shown. However, a **dbschema** of the table will show both the index and the constraint statements.

As I mentioned in the previous warning, even though you created the original index, do not simply delete the index to drop the constraint created by upgrading the index unless you want to restore from backup. Drop the constraint first; then you can drop the index.

This method of partitioning constraints works for all index-based constraints. You can create a primary key constraint created by upgrading a unique index, while you can create foreign keys from duplicate indexes.

I highly recommend this method of creating constraints even if the tables or indexes are not partitioned. It yields a database schema that can easily be stripped of indexes and constraints in preparation for exporting a database to another system. I'll explain this benefit in greater detail shortly.

Populating the Database

Once you've built a database, created and partitioned tables, and established and enforced business rules through the use of constraints, UDRs, and stored procedures, you need to insert some data. Several utilities help you perform this task, each with advantages and disadvantages that will influence your choice in any given situation. For some utilities, such as the High Performance Loader, only a cursory overview is possible here. I encourage you to seek more information in the IBM Informix manuals that accompanied your distribution of the software.

Dbimport

We discussed the first utility, **dbimport** in the database creation section of this chapter. The companion utility to **dbexport**, **dbimport** is used to create a complete database environment and then populate it by loading from ASCII flat files containing data for each table in the database. Because the database itself is created as part of the import, there are no issues with allowing or denying users access to the database while the utility runs. The database is locked in exclusive mode during the import (and export) and, as I mentioned before, should be created without any logging to prevent a long transaction from occurring. You can then switch the logging mode as explained in Chapter 5.

If the data output by the **dbexport** utility is to be stored on tape, it is possible to save the command file to disk rather than to tape. You can make minor edits to the **dbimport** command file as long as you don't change the table order in the file, materially modify the data types within a table (e.g., character to integer), or add or delete columns. These types of changes will undoubtedly cause failures when you load the data files.

Recent versions of IDS feature an updated command file format that makes the utility more pleasant to use. In the past, all the DDL statements for a table were executed and then the table was loaded with data. If you had a table with several constraints and/or indexes, unless you manually edited the command file to remove the index and constraint creation statements, the utility executed loads into indexed tables, which took a long time to be completed. In the current versions of the data server, index, index-based constraint and associated **alter table** commands come at the end of the command file, executing after the tables have been loaded. As a result, you can add or delete indexes and constraints from the file without affecting load times.

Creation statements for triggers and stored procedures also appear at the end of the import command file. As a result, there isn't any overhead resulting from the execution of triggers and stored procedures during table loads. In a practical, real-world sense, you really wouldn't want these database objects executing anyway, because the data being imported has already been processed by the stored procedures in the original database. The data should have the correct "value" already.

The SQL load Statement

The SQL **load** command provides the least amount of flexibility of all the utilities discussed here. You can use it for small to medium data sets in a logged database or for large data sets in an unlogged database or raw table. The **load** command reads a delimited ASCII flat file and simply loads it in column order into the target table. Depending on the number of indexes on the target table, data does load fairly quickly using this command. Users can access the table while a load is occurring unless the **load** statement was written to lock the table in exclusive mode.

There are a couple of potential problems when using the **load** command. In a logged database, the system handles the load as a single transaction. Depending on the amount of data to be loaded, a long transaction could occur. You can lock the table in exclusive mode to get around the creation of an excessive number of locks to support the load, but doing so eliminates any other user activity from occurring in the table.

Another problem is that no mechanisms exist to handle exceptions in the data file. If, for whatever reason, a field to be loaded into a numeric column contains a character, the data server will catch the data-type conversion error and simply abort the load. The utility does indicate how many rows were loaded, which makes it easier to find the problem row in the source file.

The dbload Utility

The **dbload** utility offers you more flexibility when working with ASCII flat files than the SQL **load** command or **dbimport**. You can perform the following functions using **dbload**:

- Load delimited or fixed-length, non-delimited files
- Load columns out of table order
- Skip *n* rows of the load file before beginning to load
- Write bad rows out to a log file for fixing while continuing the load process
- Load ASCII simple BLOBs
- Issue a **commit work** statement every *n* rows to prevent long transactions from occurring
- Substitute a value instead of **null** into a column with a **not null** check constraint

A command file controls the **dbload** utility and its functionality. This file contains the pathed name of the file to be loaded, the target table, the column order, and manipulation statements. You can also specify how many error rows can be encountered before the load process is aborted.

The **dbload** utility does not require a table to be locked in exclusive mode because it can send a **commit work** statement at predetermined intervals during the load process. However, it will suffer the same performance problems as the **load** command if indexes exist on the table.

The onload Utility

The **onload** utility is one of the fastest utilities to load data. The companion to the **onunload** utility, it reads in a binary copy of the table's data from tape and places the table and indexes in the requested dbspaces. You can set parameters for dbspace creation, to rename indexes, to rearrange the partitioning scheme, or to specify the dbspace(s) to hold index partitions.

The **onload** utility executes as a single transaction but locks the table in exclusive mode so that concurrent user access is not allowed. Because the data is written out in a format not unlike that of the **ontape** backup utility, you cannot alter or modify the data or its load order in any way.

The utility preserves original extent sizing information as well as the total table extent size at the time of export. This makes **onload** an excellent tool to use when trying to decrease the number of table extents in dbspaces. Simply use the **onunload** utility to copy all the tables out to tape, drop the tables, and then reload them using the **onload** utility. When you're done, all the tables will occupy a single logical extent within the dbspaces.

The High-Performance Loader

I'll make only the briefest explanation here about this next utility. For more information, consult the *IBM Informix High-Performance Loader User's Guide* manual that accompanied your distribution of the software.

The High-Performance Loader (HPL) is the fastest of all IDS's load and unload utilities. With the HPL, you can extract or load just a subset of data stored on disk or tape, modify the data as it is loaded or unloaded, convert formats, and more. Whereas the previously discussed utilities and commands work only with one file at a time, the HPL can use multiple files and/or tapes simultaneously, permitting parallelized operations.

The utility itself is composed of several components:

- **ipload**—A Linux/Unix X-based utility to provide a graphical interface to the utility. You can manage all aspects of creating and administering an HPL "project" through this interface if desired. The Windows ports of IDS have a native Windows GUI. As this book went to press, this utility was not available for Mac OS X ports.

- **onpload**—The actual HPL executable that loads or unloads the data. You can call it directly and pass the required parameters to execute a job if desired.

- **onpladm**—A command-line interface to define and manage all aspects of an HPL project. You can invoke a job through this interface as well.

- **onpload**—The system database created to store all aspects of an HPL project. It is automatically created the first time any of the user interfaces are called.

- **plconfig**—The HPL configuration file, a template for which called **plconfig.std** is stored in **$INFORMIXDIR/etc**. The configuration file contains parameters that control the power and parallelism of the utility.

When loading data, the HPL can execute jobs in either *deluxe* or *express* mode. In deluxe mode, all indexes, constraints, triggers, and so on are active and in force as if the user were executing a **load** operation. Large jobs in this mode can cause long transactions to occur, so best practices indicate setting *commit points* where blocks of loaded data are marked as committed in the instance so the logical log records can be advanced. During deluxe loads, the tables involved are fully accessible to end-user operations.

In express mode, the table (or tables) is locked in exclusive mode, and all indexes, constraints, and other objects are disabled. The HPL converts the table itself to raw mode by the HPL, and the load then occurs. When the load is completed, the table is converted back to standard mode. Needless to say, express loads are executed much faster than deluxe mode jobs, but a backup of the affected dbspaces is required at the end to preserve the data for recovery.

As Figure 6.4 illustrates, HPL activities and the configuration and controls for those activities are organized into projects and subsidiary structures. Multiple projects can exist within an instance, but each project has its own set of discrete jobs (which load, unload, and/or transform data) with definitions for all aspects of the operation, such as where to find the source files or tapes, the mapping of input to output elements, query and other SQL

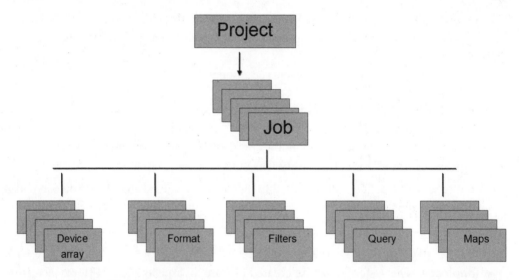

Figure 6.4: HPL project organization

operations to transform data, and so on. Each element is defined individually, although some elements can be shared across jobs and possibly across projects.

Once you've defined all the elements, you simply invoke a job using syntax similar to either of the following examples:

```
onpload -p TPC -j TPCLineitem -fl
onpladm run job TPCLineitem -p TCP -fl
```

The Server Studio graphical utility includes a nice graphical interface to managing and executing HPL operations. I strongly encourage its use when working with the HPL. It is significantly better than the **ipload** interface.

Once started, the HPL is incredibly fast. Properly configured systems can load millions of rows per minute in express mode with the HPL.

Flat File Loads Through 4GL or Other Application Languages

If none of the preceding options meet your needs, you can write an application to load data in the language of your choice. IBM Informix has a "legacy" programming language called IBM Informix 4GL that is quite powerful, although it's limited to a character-based user interface. This isn't a bad thing—keyboard-driven applications are much, much faster to use than graphical ones, which require moving back and forth to and from the mouse to accomplish anything.

In many respects, loading tables through 4GL applications doesn't really qualify for inclusion in the list of utilities we've covered. Informix 4GL was not intended to be used for creating data-load programs, although in using it you can create very robust error handling and data manipulation functionality. I mention it because there are still a good number of users with 4GL applications (either purchased from vendors or homegrown) still in operation, and it's always good to see that a viable product is not being forgotten. Second, I include it to show off a little piece of 4GL functionality buried in the product with only a cursory mention in the *IBM Informix 4GL by Example* manual.

A friend of mine, who was a very accomplished application developer using 4GL and other languages, was reading the *Example* manual and happened across two commands included in the 4GL demo distribution libraries (**$INFORMIXDIR/demo/4glbe**) that enable a 4GL application to read data in directly from ASCII flat files. The first command, **fglgets()**, takes a file name as a parameter, opens the file if it's not already open, and returns the first row of the file; if the file is already open, the command returns the next row of the file. The second command, **fglgetret**, checks the return code of the C language **pop** command that actually gets the row out of the file.

The best way to explain how it all works is to show a small snippet of code (Listing 6.9) with the commands implemented. I'll follow with some additional comments.

```
database my_test_db

main
  define fname varchar(30)
  define in_str varchar(255)
  define nrecs integer

## please be aware that no error handling is
## included in this snippet of code.

  prompt "Please enter pathed file name to load: " for fname

  let fname = fname clipped

## open file and get first row
  call fglgets(fname) returning in_str

## check the status of the open and "pop"
  while fglgetret() = 0
    let nrecs = nrecs + 1
    if nrecs mod 100 = 0 then
       display "Loading row: ", nrecs using "###,###" at 8,2
    end if
    call process_row(in_str)

## continue to get rows until EOF
    call fglgets(fname) returning in_str
  end while ## fglgetret = 0

end main
```

Listing 6.9: A simple 4GL application to load data from a flat file

Some notes on using a 4GL to load ASCII flat files:

- To use **fglgets()** and **fglgetret,** you'll need to compile the **fglgets.c** file to object form and include it with any other standard libraries you reference in makefiles.

- The **fglgets()** code opens but does not close the file.

- The **fglgets()** command travels only down the file. You cannot "rewind" the pointer in the file as you can in C.

- The maximum string length that can be read is 256 bytes.

- The Informix code lets only eight files be opened and processed at a time before you have to terminate the application using the library and restart it. The **MAXOPEN** parameter in the **fglgets.c** code controls this limit and can be changed if you desire.

- Each time **fglgets()** is invoked with a new file name, it is counted toward the MAXOPEN total, even if the file does not exist or cannot be opened.

- If the total number of files opened exceeds **MAXOPEN,** the Informix code does not return an error message to the application. It does not return any data either. From the perspective of the application, it will appear as though the file is empty. As a result, you'll need to either increase **MAXOPEN** or count the number of times an attempt is made to open a new file and stop any further attempts to open a file once **MAXOPEN** is reached.

- Placing the call to **fglgets()** in a called function has no effect on the **MAXOPEN** counter. The counter acts at an application level rather than a module level.

Concurrency and Isolation Levels

Once you've built and populated a database, protecting and controlling multiuser access to data becomes important. You implement the protection part through the use of locks in the Informix Dynamic Server instance. The control part is controlled largely by the application and determines how the instance implements the different types of locks as well as how it responds to application requests for locked data. The logging mode of the database does have an impact on both of these aspects, as I'll explain shortly.

The term *concurrency* refers to the simultaneous accessing of data by multiple users. *Isolation levels* refer to the impact a database action request should be allowed to have on other concurrent action requests. Obviously, the way these two concepts are designed and implemented is highly integrated and reciprocal. A very restrictive isolation level will significantly decrease the amount of concurrent access to the database. Depending on the operation in question, a demand for a large number of concurrent users will necessitate several levels of isolation control being used in an application, or it will require a very low isolation level or very small, tightly written transactions in the application. New functionality in IDS assists with multiuser concurrency in high isolation or potential deadlock situations.

Lock Types and Modes

To understand both issues, you must first understand how Informix Dynamic Server handles data locking and how locks can be placed. A lock can be placed on an entity as small as an index key value or as large as an entire database.

IDS has four lock types, which are described in Table 6.2.

Table 6.2: Informix Dynamic Server lock types	
Lock type	**Description**
Exclusive	All access to the data element is denied to users other than the user locking the element in this mode. The lock is placed at a row level by **update** or **delete** SQL operations and at a table or database level by user command.
Shared	A shared lock is placed by read operations to make sure data elements have been committed to disk. You can set shared locks to prevent data elements that are being read from being deleted or changed while the elements are in use by the application requesting the read.
Upgradeable or promotable	This is a shared lock that can be modified into an exclusive lock when requested. This is the type of lock used by update cursors.
Byte	A byte lock is placed on rows when the action affects columns of type **varchar**.

Users can, through SQL statements, place a shared or exclusive lock on tables or databases. Informix Dynamic Server itself will invoke an exclusive table lock if major DDL commands such as **alter**, **rename**, **drop table**, or **rename column** are executed. The instance releases its locks as soon as the action is completed, provided the user does not preface the DDL action with a separate **lock** statement. User-initiated locks remain in place for the length of the transaction in a logged database; in an unlogged database, such locks remain in place until manually removed.

Understanding and Setting Isolation Levels

An isolation level affects how the database handles read requests. These levels have the greatest impact on concurrency, or multiuser access to data. IDS provides four isolation levels, described in Table 6.3.

Table 6.3: Informix Dynamic Server isolation levels	
Isolation level	**Description**

repeatable read	The most restrictive level, **repeatable read** locks all rows read with a shared lock for the duration of the entire transaction. Locks are also placed on rows read because of a non-indexed read or sequential scan to determine eligibility for the **select** statement.
	    It's important to note that these shared locks are placed only if there is an explicit transaction surrounding the read. Simply setting the isolation level to **repeatable read** and then executing a **select** statement does not invoke the protection this level provides. Without an explicit transaction in place (i.e., **begin work . . . commit work**), other database threads can alter the rows selected.
	    This is the default isolation level for mode ANSI databases.

Isolation level	Description
	Table 6.3: Informix Dynamic Server isolation levels (Continued)
cursor stability	Similar to the **repeatable read** isolation level, **cursor stability** places shared locks on rows read by a cursor. However, once the cursor statement requests the next row of data, the lock on the previous read row is released — provided, of course, that the row was not altered. As with **repeatable read**, the shared lock is placed only if the cursor is inside an explicit transaction. This level, although an SQL statement can request it, is ineffective in ad hoc SQL sessions such as those invoked through IBM Informix SQL, **dbaccess**, and similar tools; it applies only to cursors declared in applications like those created in formalized programming languages such as C or Java.
committed read	The default level invoked by a logged database except for mode ANSI, **committed read** isolation ensures that rows read and returned to the application have been committed. The instance checks to see whether a shared lock could be placed on the row in question before it is returned to the application. It does not actually lock the row, so **committed read** acts like dirty read in terms of speed. The committed read isolation level does not prevent data being read from being changed by another database thread, even if the read is inside an explicit transaction. All a **committed read** isolation prevents is the return of data locked for update, insertion, or deletion. This can block other users from completing their work, particularly if the updating application doesn't finish its work in a reasonable amount of time. The **last committed** keywords, introduced in IDS 11, mitigate against this risk.
dirty read	The least restrictive level, **dirty read** isolation allows all rows, whether committed or not, to be returned to the application. This includes rows whose values could change because of an **update** operation and newly inserted rows in a table that have not been committed. The risk of requesting data at this isolation level is that rows returned could change or be deleted either because of a transaction rollback or the actions of another user. IDS 11's **last committed** keywords mitigate against this risk.

To set any of these levels, use the **set isolation** SQL command. You can use various isolation levels throughout an application, depending on the integrity requirements of the data being read or on restrictions you might need to impose while the application runs a particular piece of functionality.

Where non-changing reference data is concerned, dirty reads are acceptable. When requesting more critical pieces of data, consider using **cursor stability** or **repeatable read**, depending on the need for concurrent access to the data and to prevent the data from changing due to outside actions while the application is using it.

Setting an isolation level, while good for the session that requested it, can prevent other sessions from accessing the same data. For example, assume session A starts a transaction to update one or more rows in a table. Concurrently, session B tries to read one or more of the rows. Because the database is in a logged mode, both sessions are using **committed read** isolation, and session B receives a −107 SQL error from the data server instead of the data it was expecting. Before IDS 11, common application practice was to code queries with **dirty read** isolation so they always got a result back, hoping that by the time the second session was ready to make changes, the first session would be done with the row and it could be updated by the second session. This practice opened up another possible error: Imagine session B receives an interim value of the data, and based on that value the application executes certain functionality. While session B is doing its work based on the value it received, session A rolls back the transaction, returning the data values to their original state. Session B would thus have done work based on invalid data.

Another classic problem in this area is that of deadlocks. Session A locks row 2 for update and then tries to lock row 450. Concurrently, session B locks row 450 for update and then tries to lock row 2. Because neither session can get a lock on the next row it needs, they both hang until the deadlock timeout value is reached and both transactions are rolled back.

IDS 11 introduces the **last committed** isolation level modifier, which can be used with both the **dirty read** and the **committed read** isolation levels. Set through an environment variable, with an SQL command, or in the **$ONCONFIG** for all sessions, the new modifier instructs the instance to return the last committed value of the locked row to the calling session so it can continue its processing. So in the first example, session B would get the original committed value of the row that session A had locked for a potential change. Session B can accurately and reliably use that data value because it is "committed" data, not in-flight, from a data integrity perspective. In the example featuring a deadlock, both sessions would get the original committed value of the second row they want so they can continue processing.

Some SQL Statements of Interest

With each release of Informix Dynamic Server, IBM introduces new SQL functionality. The *IBM Informix Guide to SQL: Syntax* and *IBM Informix Dynamic Server Administrator's Guide* manuals that accompanied your distribution of the software explain all the changes, but I'd like to briefly cover a few statements here. We'll look at changes to some other statements, such as to the **update statistics** command, either elsewhere in this book or in *Administering Informix Dynamic Server, Advanced Topics*.

Violations and Diagnostics, Constraint and Index Enabling and Filtering

You have two choices on how to handle any errors due to updating or inserting rows into tables with unique indexes or index-based constraints. The first is to trap for the **sqlca. sqlerrd** codes in your applications, determine what error occurred, and then decide what should be done to correct the problem. Generally speaking, the offending row is kicked out to a holding table for manual intervention and processing.

The second option is to let the data server do this work for you, decreasing the amount of error handling code required in the application. To accomplish this, you set up *violation* and *diagnostic* tables for specific target tables and then turn on the error-handling features of unique indexes and index-based constraints.

Executing the **start violations table** SQL statement against a particular table causes the instance to create two tables partitioned like the target table. One table contains violation information; the other contains diagnostic information. You can set the names for these two tables if you like, but the default names are the target table name with **_vio** and **_dia** appended, respectively. You can also set the total number of rows these tables will hold.

The schema of the violation table is a duplicate copy of the target table with a couple of extra columns. These columns include a numeric counter, an abbreviation of the operation that resulted in the failure, and the user ID of the person executing the operation that failed.

The diagnostic table has a numeric column that holds the numeric cross-reference to the row in the violation table. This column and the column in the violation table are not linked by a primary-foreign key relationship, however. The diagnostic table also has a column that indicates whether an index or constraint error occurred, the name of the index or constraint that was violated, and the owner of the constraint or index.

With these two tables in place, the next step is to activate the object mode of the constraints and indexes on the table, as well as the error option. The term *object mode* simply refers to the operating state of the object and was discussed in general terms earlier in the chapter. In this case, the "objects" I'm referring to are only indexes and constraints. You can set object modes globally for all indexes or constraints on a table or individually on a constraint-by-constraint basis. Table 6.4 describes the three object modes.

Table 6.4: Constraint and index object modes	
Object mode	**Description**
enabled	The instance recognizes the existence of the index or constraint and factors those objects into its processing. Processing stops whenever a requested action (**update**, **delete**, or **insert** operation) fails. This is the default mode for an index or index-based constraint.
disabled	The instance behaves as if the index or index-based constraint does not exist.
filtering	The instance acts as if the indexes or index-based constraints are in **enabled** mode; however, only those rows that satisfy the requested action are successfully processed. Those that fail are copied out to the violation table for the target table, with the appropriate information inserted into the diagnostic table as well.

You can specify what the instance sends an application if a constraint or index is in **filtering** mode and an operation fails. This act is called setting the *error option*. You can have the instance return an error code to the application (**with error**) or not (**without error**). The application logic and follow-up procedures will determine the most appropriate option to take in any given environment.

By way of example, to implement this functionality on a table called **orders** with a unique constraint on the **order_num** column, you would execute the following commands:

```
start violations table for orders;
set constraints for orders filtering without error;
```

The violation and diagnostic tables created by these commands should not be deleted until the object mode has been changed back from **filtering** mode to **enabled** or **disabled** mode and the **stop violations** SQL command has been issued. At this point, you can drop the violation and diagnostic tables like any other normal table.

I should also note that while duplicate indexes and triggers can be placed in **enabled** or **disabled** mode by using the **set** SQL command, they cannot be put in **filtering** mode, nor will any actions pertaining to them be logged in the violations or diagnostic table.

Default Roles

Over the years, Informix Dynamic Server has added more and more functionality to secure access to instances or to data inside them. Roles have been available for some time as one method of limiting access to tables based on identity. Until recently, though, the user was required to manually invoke a role in order for its access privileges to be in effect. This requirement kind of defeated the purpose of roles and made them easy to circumvent. Recently, however, functionality has been added whereby a DBA can set up roles so that they are automatically applied when the user ID connects to the instance.

To enable this functionality, add the **default** keyword to the command as shown here:

```
grant role it_dep to jerry;
grant role hr to susan;
grant default role payroll to marilyn;
```

Iterator Functions and Derived Tables in the from Clause

Several recent IDS releases have featured functional enhancements to the **from** clause of the SQL statement. In truth, they have been extensions of the same general concept: the ability to use derived tables.

The first enhancement in this area was the ability to use an iterator function. The *IBM Informix DataBlade API Programmer's Guide* (page 15-4) defines an iterator function as "a user-defined function that returns to its calling SQL statement several times, each time returning a value. The database server gathers these returned values together in an 'active set.'" An example of such a function would be a Fibonacci sequence, which is defined as

$$F(n) = F(n-1) + F(n-2) + F(n-3) \ldots$$

where $n > 1$.

With an iterator function in the **from** clause, IDS takes the values returned from the function (the active set) and treats them as though the set was a table whose values could then be evaluated by the **where** clause of the statement.

Continuing this type of functionality, IDS 11 provides full support for *derived tables*, or the use of an additional **select** clause within the **from** clause. This capability is best illustrated with a series of examples, shown in Listing 6.10.

```
select sum(virt_col1) as sum_vc1, vc2
  from (select col_1, col_2 from tab_1)
    as virtual_tab(virt_col1, virt_col_2)
  group by vc2;

select * from
  ( (select col1,col2 from tab_3) as
       virt_tab_3(vcol_31,vcol_32)

  left outer join
    ( (select col1,col2 from tab_1) as
         virt_tab_1(vcol1,vcol2)

       left outer join
         (select col1,col2 from tab_2) as
            virt_tab_2(vcol3,vcol4)
          on virt_tab_1.vcol1 = virt_tab_2.vcol3 )
      on virt_tab_3.vcol_31 = virt_tab_2.vcol3 );

select *
  from table(fib_function(5))
    as virt_t(a), tab1 t where virt_t.a = t.x;
```

Listing 6.10: Creating derived tables in IDS 11

With this functionality, you can execute very powerful and intuitive SQL operations without having to create and use temporary tables.

Date and Date-Time Functions

In addition to letting you use date and date-time functions in the partitioning scheme, IDS 11 introduces some new date and date-time manipulation functions.

The **round()** function returns the desired date-oriented precision of the **date** or **datetime** data type passed to the function. The options for precision include nearest year, month, day of month, day of week, hour, or minute. For example, suppose a row in a table has the value **2008-02-26 14:30:1213455** in its **datetime** field. The following SQL statements would return the results shown.

```
select round(col_dt, 'YEAR') from mytab;
(expression)  2008-01-01 00:00

select round(col_dt, 'DD') from mytab;
(expression)  2008-02-27 00:00

select round(col_dt, 'HH') from mytab
(expression)  2008-02-26 15:00

select round(col_dt, 'MI') from mytab
(expression)  2008-02-26 14:30
```

The **trunc()** function returns the desired date-oriented truncation of the **date** or **datetime** data type passed to the function. The truncation options are identical to the **round()** options. Using the same **datetime** value, the following SQL statements would return the results shown.

```
select trunc(col_dt, 'YEAR') from mytab
(expression)  2008-01-01 00:00

select trunc(col_dt, 'YEAR')::date from mytab
(expression)  01/01/2008

select trunc(col_dt, 'MONTH') from mytab
(expression)  2008-02-01 00:00

select trunc(col_dt, 'DD') from mytab
(expression)  2008-02-26 00:00
```

At first glance, the values returned from **trunc()** appear to be identical to those returned by the **round()** function, but they are not. Look carefully at the values returned, not the format of the string.

The **add_months()** function receives a **date/datetime** data type and an integer representing the number of months to be added to the date and returns the modified date.

The **last_day()** function returns the last date in the month of the **date/datetime** data type passed to the function. I really need this function because I can never remember how many days are in any given month!

The **next_day()** function gives you the date for the next desired day of the week for the **date/datetime** data type passed to it. You specify the day of the week using a three-letter abbreviation, such as **SUN**, **MON**, and so on. For example:

```
select next_day(col_dt, 'MON') from mytab;
(expression)  2008-03-03
```

The **months_between()** function calculates the difference in months between two **date/datetime** data types passed to it. The returned value, a decimal, is based on all months having 31 days. As a result, the returned expression will always have fractional values unless the dates entered are exact multiples of 31 days apart. For example, suppose you want to know the difference between November 1 and December 7:

```
select months_between(date_1, date_2) from mytab;
(expression)  1.2009453
```

You can pass either date into the function first, followed by the second. If the first date passed is the later of the two, the returned value will be a positive number. Otherwise, a negative value will be returned.

String Manipulation

IDS 11 also adds new functionality to manipulate character strings, namely the ability to delete all characters from either the right or left side of a string based on a target substring. Suppose, for example, we store the following string in a column of the **mytab** table: "If the first date passed is the later of the two, the returned value will be a positive number." The **ltrim()** function would produce the following output:

```
select ltrim (strngcol, "If the first date ")
   from mytab;
(expression) "passed is the later of the two, the
             returned value will be a positive number"
```

The **rtrim()** function performs the same type of operation but deletes from the right side of the string based on the target substring passed in.

Sequences

Truth be told, the **sequence** object was a little long in coming to IDS. Other data servers have supported sequences for a while. But they're here now and can be useful in the right circumstances.

The **sequence** object is somewhat like the **serial** or **serial8** data types in that it generates one or more values depending on how you create and call the object. Unlike **serial** and **serial8**, though, a **sequence** is a database-level object, not table-specific. As you'll see in a moment, this difference makes sequences considerably faster and better suited for generating global unique ID (GUIDs) and other identifiers within your data processing system.

A **sequence** object is composed of two parts: the sequence itself, configured as shown below, and an optional access table that triggers the sequence functionality. You create a **sequence** with the **create sequence** SQL command, which has several flags associated with it. You can set the sequence to start at a specific value, generate increasing or decreasing values, set a maximum and minimum value, and specify whether the values are generated in sequential order or stepwise, skipping *n* values between returned numbers. You can also specify whether the **sequence** generates unique values or is allowed to cycle from its minimum to maximum value repeatedly.

Once a **sequence** object has been created, you can access it directly to retrieve a new value or the current value. The syntax shown in Listing 6.11 illustrates new functionality introduced in IDS 11, the **sysdual** access table in the **sysmaster** database.

```
create sequence my_seq_1 increment by 2
  start with 2 nocycle;

select my_seq_1.nextval from sysmaster@mproduction:sysdual;
nextval  2

select my_seq_1.nextval from sysmaster@mproduction:sysdual;
nextval  4

select my_seq_1.currval from sysmaster@mproduction:sysdual;
currval  4

select my_seq_1.nextval from sysmaster@mproduction:sysdual;
nextval  6

select my_seq_1.currval from sysmaster@mproduction:sysdual;
currval  6
```

Listing 6.11: Creating and using sequence objects in IDS

Sequences can generate more than one value at a time depending on the number of *rows* in the access table, so be very careful if you use an object other than the **sysdual** table, which only has one row in it. I found this out the hard way as I was testing sequence functionality and kept getting back the "wrong" values. Make sure your access table has only the number of rows for the number of values you want returned from the **sequence** object. Listing 6.12 illustrates this caution using a new but simpler sequence.

```
create sequence my_seq_2 start with 1 nocycle;

create table yoyo (col1 char(1));
insert into yoyo values ("a");
insert into yoyo values ("b");
insert into yoyo values ("c");
insert into yoyo values ("d");

select my_seq_2.nextval from yoyo;
nextval  5
         6
         7
         8

select my_seq_2.currval from yoyo;
currval  5
         6
         7
         8

create table yoyo_2 (col1 char(1));
insert into yoyo_2 values ("z");

select my_seq_2.nextval from yoyo_2;
nextval  9

select my_seq_2.nextval from yoyo;
nextval  10
         11
         12
         13
```

Listing 6.12: Sequence functionality based on the number of rows in the access table

As you can see, with four rows in the access table, the **my_seq_2** object returned four values. When, however, I pointed the same sequence object to an access table with one row (**yoyo_2**), only one number was returned.

You can also use sequence values directly in DML statements as shown here:

```
insert into my_table
  values (my_seq_2.nextval, . . .);
insert into my_other_table
  values (my_seq_1.nextval, my_seq_2.currval,
          my_seq_3.nextval, . . .);
```

Triggers on Views

For the most part, designers consider views as read-only objects whose purpose is either to obscure data elements from end users or to make specific SQL operations easier to execute. Views can be updatable objects as well. Originally, this capability was limited to views created on a single table, but recent enhancements have enabled **insert**, **delete**, and **update** operations to be executed on multitable views.

The new functionality is available through **instead of** triggers created on the views. When the triggering action occurs, the trigger executes "instead of" the operation. The trigger typically calls a UDR that performs whatever the operation was supposed to do one table at a time.

A couple of rules are associated with **instead of** triggers on views:

- Depending on the triggering action, you can have **referencing new** (insert), **referencing old** (delete), or both (update) clauses, but you cannot have **before** or **after** blocks in the trigger.

- A **for each row** statement is required in the trigger.

- Neither **select** nor **when** clauses are supported.

Listing 6.13 shows a brief syntax example of an **instead of** trigger on insert.

```
create trigger my_ins_trig_on_view
instead of insert on my_view
referencing new as new
    for each row
(execute procedure ins_basetables(new.value1, new.value2, new.value3));

create procedure ins_basetables (var1 int, var2 int, var3 int)
    insert into table_1 values (var1);
    insert into table_2 values (var2, var3);
    insert into table_3 values (var1, current);
end procedure;
```

Listing 6.13: Executing an instead of trigger on insert into a multitable view

Order-by Not in Select List

This next capability is not a major enhancement, nor does it fall into the "go to market" or "customers will immediately upgrade to get it" category of functionality, but it does solve a problem that always bothered me when I was creating applications.

Back in the dark ages, if I wanted to execute a **sort** or **order by** operation, I always had to include the column(s) I wanted to order with in the **select** statement and receive them back as part of the result set even though I had no use for them in the application. This meant I had to create variables with extra column(s) or larger temporary tables just to throw the data away later. That is no longer the case.

Now, the following syntax is legal and will be correctly executed by the instance:

```
select a.col1, b.col3, a.col4
from my_table a, my_other_table b
where a.col1 = b.col9
order by b.col7
```

What actually happens behind the scenes is that the query optimizer rewrites the **select** statement to include **b.col7** and then uses the values to perform the **order by** operation. Once the result set is ready to be returned, the column (**b.col7**) is stripped so that only the three requested columns are sent back.

The dbschema Utility

The **dbschema** utility enables you to view and save the DDL or "schema" statements that were used to create the objects in a database. In addition, it can display information that the query optimizer uses when it evaluates the range of values a particular column or set of columns can have—commonly called the *data distribution*.

Although several flags can effect the output this utility produces, there is one that in my opinion should be mandatory every time you execute the utility: the **-ss** (lower case), or server-specific, flag. Consider the difference between the output of the two commands shown in Listing 6.14. I extracted out a portion from both that looks at the same table.

```
dbschema -d my_db

{ TABLE "informix".my_stock row size = 51 number of columns
  = 8 index size = 18 }
create table "informix".my_stock
  (
    stock_num smallint,
    manu_code char(3),
    description char(15),
    unit_price money(6,2),
    unit char(4),
    unit_descr char(15),
    ifx_insert_checksum integer
        default null,
    ifx_row_version integer
        default 1,
    primary key (stock_num,manu_code)
  );
revoke all on "informix".my_stock from "public" as "informix";
```

Listing 6.14: Sample dbschema output with and without the server-specific flag (part 1 of 2)

```
dbschema -d my_db -ss
{ TABLE "informix".my_stock row size = 51 number of columns
  = 8 index size = 18 }
create table "informix".my_stock
  (
    stock_num smallint,
    manu_code char(3),
    description char(15),
    unit_price money(6,2),
    unit char(4),
    unit_descr char(15),
    ifx_insert_checksum integer
        default null,
    ifx_row_version integer
        default 1,
    primary key (stock_num,manu_code)
  )
first extent 5600 next size 560
fragment by expression
(stock_num > 6000) in data_3,
(stock_num > 4000) in data_2
(stock_num > 2000) in data_1
(stock_num <= 2000) in my_old_data;
revoke all on "informix".my_stock from "public" as "informix";
```

Listing 6.14: Sample dbschema output with and without the server-specific flag (part 2 of 2)

The **-ss** flag displays extent size and both table and index partitioning schemes if they exist. With the **-ss** flag on the second command, you can now see that the table is partitioned by expression. You can also see what sizes were specified for the first and succeeding extents of the table. You can, and should, use this same flag when exporting a database with the **dbexport** utility.

Another flag I often use is the one that limits the **dbschema** utility to only displaying the schema for one table or view. Simply add **-t** *table_name* to the command as follows:

```
dbschema -d test1 -t store_sales -ss
```

Without the **-t** flag, the utility generates the schema for all tables and views in the database specified with the **-d** flag.

The **-hd** flag displays information called data distributions that the IDS optimizer uses when it is trying to find the most efficient route to the data requested by user sessions. Data distributions are discussed in greater detail in *Administering Informix Dynamic Server, Advanced Topics*.

Table 6.5 lists some of the more popular flags used in conjunction with the **dbschema** utility.

Table 6.5: Commonly used dbschema utility flags	
Flag	**Description**
-d *database_name*	The name of the database in the active instance against which the command should be executed.
-t *table_name*	The table or view whose schema should be returned. If this flag is not set, the utility returns the schema for all tables and views in the database.
-ss	Produces the full SQL commands required to completely re-create a table or view. Included in the output generated is table extent size information as well as table and index partitioning schemes, if any.
-p *[account_id]*	Displays permission–related information or, in other words, the **grant** commands. By using the -**p account_id flag**, you can restrict the utility to returning only the permission information for the **account_id** user account or role.
-f *[function_name]*	Displays information about the specified user-defined function or stored procedure. You can use this flag without a function or stored procedure name to obtain all registered functions and stored procedures in the database.
-r *[role_name]*	Displays information about the specified role. You can use this flag without a role name to retrieve all the defined roles in the database.
-u	Displays just the DDL statements for user-defined types. An additional flag can be added, either **all** for all types or **i type_name** to output the inheritance tree for the named type. The second option helps discover types created **under** another type.
-si	Excludes the partitioning statements for any indexes created on non-partitioned tables.

Summary

We covered a wide range of topics oriented toward administering a database in this chapter. Although I didn't explain every database administration function, you should now be able to create a database as well as tables and indexes. You should be able to determine whether partitioning indexes or tables would be effective for your environment. You should be able to implement round-robin and by expression partition schemes on tables and indexes as appropriate and be able to populate the tables in the most efficient way. Last, you should understand the balance between data integrity and multiuser access that resolves itself through isolation levels.

When administering your databases, keep the following points in mind:

- Even though it requires more keystrokes to achieve the same result, you may well find that you have greater control and can get things done more quickly using SQL statements via the **dbaccess** utility rather than the graphical tools. For the purpose of remote administration, it is imperative that you be familiar with the raw SQL commands to perform the various DBA functions.

- While round-robin partitioning has all the weaknesses of RAID striping, this method can still provide an increase in performance over leaving a table in a single dbspace. Just remember that any indexes created on tables using round-robin partitioning *must not* be created "co-resident" but should, at the very least, be created in another dbspace.

- Write partitioning expressions with the most restrictive conditions first. When using ranges in a condition, put the most restrictive portion of the range on the left side of the condition statement. Remember to keep the expressions simple because they are evaluated each time data is updated or inserted. Avoid using raw **serial**, **date**, or **datetime** columns in expression statements if possible. Instead, use the new date and date-time functions to create effective partitioning schemes without constant ongoing maintenance.

- Whenever possible, avoid using the **remainder** attribute in partitioning expressions. Its use implies variability of the data it contains and will result in the partition being sequentially searched by each query. It will also impact your ability to quickly detach or drop partitions to remove unwanted data from the table.

- Review the notes in the "Attaching Tables" section of this chapter for some points to consider when attaching tables.

- Create a **dbschema** with the **-ss** flag whenever you make major changes to a table or index—most particularly its partitioning scheme—to make sure the scheme is "correct."

- Don't allow too many in-place table alters to exist on any table. This can have a negative impact on performance over time. Periodically executing a table-wide **update** command that replaces a column's value with its original value will synchronize the table's rows to the latest schema version.

In this chapter, we discussed many of the jobs a DBA performs. One of the most important jobs, though, is ensuring the recoverability of the database in the event of a catastrophic failure. In the next chapter, we'll return to being an Informix Dynamic Server Administrator and examine the backup and recovery utilities and how to create backups as well as restore from them.

7

Backing Up and Restoring

In this Chapter

- ▸ Backup design methodologies
- ▸ Backing up the logical logs
- ▸ Tape device options
- ▸ How the backup process works
- ▸ Using the ISM and the **ON-Bar** utility suite

I n every job, there is a mundane task, or set of tasks, that must be done on a regular basis regardless of how dull, boring, or quotidian it might be. In some cases, the task itself isn't terribly significant; it's just part of a larger process. In other cases, the task is important enough that its completion, or failure, can have a serious and irrevocable impact on other processes.

Informix Dynamic Server backup and restoration operations fit into the latter category. A relatively boring task when viewed individually, few people make it their life's goal to handle the process of backing up IDS instances. Yet whenever a restore from backup is required, nothing matters more to the enterprise than the existence and viability of the backup created by that process.

In this chapter, we'll discuss several different philosophies regarding the backup process. I'll describe how Informix Dynamic Server can create backups while the instance is online and active, as well as the types of storage devices IDS supports. I'll cover the syntax required to create or restore from backups using the **ontape** utility, and I'll introduce the **ON-Bar** utility suite and explain how you can use it, in conjunction with a tape management system, to back up and restore instances and their logical logs. I'll also review the configuration and use of the Informix Storage Manager (ISM), a basic tape management system bundled into IDS, including the cloning of individual backup sets or entire tape volumes. By the end of the chapter, you should be able to design and implement a backup process that will work in your environment.

Let me state up front one assumption I'll make in this chapter: that your backups, whether instance or logical log, will be written out to one or more tape devices. I realize this may not be the case in your environment, particularly with the recent enhancements to **ontape** that make backup to disk an extremely attractive option. As a result, I'll use the phase "to tape" to refer to backups written either to tape or to disk. Although your backups may first go to disk, best practices dictate that eventually you copy the files to tape and store them off-site in the event of a comprehensive site failure.

Backup Strategies

It's a fact of life that from time to time you'll need to perform either a partial or complete restore. Whether due to a major mistake made by a user or some sort of catastrophic mechanical failure, the inability to recover an instance back to a particular moment in time could cost you your job. It only makes sense, then, to ensure you have the proper backup strategy in place as well as the hardware to support it.

Informix Dynamic Server provides two tools for backing up an instance: the **ontape** utility and the **ON-Bar** utility suite. The former is self-contained, while the latter enables third-party tape management solutions to back up and restore instances or specific dbspaces. A limited tape management utility called the Informix Storage Manager is bundled as part of the data server, permitting sites without full third-party tape management solutions to use **ON-Bar** functionality with a limited set of locally connected tape or disk devices.

The **ON-Bar** suite and associated management products can make designing and implementing your backup and recovery plan pretty easy. Using **ON-Bar** and either the ISM or a third-party tape management solution frees you from the media-handling and management issues that exist when using the **ontape** utility to tape. Several third-party vendors have written software to interface their media management systems, and all the supported backup hardware, to the Informix Dynamic Server **ON-Bar** utility. As a result, you can incorporate newer, higher-capacity, and faster tape drives and tape drive configurations into your plan. If supported by the management software, the data server can provide multiple data streams in parallel out of the instance(s) to the backup devices, decreasing the amount of time required to create a backup or execute a restore.

In establishing a backup strategy, a number of factors can and should influence its creation:

- What granularity of restore could be required?
- How much data is there to back up and possibly restore in the instance?
- How easily could lost data be re-created?
- How much time is available to create a backup if the backup process had to occur in a quiet or maintenance period?
- What would be an acceptable amount of time to restore from a backup?
- What physical devices are available on which to create the backup?
- What are the retention and recycle periods for the tapes used to back up the instance?

The importance of each of these factors, and their interrelationships, will determine whether you use what I call a "whole-istic" approach to backing up an instance, a more individualized or focused approach on a dbspace level, or a combination of the two.

While most sites use what I call a whole-istic approach, there are advantages to taking a more focused approach. The most important is that you can direct your efforts at those tables that really need backing up rather than having to deal with the entire instance. This ability yields a higher degree of granularity when you're faced with having to restore. The focused approach can tend to be more complicated to implement and maintain, depending on whether you choose to create the backups through **ON-Bar** and a storage manager or via command-line utilities, which would require significantly more manual intervention.

The Focused Approach

Because the IDS data server does not natively support table-level restores from **ontape** or through **ON-Bar** (although with a proper partitioning scheme or the table-level restore functionality of the **archecker** utility, it is possible to do), if specific tables require special attention from a restoration point of view, most often this calls for a series of table-oriented backup procedures. These table-level backups should be supplemental to the whole-instance backups you create on a regular basis.

A table-oriented backup procedure usually involves some sort of table unloading. Depending on the size of the table and the need for concurrent access during the backup, you can achieve this unloading either by using the SQL **unload** command to create an ASCII dump to disk and then executing the **onunload** command to create a binary copy of the locked table to tape or by executing an unload job through the High-Performance Loader (HPL). These key tables can be unloaded and backed up several times each day or week, depending on need. You could also run this type of focused backup to generate table copies for the updating of remote servers if full data replication is not possible or required.

Another variation on this method of backing up is particularly relevant in OLAP environments—that is, to back up the load data rather than the database itself. This technique is helpful when multiple aggregate tables are affected by a single load file, as is often the case.

Simply reloading the source files will regenerate the same aggregate values as before, so there's no need to capture the changes with an instance backup. On the other hand, the restoration process will take longer to complete depending on the number of source files that need to be processed and the length of time required to process each one.

To be sure, it's important to create a baseline backup of the entire OLAP instance from time to time. In this way, you can reduce the number of source files to carry forward for potential use in restoring the database/instance. Those source files can then be removed to permanent offsite storage.

With the **ON-Bar** utility suite, it's possible to back up a group of one or more dbspaces. If you follow Informix's general recommendation of one critical table to a dbspace, creating dbspace-level backups through **ON-Bar** would be the equivalent of a table-level or focused approach. As I'll explain later, recovering from this type of backup will affect more than just the table(s) stored in the dbspace(s). This is a positive thing, however, because it ensures the logical consistency of the data in the instance.

Last, it's possible to restore a single table, or parts thereof, using recent functionality added to the **archecker** utility. As you will see, this is not a direct restore to table; rather, the data is restored to a new table and then moved into the final target table. With this method, you can "have your cake and eat it too" by generating full system backups along the whole-istic approach yet being able to restore as if you designed a focused approach.

The "Whole-istic" Approach

The method I refer to as the *whole-istic* approach is the most common approach to backing up an instance. Using the **ontape** utility or the **ON-Bar** utility suite, you can back up the entire instance—or, as needed, portions thereof—to tape on a regular basis. Using **ontape**, you must back up the entire instance, but you can restore to a dbspace level if needed. Going one step further, most dbspace restore operations can be executed with the instance online and fully functional.

With the **ON-Bar** utility suite, you can back up the whole instance or individual spaces within the instance. Obviously, the backup you use to restore from will have an impact on what you can restore. From a full instance backup, you can restore individual spaces, the entire instance, or, in conjunction with the logical logs, the entire instance to a specific moment in time. From a dbspace-level backup, you can restore only the individual dbspace, although the logical logs will be used to roll forward transactions that affect the instance as a whole.

> Whether executed through **ontape** or the **ON-Bar** utility suite, online dbspace restores are possible only for dbspaces that don't contain critical Informix Dynamic Server structures, such as the logical logs, physical log, or rootdbs. If you lose a dbspace containing those structures, the instance will abort processing and you will have to restore the entire instance.

Looking at the **ontape** utility in a little greater detail, the frequency and depth of the backups created with this utility are bounded by the amount of time required to create the backup, the acceptable amount of time to effect a restore, and, to a lesser degree, the tape device itself. I'll discuss tape devices in somewhat greater detail later in the chapter; for now, it's the speed of the device that's important.

Obviously, the speed of the tape device directly affects the time required to back up or restore an instance. That said, don't be completely discouraged if you have a slow device. Informix Dynamic Server has always permitted you to create backups while the instance is online and actively being used. Provided there is not a business requirement for complete inactivity in an instance during a backup, you can still use a slow device to create your backups. The backup process normally has little to no effect on the normal end-user activity that occurs in an instance.

The only case where an **ontape** backup operation will have an impact on normal instance processing occurs when the backup device (**TAPEDEV**) and logical log tape device (**LTAPEDEV**) are the same and databases in the instance are in a logged mode. In this case, it is possible for the logical logs to fill up with records from database activity while an instance backup is being created. If the dynamic addition of logical logs has not been turned on (**DYNAMIC_LOGS = 2**), with the logical log backup operation terminated in order to create the instance backup, the instance will suspend all activity until the logs are written out to tape. All user sessions will stall until the backup operation is canceled and the logical logs are backed up. Once the logs are written to tape, the instance will resume normal processing. The instance backup will need to be restarted during a period of lower instance activity because it was aborted and unusable.

Regardless of which Informix backup utility you use, there are three *levels* of granularity to backup operations, as explained in Table 7.1.

Table 7.1: Informix Dynamic Server backup levels	
Backup level	Description
0	All used pages in the instance are written to tape.
1	Only those pages that have changed since the time stamp of the last level 0 backup are written to tape.
2	Only those pages that have changed since the time stamp of the last level 1 backup are written out to tape.

Your job as an administrator is to strike a balance between what you can achieve with these three levels of backups and your requirements to protect and recover the instance's data. For a production OLTP environment, I recommend the following:

- The databases be in an unbuffered logging mode
- The logical logs be backed up to tape continuously
- A daily level 2 backup of the instance be created

Depending on your level of paranoia and the length of time required to create and restore a full backup, you could create a level 0 (zero) backup either on the first of the month or on the first and fifteenth of the month. In addition, you could create a level 1 (one) backup once a week to decrease the length of time required to create the daily level 2 backups.

With this type of design, a restore would require the level 0 tape from either the first or the fifteenth, the closest intervening level 1 (if any), the last level 2, and the logical logs written out to tape following the level 2 backup, as illustrated in Figure 7.1. We'll discuss how and when to back up the logical logs in the next section.

Figure 7.1: Precedence of Informix Dynamic Server backup levels

Obviously, you have to decide what is best for your environment. While I say you "could" execute a level 0 backup twice a month, it might not be feasible in your environment due to time, media cost, or other constraints.

In an OLAP environment, you have a couple of additional factors to consider. First, the size of the data store is usually much larger than for an OLTP environment. This means the amount of time required to create or restore from a backup will be longer. Second, as the warehouse grows, there will be an ever-*decreasing* percentage of pages in the database that will be changing over time. This should require a different approach to the backup process.

Unbuffered logging of the databases in the instance and the backing up of logical logs to tape are less important in OLAP environments. Backups can be made less frequently than daily depending on the frequency of updates to the warehouse, the average amount of data loaded, and the rate at which the load and update process occurs. As I mentioned earlier, it might make more sense to back up the raw data load files rather than the instance itself. Certainly, you occasionally need to make a full instance backup to establish some sort of a moment-in-time baseline against which the raw data is reloaded. In this case, you might generate a level 0 backup once or twice a quarter rather than once or twice a month. A level 1 backup could be created perhaps once a month, with a level 2 backup created once a week.

Restoration with this type of design is similar to that already explained for an OLTP environment. However, instead of using logical log backups to restore back to the last recorded moments in time, you would use data load files to reload the warehouse.

Although I would not of necessity change the backup procedure for OLTP environments, all the suggestions just made for OLAP environments can become moot, as I'll explain in a moment, if you use the **ON-Bar** utility suite. Looking at OLTP environments first, though, with multiple tape devices and the ability of the data server and backup suite to stream data in parallel to those devices, you could create level 0 backups daily or at least weekly, creating level 1 backups on the other days of the week. A total restore would require less time to be completed because you would have eliminated at least one complete backup level from the process.

With enough tape devices thrown into the backup design, and with the ever-expanding storage capacities of the devices and media, you could completely back up an OLAP or data warehouse environment much more frequently than quarterly, as I previously mentioned. This would reduce the amount of tape management required to store the load files as well as the effort needed to use the load file backups in a restore situation.

With the data stream parallelization available through the **ON-Bar** suite, you can almost treat an OLAP environment as though it is an OLTP instance and capture daily changes to the instance through level 1 backups or dbspace-specific backup operations. Dbspace-specific backups would require the proper placement of tables to isolate changed pages to known dbspaces within the instance. You would want to put tables receiving newly loaded data in specific dbspaces while leaving older, more static data in other dbspaces. Then, on a regular basis, you would invoke the **ON-Bar** backup process to capture just those spaces with the new data while ignoring the others. A full instance backup would support these daily dbspace-specific incremental backups, but the full backup could be created perhaps twice a year.

Understand that this is just one way of thinking about backup and recovery. If your company or industry has specific best practices in this area, give careful consideration to those recommendations. When in doubt as to which approach to use, always choose the one with the greatest amount of data security and ability to recover your environment in the shortest amount of time.

Logical Log Backup

As you learned in Chapter 6, IDS uses the physical log and logical logs to store information about the changes that occur to data in an instance. Depending on the logging mode of a database, either very little information will be stored in these logs, as is the case with a database in unlogged mode, or every action (save most queries) will be tracked and recorded, as happens with a database in a logged mode.

These data changes might, or might not, be of value to you in terms of recovering to a moment in time and will determine which logging mode you choose for an individual database. Generally speaking, most environments (except OLAP) cannot sustain a loss of transaction information and will require these records. As a result, you need to know when, and how, logical logs can be backed up.

Depending on whether you're using buffered or unbuffered logging, transaction information is stored for a period of time in the physical and logical log buffers and then is written to the logical log structures on disk. Naturally, these structures will fill up over time. When all the logical logs fill up and are not backed up, and new ones are not added either manually or dynamically, a message indicating that the logical logs are full is entered into the **MSGPATH**, and the instance suspends operation until the logs are backed up and freed for reuse.

With this point in mind, you need to decide how and when to back up the logs. You have three choices to consider: never, on demand, and continuous.

Never

To never back up the logical logs, you set the **LTAPEDEV** parameter to **/dev/null** on Linux, Mac OS X, and Unix ports or to **NUL** on Windows ports. As each logical log fills, it is immediately marked as though it is backed up. The log is immediately made available for use whenever the instance cycles back to it. I set **LTAPEDEV** to **/dev/null** in development instances, where I need a logged database environment but I don't care about capturing the changes that occur to the test data in the database. Setting **LTAPEDEV** to **/dev/null** might also be appropriate for data warehouse environments where little to no logical log activity occurs. Your backup options are strictly limited, however, as explained in the warning that follows.

WARNING There is a serious side effect to using **/dev/null** as a logical log backup device if you plan to use **ON-Bar** commands to back up your instance. The utility is structured such that all critical instance structures must be captured to a valid backup device. This requirement ensures not only that a re-store can be successfully accomplished but also that the logical consistency of the instance is preserved.

Because logical log backups do not occur when **LTAPEDEV** is set to **/dev/null**, you will not be able to use the **ON-Bar** utility to create or restore backups.

On Demand

In the on-demand scenario, the logical logs are backed up to tape as a result of executing an **ontape -a** or an **onbar -b -l** command. Full logs as well as the current logical log are backed up to tape and marked free for reuse. This choice is acceptable for instances containing unlogged databases because the logs usually will not fill quickly enough to justify continuously backing them up. Extreme care must be taken when using this option in instances with logged databases. If you don't back up the logical logs frequently enough and dynamic logical log creation has not been enabled, a log-full condition could occur that will affect the entire instance as I've already explained.

Continuous

With a continuous approach to the backup of the logical logs, each logical log is automatically backed up to tape as it fills. You can achieve this type of backup in one of two ways. The first is by executing the **ontape -c** command from a shell window of a terminal device connected to the physical server. This command invokes a log backup process that runs in foreground mode in the window. Do not close the window (you can minimize it, though), or the logical log backup process will abort. The **ontape** utility will indicate when a backup tape has filled and will request that a new tape be used.

The second method is to use the **ON-Bar** suite with the **ALARMPROGRAM** parameter and turn on automatic backup of the logical logs. The default setting for this parameter is to use the **$INFORMIXDIR/etc/alarmprogram.sh** shell script. At the top of this script is a small set of configuration parameters:

```
# ########################################
#
# PUBLIC SECTION : CONFIGURATION VARIABLES
#
# ########################################
BACKUPLOGS=N
ALARMADMIN=0
ALARMPAGER=0
ADMINEMAIL=
PAGEREMAIL=
MAILUTILITY=/usr/bin/mail
```

If one of these parameters, **BACKUPLOGS**, is set to Y, the script will automatically trigger the **onbar -b -l** command when a logical log fills. Understand, though, that the script will check the value of the **LTAPEDEV** parameter and if it finds it's set to **/dev/null** (or the Windows equivalent), it will change the **BACKUPLOGS** parameter so no backups are triggered.

Decisions Regarding Logical Log Backup

There are those who disagree with the interface design of the **ontape** utility as well as dedicating a tape device to the logical log backup process. Unfortunately, there are not too many other ways of handling this task in my opinion. It's also easy to deal with. When considering tape devices, 4mm DAT devices and many other medium-capacity tape formats are inexpensive and more than fast enough to handle the amount of logical log data that will be pushed to them under normal and reasonable conditions. These devices can easily be added to the physical server's I/O bus, either as an internal or external device. The media itself is rather compact and easy to store, too. With an 8 GB capacity for 120-meter tapes in DDS2 drives, you can store a lot of logical log information before having to change tapes. For those who don't want to use tape, recent changes to **ontape**'s ability to intelligently manage on-disk backups of instances and logical logs practically make it a no-brainer to use it with **LTAPEDEV** set to a directory (more about this configuration option in the next section). You'll have to keep a terminal window open, though, for the utility to work. Last, if you don't like the idea of keeping a terminal window open somewhere to support the **ontape** command, you can use the **ON-Bar** equivalent.

In my opinion, choosing to continuously back up the logical logs is the best option for instances with production databases in logged mode. The tapes used to back up the logical logs can and should be switched out on a regular basis in conjunction with the daily backup process. Rotate them off-site along with the companion backup tapes so you can use them to restore to a moment in time if necessary following a catastrophic disaster.

There is one other factor to consider in deciding when and how to back up the logical log records: the impact smart and simple BLOBs will have on the process. Because simple BLOBs bypass the instance's shared memory structures, writes of these

BLOB types are not considered committed until the simple BLOB information is written to the logical log. Depending on the size of the simple BLOBs, the frequency at which they are written, and the size of the logical logs themselves, a logical log could fill quickly. Remember, too, that simple BLOB deletes are not considered committed, nor is the disk space the BLOB was stored on freed up, until the logical log containing the delete record has been backed up. This could require more effort to back up the logs if you choose to use the on-demand method discussed earlier. Continuous logging would be easier and better in this type of situation; you wouldn't have to baby-sit the backup process as much. Nevertheless, if your environment has a lot of simple BLOB activity, your log space will fill in a shorter amount of time. The log backup process will require a bit more careful monitoring to make sure the tape has not filled up and needs to be exchanged for another.

With smart BLOBs, the **LOGGING** option of the sbspace creation command determines whether changes to the objects are logged. Unlike simple BLOBs, where the entire BLOB is written to the logical logs along with the simple BLOBspace, logged updates of smart BLOBs generate twice the logical log volume as the BLOB itself. The original as well as the new version are written to the logs in order to have a rollback image. In addition to the smart BLOB data, the metadata area of the sbspace(s) is always logged. Although the size of these records is much smaller, you need to consider the total impact on logical log use when deciding how to manage backing up the logical logs.

Backup Devices

For both the **ontape** and **ON-Bar** utilities, you can use either tape or flat files as backup devices. Both options have advantages and disadvantages, but each can adequately serve your needs depending on the level of risk you are willing to assume, the amount of media management and administration you can perform, and the potential requirement to be able to restore to any given moment in time.

In brief, backing up to tape is the most reliable as far as failure protection is concerned, and it provides the greatest number of restore options over time. There is a corresponding administration cost to manage the media, but this cost is offset to a large degree if you use **ON-Bar** with the ISM or a third-party management solution.

Using flat files should be, at best, an interim step in a bigger backup process from a safety and resiliency perspective. Once the instance or logical logs are backed up to a directory on the server, they should be backed up to tape as part of the server backup operation. The idea is to prevent file loss due to disk failure on the server or disk subsystem.

I should note that there is one other option to backing up an instance environment other than using **ontape** or **ON-Bar**: You can use the operating system's backup utility to back up the system, including the data directories, or create a unique backup job that gets only the data directories (cooked files) or mount points (raw disk). A couple caveats to this approach make it less than appealing, however.

First, the O/S method requires an instance outage. Some O/S utilities will pause and then skip the open dbspace cooked files if you don't quiesce the instance(s). In my opinion, this hardly qualifies as an effective backup procedure! Other utilities, such as the **dd** command used on Linux, Mac OS X, and Unix systems to copy raw partitions, require more than a passing familiarity with system administration skills to execute backup and restore operations successfully. When used, this command will grab the partition's pages as they exist without regard to what is in operation against them at that moment in time. Shutting down the instance, though, eliminates one of the many key technical advantages of Informix Dynamic Server compared with competitors' products.

The second caveat is that you have no referential integrity process at work during a restore. If somehow you are able to get the backup utility to capture a dbspace while it is online, when you restore it, all you will get back is the dbspace itself. An operating system restore of a dbspace file will not check to make sure other components of the instance and database(s) are intact. This will cause data integrity problems within the instance that could range from minor to significant depending on how many parent-child relationships are affected.

For example, imagine, as could very easily happen, that a dbspace containing a parent table was backed up and that then, during the course of backing other dbspaces, a set of parent and child rows is inserted. The child table, though, is in the last dbspace to be backed up. If you attempted a restore with this backup and the backup was successful, you would have an instance with orphaned child rows. I don't think I need to say more about this backup option. Use what's in IDS. It offers the safest and best options.

Tape Devices

The market today is able to provide several different technologies and media to back up your instances and logical logs. Historically, these options have included QIC, 4mm digital audio tape (DAT), and 8mm helical-scan tape technology, all of which traditionally have been used to store backups. Each of these alternatives has its own advantages and disadvantages, ranging from the size of the tape itself to the amount of data each type of tape can hold. New medium-capacity formats and drives have appeared in the past decade or so and are excellent candidates for table-driven, focused backups or even for logical log backups.

With data warehouses becoming more popular and larger, as well as larger production OLTP environments, digital linear tape (DLT) technology and other high-capacity formats have become the preferred tape commodity. Boasting a compressed capacity of double to triple digits of gigabytes and an acceptably fast transfer rate, these technologies should be able to work with nearly any backup design in either OLTP or OLAP database environments. In addition, you can select write once, read many (WORM) optical disks or rewritable optical media for long-term storage of data accessed so infrequently that response time is not a factor.

With the Informix Storage Manager, you can take advantage of almost all of these technologies as well as several more that I have not mentioned yet. You are, however, limited to four locally connected devices, including flat files. The tape devices must be "simple," too. By that I mean that robots, autochangers, and jukeboxes are not supported, just individually addressable devices. The ISM supports 4mm and 8mm, 8mm/5 GB, 3480, 3570, 4890, 9490 Timberline, DLT, some optical, VHS, QIC, and half-inch tape drives in addition to flat files as valid backup devices.

Your tape drive options for use with the **ontape** utility are a little different. This utility's biggest weakness is its tape handling and tape technology support; basically, there is none. A double-edged sword, this is both a bad and a good thing.

On the down side, you have no direct device support. You're at the mercy of whatever devices the operating system supports natively. On the positive side, Informix development isn't spending valuable engineering time fiddling around with tape drive commands, robotic control extensions, and related issues. They do not have to make sure they have support ported into each release of IDS for every possible tape/cartridge/optical device that could be attached to a machine, thereby bloating the code. Instead, they concentrate on what they do best and use their engineering resources to improve and enhance the functionality, performance, and scalability of the data server.

So, what can you use to back up with if you're going to use the **ontape** utility? The bottom line is this: You can use any single-tape device you want as long as you have a driver for it and it operates in native, uncompressed mode. Like the ISM, **ontape** has no support for autochangers or jukeboxes. You need to manually swap tapes, write shell scripts to wrap around the **ontape** utility, or pick up its output to standard I/O (**STDIO**) to get it to work with multitape devices.

A commonly asked question by those new to Informix Dynamic Server is how much data will the data server support via the **TAPESIZE** and **LTAPESIZE** configuration parameters to **ontape**. In the past, considerable confusion and uncertainty existed about what the right answer was, and previous discussions went into quite a bit of detail explaining the technical details that governed the actual size you could use with the earlier releases of IDS.

Today, the real answer to this question is "It depends." In writing to a backup file on disk, the data stream is actually *mapped* into blocks in the file system. These blocks are not contiguous, and they are managed by a series of pointers within the file system itself. The file system limits the number of blocks and pointers any one file can have. This limit, commonly referred to as the *maximum file size*, varies depending on, among other things, the number of bits (32 or 64) the operating system is compiled to operate in. On most 32-bit operating systems, the maximum file size was originally 2 GB but has been increased over the years. The maximum file size in 64-bit operating systems is significantly larger.

When a data stream is directed to a tape device, the file system block and pointer system is bypassed completely. As a result, the operating system's file size limit does not apply to data written to tape. When data is written to tape, the write is actually an append operation, with each byte placed on the media as directed by the tape device until the media reaches its maximum storage capacity.

Is there a limit inside **ontape** to how much data it will stream? Yes, there is. The answer is:

- The maximum file size supported by the operating system if **TAPEDEV** or **LTAPEDEV** point to flat files, or

- The maximum uncompressed storage capacity of the tape device and media combination if **TAPEDEV** or **LTAPEDEV** point to a tape device.

In either case, the amount of data streamed cannot exceed 4 TB.

There is one other option you can use quite effectively, albeit in a limited capacity, for a tape device from time to time with the **ontape** utility: **/dev/null** or the Windows equivalent.

Setting **TAPEDEV** or **LTAPEDEV** to **/dev/null** lets backup commands execute in just a few seconds. When **TAPEDEV** is set to **/dev/null** and a backup operation is executed, the backup-related flags in the instance's reserved pages are instantly updated and the operation then terminates. This technique is handy when you need to change logging modes on a database or you want to back up and close the current logical log so newly created BLOBspaces can be activated. In making the change to **/dev/null**, you do not need to erase the information regarding tape size or block size for that tape device; the data server ignores these values.

Needless to say, you cannot restore anything from a backup created to **/dev/null**. There are other implications with regard to **ON-Bar** backups as well, which we've already covered. Should you temporarily change either of your tape devices to **/dev/null** to execute some commands, remember to change it back to a valid device as quickly as possible.

There is one additional caveat to selecting a tape device to use with the **ontape** utility: The device must not automatically rewind the media when the device is opened or closed. Before writing to or reading from a tape, **ontape** performs a series of compatibility checks, one of which is media rewind.

There is another option for creating a "fast" backup that doesn't require manipulation of $ONCONFIG tape device parameters: the ON-Bar and ontape "fake" backup option. You can execute a fake backup even if ON-Bar and/ or the ISM have not been configured. Later in the chapter, I'll explain how to create fake backups using these two utilities.

Backup to Directory and File Handling

Your other option for storing instance and logical log backups is on disk. As you undoubtedly are aware, this choice does add an element of risk to your backup procedure. Having instance or log backups on disk does you no good if you don't back up that disk to tape or another media on a regular basis. When the disk fails—and they all will at some time or another—you've lost your database backups. If the disk also contains some or all of your instance chunks, you're really in trouble. What you should do if you're going to back up instance or log information to disk is immediately launch a backup of the physical server's directory after the IDS backups are completed.

When backing up to disk, the created files and their locations will vary depending on which backup utility you use. As you'll see later when we discuss the ISM, when configuring a disk device for a backup medium, you specify a directory for the instance as well as for the logical log backups. When an **ON-Bar** backup operation is executed, a uniquely named file is created in that directory for each instance storage object (e.g., dbspace) backed up as part of the operation. Likewise for the logical logs—when backed up, each log is written to a uniquely named file in the specified directory.

The file names themselves have a numeric value that is incremented for each dbspace or logical log backed up. Both instance and log backup files use the same sequential numbering system to ensure uniqueness of the file names, with the serial number generator starting in the 15800 range. You cannot change this value, nor should you change the names of the created files. As you'll see, these names are stored in **ON-Bar** and ISM control files as part of the backup result set and are used in the restoration process.

When you use the **ontape** utility, recent enhancements to IDS give you three choices. First, you can use the original configuration, a fully pathed file name for the **TAPEDEV** and/or **LTAPEDEV** devices in the **$ONCONFIG** file. For example:

```
TAPEDEV    /data/tagus_inst_bkup
.
.
.
LTAPEDEV   /data/tagus_logical_bkup
.
```

When **ontape** creates an instance or logical log backup to a disk file under this type of configuration, it overwrites the existing file with the output of the current command. As a result, it is incumbent on you as the administrator to make sure the file is both moved and renamed or backed up in some form or another for later retrieval before executing another backup and overwriting the file. You also will need to track which backup type was created and when in order to retrieve the correct file in a restore situation.

The only minor exception to this is if you are archiving the logical logs to disk continually via the **ontape -c** command. In this case, a lock is placed on the file and the file itself is appended until the backup is interrupted. You still will need to rotate the logical log backup file before initiating another **ontape**-based continuous log backup operation.

Your second option is configure the **TAPEDEV** device parameter to **STDIO**, or standard I/O. You can also use the **-t STDIO** flag to the **ontape** command to override the **$ONCONFIG** value for that invocation of the command. When a backup is created to **STDIO**, the data stream is passed to a system "pipe" that can be captured by a program or utility and manipulated as needed. For example, you can pass the data stream to a shell script which, in turn, redirects the stream to a data file with a naming convention you choose:

```
ontape -s -L 0 | my_bkup_util.sh -t STDIO
```

Or, if the **TAPEDEV** parameter is already set to **STDIO**, you can pass the stream to compression utility:

```
ontape -s -L 0 |gzip > /data/bkups/mon_bk_L0.gz
```

My favorite use, though, of this option is to simultaneously execute a backup and restore on another server to instantiate High Availability Data Replication (HDR) or MACH-11 instances:

```
ontape -s -L 0 | rsh mirror_server "ontape -p"
```

The third option for **TAPEDEV** and **LTAPEDEV** was released with IDS 11: the ability to use a directory and have the data server manage the file naming for you! I personally think this is a great thing and is enough to make me waffle a bit (albeit a very small amount) on recommending backups to disk as opposed to tape.

With **TAPEDEV** or **LTAPEDEV** set to a value such as **/opt/IBM/informix/backups/** (notice the trailing slash, or /), when **ontape** creates an instance backup, it will create a file in the specified directory. Because the size of the file will be the smaller of either 4

TB or the maximum file size the O/S supports, most likely only one file will be created per backup operation.

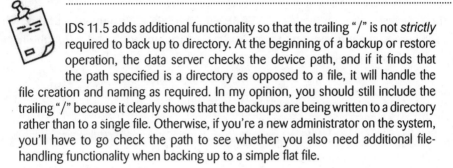

IDS 11.5 adds additional functionality so that the trailing "/" is not *strictly* required to back up to directory. At the beginning of a backup or restore operation, the data server checks the device path, and if it finds that the path specified is a directory as opposed to a file, it will handle the file creation and naming as required. In my opinion, you should still include the trailing "/" because it clearly shows that the backups are being written to a directory rather than to a single file. Otherwise, if you're a new administrator on the system, you'll have to go check the path to see whether you also need additional file-handling functionality when backing up to a simple flat file.

The instance uses a default naming convention for the files it creates, which can be overridden. The default name for instance backups is composed of three parts:

- The physical server name
- The **DBSERVERNUM** value of the instance being backed up
- The backup level with an "L" prefix

Using **ontape** with the tape devices set to a directory would create the following examples of named files in the target directory. I've edited these examples somewhat to remove permission, ownership, and other parts of the file name string.

```
Jan 26 03:51 nichole_123_L0
Jan 27 00:34 nichole_123_L1
```

If there is an existing file for a previous backup of that level, it is renamed with the time stamp of when the backup was created. In this way, you can easily find the latest backup of any level—it just has the **L***n* suffix in the file name, where *n* indicates the backup level:

```
Jan 25 04:34 nichole_123_20080125_043421_L1
Jan 26 03:51 nichole_123_L0
Jan 27 00:34 nichole_123_L1
```

The naming convention for logical log backups is similar. The third position, though, contains the word **Log** and 10 places of precision to hold the logical log number. For example:

```
Jan 26 10:34 nichole_123_Log0000000387
```

I don't know about you, but I don't remember or use the **DBSERVERNUM** values when referring to instances. I use something easier, such as the instance name or one of its more commonly used aliases. You can leverage this (or any other) string to override the file-naming convention with the **IFX_ONTAPE_FILE_PREFIX** environment variable. When set, the file names created contain the environment variable string and either the instance backup level or the logical log number, as shown in edited format here:

```
Jan 15 14:57 mproduction_20080115_145734_L0
Jan 16 15:14 mproduction_20080116_151436_L0
Jan 26 23:51 mproduction_L0
Jan 27 00:34 mproduction_L1
Jan 26 19:59 mproduction_Log0000000008
Jan 26 20:30 mproduction_Log0000000009
```

One final note about **ontape** configuration values: They are dynamically read each time you invoke **ontape**. As a result, you can change these values more or less at will without having to shut down and restart the instance. This gives you the flexibility to perform several administrative functions that require a backup without dramatically affecting the instance as a whole.

For example, adding a simple BLOBspace requires a backup to occur before the new simple BLOBspace is brought to an online state and is ready for activity. Using the **ontape** utility and leveraging the runtime read of its configuration parameters, you can temporarily change **TAPEDEV** to **/dev/null**, create a backup to bring the simple BLOBspace online, and then change **TAPEDEV** back to its original value. (Another option is to use the **ontape** and **ON-Bar** fake backup options, discussed later in the chapter).

Understanding the Backup Process

Another question commonly asked by administrators new to Informix Dynamic Server is how the data server can create backups at all, much less at different levels, while an instance is fully active and in a multiuser state. This is one of the nice features Informix Dynamic Server enjoys over its competitors in the market today. The answer lies in a part of the data page structures called the *page header* and is called the *page-ending time stamp*. In this section, I briefly explain how the online backup process works. In general, the algorithm discussed here is valid regardless of which Informix backup utility you use. I'll use an **ontape** backup as an example in this discussion.

Every time an element on a data page changes, an overhead structure on the page called a *time stamp* is updated. The relative value of any given page's time stamp to another page in an instance determines whether one page was modified before or after another.

The data server also uses the time stamp to determine whether a page was modified before or after any given moment in time. This is the key to creating online backups.

When you initiate a backup at any of the three levels, the first thing that happens is a checkpoint. The checkpoint flushes all the buffers to disk and synchronizes the disk images to those in the logical log buffers if buffered logging is set on any database in the instance.

Then, the data server sets what I'll call the *backup time stamp* for the instance. This is the moment in time when the checkpoint was completed, and it is one of the standards against which the backup process evaluates all page time stamps to determine qualification for being backed up.

Depending on the requested backup level, the data server will read and stream out either of the following:

- Pages with time stamps younger (or newer) than the backup time stamp of a previous backup of the appropriate lower level, as happens with level 1 or level 2 backups. For example, a level 1 backup would stream only pages with a time stamp newer than the last level 0, while a level 2 would stream only pages with a time stamp newer than the last level 1 time stamp.

- All used pages, but the pages copied will be as they were when their page time stamp was older than or equal to the backup time stamp, as occurs in a level 0 backup.

The backup process looks at each used page in a chunk and evaluates the time stamp on the page to see whether it matches the criteria for backing up. If it does, it is streamed out of the appropriate backup API. But what happens when the next checkpoint needs to occur and pages are going to be updated that haven't been backed up yet? This is where the physical log assumes a role other than that of ensuring the ability to roll back a transaction.

Before the checkpoint flush to disk, **ontape** and **ON-Bar** look at all the pages in the physical log. In looking at a page in the physical log, if the backup utility has already evaluated that page in the chunk to determine whether it should be backed up, nothing more happens with that page, and the next page from the physical log is read. If the next page stored in the physical log belongs to a chunk that the backup operation has not yet processed, the backup utility jumps to and evaluates the existing time stamp on that page in the chunk. If the time stamp qualifies the page for backing up, the page on disk is immediately streamed out of the backup API.

Once all the pages from the physical log are read and qualifying pages on disk are backed up, the checkpoint is allowed to continue, and the backup utility resumes work from where it stopped before the checkpoint. As part of the checkpoint process, the page time stamps of all pages affected by the checkpoint are updated. When the backup process gets to one of those pages that was backed up earlier as part of the checkpoint process, the time stamp on the page will be newer than the backup time stamp, disqualifying that page for backup. The backup utility will continue on and evaluate the next page in the chunk. This behavior is of little consequence to us because the page, as it existed before the start of the backup, was already copied to tape.

Looking at the difference between **ontape** and **ON-Bar** backups, **ontape** backups always execute serially and follow the chunk creation order explained earlier. As I've already described, with **ON-Bar** you can either emulate that functionality or create backups in parallel mode. You invoke **ON-Bar** parallel mode with the **onbar –b** command, while the serial mode includes an additional flag: **onbar –b –w**.

IDS 11 brings some significant changes to the way **ON-Bar** backs up data that I need to explain. As I noted earlier, **ontape** backs up spaces in chunk creation order starting with the rootdbs. Before IDS 11, **ON-Bar** serial backups performed the same way. A single time stamp was used, and chunks were backed up in the same manner as with the **ontape** utility. **ON-Bar** parallel backups were a different story, though.

With multiple backup devices configured into the storage manager system, you could back up several dbspaces in parallel using the **onbar –b** command. Each dbspace had its own backup time stamp, though, because each was backed up independently of the others. The backup process used this time stamp to determine whether pages within the space were eligible for backup depending on the backup level used. Likewise, during a checkpoint, pages in the physical log were compared with the spaces currently being backed up to determine whether to stream them out before flushing them to disk.

The net result of this old algorithm was that parallel **ON-Bar** backups required restoration of the logical logs as well as the dbspaces to ensure transactional integrity. After all the spaces were restored to their individual time stamp, the logical logs were used to restore transactions throughout the system to the time stamp of the last space backed up. This could be a very time-consuming process, depending on the size of the system in terms of the number of spaces, the number of transactions that occurred during the backup, the degree of parallelism involved, and so on.

IDS 11 brings two important changes to this process. First, regardless of whether the backup operation is a parallel or a serial one, **ON-Bar** now uses a single, operation-wide time stamp. As a result, a logical roll-forward operation is no longer required in an **ON-Bar** restore. The second change is that parallel **ON-Bar** operations use a different algorithm to stream spaces out of the backup API. Where as older versions of IDS used chunk creation order, with IDS 11 spaces are streamed according to their used size once the critical spaces are backed up.

With IDS 11, you can set the **BAR_MAX_BACKUP** parameter to a value greater than 0 (zero), and the instance will re-order how chunks are sent to the backup devices to reduce the total time of the backup operation. For the ordering to be as effective as possible, the value of this parameter should correspond to the number of available backup devices. If you neglect to put a value here, the system default of 4 is used.

Figure 7.2 illustrates how this new functionality is of value.

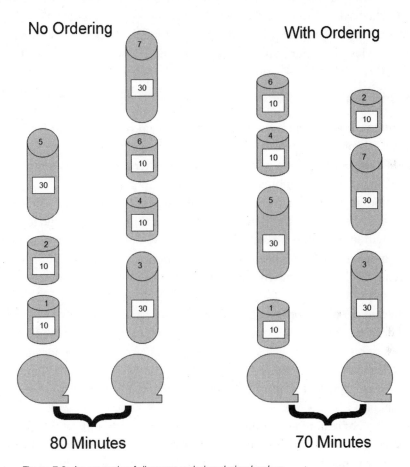

Figure 7.2: An example of dbspace ordering during backup

In this rather simple example, there are seven spaces to back up, with the backup time for each space shown in the box inside the space. Without ordering, the spaces are spooled in creation order with a large space at the end. With ordering, the largest spaces are backed up first (following the rootdbs, which is always the first thing backed up) followed by the smaller spaces. In this case, the backup operation is completed 10 minutes sooner. As the number of spaces and the size of the spaces increases, reordering the dbspaces will yield greater and greater dividends. This enables IDS to better leverage the parallelism available when you have multiple backup devices and reduces the total time required to create (and restore from) a backup.

As you can see, Informix Dynamic Server backups are literally a moment-in-time snapshot of the instance's contents. The last two reserved pages in the rootdbs contain all the relevant information about the last two backups, of different levels, created within the instance. The backup level, the real time the backup occurred, the backup time stamp, and information about the current logical log at the time the backup operation started are stored. You can view this information by executing the **oncheck -pr** command.

Restore Options

You have only two options when restoring from a backup. You can either restore the entire instance, commonly called a *cold restore*, or you can restore one or more dbspaces, referred to as a *warm* or *online restore*. The conditions requiring the restore will dictate which option, or whether a combination of the two, is appropriate.

A cold restore is required if a catastrophic failure occurs on an unprotected disk supporting the dbspaces containing the rootdbs, physical log, or any of the logical logs. The instance will immediately go offline because of the failure, and you won't be able to restart it. A complete restore or instance reinitialization is your only option. You can, of course, execute a cold restore at will, but the instance must be offline for the restore to proceed.

If unprotected disks supporting other dbspaces fail, or if you simply need to recover a space (other than the rootdbs or one containing the physical or logical logs), you can execute warm or online restore. This type of restore can occur with the instance in an online, fully active operating mode, although the dbspace(s) to be restored must be in a down state. (See Chapter 5 for information about deliberately changing the status of a dbspace or chunk.)

One other kind of restore operation became available to administrators with IDS 10. The *point-in-time table-level restore* uses new functionality in the **archecker** utility to extract the contents of one or more tables from a backup and restore the data to one or more staging tables. I'll discuss this feature, as well as the details of cold and warm restores, in more depth later in the chapter.

Redirected Restores

Although it's not a formal restore option, a recent change in the restore functionality of both **ontape** and **ON-Bar** bears mentioning. In the past, a restore operation was absolute in terms of a target space and where it was created; the restore process would only recover to the exact same location. This was another reason why using symbolic links when defining device paths was so important. The physical device, partition, or file could change as needed within the system, yet the path statements from which IDS worked never varied; they just pointed to where they needed to at the time.

Recently, it became possible to "rename" or redirect the data stream for a space (or spaces) as part of the restore operation. For example, if the original device path of one of the chunks in an instance was **/opt/IBM/informix/inst_1/some_name**, you could direct the restore operation to write the data being restored to **/ifmx_data/dif_inst/chunk_1**. The original goal of the feature was to enable you to restore a backup taken from server A onto a compatible server B even though the physical paths of the devices were different. You can certainly use this technique within the same physical server if you need to restore and it is not possible to re-create the symbolic links or if no links exist and actual device paths were used.

You could do this for a single device or for as many devices as you need. Available in both **ontape** and **ON-Bar**, this option requires only that you provide the original location information (path and offset) and the new device path and offset. With either utility, you use the **–rename** flag along with the **–p** and **–n** flags to indicate the old and new path/offset information, respectively. You can list as many devices as you need in the command string, but you run the risk of typos if there are multiple devices to rename. As an alternative, you can use a file flag and the path to a flat file containing the same device information.

Using the Ontape Utility

You can use the **ontape** utility to back up and restore all or part of Informix Dynamic Server instances and logical logs. In this section, we examine the required syntax to perform these operations. You'll see that one of the advantages of using this utility is its simplicity. It just works without a lot of convoluted setup.

Creating Backups (Including Fake)

First, let's look at how to back up the logical logs. As I mentioned in the discussion of logical logs, you can back up the logical logs on demand or continuously. To back up the logs on demand, execute the **ontape -a** command. This command copies the full logs to tape and then asks whether you want to back up the current log as well. If you answer yes, the current active log will stop recording transaction information and be copied to tape, regardless of how much of the log was used. While this is occurring, the next free log becomes the active log and begins to record transaction information.

To continuously back up the logical logs, execute the **ontape -c** command. This operation starts the log backup process in foreground mode in the command window in which it was invoked. Hardly any status messages are displayed from this command. When a tape is filled to **LTAPESIZE**, a message stating the log numbers that the tape contains followed by a prompt asking for a new tape to be inserted appears in the window. Other than that, there are no other messages or reports. Obviously, if you're backing up to directory using the IDS 11 functionality, individual files for each logical log are being created, and these messages do not occur.

Now let's look at the syntax required to back up the instance itself. The only flag you need to set is the backup level. The syntax is as follows, where *backup_level* is replaced with a **0** (zero), **1** (one), or **2**.

```
ontape -s -L backup_level
```

A few other flags can be set in conjunction with this command. Table 7.2 lists several of these.

Table 7.2: Backup flags for the ontape utility	
Ontape backup flag	**Description**
–F	Creates a "fake" backup. No data is streamed to the backup API, but instance flags are set indicating a backup occurred. This option can be useful when you're activating newly created simple BLOBspaces.
–t STDIO	Overrides the **TAPEDEV** parameter and redirects the backup stream to standard I/O for capture by the operating system process waiting there.
–v	Specifies verbose mode, which displays descriptive information about the status of the backup operation.
–y	Answers affirmatively to all command prompts. This option can be useful if you're trying to script **ontape** operations to devices other than a directory.

There is one other set of flags not covered in this table. As you learned in Chapter 5, database logging modes are changed in conjunction with a level 0 (zero) backup. This can involve appending a flag for the desired logging mode as well as the name of the database to the backup command. If you need to make a logging mode change to more than one database in the instance, using the **ondblog** utility eliminates the need to execute a level 0 backup for each database that needs to be changed. With **ondblog**, the target databases are flagged with their new logging mode, and then the change occurs when a single level 0 backup is executed.

While an instance backup is running, the approximate percent completed will be displayed. Be aware that this number may or may not be completely accurate. Before writing backup data to tape, the data server sums up all the allocated table extents in the instance. As the **ontape** backup operation reads through the pages, it calculates the percentage of the total allocation that has been read and echoes out the result in increments of 10 percent.

If a large number of tables have actually used only a small amount of the total number of pages allocated, the percentage calculation can be skewed. Because unused table pages will not need backing up, the backup process will bypass the rest of the pages in that table and move to the next set of used pages. The total page count read will be updated to reflect the current read position of the backup operation as well. As a result, the percent-complete calculation can appear to display erratic and inconsistent progress. This behavior should not cause you any concern.

Restoring from Backups

The syntax to execute a restore is as straightforward as the syntax for a backup. The following command performs a cold restore:

```
ontape -r
```

The following command restores a named dbspace:

```
ontape -r -D dbspace_name
```

By replacing *dbspace_name* with a whitespace-separated list of dbspace names, you can restore multiple dbspaces at one time. The **ontape** utility does not support moment-in-time restores per se; you are restricted to a logical log level of granularity.

During the restore operation, you can stop the process whenever you reach the end of a backup level to restore to the moment in time when that backup level was created. Or, you can continue when prompted by inserting either the tape for the next backup level or, if all levels have been restored, the logical log backup tape(s) and roll forward transactions one log at a time until you reach the latest log you want restored. Because **ontape** backups, and their corresponding restores, are based on a single backup time stamp, you are assured of logical consistency at the end of the restore operation.

You can also rename or redirect the data stream for one or more spaces as noted earlier. The syntax for this is operation is

```
-rename [ -f pathed_file_name | -p original_path \
   -o original_offset -n new_path -o new_offset ]
```

Using ON-Bar and the Informix Storage Manager

As the Informix Dynamic Server data server has progressed over time, IDS development has listened to its customers and how they have been creating and using increasingly larger and more complex databases to run their business. Along with size and complexity, these databases have assumed an even more critical role in the overall ability of the company to succeed and meet its business objectives.

IDS development recognized that the ability to protect these databases against a catastrophic system failure was critical. They also realized that something else more flexible in terms of granularity and scope than what the **ontape** utility provided was needed. In the sections that follow, I'll discuss the technology that was created or implemented to meet this need and how to use this functionality to protect your instances against failure.

The ON-Bar Utility Suite and the ISM

As I noted in Chapter 4, the **ON-Bar** utility suite, the Informix Storage Manager, and the Tivoli Storage Manager (TSM) client are optional components. They are installed as part of a default installation, but you can opt not to install any or all of these components.

The **ON-Bar** utility suite and the ISM are not the first attempt by the data server's development team to satisfy the demand for a better backup tool. The first tool didn't do very well and was allowed to fade to oblivion after a year or two. In its place, IBM released the **ON-Bar** utility suite (short for *ON*line *B*ackup *A*nd *R*estore), or **ON-Bar** for short. **ON-Bar** is IDS's implementation of the client component of the Open Systems Backup Services Data Movement (XBSA) API defined by the X/Open organization.

The utility was initially released as a standalone interface for third-party storage management products, but not long afterward a limited functionality storage manager called the Informix Storage Manager was bundled with the data server. The ISM was provided to give customers who didn't need a full-scale, enterprise-wide tape management solution the ability to leverage the functionality and flexibility provided by the **ON-Bar** utility.

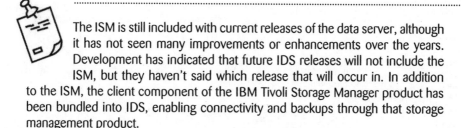

The ISM is still included with current releases of the data server, although it has not seen many improvements or enhancements over the years. Development has indicated that future IDS releases will not include the ISM, but they haven't said which release that will occur in. In addition to the ISM, the client component of the IBM Tivoli Storage Manager product has been bundled into IDS, enabling connectivity and backups through that storage management product.

The X/Open XBSA API itself was created as a standard through which applications could communicate to create and restore backups regardless of platform. It was designed to provide five basic functions:

- Concurrent services—The ability to concurrently back up and/or restore defined data sets of any type in a heterogeneous environment
- Object searches—The ability to search for a given backup object to initiate a restore operation
- Scalability—The ability to reliably store and retrieve a data set of any size
- System configuration independence—The ability to support a wide range of heterogeneous computing platforms and network configurations
- Integrity—The ability to configure and run backup and restore operations as independent events so that the actions of one operation do not adversely affect other operations

The interface contains four basic operational components, as illustrated in Figure 7.3. These components include the following:

- XBSA Client—This software sits next to the data that is to be backed up and responds to requests from the XBSA Manager to provide or receive data.
- XBSA Manager—This component handles the communications and administrative overhead between the actual backup software and the client component. It provides an interface into the image database catalog maintained by the Backup Service component (described next).
- Backup Service—This component is the software that actually handles the read and write operations to the storage media. It also builds and maintains a database that tracks the backup images that are available for use on an "as needed" basis.
- XBSA application—A user of the API, this is a generic term that can refer to either an XBSA client or an XBSA Manager.

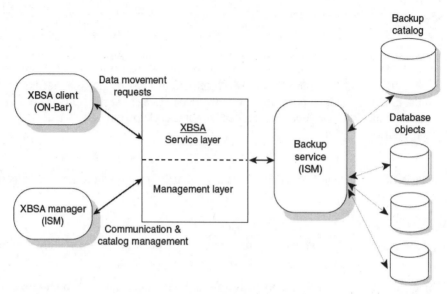

Figure 7.3: Overview of the XBSA operational components

In the implementation shipped with Informix Dynamic Server, the XBSA client is the **ON-Bar** utility suite, while the ISM fulfills the role of XBSA Manager and Backup Service. **ON-Bar** is called a *utility suite* because it is composed of two utilities:

- **onbar**—An executable that resides in **$INFORMIXDIR/bin** that calls the **onbar_d** driver. In Windows ports of the data server, this is a **.bat** file.
- **onbar_d**—The IDS driver that interfaces with the storage manager and actually executes the commands within the data server to manipulate data to and from the target instance as part of the backup or restore operation.

With the **ON-Bar** utility suite, IDS development got out of the business of trying to write backup and tape management software. Through the utility, the data server could interface with any number of compliant storage managers and provide the ability to back up groups of one or more dbspaces, whole instances, or the logical logs and to restore any of them. In some cases, the restore can be executed to an exact second in time if required.

As customer feedback on the **ON-Bar** strategy was received, it became clear there were some customers that did not need, or might not be able to afford, a full-fledged, enterprise-oriented tape management system yet could benefit from the functionality **ON-Bar** provided. Drawing on the lessons learned earlier, rather than designing and building a new backup solution, IBM acquired the rights to use a restricted-use edition of a now very old version of a third-party tape management product, and the product was bundled into IDS. This product is the ISM.

Functionally, the pieces of IDS's backup solution interact as shown in Figure 7.4. With the combination of **ON-Bar** and the ISM, sites can perform parallelized backups to a limited number of devices and take advantage of the media management that is included in the ISM product.

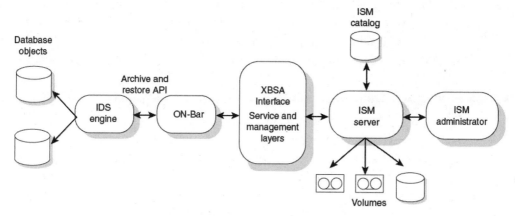

Figure 7.4: Functional interaction of the ON-Bar and ISM products

In preparing to configure and use the ISM or any tape management system, a few terms are worthy of review, particularly if you're not familiar with storage management products:

- *Save set*—The logical name for data backed up as part of a specific backup operation.

- *Device*—A physical device on which save sets are created. There are two basic classes of devices: tape and file. Depending on the resources available on your physical server, a single save set can be created on multiple devices of differing types. Note that with the ISM, you are limited to four devices. If you need more, you'll need to purchase and install a full-featured version of a tape management product. Best practices indicate that you do not use more than two devices of type file with the ISM so that you can use tape-type devices to make copies of the backups made to disk files.

- *Backup volume*—Also referred to as *volume* or by the generic term of *media*, this is the actual media used by the backup device. In the case of a file-type device, it is the file created on disk.

- *Standalone device*—A single storage device that contains no robotic or automatic tape-handling mechanism. The ISM supports only standalone devices, so you'll need to manually mount and unmount backup volumes for any given backup or restore operation.

- *Volume name*—The logical name given to a particular backup volume. Save set information is displayed as being created on **volume_name_1 . . . volume_name_n**.

- *Volume pool*—The logical name given to a defined set of volumes. As you'll see when we discuss how you actually use the ISM, it is a common practice to define and populate different pools based on their intended use. For example, you can create one pool of tapes for full and complete backups of the instance, another for the archiving of the logical logs, and yet another for making copies of other volumes. Each of these pools will have its own unique set of volumes used for backup or restore operations.

- *Volume label*—A logical identifier written by the ISM to a volume, not unlike a *header*. The volume label is used to identify media within a volume pool. All volumes within a given volume pool will share a common volume label that incorporates the volume name as part of the label. By default, all volume labels expire two years after being applied to the volume. This is done to promote the refreshing of the physical media because it will wear out over time. When a label expires, the ISM will no longer write to the volume even though save set information can be read off the volume provided the save set information is still available in the ISM catalog.

- *ISM catalog*—The database maintained by the ISM itself that lists the individual save sets, the pools and volumes used, and so on. This catalog is regularly written out to a volume in the **ISM_DATA_POOL** volume pool as part of the instance backup process.

- *Bootstrap file*—A subset of the ISM catalog, the bootstrap file is required to recover the ISM catalog after a catastrophic failure. It is backed up as a separate "object" in every **ON-Bar** backup operation. By default, this file, along with some other critical backup information, is written out to a volume in the **ISMData** volume pool. If you choose to back up your instance to another volume pool, the backup destination of the bootstrap file and the other objects must be configured as I'll explain later. Given the critical nature of these files, I strongly encourage configuring this destination if you'll be backing up to a different pool.

- *Retention period*—The length of time during which information about save sets will be kept in the ISM catalog. At the end of a save set's retention period, it is said to have *expired*, and although the data is not erased from the volume itself (unless it was overwritten somehow), all entries for that save set are removed from the ISM catalog. If you need to recover from a save set that has expired, you can recover either the entire ISM catalog from a backup or, more appropriately, just the save set information and update the ISM catalog by executing an **ism_catalog -recreate_from** command.

- *Recycle status*—Indicates whether all the save sets written to a particular volume have expired and the volume is now available for reuse. Although the default retention period is set for all volumes through the ISM and thus affects the recycle status of any given volume, you can disable the recycle process for a volume by changing its recycle status to **manual**. This setting preserves the save set information in the ISM catalog until such time as you manually recycle the volume.

- *Clones*—Within the ISM, you can make copies of entire volumes or save sets. The clones themselves inherit all the characteristics of the original, however; so if you clone a save set that is about to expire, the clone copy will expire at the same time as the original save set. You can extend the retention period by altering the property for the save set and changing the recycle period to **manual** to prevent the save set from expiring.

The **ON-Bar** backup and recovery mechanism itself is supported by several database structures. I have already mentioned the ISM catalog, which stores information about save sets, their expiration date, and their location in the various volumes, among other things. There is also a set of tables in the **sysutils** database that support and track **ON-Bar** operations.

You can get a rudimentary understanding of what these tables do by looking at their creation script in the **$INFORMIXDIR/etc** directory or by referring to the *IBM Informix Backup and Restore Guide* that accompanied your distribution of the software. In brief, the **bar_action** table tracks the success or failure of **ON-Bar**-based backup or restore operations. This table is the key to the restartable restore option of the **ON-Bar** command set.

The **bar_instance** table tracks successful backup operations. This table interfaces closely with the ISM catalog because it contains two numeric values that, when combined with information from the catalog, form a seed value that indicates where on a volume a particular save set is located for the given database object.

The **bar_object** table contains a list and overhead information about all the database objects (e.g., dbspaces, BLOBspaces, logical logs) against which an **ON-Bar** backup operation has been attempted.

Having established the underlying foundation and basic terminology that will be used to describe various components and functionality of **ON-Bar** and the ISM, let's look at how you actually configure and use these utilities to back up and restore an instance and logical logs.

Configuring the ISM and ON-Bar

Several configuration parameters in the **$ONCONFIG** file affect the performance of the ISM or the way **ON-Bar** interacts with any tape management system, including the ISM. Table 7.3 briefly describes these parameters.

Table 7.3: ON-Bar–oriented configuration parameters	
Parameter	Description
BAR_MAX_BACKUP	Think of this setting as the number of data streams output to backup devices during a parallel backup operation. It should be set to the number of tape/disk devices available.
BAR_XFER_BUF_SIZE	This parameter is used to calculate the amount of memory used for transfer buffers. It is an integer representing a number of pages with a total size limit of 64 KB. To obtain a maximum value for the parameter, divide 64 by the largest dbspace page size (in kilobytes). For example, if you were using 8 KB pages, the value would be 8.
ISM_DATA_POOL	This optional parameter specifies the volume pool to be used when backing up instances.
ISM_LOG_POOL	This optional parameter specifies the volume pool for backing up logical logs.
BAR_NB_XPORT_COUNT	This value establishes the number of data buffers each **ON-Bar** stream will use to exchange data between the instance and the tape management system.
BAR_PERFORMANCE	This parameter's value, from **0** (zero) to **4**, indicates the type of statistical information output to the **ON-Bar** log.
BAR_RETRY	The number of additional attempts an ON-Bar operation should execute should the first attempt fail.
BAR_BSALIB_PATH	This optional parameter specifies the path to the tape management system's shared library used to exchange data to and from the **ON-Bar** API.

As I mentioned earlier, the value of the **LTAPEDEV** configuration parameter is also important. If you plan to use **ON-Bar** to back up the logical logs, **LTAPEDEV** cannot be set to **/dev/null** or the Windows equivalent; otherwise, when a logical log fills, the instance automatically marks the log as "backed up." As a result, there is nothing for **ON-Bar** to back up. Setting the parameter to null also prevents instance backups from occurring.

Preparing to use **ON-Bar** for the first time requires setting the parameters mentioned as well as configuring the storage management system you'll be using. The setup for these systems varies widely and cannot be explained to any degree of satisfaction here. Instead, what I'll do is use the ISM as proxy for the overall process.

To begin with, you must tell the instance where the shared library interface is to the tape management system. There are a couple ways of doing this.

The first is to use the **BAR_BSALIB_PATH** configuration parameter. Set this parameter to the full path of the systems shared library. The second option is to re-create the **$INFORMIXDIR/lib/ibsad001.*platform_extension*** symbolic link and have it point to the management system's shared library. The third option is to include the management systems shared library directory in the **LD_LIBRARY_PATH** string.

The ISM's library is created in **$INFORMIXDIR/lib** and is called **libbsa.*platform_extension*,** so it would be easy to use either the first or second option. This file may not exist at first when you look for it. It may be created as a function of the next step.

Next, you must install and configure the tape management system. For the ISM, that means executing the **ism_startup -init** command found in **$INFORMIXDIR/bin** as root. This operation adds a series of binaries and libraries to **$INFORMIXDIR/ism** and creates the **sm_versions** file in **$INFORMIXDIR/etc** if it doesn't already exist. The tape management system you're going to use must have an entry in that file. For information about this file's format, consult the *IBM Informix Backup and Restore Guide*.

The ISM, like any third-party tape management system that could be running on the same physical server as the IDS instance(s), is a separate application and does not start as part of any instance startup procedure. If you want the ISM to start (**ism_startup**) or stop (**ism_shutdown**) automatically when the physical server is shut down or started, you must add the appropriate entries in the **/etc/rc2.d** and **/etc/rc0.d** directories.

Once you've started the ISM, you ought to grant administrative privileges to the user IDs that will be executing ISM operations. You accomplish this task with the **ism_add** utility:

```
ism_add -admin user_id@local_host_name
```

If you chose to use role separation during the installation process, you may want to add the account names specified during installation to the list of users able to make ISM configuration changes.

Setting the Server Properties

Perhaps the most important property you can set is how long individual save sets will remain active and available for use before they expire. In setting what is referred to as the *retention level*, you need to consider what your backup strategy is and the number of complete backup sets you would like to have available to restore from if necessary.

If your strategy is such that through a combination of full and incremental backup operations you'll have a complete backup of the instance(s) each week, you might consider setting the retention level at some number of weeks. The exact number would depend on how likely you think it would be necessary to go back *n* weeks to grab some data element.

You should also add some amount of time for what I call the "Oh, crud!" factor. This factor comes into play when, for some reason, a particular piece of media fails and you are not able to complete the restore without going back to an earlier backup set. Your choice of words in these types of situations may vary a bit from mine, but I usually add one to two more complete time periods on to the value of *n* for a little added insurance.

In setting the expiration period, you should know that not all save sets automatically expire at the end of their time period. Suppose you set the retention period for five days and create a level 0 backup on Monday and a level 2 backup on Thursday. While the level 0 backup would be set to expire on Saturday, it would remain active until one of two things happened: either another three days passed without any other incremental backup occurring, at which time the level 2 backup would also expire, or another level 0 backup was created. A save set will not expire if other save sets depend on it to complete a full restore.

Be aware that you can override the scheduled expiration of a save set if necessary. You do so by the **recycle status** of the entire volume to **manual** instead of leaving it at the default of **automatic**. With the **manual** setting, all unexpired save sets on the volume will remain active in the ISM catalog. When the setting is returned to **automatic**, the save sets will expire as appropriate for their time setting.

If you're using a third-party management system, you will need to execute the correct commands to review and set retention and other properties.

With the ISM started, execute the **ism_show –config** command as shown in Figure 7.5 to see its basic properties.

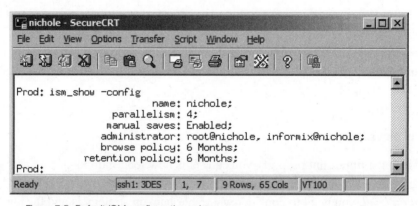

Figure 7.5: Default ISM configuration values

With the exception of an additional administrative user, Figure 7.5 shows the default configuration values for the ISM. To change the default retention period of six months, or to set the number of parallel data streams you want to use if the appropriate **ON-Bar** commands are issued, use the **ism_config** command like this:

```
ism_config -retention num_days
ism_config -streams num_streams
```

The maximum streams value you can enter is **4** in the ISM. In a full-featured tape management system, you'd want to configure the number of streams to match the potential number of devices to be used when executing a backup or restore operation.

Log Files

A number of log files can help you monitor various aspects of the ISM and **ON-Bar** operations.

ON-Bar Activity Log

The **ON-Bar** activity log contains a description of **ON-Bar** actions not unlike that contained in the **MSGPATH** file. Its name and location are set via the **BAR_ACT_LOG** configuration parameter in the **$ONCONFIG** file.

ON-Bar Debug Log and Debug Level

This optional log is used by IBM Informix's Technical Support department to help isolate problems within the **ON-Bar** utility suite. To activate it, you must indicate its fully pathed location via the **BAR_DEBUG_LOG** configuration parameter in the **$ONCONFIG** file. In addition, you need to set, via the **BAR_DEBUG** configuration parameter, the level of message granularity you would like. The levels range from **0** (zero) to **9**, with increased logging occurring as you go up the scale. At levels **7** and above, there is a considerable amount of output to the log file. You'll need to monitor the log's size to avoid any problems in the file system.

ISM Server Log

This log, residing at **$INFORMIXDIR/ism/logs/daemon.log**, records all ISM operations. When monitoring it in real time via a **tail -f** command, you can watch the ISM as it connects to its daemons, opens the ISM catalog, and mounts and uses volumes to create backups or to restore.

Legato Message Log

Okay, I haven't mentioned from whom the ISM was licensed. It was Legato, and this log, which resides in **$INFORMIXDIR/ism/logs/messages**, records messages from the Legato product itself. An abbreviated list of ISM catalog backups is regularly output to this log as well. This list is crucial if you're faced with restoring after a catastrophic failure, as I'll explain later in this chapter.

ISM Debug Level and Log

Similar to the **ON-Bar** debug log and level, this log with its associated level records debugging information about the ISM. It is located at **$INFORMIXDIR/ism/applogs/xbsa. messages**. Debugging activity to this log is triggered by setting the **ISM_DEBUG_LEVEL** parameter in the **onbar** file located in **$INFORMIXDIR/bin**. The debug level is not included in the **onbar** file; you'll need to add the parameter manually. Acceptable values for this parameter are similar to those for the **ON-Bar** debug log: whole numbers between **0** (zero) and **9**.

You can set the ISM debug configuration parameter in only one area of the **onbar** file, shown in Figure 7.6. This area, close to the beginning of the file, is where you can add any custom ISM configuration parameters. In this particular example, the ISM debug level is being set to **6**, which will automatically trigger output to the **xbsa.messages** file in the **$INFORMIXDIR/ism/applogs** directory. To terminate ISM logging, you could either comment out the line that sets the **ISM_DEBUG_LEVEL** or set it to **0** (zero). An ISM restart, performed by executing the **ism_shutdown** and **ism_startup** commands, is required for changes to this file to take effect.

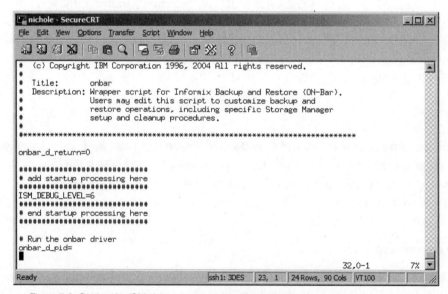

Figure 7.6: Setting the ISM debug parameter in the onbar file

You can also set this parameter as an environment variable, as documented in the *IBM Informix Storage Manager Administration Guide* that accompanied your distribution of the software.

Configuring Storage Devices

Your first step in preparing to use **ON-Bar** commands with the ISM is to configure one or more storage devices. With the ISM, you are limited to four devices, although each device can operate independently, enabling you to back up four dbspaces at a time if you use the parallelized backup command.

Before you attempt to configure a device, it has to be "known" to the system. By that I mean that if you're going to use a device of type **file**, the directory in which the files will be created must already exist. If you're going to use a tape device, it needs to be configured into the operating system through the appropriate setup routine. It also must be one of the supported devices within the ISM itself. (For a list of supported devices, see the *IBM Informix Storage Manager Administrator's Guide* that accompanied your distribution of the software.) If given the option when configuring a tape device, set the device property to **no rewind** so that the ISM can control the device.

To configure a device from the command line, you would execute the following command:

```
ism_add -device device_name -type device_type
```

Replace **device_name** with the fully pathed name of the device (e.g., **/dev/rmt/tape0** or **/ifmx_data/backup_dir**). For **device_type**, enter one of the media types supported by the ISM (e.g., **4mm**, **8mm 5GB**, or **dlt**). For example, to add a tape device intended for logical log backups, you could execute the following command:

```
ism_add -device /dev/rmt/4_tape0 -type 4mm
```

To check the operational status of the devices, you can execute the **ism_show -devices** command as illustrated in Figure 7.7. In the test machine I used for this book, there isn't a tape device available, so I have to configure file-based devices.

The next step in setting up a device in the ISM is to check whether it is enabled for use. This task requires using the **nsradmin** utility while logged in as the **root** user ID. Start by executing a **nsradmin -c** command to bring up the utility's main screen, shown in Figure 7.8.

Choose the **Select** option followed by the **NSR device** option. The utility will display the first configured device, and you can review its settings as illustrated in Figure 7.9.

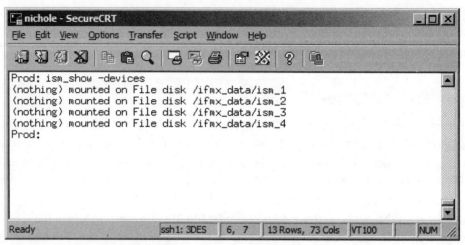

Figure 7.7: Displaying configured ISM devices

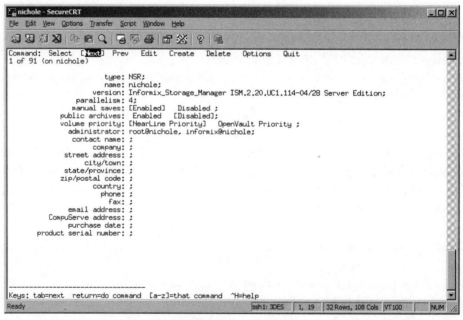

Figure 7.8: Main screen from the nsradmin utility

The current properties for the device are enclosed in brackets. You want to look at the **enabled** line midway in the screen to ensure the device can be used. If the device is not enabled, or if any other value needs to be changed, select **Edit** from the menu ring and make the necessary changes.

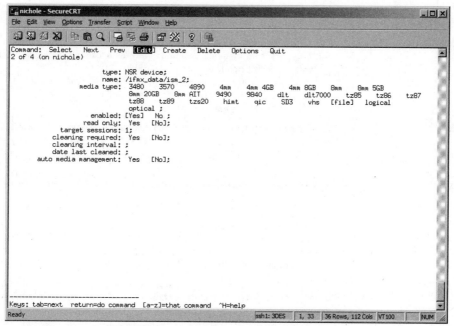

Figure 7.9: Utility nsradmin device configuration screen

Labeling Volumes

Once you've created one or more devices, you need to load and label the volumes and assign them to a volume pool before they can be used. To begin, you must create the directories for disk devices; for tapes, insert the media.

The process for creating labels on new volumes is exactly the same as re-labeling existing volumes to destroy any save sets that may exist on the volume. You must first decide which volume pool a particular volume will be part of. As you learned earlier, a volume pool is a logical grouping of volumes that contain the same type of data. For example, you could have a group of volumes that contains just instance backups or only logical log information. Once a volume has been assigned to a pool, it will be used only when mounted and an operation occurs for that pool. By that, I mean that if all four possible devices have instance backup volumes in them and a logical log backup operation starts, the logical log backup will be suspended until at least one volume is unmounted and a volume from the logical log backup volume pool is mounted in its place.

Table 7.4 lists the nine major volume pools that are configured into the ISM.

Labeling a volume requires using the **ism_op** utility. Its syntax is relatively simple:

```
ism_op -label device_name -pool volume_pool -volume volume_name
```

Table 7.4: Preconfigured ISM volume pools	
Volume pool category	**Description**
ISMData	This category is for instance backups of any level. Dbspace-specific backups are written to this pool as well. Two separate volume pools fall into this general category: **ISMDiskData** and **ISMData**. The first is only for file devices, while the second will accommodate file or tape devices.
ISMLogs	This category is for logical log backups. Like the **ISMData** category, it contains two separate volume pools: **ISMDiskLogs** for file devices only and **ISMLogs** for tape or file devices.
ISMDataClone	This pool is for making copies of **ISMData** or **ISMDiskData** pool volumes or save sets.
ISMLogsClone	This pool is for making copies of **ISMLogs** or **ISMDiskLogs** pool volumes.
Default	This pool is inherited as part of the Networker product and normally is not used. See the warning at the end of the "Mounting Volumes" section for more information about this pool.
Default Clone	Another pool inherited as part of the Networker product, this pool supports making copies of volumes in the **Default** pool. It is not used in Informix's application.
Full	A pool inherited as part of the Networker product.
Non Full	A pool inherited as part of the Networker product.
Offsite	You could use this pool to create a set of tapes for permanent or rotating off-site storage as part of your disaster recovery plan.

Replace *device_name* with the name of the device (e.g., **/opt/IBM/Informix/devices/tapes/tape0** or **/ifmx_backups/dev_1**). Replace *volume_pool* with one of the preconfigured ISM volume pools listed in the preceding table (e.g., **ISMData** or **ISMLogs**), and replace *volume_name* with the name you want the volume to have. For example, to label an instance tape volume with the name **inst_tape_1**, you would execute the following command:

```
ism_op -label /opt/IBM/Informix/devices/tapes/tape0 \
-pool ISMData -volume inst_tape_1
```

To label a disk-based logical log volume, you would execute

```
ism_op -label /ifmx_backups/dev_1 -pool ISMDiskLogs \
-volume danube_logs
```

You can use the **ism_config** utility to set the **recycle status** for the volume(s) you create.

You can use the **ism_show –volumes** command to see which volumes have been configured. If you need to delete a volume, you can use the **ism_rm –volume** command.

Mounting Volumes

For the ISM to read or write to the labeled volumes, they first must be *mounted* within the ISM. This is more a logical mount than a physical mount (although a tape does need to be in the device before you try to mount it in the ISM), which explains why disk-based volumes (which by their very nature are usually always available) need to be mounted before use as well.

Before trying to mount a volume in a device, select the device and then "detect the volume." Invoked by an **ism_op** command, the ISM will read the label of the volume in the device and update its metadata to reflect what volume is actually inserted into the device. To then mount (or unmount) the volume, issue the next **ism_op** command.

The syntax tree for these **ism_op** operations is rather simple:

```
ism_op [ -detect | -mount | -unmount ] device_name
```

Replace ***device_name*** with the device containing the volume.

For example, to detect and then mount a volume in a tape device, you would execute the following commands:

```
ism_op –detect /opt/IBM/Informix/devices/tapes/tape0
ism_op –mount /opt/IBM/Informix/devices/tapes/tape0
```

Figure 7.10 illustrates the whole process for the four devices I've configured into my test system.

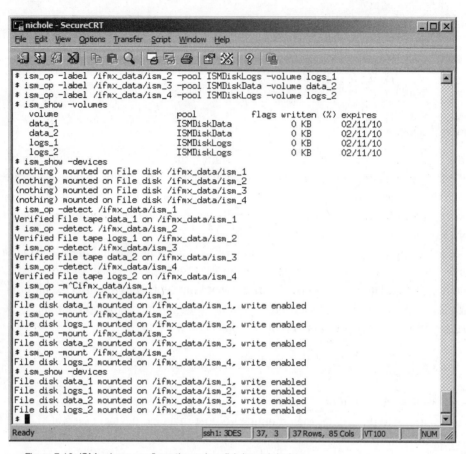

```
nichole - SecureCRT                                                    _|□|×
File  Edit  View  Options  Transfer  Script  Window  Help

$ ism_op -label /ifmx_data/ism_2 -pool ISMDiskLogs -volume logs_1
$ ism_op -label /ifmx_data/ism_3 -pool ISMDiskData -volume data_2
$ ism_op -label /ifmx_data/ism_4 -pool ISMDiskLogs -volume logs_2
$ ism_show -volumes
   volume                       pool            flags written (%) expires
   data_1                       ISMDiskData           0 KB        02/11/10
   data_2                       ISMDiskData           0 KB        02/11/10
   logs_1                       ISMDiskLogs           0 KB        02/11/10
   logs_2                       ISMDiskLogs           0 KB        02/11/10
$ ism_show -devices
(nothing) mounted on File disk /ifmx_data/ism_1
(nothing) mounted on File disk /ifmx_data/ism_2
(nothing) mounted on File disk /ifmx_data/ism_3
(nothing) mounted on File disk /ifmx_data/ism_4
$ ism_op -detect /ifmx_data/ism_1
Verified File tape data_1 on /ifmx_data/ism_1
$ ism_op -detect /ifmx_data/ism_2
Verified File tape logs_1 on /ifmx_data/ism_2
$ ism_op -detect /ifmx_data/ism_3
Verified File tape data_2 on /ifmx_data/ism_3
$ ism_op -detect /ifmx_data/ism_4
Verified File tape logs_2 on /ifmx_data/ism_4
$ ism_op -m^Cifmx_data/ism_1
$ ism_op -mount /ifmx_data/ism_1
File disk data_1 mounted on /ifmx_data/ism_1, write enabled
$ ism_op -mount /ifmx_data/ism_2
File disk logs_1 mounted on /ifmx_data/ism_2, write enabled
$ ism_op -mount /ifmx_data/ism_3
File disk data_2 mounted on /ifmx_data/ism_3, write enabled
$ ism_op -mount /ifmx_data/ism_4
File disk logs_2 mounted on /ifmx_data/ism_4, write enabled
$ ism_show -devices
File disk data_1 mounted on /ifmx_data/ism_1, write enabled
File disk logs_1 mounted on /ifmx_data/ism_2, write enabled
File disk data_2 mounted on /ifmx_data/ism_3, write enabled
File disk logs_2 mounted on /ifmx_data/ism_4, write enabled
$ 

Ready                        ssh1: 3DES   37, 3   37 Rows, 85 Cols  VT100      NUM
```

Figure 7.10: ISM volume configuration using disk-based devices

WARNING What is not shown in this figure is the creation of, and mounting of media in, the **Default** volume pool. A pool inherited as part of the OEM software, you normally will not use the **Default** pool. There is a single use case, though, where it is critical.

While a normal backup operation now copies bootstrap information along with instance data, if you want to create a separate backup of the bootstrap information with the **ism_catalog** utility, this information is backed up only to this volume pool. As such, you will need to create this volume pool and mount a volume for the operation to be completed. You can monitor this process through the **ism_watch** utility, described later.

When using tape-based devices, the ISM does not put any sort of a media lock on the device when a volume is mounted. As a result, nothing prevents you from ejecting a volume while it is mounted but inactive. I recommend, though, that you unmount any volume before ejecting it from the device.

If you don't unmount the volume before ejecting, you should always detect the new volume before trying to use the device again. This action not only synchronizes the ISM metadata to what has happened (volume **instdata.2** is in the device now), but it resets the physical media as well. Because ISM devices are no-rewind devices, without the redetection the ISM will think that it is at position x of volume n when it next attempts to write. In actual fact, it will be close to, or on, the label of the new volume and, if written over, the volume will become useless.

With devices configured and volumes labeled, assigned to volume pool, and mounted, you are now ready to use **ON-Bar** to back up and restore your instances and logical logs.

Creating Backups with ON-Bar

Creating **ON-Bar** backups using the command line, as opposed to a potential graphical option, has several benefits. First is the ability to parallelize the backup process across the four devices allowed in the ISM or however many are configured in your third-party management product. Second, you have the added flexibility of restoring to a logical log level or to the second in a moment-in-time restore situation.

Given the differences in the way parallel and serial backups are created, they are not compatible with each other as far as restore operations are concerned. For this reason, if you plan to use the **ON-Bar** command-line commands to back up your instance(s), you should standardize on the backup format you will use.

The command syntax for creating parallelized **ON-Bar** backups is as follows, where *level* is **0** (zero), **1** (one), or **2** as with **ontape** backups:

```
onbar -b [ -L level ] [ space_name | file_name ]
```

If no level is specified, a level 0 backup is executed by default. In addition to specifying a backup level, you can use one of two methods to list one or more individual dbspaces that are to be backed up. By default, all spaces are backed up, but if you have a business need to back up only specific spaces, you can do so with either of these options. The first method is to replace *space_name* with one or more dbspace names separated by a white space. The second is to replace *file_name* with a fully pathed file name containing a list of dbspace names to be backed up. This file should have one dbspace name to a line, with no other punctuation or dividers.

The command syntax for creating a serialized backup is as follows:

```
onbar -b -w [ -L level ]
```

As illustrated with the parallelized version of the command, you can specify the backup level you want by replacing *level* with **0**, **1**, or **2**. If the level is omitted, a level 0 backup is created. Because a serial-mode **ON-Bar** backup behaves almost exactly like **ontape**, individual or dbspace group backups are not supported.

Another distinction can be made between serial and parallel mode backups. When you use the serial command, the backup operation executes and then terminates. With the parallel command, once the backup is completed, a verification process occurs to check the volume label and the save sets. This does add some time to the overall backup process and so should be factored into configuring the time window for backups. During the verification process, the instance and its dbspaces are completely available for end-user access, just as during the rest of the backup operation; the volumes and devices used for the backup, however, are not.

Creating a "Fake" Backup

As I noted in the section on creating **ontape** backups, certain administrative tasks require a level 0 backup before taking effect. These tasks include switching the logging mode of one or more databases, managing simple BLOBspaces, and being able to reuse chunks that were dropped from a dbspace. Depending on the size of the instance and the amount of time available in the maintenance window, creating this type of backup may not be possible. You can, though, create a "fake" backup by using the **-F** flag to the **onbar** backup command. For example:

```
onbar -b -F
```

As should be abundantly clear, no backup is actually performed. As a result, there is nothing to restore from. You should perform fake backups for administrative purposes only.

The ism_watch Utility

One closing note: If you are using the ISM, you can monitor its operations as they execute. Invoke the **ism_watch** utility to monitor logging-oriented messages as well as activity on configured devices and mounted volumes as illustrated in Figure 7.11.

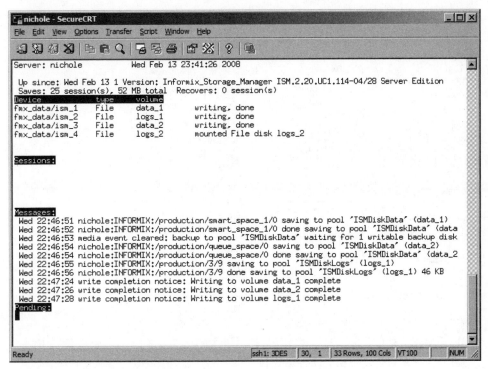

Figure 7.11: Monitoring information from the ism_watch utility

Volume Inventories

From time to time, you will wonder what save sets are stored on a particular volume or whether all the save sets on a volume have expired. You can try to dig some of these facts out of the **ixbar** file, but the easiest way to gather this information if you're using the ISM is to use the volume inventory management component of the **ism_show** utility as illustrated in Figure 7.12. If you're using a third-party product, it will undoubtedly have some sort of interface to display the same type of information.
Invoked by the command

```
ism_show -volume volume_name
```

where **volume_name** is a specific volume name, this component reads and displays what is recorded in the ISM catalog regarding the contents of each volume and the status of each save set.

The lower part of the sample display shows the save set information. Each save set in the volume is listed by its save set ID as well as by name. The third column hopefully will always be empty, but it may contain a **-S** (upper case) flag if the ISM considers the save

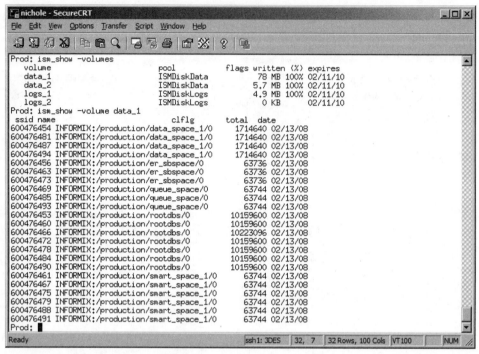

Figure 7.12: Volume inventory from the ism_show utility

set "suspect." The fourth column reports the size of the save set in bytes, while the fifth column contains the date the save set was created. You can use this date to calculate the expiration for the save set based on the configured retention period.

Restoring and Recovering from an ON-Bar Backup

At some point, a situation will occur where you'll have to use the backups you've been creating. Fortunately, restoring **ON-Bar** backups is not terribly difficult. As with the **ontape** utility, you can either restore one or more down dbspaces (a warm restore) or restore the entire instance (a cold restore). An added benefit with **ON-Bar** is that you can restrict the restore process with a finer degree of granularity. For example, you can specify that a restore operation terminate after the transactions in a particular logical log are rolled forward. You can increase the granularity of the restore operation by specifying a time value down to the second as well.

Restoring Instances and/or Dbspaces

You can execute **ON-Bar** restore operations from the graphical interface of your tape management software or from the command line. It's generally best to remain consistent in your approach, though; if you created the backup with a graphical interface, use it to restore as well.

Regardless of which interface you use, you can restore only save sets that have not expired. This restriction requires that you create backups on a regular basis and that your retention period be set such that you can have at least two unexpired save sets available at all times.

You can monitor the progress of a restore operation by executing a **tail -f** command on the **BAR_ACT_LOG** file or through the **ism_watch** utility if using the ISM. If a tape swap is required, the appropriate messages will be displayed here. If you're using a different tape management system, I'm sure it provides an interface to monitor operations.

As you already know, the parallel and serial **ON-Bar** backup modes are not compatible from a restore perspective. This lack of compatibility stems not from a dissimilar output format, although in the past it was due to the difference in how the logical or transactional integrity of the backup was fixed during the backup process. With IDS 11, that has changed so that both serial and parallel backups share a single backup time stamp. Today, the only difference is whether the backup was created to multiple devices or not. As a result, it is important to match the correct restore command with the format of the backup to be restored. Tables 7.5 and 7.6 describe the most commonly used syntax for serial and parallel restores, respectively.

Table 7.5: ON-Bar serial mode restore syntax	
ON-Bar restore command (serial mode)	**Description**
onbar -r -w	Performs a full-system, or cold, restore using the last full set of save sets. The instance must be offline for this command to be executed. When the restore is completed, the instance will be logically consistent.
onbar -r - w -p	Performs a physical restore of all dbspaces without rolling forward any transactions stored in the logical logs. When the restore is completed, the instance is logically consistent because the dbspaces are restored to the backup time stamp generated at the beginning of the backup operation.
onbar -r -w -l	Performs a logical restore by rolling forward transactions from the logical logs to dbspaces that have been restored only to a physical level. When the restore is completed, the instance will be logically consistent.
onbar -r -w -t moment_in_ time	Performs a full restore up to the specified moment in time specified. The format for the time value is *yyyy-mm-dd hh:mm:ss*. When completed, the instance will be logically consistent.
onbar -r -w -n log_num	Performs a full restore up to and including the indicated logical log number. Any transactions recorded in logical logs subsequent to the specified log are not restored. When the restore is completed, the instance will be logically consistent.

ON-Bar restore command (parallel mode)	Description
Table 7.6: ON-Bar parallel mode restore syntax	
onbar –r	Performs a full-system, or cold, restore using the last full set of save sets. The instance must be offline for this command to be executed. When the restore is completed, the instance will be logically consistent.
onbar –r –p	Performs a physical restore of all dbspaces without rolling forward any transactions stored in the logical logs. Starting with IDS 11, when the restore is completed, the instance will be logically consistent. In earlier versions of IDS, the instance will not be logically consistent because each dbspace is restored to the backup time stamp for that dbspace rather than to an instance-wide time stamp. A logical restore is required to bring the instance into transactional consistency and an operating mode that will allow user access.
onbar –r –l	Performs a logical restore by rolling forward transactions from the logical logs to dbspaces that have been restored only to a physical level. When the restore is completed, the instance will be logically consistent.
onbar –r –p [spaces | –f file_name]	Performs a warm restore of noncritical dbspaces that are down. The dbspaces to be restored can be listed in one of two formats, the first being a simple list of dbspace names separated by whitespaces. The second **format** uses the –f flag and a fully pathed file name containing the dbspace names, one to a line.
onbar –r –t *moment-in-time*	Performs a full restore up to the specified moment in time. The format for the time value is *yyyy-mm-dd hh:mm:ss*. When the restore is completed, the instance will be logically consistent.
onbar –r –n *log_num*	Performs a full restore up to and including the indicated logical log number. Any transactions recorded in logical logs subsequent to the specified log are not restored. When the restore is completed, the instance will be logically consistent.

Both modes have other flags you can use to modify the restore operation. Table 7.7 describes a few of the most commonly used **ON-Bar** flags.

For both serial and parallel restore operations, you can also rename or redirect the data stream for one or more spaces, as I described earlier in the chapter. The syntax for this operation is

```
-rename [ -f pathed_file_name | -p original_path \
   -o original_offset -n new_path -o new_offset ]
```

When you execute a restore operation, any logical logs that have not been backed up will be copied out to tape. This action is referred to as *salvaging* the logical logs. During the logical restore portion of a full instance restore operation, the logical logs will be overwritten with transaction data to be rolled forward. The existing logs are first salvaged

Table 7.7: Additional ON-Bar restore flags	
ON-Bar restore flag	**Description**
–O (capital "O")	Usable with all flags except for the **-n** and **-l** flags, this flag can be used to effect several restore operations, specifically: • Perform a warm restore of online dbspaces. You can either restore all dbspaces or use one of the options listed in Table 7.6 to pass in a list of dbspaces. When completed, the instance will be logically consistent because the logical logs are rolled forward. • Forcibly re-create a nonexistent chunk. Regardless of whether the original chunk was created in raw or cooked space, the chunk device created with this operation will be a cooked file. • Continue executing the restore even if a critical dbspace does not exist within the instance. At the beginning of the restore process, all chunk paths are checked to make sure they exist. Occasionally, a false error is raised that a path/dbspace cannot be written to. This flag forces the restore process to continue and attempt the restore. If the space is actually unavailable, the restore will fail.
–restart	For information about this flag, see the "Restartable Restores" section of this chapter.
–e	This flag executes an external restore. Briefly, an "external" backup and restore occurs within a centralized disk farm environment, using its ability to maintain fully synchronized copies of the disks. Copies can be "split off" or "frozen" as needed by suspending instance operations and executing the freeze/split. Obviously, a copy will contain a full image of the instance at that moment in time. To execute an external restore, instance operations are suspended while the old copies of disk replace those being used. The **onbar -r [-w] -e** command is issued to synchronize instance memory with instance metadata stored in the "restored" disks.

to preserve the information they contain in case it is needed for another restore operation to a later moment in time. Thus, the first step in restoring should be to mount a volume from the volume pool for logical log backups if one is not already available.

Performing a warm restore through the command line is a two-step process. The first step is a physical restore:

```
onbar –r [ –w ] –p –O [ space_name(s) | pathed_file ]
```

The physical restore is followed by a logical restore:

```
onbar –r –l
```

If the backup was created in serial mode, include the **-w** flag to the restore command.

During the restore operation, the space or spaces being restored are taken offline and placed in maintenance mode, effectively blocking all user access to it or them. Because during a warm restore the instance is up and most likely recording transaction information in the logical logs for end-user activity, the restore cannot affect these logs. As a result, the engine creates temporary logical log structures in the instance's temporary dbspaces to store the transaction information extracted from the logical log backup(s) to roll forward during the logical restore portion of the operation. Without sufficient space in the temporary dbspaces to store these log records, the restore process will fail.

One other insight about warm restores: Although you can append a time element to a warm restore, as in the following example, the extra time flag has no real effect on the restore:

```
onbar -r -p -O danube_5 -t 2008:01:04 23:45:31
```

During the logical restore portion of the operation, all transactions will be rolled forward, bringing the dbspace(s) current to the last checkpoint. This is the only way to guarantee transactional integrity in the instance.

Suppose, for example, that there was a parent table in one dbspace with one or more child tables in another dbspace. If you were to restore the dbspace containing the parent table to a moment in time several hours earlier than the existing state of the child tables, you could have a situation where committed child rows no longer had a parent row to reference.

If the goal in performing a warm restore is to recover to a moment in time just before a user or programmatic error occurred that had a seriously negative impact on data in one or more dbspaces, consider using the table-level restore functionality discussed later in this chapter.

Restartable Restores

One of the great things about the **ON-Bar** utility suite is the ability to restart a restore operation that stopped for some reason and have it pick up where it left off rather than begin all over again. This functionality is available because of the database-driven implementation of the **ON-Bar** suite.

In the introduction to **ON-Bar** and the ISM, I mentioned that the **bar_action** table tracks the success or failure of each **ON-Bar** operation. When you use the **-restart** flag to initiate a restore operation (e.g., **onbar -restart**), the operation queries this table for the last attempted restore operation. For those instance objects whose individual restore job failed, another job will be forked to restore just that object. Through the associated join to the **bar_instance** table with its location seed values, the restore operation can advance the media in the appropriate volume to the right location and begin reading the backup set. When the restore is successfully completed, the instance or dbspace(s) will be in whatever logically consistent state is appropriate for the original restore request.

To use this feature, you must enable it by setting the **RESTARTABLE_RESTORE** parameter in the **$ONCONFIG** file to **on**. This parameter is not read dynamically by the **ON-Bar** utility suite, so any change to its value requires an instance shutdown and restart for the new value to take effect. You cannot turn this parameter on immediately before attempting to restart a restore, either. It must be set before the initial restore operation. I generally recommend setting on **RESTARTABLE_RESTORE** when you initialize the instance and leaving it on.

By way of an example, here is how the restartable restore feature works. After ensuring that the **RESTARTABLE_RESTORE** configuration parameter was turned on and that the instance had been restarted at least once, I created a full backup of the test instance I used for this book. When the backup was completed, I dropped one of the six dbspaces in the instance with the **onspaces -d** *dbspace_name* command. I then restored the entire instance to a moment in time a couple of minutes before the time when I dropped the dbspace. With this restoration, I could test the backup to make sure it could restore all the dbspaces.

When the restore operation was successfully completed and all the dbspaces were recovered and checked for logical consistency, I not only dropped the dbspace but I also deleted the file in the data directory that supported the dbspace. I then started another restore to the same moment in time as the first restore operation. The **MSGPATH** and **BAR_ACT_LOG** files recorded errors attempting to access the physical device that was supposed to support the dropped dbspace, but the restore operation continued. When the restore was completed, the instance was in fast recovery mode with each of the dbspaces in an inconsistent state.

I re-created the disk file for the dropped dbspace and then executed an **onbar –restart** command. The dropped dbspace was recovered, a logical restore rolled transactions forward to each of the dbspaces, and when the restore was completed, the instance was in quiescent mode.

Recovering from a Catastrophic Failure

As you can surmise by now, a couple of files and database structures are critical to the health and welfare of **ON-Bar**-based operations. In this section, I briefly cover each one and describe how to recover or rebuild it in the event of a catastrophic server failure.

The **sysutils** database is created automatically in the rootdbs during instance initialization. As such, it is backed up whenever a backup operation includes the rootdbs. You can also create an ASCII copy of the **sysutils** contents using the **dbexport** utility, provided you are logged in using the **informix** user ID. Recovery would require a whole instance restore or selective SQL **insert**, **update**, or **delete** commands using the data files created by the **dbexport** utility.

The **ixbar** and **$ONCONFIG** files are *not* backed up as part of a whole instance backup operation. You would be wise to occasionally create a separate backup of just these files to a different media type (the files themselves are relatively small) and rotate them off-site for additional disaster protection. Recovery consists of simply copying these files back into the **$INFORMIXDIR\etc** directory.

The ISM bootstrap information is now backed up as part of the instance backup process. You can usually find the latest version on one of the volumes used for the instance backup. There is no recovery requirement for this file as far as **ON-Bar** operations are concerned, but the information this file contains can greatly simplify the process of restoring the ISM catalog.

The ISM itself generates and maintains the ISM catalog. The ISM uses this database to track the location and viability of all save sets created through its interface. Without the ISM catalog, you cannot hope to restore a single bit to your instance. There are two "recovery" methods for its information, the first focused on re-creating the catalog itself. The second method is oriented toward recovering information about save sets that have expired so that the sets can be used in a restore operation. Both methods require command-line activities.

If, for some reason, the ISM catalog becomes corrupted or is deleted, you can recover it from a save set created as part of an instance or dbspace backup operation. The key is knowing which save set to recover. In later versions of the ISM, this information is most often stored in the **Default** media pool. If the information is not readily available, you'll need to scan the volumes themselves to find the latest ISM catalog save set each contains. After mounting the volume, you can execute the following command, replacing ***device_name*** as appropriate:

```
ism_catalog -find_bootstrap device_name
```

This operation scans the volume and returns one row containing save set information about the last ISM catalog backup stored on the volume, as shown in Figure 7.13. As you can see in the figure, the latest version of the catalog could be recovered from save set number 600476500 on volume **deflt_1**.

With the volume and save set number, executing the **ism_catalog -recover** command restores the catalog off the volume to disk. The catalog recovery command first prompts for the device name where the save set is mounted. This is followed by a prompt for the save set number. The command also asks for a "starting file number" as well as a "starting record number"; choose the default of **0** (zero) for both values. After a confirmation prompt verifying that the volume is mounted, the catalog will be recovered from the volume. Figure 7.14 illustrates this process.

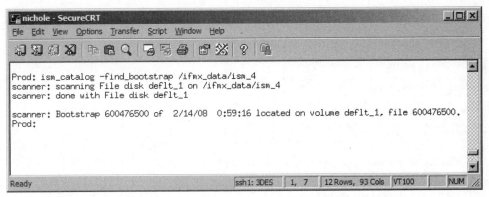

Figure 7.13: ISM catalog backup information saved as part of the backup operation

As you can see in the figure, one part of the catalog recovery operation is the re-creation of several critical ISM background configuration files, including the **nsr.res** file, which contains a lot of ISM configuration and operational settings. When the catalog recovery operation is completed successfully and the catalog is back in place, you should have full access to your unrecycled volumes and unexpired save sets.

You can recover expired save sets as well provided the volume itself has not reached its recycle date. This process does not actually restore the save set; it simply re-creates entries in the ISM catalog for save sets found while scanning the volume.

To recover expired save sets, mount the volume and then execute the following command, replacing ***device_name*** as appropriate:

```
ism_catalog -recreate_from device_name
```

As this command is executed, it echoes information such as the save set number found and its size while it updates the catalog. Upon completion, the volume itself will be changed to a **disabled** status to protect its contents from being overwritten. This does not prevent the volume from being recycled, though. To prevent this from occurring, you would have to change its status to a **manual** recycle using the **ism_config** command.

Logical Log Backups Through ON-Bar

Using the **ON-Bar** utility suite to manage the backing up of an instance's logical logs is a rather uncomplicated procedure. As you have already seen during the discussions on backing up and restoring the instance or a group of dbspaces, as of IDS 11 the logical logs are no longer strictly required for a whole-instance restore operation. Generally speaking, though, the current logical log is backed up as part of instance backup operations. These

```
nichole - SecureCRT                                                    _ □ ×
File  Edit  View  Options  Transfer  Script  Window  Help

Prod: ism_catalog -recover
ism_catalog: Using nichole as server

NOTICE: ism_catalog is used to recover the ISM
server's on-line file and media indexes from media
(backup tapes or disks) when either of the server's
on-line file or media index has been lost or damaged.
Note that this command will OVERWRITE the server's
existing on-line file and media indexes.  ism_catalog
is not used to recover ISM clients' on-line
indexes; normal recover procedures may be used for
this purpose.  See the mmrecov(8) and nsr_crash(8)
man pages for more details.

/ifmx_data/ism_1 /ifmx_data/ism_2 /ifmx_data/ism_3 /ifmx_data/ism_4
What is the name of the device you plan on using [/ifmx_data/ism_1]? ifmx_data/ism_4

What is the name of the device you plan on using [/ifmx_data/ism_1]? /ifmx_data/ism_4
/ifmx_data/ism_4: unmounted deflt_1

Enter the latest bootstrap save set id []: 600476500
Enter starting file number (if known) [0]:
Enter starting record number (if known) [0]:

Please insert the volume on which save set id 600476500 started
into /ifmx_data/ism_4.  When you have done this, press <RETURN>:

Scanning /ifmx_data/ism_4 for save set 600476500; this may take a while...
scanner: Reading the file label
scanner: Reading the file label
scanner: scanning File disk deflt_1 on /ifmx_data/ism_4
scanner: volume id 976223529 record size 32768
  created  2/14/08  0:54:02 expires  2/13/10  0:54:02
scanner: searching for ssid(s): 600476500
scanner: scanning file 600476500, record 0
scanner: ssid 600476500: found beginning of nichole:bootstrap
scanner: spawning `uasm -r -v -iY` for ssid 600476500 (nichole:bootstrap)
/nsr
/nsr: file exists, overwriting
/opt/IBM/informix/11/ism/res/nsrla.res
/opt/IBM/informix/11/ism/res/nsr.res
/opt/IBM/informix/11/ism/res/nsrjb.res
/opt/IBM/informix/11/ism/res/
scanner: ssid 600476500: scan complete
scanner: ssid 600476500: 52 KB, 16 file(s)
/opt/IBM/informix/11/ism/mm/
nsrmmdbasm -r /opt/IBM/informix/11/ism/mm/mmvolume/
/opt/IBM/informix/11/ism/index/nichole/
/opt/IBM/informix/11/ism/index/
/opt/IBM/informix/11/ism/
/opt/IBM/informix/11/
/opt/IBM/informix/
/opt/IBM/
nsrindexasm -r /opt/IBM/informix/11/ism/index/nichole/db/
/opt/
/
nichole: 11 records recovered, 0 discarded.
/ifmx_data/ism_4: mounted File disk deflt_1 (write protected)

The bootstrap entry in the on-line index for nichole has been recovered.
The complete index is now being reconstructed from the various partial
indexes which were saved during the normal save for this server.

If your resource files were lost, they are now recovered in the 'res.R'
directory.  Copy or move them to the 'res' directory, after the index
has been reconstructed and you have shut down the daemons.  Then restart
the daemons.

Otherwise, just restart the daemons after the index has been reconstructed.
Prod: nsrindexasm: Pursuing index pieces of /opt/IBM/informix/11/ism/index/nichole/db from ni
chole.
Recovering files into their original locations.
nsrindexasm -r ./nichole/db/
merging with existing nichole index
nichole: 45 records recovered, 0 discarded.
Received 1 matching file(s) from NSR server `nichole`
Recover completion time: Mon Mar  3 21:25:43 2008

The index for `nichole` is now fully recovered.

Prod:

Ready                                     ssh1: 3DES    82, 7    82 Rows, 93 Cols   VT100         NUM
```

Figure 7.14: Recovery of ISM catalog information from a save set

backups of the logical logs, however, should not be considered sufficient in and of themselves for protecting the instance against failure. For this level of protection, you need to be backing up the logs as they fill.

This process is handled through what is generally called the *alarm program*. When certain instance events occur, such as the filling of a logical log, the engine calls the program or shell script referenced by the **ALARMPROGRAM** configuration parameter (default value **$INFOR-MIXDIR/etc/alarmprogram.sh**) and passes a couple of parameters that enable the program or shell script to determine the correct course of action to take. Within the default shell script for **ALARMPROGRAM** is a parameter that triggers whether full logical logs are backed up. When turned on, the **ALARMPROGRAM** script calls a baseline template called **logs_full.sh** (also located in **$INFORMIXDIR/etc**). For the "logical logs full" event, the default action of this script is to invoke the **ON-Bar** logical log backup command, **onbar –l** (lower case "l").

As you know, you are not required to automatically back up the logical logs as they fill. Provided you have sufficient free log space so instance operations aren't affected, you can back up the logical logs from the command line with the same command used in the **logs_full.sh** script, **onbar -l**.

Cloning Volumes or Save Sets

Depending on how the backup operation has been configured, the amount of time available in which to create the backups, media quantity, and a general desire for disaster protection through off-site storage, there may be a need to create copies of either entire volumes or specific save sets. This practice is called *cloning* the volume or save set.

Cloning volumes and save sets provides more than just disaster preparedness. In the cloning process, the save sets are interrogated for integrity. If a set is bad or a volume has media problems, the cloning process will note that fact. With this knowledge, you are then better able to determine what, if any, remedial steps you need to take to either re-create or generate new save sets. As you'll see in the next section, there is another utility you can use to verify the integrity of your backups and mitigate the shock of discovering, during a restore operation, that the save set or volume has problems and cannot be used.

Cloned volumes or save sets are stored as separate entities in the ISM catalog, and you can view them like any other entity in the result set of an **ism_show –volumes** command. However, although clones are separate entities, they are not completely independent of the originals. A clone inherits the same retention and recycle characteristics of the original, so if the goal in cloning a save set is to extend its useful life because it is about to expire, you'll need to set the expiration period on the clone to **manual**.

By default, you cannot use cloned volumes or save sets in restore operations. When you request a restore, the ISM always searches for, and uses, the original volume and save set combination. If these are not available, or if you detect a defect after a clone was created, the clone can be used provided you perform one of the following actions before attempting to execute the restore operation:

- Either delete the volume:

  ```
  ism_op -volume volume_name
  ```

- Or change the status of the volume's save sets to **expired**:

  ```
  ism_config -volume volume_name \
  -disable_restore save_set_id
  ```

When the restore operation begins, the ISM will note that the original volume or save set (or sets) is not available, recognize that a clone exists, and request that the clone volume (or volumes) be mounted for use.

To clone a volume or a group of save sets, you need two backup devices. One device would have a mounted volume from either the **ISMDataClone** or the **ISMLogsClone** volume pool (or their disk-based equivalents), depending on what it is you are going to clone. The other device would have the original volume to be cloned. To initiate the clone operation, use the **ism_clone** command.

Cloning volumes provides a nice way to have your cake and eat it too. If, for example, the physical server does not have terribly fast tape devices, or for some reason backups are possible only during a very small maintenance window, you can create the backups to disk-based volumes. After completing this backup, you can clone the volumes to tape without affecting instance operations. With this strategy, the instance backup requirements are met, and the save sets are stored on more stable media for disaster recovery purposes.

Verifying Backups with Archecker

I believe it was in IDS 9.2, or possibly IDS 9.3, that a utility written by John Miller for use by the Technical Support organization was incorporated into the data server. Called **archecker**, this tool gives users the ability to verify backup images created using **ontape** and **ON-Bar** without actually executing a restore. The utility scans through the latest level 0 backup image, ensuring the format of the data contained therein is consistent with that required to pass through the restore API and be applied to disk. If run against **ON-Bar** backups, **archecker** also checks the integrity of the tape management system's control information by verifying that this system retrieves the correct volumes to execute the restore.

You use a control file to manage **archecker** operations. Simply copy the template called **ac_config.std** located in **$INFORMIXDIR/etc** and modify it to meet your needs. Set the **AC_CONFIG** environment variable to point to the new file name or location.

The provided template contains only three parameters, one of which is the log file location for the utility, but there are eight other parameters you can set to specify the tape block size, the location of the **ON-Bar IXBAR** file, the tape device to use, the timeout value, the file system location where **archecker** builds its bitmap structures to check backup data, and more.

Once you've set the configuration file, you can invoke the **archecker** utility in either of two ways. From the command line, point **archecker** toward either an **ontape** or an **ON-Bar** backup. Or invoke the utility through the **ON-Bar** API itself to check the latest **ON-Bar** backup. In either case, as the utility executes, status messages such as those shown in Figure 7.15 are stored in the utility's log file as defined in the configuration file.

The information shown in the figure has been heavily edited to reduce the line count, but you can see that the utility performs an exhaustive check of the tables in the system databases stored in the rootdbs and then proceeds to check the integrity of each dbspace's control structures. If the dbspace contains an end-user–created database, **archecker** checks the control tables for the database(s) exhaustively as well. After checking each dbspace's control structures, the utility parses the data stream for the dbspace to make sure it can be restored. After checking all spaces, the utility responds with an overall pass or fail result.

The command-line syntax for the utility is simple:

```
archecker -b (for ON-Bar)
archecker -t (for ontape)
```

With either form, you can also append a **-v** (lower case) to specify verbose output, although this option does little to change the functionality of the command. You're better off using the **AC_VERBOSE** parameter in the configuration file. There is also a **-s** (lower case) flag that copies the output sent to the **archecker** log to the screen.

If you use the **ON-Bar** "validate" option, the utility suite calls the **archecker** utility directly. In addition to the output in the **archecker** log, information is recorded in the **BAR_ACT_LOG** for the instance as shown in Figure 7.16.

Using the **ON-Bar** interface to the utility provides additional validation options not available from the command line. You can validate to a specific moment in time by using the logical logs as well as specify a subset of dbspaces to check. The syntax to use this option is

```
onbar -v [ -t time_stamp] [-w] [ -f file_name | list_of_spaces]
```

where the **-w** flag indicates "whole system" or serialized **ON-Bar** backups. You can either list the dbspaces to check or specify a file containing the names after the **-f** flag.

Figure 7.15: Archecker operational messages in its log file

```
nichole - SecureCRT                                                                    _|□|×|
File  Edit  View  Options  Transfer  Script  Window  Help

2008-03-05 23:42:52 3596  3594 /opt/IBM/informix/11/bin/onbar_d -v
2008-03-05 23:42:54 3596  3594 Successfully connected to Storage Manager.
2008-03-05 23:42:54 3596  3594 Begin backup verification of level 0 for rootdbs (Storage Manager copy ID: 600476501 0).
2008-03-05 23:42:57 3596  3594 Begin backup verification of level 0 for data_space_1 (Storage Manager copy ID: 600476502 0).
2008-03-05 23:42:59 3596  3594 Begin backup verification of level 0 for er_sbspace (Storage Manager copy ID: 600476504 0).
2008-03-05 23:43:00 3596  3594 Begin backup verification of level 0 for queue_space (Storage Manager copy ID: 600476503 0).
2008-03-05 23:43:02 3596  3594 Begin backup verification of level 0 for smart_space_1 (Storage Manager copy ID: 600476505 0).
2008-03-05 23:43:03 3596  3594 Completed level 0 backup verification successfully.
2008-03-05 23:43:03 3596  3594 /opt/IBM/informix/11/bin/onbar_d complete, returning 0 (0x00)

                                                                    495,2            Bot
Ready                                         ssh1: 3DES    9, 2    12 Rows, 130 Cols  VT100        NUM
```

Figure 7.16: ON-Bar log information from a backup validation

Using the Table-Level Restore Functionality

IDS 10 brought a significant enhancement to the **archecker** utility, one that IDS administrators had requested for quite a while. This feature, called *table-level restore (TLR)*, gives you the ability to restore a single table rather than the entire instance (**ontape** and **ON-Bar**) or one or more dbspaces (**ON-Bar**).

Before this version, if intentional or unintentional data corruption occurred, the administrator had to go through a slow and painful exercise to recover as much of the pre-corrupted data as possible. The administrator would back up the instance and then, using a prior backup, restore the instance or space to just before the corruption occurred, extract the data from the table(s) to another set of dbspaces, restore the instance to its most current state, and then replace the current, corrupt data with the data extracted from the earlier backup.

With the new functionality in **archecker**, you can now recover the data without taking the instance or dbspaces offline. Through the control file discussed later in this section, you can define the extract up to a specific moment in time based on conditions within the data (e.g., **column_1 <= 50**) and redirect it as necessary. All of these options are very powerful, but none is more so than being able, for the first time, to restore a backup created on a physical server running one operating system to another physical server using a different operating system! Finally, users had the ability to migrate databases across systems without having to use the slow and storage-space-hungry **dbexport** and **dbimport** utilities. They could extract from one instance's backup and send it directly to another instance anywhere on the network through a type of distributed transaction operation.

TLR can operate in one of two modes: physical or logical. When executed in physical mode, it uses the last level 0 **ontape** or **ON-Bar** backup and extracts all the data that match the control file conditions. If a table was partitioned into several dbspaces and the backup was created using **ON-Bar** parallel mode, you can perform parallel physical-mode TLR operations, each with a separate control file, to recover the table more quickly. In logical mode, after the level 0 backup has been processed, the logical log records created after

339

the backup are parsed as well for transactions executed on the source table that also need to be applied. You can control whether the log records are just extracted or are extracted and then applied. The default operation is if the data in the transactions match the control file conditions, the log records are staged in a temporary table, where they are replayed against the target table(s) through a type of roll-forward operation. In this way, you can bring the source table back as close as possible to the moment in time when the corruption occurred. Parallelized logical TLR operations are not supported, however.

But what happens if, for example, you don't know precisely when a critical table was somehow deleted from the database? Not to worry. As one of the primary business cases behind the development of the TLR, the **drop table** command is ignored as logical log records of operations on the source table are processed. You can execute a TLR operation to any time after you think the table was dropped and be able to recover the table.

Because it is an extension of the **archecker** utility, you are already familiar with all but one of the major components required for TLR. The control file, also called the *schema command file*, controls the TLR operation. In this file, you use basic SQL commands to define the source and destination database(s), table(s), table schema(s), the moment in time to restore to, and other conditions. You can define the full path to this file in the **AC_CONFIG** file or pass it as an argument when invoking **archecker** to perform a TLR operation.

There are only five major SQL statements in the control file. They are **database**, **create table**, **insert into**, **restore**, and **set**. Additional SQL **select** and **insert** commands within the **insert into** statement are supported.

The structure of the file is pretty simple. First, you open a database. Then you define the exact schema of the source table(s) from which data will be extracted. The target table(s) to receive the extracted data are also defined. The schema of the target table(s) need not match the source table(s); they can be completely different in terms of column count, column name, and partitioning scheme if desired. The data types of the columns to be loaded must be compatible (e.g., loading a **smallint** source into an **int**) if not exact, though. With the **restore** statement, you can indicate whether the TLR operation is to execute in physical or logical mode, with the additional option of indicating a specific moment in time to restore to. With the **set** statement, you can set the transaction interval or number of rows to be processed before a **commit work** statement is executed to prevent a long transaction from occurring. You can also specify which dbspaces to use to hold the temporary logical log staging tables during a logical TLR operation; these tables cannot be created in instance temporary dbspaces, however.

Let's look at some examples of command files. Listing 7.1 shows the first one.

```
database stores;

create table my_source_table
  ( customer_num serial,
    fname char(15),
    lname char(15),
    company char(20),
    address1 char(20),
    address2 char(20),
    city char(15),
    state char(2),
    zipcode char(5),
    phone char(18)
  ) fragment by expression
(customer_num < 114) in data_space_1,
     (customer_num >= 114) in data_space_2;

create table mytest
  ( customer_num serial,
    fname char(15),
    lname char(15),
    company char(20),
    address1 char(20),
    address2 char(20),
    city char(15),
    state char(2),
    zipcode char(5),
    phone char(18)
  ) in data_space_12;

insert into mytest select * from my_source_table;
```

Listing 7.1: Simple control file for a table-level restore (TLR)

In this first, very basic example, there are several things to notice:

- The source table's schema definition is fairly complete. It includes the column names and data types along with the partitioning scheme (if any), but constraints, keys, and indexes are not listed.

- If the destination table does not exist in the database, it, too, must be fully defined. In this example, the column names are identical between the two tables, but this is not required. If the target table (or tables) already exists in the database, you can go to the **insert** statement.

- Because there are no other conditions expressed in the file, **archecker** will execute in logical mode and restore to the most current moment in time.

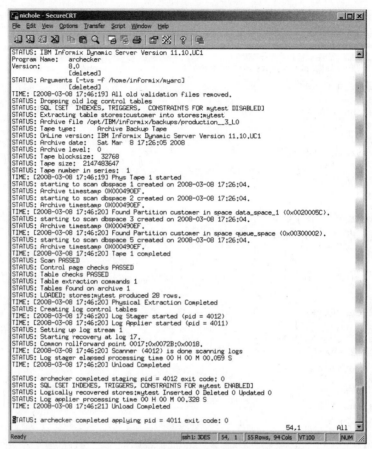

Figure 7.17: ON-Bar log information from a TLR operation

Figure 7.17 shows the slightly edited output from the **archecker** log file when a TLR operation with this control file is executed.

If you're trying to recover one or more dropped tables, you need to define only the tables that were dropped. The next example, shown in Listing 7.2, illustrates this scenario.

```
database stores;

create table my_source_table
  ( customer_num serial,
    fname char(15),
    lname char(15),
    company char(20),
    address1 char(20),
    address2 char(20),
```

Listing 7.2: TLR control file to recover a dropped table (part 1 of 2)

```
      city char(15),
      state char(2),
      zipcode char(5),
      phone char(18)
   ) fragment by expression
(customer_num < 114) in data_space_1,
      (customer_num >= 114) in data_space_2;

insert into my_source_table select * from my_source_table;

set workspace to work_1, work_2;
```

Listing 7.2: TLR control file to recover a dropped table (part 2 of 2)

In this case, the table will be re-created as it originally existed on disk. Because the command executes in logical mode, the logical logs will be replayed but the **drop table** command will be ignored. The control file also designates the **work_1** and **work_2** dbspaces to hold the temporary data tables generated as **archecker** parses the backup objects.

So far, we've looked at examples with just one table, but **archecker** can extract from more than one table and can populate multiple tables within a single operation, as the next two examples illustrate. In the control file shown in Listing 7.3, two source tables are used to populate a single target table. In Listing 7.4, the inverse occurs. One thing to keep in mind with these two examples, although it is not shown in the source code (to keep the listings small), the schemas for all the tables are identical in terms of column counts and data types; otherwise, an insert failure would occur.

```
database stores;

create table my_source_table_1
  ( columns ) in data_space_2;

create table my_source_table_2
  ( columns ) in data_space_6;

create table my_target_table
  ( columns ) in data_space_12;

insert into my_target_table select * from my_source_table_1, my_source_table_2;

set workspace to work_1, work_2;
```

Listing 7.3: TLR control file to restore a single table using multiple source tables

```
database stores;

create table my_source_table
  ( columns ) in data_space_2;

create table my_target_table_1
  ( columns ) in data_space_12;

create table my_target_table_2
  ( columns ) in data_space_13;

insert into my_target_table_1 select col_1, col_2, col_3 from my_source_table;

insert into my_target_table_2 select col_4, col_5, col_6 from my_source_table;

set workspace to work_1, work_2;
```

Listing 7.4: TLR control file to restore multiple tables from a single source table

Listing 7.5 shows one last example with everything thrown in.

```
database mac_stores;

create table mac_customer
( customer_num serial,
  fname char(15),
  lname char(15),
  company char(20),
  address1 char(20),
  address2 char(20),
  city char(15),
  state char(2),
  zipcode char(5),
  phone char(18)
) in data_space_9;

database hpux_stores;

create table my_customer
( customer_num serial,
  fname char(15),
  lname char(15),
  company char(20),
  address1 char(20),
  address2 char(20),
  city char(15),
  state char(2),
  zipcode char(5),
```

Listing 7.5: Distributed TLR operation (part 1 of 2)

```
phone char(18)
) in data_space_8;

insert into mac_stores@mac_instance.mac_customer
select * from my_customer where zipcode matches "75*";

restore to '2008-03-08 21:23:02';

set workspace to work_1, work_2;
```

Listing 7.5: Distributed TLR operation (part 2 of 2)

In this case, a distributed TLR operation will occur, with data extracted from a backup created on an HP-UX–based instance and restored to a Macintosh-based instance. The records to be extracted are filtered with a **where** clause limiting the data to an area of North Texas as it existed in the table up to a specific moment in time. When writing filtering conditions, you have the full range of basic SQL conditions, such as =, <=, **and**, **or**, **is [not]null**, and so on. You cannot use UDRs, aggregates, views, subqueries, or other advanced SQL syntax, though.

The syntax to use TLR functionality is as follows:

```
archecker [-b | -t] -X [-f pathed_file] [-v] [-s] \
[-l phys|stage|apply]
```

As before, you use **-b** or **-t** to indicate whether the backup media is from an **ON-Bar** or an **ontape** operation, respectively. Use the **-f** flag if you do not include the full path to the control file in the **AC_CONFIG** file. The **-v** and **-s** (both lower case) flags specify verbose mode and the redirection of **archecker** log information to the screen, respectively. You can also indicate whether the TLR operation executes in physical or logical mode with the **-l** (lowercase "l") flag. As I mentioned previously, the default is to execute all three stages, but you can specify just one or two stages provided they are comma-separated—for example, **-l phys,stage**. In this case, the data will be extracted and stored in the temporary staging tables but not applied.

Summary

Although the **ontape** utility has long been the workhorse for Informix Dynamic Server backup and restore operations, with the **ON-Bar** utility suite and ISM bundle or another third-party tape management system, you now have considerably more flexibility in creating a backup and restore strategy. While both options enable you to back up entire instances (or with **ON-Bar**, groups of dbspaces), you can also create table-level backups by using SQL commands or IDS utilities such as **onunload**. You can periodically verify your backup images with the **archecker** utility and use its extended functionality to restore one or more tables from backup images without having to take the instance or dbspaces offline.

When designing or implementing a backup and restore methodology, keep the following points in mind:

- Regardless of the size of the instance or the backup methodology you use, you need to periodically create a complete baseline backup. The amount of time between baseline backups will vary depending on

  - The size of the instance

  - The amount of time required to create the backup

  - The amount of change that occurs in the instance

  - The acceptable amount of risk and time required to re-create changes occurring after the baseline backup

- Starting with IDS 11, there is official support for **ontape** or **ON-Bar** backups created on tape media with compression. With this release, you can use "backup filter" technology to insert a compression and/or an encryption algorithm into the data stream as it passes from the instance to the backup and restore API. The ISM utility has its own internal compression utility, which you can invoke by setting the **ISM_COMPRESSION** environment variable. This is a software-based compression algorithm, however. You will obtain better performance using any hardware-based compression your backup device provides.

- When using the **ontape** utility to create backups, set the **TAPESIZE** and **LTAPESIZE** parameters to **0** (zero) if **TAPEDEV** and/or **LTAPEDEV** are pointed to tape devices. This setting will enable the entire capacity of the media to be used for operations. **Ontape** will also gracefully handle end-of-media events without causing the operation to fail. Set these parameters to whatever maximum file size is available in the selected drive and file system if **TAPEDEV** and/or **LTAPEDEV** point to disk files or to the new directory option.

- When you use **/dev/null** as an **ontape** backup device, you can accomplish certain functions, such as changing database logging modes or automatically freeing logical logs, rather quickly. Obviously, backups created to **/dev/null** cannot be restored. Be aware, however, that the practical value of **/dev/null** as a backup device for instance changes is not that great with the availability of the fake backup option in the **ON-Bar** utility suite as well as in **ontape**. Setting **LTAPEDEV** to **/dev/null** effectively eliminates using the **ON-Bar** utility suite for backup and recovery operations as well. Although the logical logs are no longer required for parallelized full-instance restores, they are required for moment-in-time or partial restores where transactional integrity must be assured through a logical roll-forward operation.

- Regardless of which backup utility you use, the availability of various backup levels lets you reduce the total time required to create or restore from a backup.

- If an instance has databases operating in logged mode and only one tape device is available to the system, make sure you run your backups during a period of time that will enable them to be completed without the logical logs filling up.

- Some DML and DDL statements, such as dropping a BLOB or creating a BLOBspace, require the logical log recording the transaction to be closed and backed up before being completed. The **ontape** utility and the **ON-Bar** suite both have flags to invoke an immediate logical log backup operation to close and backup the current log.

- **ON-Bar** backup and restore operations can operate in serial or parallel mode depending on the commands used. If you have multiple backup devices available, you can drastically reduce the amount of time required to back up a large instance by using the parallel **ON-Bar** commands with the dbspace reordering functionality that was introduced in IDS 11. **ON-Bar** parallel restore operations no longer require the rolling forward of logical log information as a separate step to achieve logical consistency.

- Depending on the backup operations executed, additional ISM and instance configuration files should be backed up to another media form or, in some cases, printed. They will help you recover in the event there is a complete system failure and you must manually recover all aspects of the IDS system, including **ON-Bar** functionality.

- You can clone **ON-Bar** volumes or save sets for disaster recovery, creating remote environments, or to validate the integrity of a volume and the save sets it contains. Cloned volumes or save sets inherit the expiration and recycle parameters of the originals. Clones cannot be used for restores unless you declare the originals unavailable in the ISM catalog.

- You should periodically check the integrity of your backups with the **archecker** utility.

In the next chapter, we'll explore the various utilities you can use to look inside the instance as a whole, or into an individual user session, to see what tasks are being executed and resources used.

8

Monitoring the Instance

In this Chapter

‣ Finding out what SQL statement a user session is executing

‣ Determining how efficiently the instance is reading or writing data

‣ Seeing how much table interleaving is occurring in the dbspaces

‣ Checking whether an index is corrupted

‣ Determining the values with which the instance was brought online

‣ Monitoring key instance elements or functionality from a graphical interface in real time

As you already know, high-performance database environments are not plug-and-play ready. In complex environments, data servers require daily care, feeding, and maintenance. Depending on the vendor, they may require a lot of care and attention. Luckily for you, Informix Dynamic Server does not. In fact, many customers using IDS are not even aware of it. IDS powers their corporate telephone and video conferencing systems, enabling them to place or receive calls and voicemails or to conduct meetings with participants from all over the world as though everyone were on-site. Elsewhere, IDS captures and processes results from life-critical medical tests so doctors and others can properly treat patients. IDS makes it possible for subscribers to send and receive text messages on mobile telephone systems and to purchase video on demand (VOD) from satellite and other providers. IDS reconciles the billing transactions for the world's largest credit card company. (Unfortunately, this means you'll always get your charges! Sorry, but that's the reliability of Informix Dynamic Server for you.)

In short, IDS just runs and runs without any administrative intervention. To be sure, backups and other administrative tasks must be performed, but one Dynamic Server

Administrator can easily support a healthy number of IDS instances spread across the enterprise, however far it reaches geographically.

There are times, though, when you'll need to know what is going on in an instance or database. This chapter introduces several utilities to help you look into the bowels of the IDS data server and monitor what's happening. Two of the utilities function from the command line and are the primary tools you'll use. I'll also briefly cover the functionality available through the OpenAdmin Tool for IDS (OAT). By the end of the chapter, you should understand the purpose of each tool and how to use each one to generate the type of information you want.

The New System Administration Interface

One of the few complaints new administrators make about IDS is that it's "difficult" to understand the IDS command-line utilities. As a data server deeply rooted in the Unix world, IDS's primary administrative interface has been a series of command-line interface (CLI) tools. That's not to say graphical utilities don't exist; several have come and gone as I've worked with the data server. Today, some very good ones are available, including OAT, Server Studio, and DBSonar from Cobrasonic Software. Regardless of whether you prefer to use graphical versus command-line tools, starting with IDS 11, there's a new way to administer IDS that requires neither a GUI nor learning the intricacies of the **onspaces** or **onparams** utility: the SQL Administration API.

Built on top of the **sysadmin** database, a new instance-level database, and about 16 new tables in the **sysmaster** database, the SQL Administration API gives members of the Database Server Administrator (DBSA) group access to a broad range of functionality, including alerts, performance monitoring, and baseline generation as well as instance maintenance. Because the API is SQL-based, you can execute commands from any machine with basic instance connectivity—there's no need to have the overhead of a Web server or a heavyweight client application.

Focusing on the administration part for the moment, the API provides a set of functions to perform routine operations and manage storage spaces, instance configuration, and validation. Executed commands and their results are captured for forensic purposes should the need arise to review what's changed in the instance.

The API's **task()** function accepts a series of string fields that specify the operation to perform and any parameters for the operation. The function returns plain text indicating whether the command succeeded. For example:

```
execute function
  task ('add log', 'logs_space', '10 MB', '1');

(expression) created logical log number 15 in logs_space

execute function task('archive fake');

(expression) backup complete
```

The API's **admin()** function accepts the same set of parameters but returns an integer based on the success or failure of the command. If the returned value is positive, the command succeeded and the returned value represents the serial number for the row in the **command_history** table that recorded the transaction. If the function returns **0** (zero), the command succeeded but the data server wasn't able to insert a new row into the history table (time to check your free space!). If the returned value is a negative number, the command failed. Here are a couple **admin()** function examples:

```
execute function
  admin('create with_check dbspace','tagus_data_1',
        '/opt/IBM/Informix/devices/tagus/data_1',
        '300 MB', '0');

(expression) 234

execute function admin('shutdown');

(expression) 400
```

To minimize the amount of typing, path names can start with an environment variable provided the variable exists in the target server's environment. You can also use "real" units (e.g., **KB**, **MB**, **GB**) for sizes as opposed to trying to remember whether to use pages or kilobytes, as is sometimes required with the CLI utilities.

All told, you can execute about 80 operations or tasks through the SQL Administration API, making it a serious contender for my preferred IDS administration tool! In IDS 11.5, Chapter 6 of the *IBM Informix Guide to SQL: Syntax* manual documents the full syntax for each of the commands, so you no longer have to guess at parameter order. The OAT utility, introduced in Chapter 5 and described further later in this chapter, makes extensive use of this new API.

Command-Line Utilities

Every port of Informix Dynamic Server contains the **onstat** and **oncheck** utilities. Together, these two utilities form the lingua franca of Informix investigative tools. The functionality of the two utilities has increased substantially over the years as new flags have been added, giving IDS DBAs and administrators more information about instance operations and database structures.

You use the **onstat** utility to monitor the operational "status" of an instance or a thread. The output returned by this utility is almost exclusively derived from queries into the System Monitoring Interface (SMI). (Chapter 4 provides more information about the SMI.) Given that the **onstat** utility commands are moment-in-time snapshots from the instance's shared memory, the returned results can be highly volatile if viewed individually.

You use the **oncheck** utility to verify instance or database configuration information that primarily resides on disk. There is much less volatility in the information **oncheck** displays.

The *IBM Informix Dynamic Server Administrator's Reference* describes both of these utilities and their flags fairly well. That said, some parts of the output from many of the flags are not documented for public consumption. Over time, more and more of this output has been explained in the documentation, but the coverage is not yet complete. I won't try in this chapter to re-explain every flag option or what the output generated by each flag looks like. What I will do, however, is cover some of the flag options of each utility that I find most helpful to use. A couple of commands, such as **onstat -p**, are described in other chapters, and I won't go over them again here.

Engine Status Reports: The onstat Utility

For newcomers to Informix Dynamic Server, the **onstat** utility is the most difficult to master. That's not because it is complicated to use; it's just that there are so many flags and options to remember and use. Some of the options are driven by a single flag with either a lower- or an uppercase letter, while the **-g** flag requires additional parameters, such as a three-letter root often followed by still other parameters. Listing 8.1 provides a complete key to the **onstat** flags.

```
USAGE: onstat [ -abBcCdDfFgGhjklmOpPRstTuxXz ] [ -i ]
              [ -r [<seconds>] ] [ -o [<outfile>] ] [ <infile> ]

FLAG      DESCRIPTION
--        Print this help text
<infile>  Read shared memory information from specified dump file
-a        Print all info
-b        Print buffers
-B        Print all buffers
-c        Print configuration file
-C        Print btree cleaner requests
-d [update]
          Print spaces and chunks
             update - Ask server to update BLOB chunk statistics
-D        Print spaces and detailed chunk stats
-f        Print dataskip status
-F        Print page flushers
```

Listing 8.1: Flags and parameters for the onstat utility (part 1 of 5)

```
-g <cmd>  MULTITHREADING COMMAND or
          ENTERPRISE REPLICATION COMMAND (see below)

-G        Print global transaction IDs
-h        Print buffer hash chain info
-i        Interactive mode
-j        Print interactive status of the active onpload process
-k        Print locks
-l        Print logging
-m        Print message log
-o <file_name>
          Put shared memory into specified file (default: onstat.out)
-O        Print optical subsystem memory and staging cache information
-p        Print profile
-P        Print partition buffer summary
-r <seconds>
          Repeat options every <seconds> seconds (default: 5)
-R        Print LRU queues
-s        Print latches
-t        Print tablespaces
-T        Print tablespace information
-u        Print user threads
-x        Print transactions
-X        Print entire list of sharers and waiters for buffers
-z        Zero profile counts
```

MULTITHREADING COMMANDS:
```
act       Print active threads
afr <pool_name | session_id>
          Print allocated pool fragments
all       Print all multithreading information
ath       Print all threads
buf       Print profile information related to buffer pools
ckp       Print checkpoint statistics
cmsm      Print Connection Manager statistics
con       Print conditions with waiters
cpu       Print CPU info for all threads
dbc       Print dbScheduler/dbWorker thread info
ddr       Print DDR log post processing information
dic       Print dictionary cache information
dis       Print a list of database servers and the status of each
dll       Print dynamic library statistics
dmp <address> <length>
          Dump <length> bytes of shared memory starting at <address>
dri       Print data replication information
dsc       Print a list of distribution cache information
env [all | [<session-id>]] [<variable-name>[,<variable-name>...]]
          Display environment variable settings
ffr <pool_name | session_id>
          Print free pool fragments
```

Listing 8.1: Flags and parameters for the onstat utility (part 2 of 5)

```
glo       Print global multithreading information
his [<ntraces>]
          Print SQL statement tracing information for <ntraces>
              no <ntraces> - Complete output from trace buffer
idxscan   Print index scan profiles
imc       Print information about connected MaxConnect instances
iob       Print big buffer usage by I/O VP class
iof       Print disk I/O statistics by chunk/file
iog       Print AIO global information
iov       Print disk I/O statistics by VP
ipl       Print index page logging status
lap       Print light append information
lmx       Print all locked mutexes
lsc       Print light scan information
mem [<pool_name> | <session_id>]
          Print pool statistics
mgm       Print Memory Grant Manager information
nbm       Print block map for nonresident segments
nsc [<client_id>]
          Print net shared memory status
nsd       Print net shared memory data
nss [<session_id>]
          Print net shared memory status
ntd       Print net dispatch information
ntm       Print net message information
ntt       Print net user thread access times
ntu       Print net user thread profile information
opn [<tid>]
          Print open tables
plk       Print partition lock profiles
pos       Print /INFORMIXDIR/etc/.infos.DBSERVERNAME file
ppf [<partition_number> | 0]
          Print partition profiles
prc       Print information about SPL routine cache
qst       Print queue statistics
rbm       Print block map for resident segment
rea       Print ready threads
rss [verbose | log | <RSS_server_name>]
          Print RSS server-related information
rwm       Print read/write mutex lists
sch       Print VP scheduler statistics
sds [verbose | <SDS server name>]
          Print SDS related information
seg       Print memory segment statistics
ses [<session_id>]
          Print session information
sle       Print all sleeping threads
smb       Print smart large object usage
smx [ses]
          Print server multiplexer-related information
```

Listing 8.1: Flags and parameters for the onstat utility (part 3 of 5)

```
spi        Print spin locks with long spins
sql [<session-id>]
           Print SQL information
src <pattern> <mask>
           Search memory for <pattern>, where <pattern>==(memory&<mask>)
ssc [pool | all]
           Print SQL statement cache pool summary, or SQL statement cache
              summary and entries, including key-only entries (all)
stk <tid>
           Dump the stack of a specified thread
stm [<session_id>]
           Print the approximate memory usage of all prepared statements
           in a session
stq [<session_id>]
           Print stream queue information
sts        Print max and current stack sizes
tgp        Print generic page thread profiles
tpf [<tid> | 0]
           Print thread profiles
ufr <pool_name | session_id>
           Print pool usage breakdown
vpcache    Print CPU VP memory block cache statistics
wai        Print waiting threads
wmx        Print all mutexes with waiters
wst        Print thread wait statistics
```

ENTERPRISE REPLICATION COMMANDS:
```
cat [scope | replname ]
           Print Enterprise Replication global catalog information

cdr
           Print Enterprise Replication statistics

cdr config [parameter_name] [long]
cdr config CDR_ENV [variable_name] [long]
           Print Enterprise Replication configuration information.
           Not specifying a parameter will display the name of and
           information about all available parameters.

dtc
           Print statistics for the Enterprise Replication delete table cleaner

dss [ UDR | UDRx ]
           Print statistics about data sync threads and user-defined data types

grp [ A|E|Ex|G|L|Lx|M|Mz|P|pager|R|S|Sl|Sx|T|UDR|UDRx ]
           Print statistics about the Enterprise Replication grouper

nif [all | sites | serverid | sum]
           Print statistics about the Enterprise Replication network interface
```

Listing 8.1: Flags and parameters for the onstat utility (part 4 of 5)

```
que
        Print statistics for the Enterprise Replication high-level queues

rcv [serverid]
        Print statistics about the Enterprise Replication receive manager

rep [replname]
            Print events that are in the queue for the schedule manager

rqm [ ACKQ | CNTRLQ | RECVQ | SENDQ | SYNCQ | SBSPACES | FULL |
      BRIEF | VERBOSE ]
        Print statistics of the Enterprise Replication low-level queues

sync
        Print the Enterprise Replication synchronization status
```

Listing 8.1: Flags and parameters for the onstat utility (part 5 of 5)

The functionality in the **onstat** utility gives you the ability to see what's happening in the instance to which your environment points. This type of functionality has existed for years in mainframe-based data servers but was sorely lacking on data servers on distributed platforms. Although I don't pretend that complete parity exists in feature sets between mainframe and IDS analysis tools, what IDS offers is at least comparable to, and in some cases better than, mainframe systems.

The functionality of the **onstat** utility is a significant differentiator from other Unix/ Windows-based data servers on the market today. You can literally see *everything* that is occurring in the instance at any moment in time. I'll be honest and say that some of what you see will be a bit cryptic because the output is in hexadecimal. You may need to link identifiers from several different command outputs that examine one aspect of instance functionality to get a complete picture of what's happening, but the information is all there. Many data servers don't provide this level of diagnostic access or insight into their operations. Instead, they force administrators to rely on the vendor and its support organization (via paid contracts!) to "work their magic" when problems arise. Not so with IDS—you have the tools you need to do your job. That said, I still strongly encourage you to purchase an IBM support contract on your IDS environment. You will want to master the basics, but you may not have the time to devote to learning all the intricacies of the data server. The support organization can help you quickly solve any issue you might have so you can focus on more important tasks that add greater business value to your company.

There is one option to the **onstat** command you might find particularly handy: the -**i** flag. By executing an **onstat –i**, you put the **onstat** command in interactive mode. The shell prompt changes to reflect that **onstat** is running. At this point, you can simply enter the flags and qualifiers you need, as demonstrated in Listing 8.2. Be aware that the lower and uppercase versions of the flags perform different functions.

```
M_Prod: onstat -i

IBM Informix Dynamic Server Version 11.50.UC1
-- On-Line (Prim) -- Up 00:01:46 -- 105120 Kbytes

onstat> -p

IBM Informix Dynamic Server Version 11.50.UC1
-- On-Line (Prim) -- Up 00:01:54 -- 105120 Kbytes

Profile
dskreads   pagreads  bufreads   %cached  dskwrits  pagwrits  bufwrits  %cached
1290       1346      39396      96.73    64        393       8075      99.21

isamtot   open   start   read   write   rewrite   delete   commit   rollbk
28057     2433   3859    7923   1013    15        276      1008     0

gp_read  gp_write  gp_rewrt  gp_del   gp_alloc  gp_free  gp_curs
4        0         0         0        0         0        4


-------------------------------------------------------------------------------
onstat> -d

IBM Informix Dynamic Server Version 11.50.UC1
-- On-Line (Prim) -- Up 00:01:57 -- 105120 Kbytes

Dbspaces
address   number  flags   fchunk  nchunks  pgsize  flags  owner      name
45d757f8 1        0x40001 1       1        2048    N  B   informix   rootdbs
45e3d8c8 2        0x40001 2       1        2048    N  B   informix   data_space_1
    .
    .
    .

6 active, 2047 maximum

Chunks
address   chunk/dbs  offset  size    free    bpages  flags  pathname
45d75958 1      1    0       40000   12985           PO-B   root_space
45e2bc30 2      2    0       50000   48528           PO-B   data1
    .
    .
    .

6 active, 32766 maximum
```

Listing 8.2: Using the onstat utility in interactive mode (part 1 of 2)

```
dataskip is OFF for all dbspaces

----------------------------------------------------------------------
onstat> -g glo

IBM Informix Dynamic Server Version 11.50.UC1
-- On-Line (Prim) -- Up 00:02:14 -- 105120 Kbytes

MT global info:
sessions  threads   vps   lngspins
0         33        18    0

          sched calls    thread switches   yield 0    yield n    yield forever
total:    1691554        8642              1683331    1444       4344
per sec:  0              0                 0          0          0

Virtual processor summary:
  class     vps      usercpu   syscpu    total
  cpu       1        5.59      0.51      6.10
  aio       12       0.00      0.00      0.00
  lio       1        0.00      0.00      0.00
  pio       1        0.00      0.00      0.00
  adm       1        0.00      0.01      0.01
  soc       1        0.00      0.00      0.00
  msc       1        0.00      0.00      0.00
  total     18       5.59      0.52      6.11

Individual virtual processors:
  vp    pid      class     usercpu   syscpu    total     Thread    Eff
  1     3454     cpu       5.59      0.51      6.10      10.93     55%
  2     3455     adm       0.00      0.01      0.01      0.00      0%
  3     3456     lio       0.00      0.00      0.00      0.00      0%
  4     3457     pio       0.00      0.00      0.00      0.00      0%
  .
  .
  .
          tot            5.59      0.52      6.11
```

Listing 8.2: Using the onstat utility in interactive mode (part 2 of 2)

Because the **onstat** command is already running and attached to the instance's shared memory, the response to commands entered will be almost instantaneous. All the **onstat** command flags are available in this mode, including the -r *seconds* flag, which will repeat the command every *n* seconds as entered. There is another option, **-rz** *seconds*, available only in this mode. This command combines the "repeat every *n* seconds" option with the "zero statistics" option to repeat the command at the specified interval and to zero out the statistical counters between each iteration of the command.

The repeat flag is also commonly used to monitor statistics during a set of operations or to try and determine session or instance resource changes. As you would expect, if you want to repeat the **-u** (print user threads) flag every five seconds to see what user sessions are connected to the instance, you would execute the command **onstat -u -r 5**. Press **Ctrl-c** to interrupt the repeating command. Press **Ctrl-d** to exit the interactive mode interface.

Looking at User Threads

One of your most common tasks will be to determine what any given user thread is doing and what resources it is taking to complete its tasks. Listing 8.3 shows the output of the **onstat -u** command, which outputs all the active sessions and their IDs, the first step in looking at a specific user session and the threads associated with it.

```
M_Prod: onstat -u

IBM Informix Dynamic Server Version 11.50.UC1
-- On-Line -- Up 00:40:42 -- 105120 Kbytes

Userthreads
address    flags    sessid  user      tty  wait      tout locks  nreads  nwrites
45dfd018   ---P--D  1       informix  -    0         0    0      36      76
45dfd5f0   ---P--F  0       informix  -    0         0    0      0       131
45dfdbc8   ---P--F  0       informix  -    0         0    0      0       0
45dfe1a0   ---P--F  0       informix  -    0         0    0      0       0
45dfe778   ---P--F  0       informix  -    0         0    0      0       0
45dfed50   ---P--F  0       informix  -    0         0    0      0       0
45dff328   ---P--F  0       informix  -    0         0    0      0       0
45dff900   ---P--F  0       informix  -    0         0    0      0       0
45dffed8   ---P--F  0       informix  -    0         0    0      0       0
45e004b0   ---P---  5       informix  -    0         0    0      0       0
45e00a88   ---P--B  6       informix  -    0         0    0      0       0
45e01060   Y--P--D  20      informix  -    440a7e1c  0    0      0       0
45e01638   ---P---  19      informix  -    0         0    2      394     196
45e01c10   ---P--D  10      informix  -    0         0    0      0       0
45e021e8   ---P---  18      informix  -    0         0    2      608     205
45e027c0   ---P---  17      informix  -    0         0    1      169     2
45e02d98   Y--P---  220     carlton   2    46d60798  0    1      0       0
   17 active, 128 total, 25 maximum concurrent
```

Listing 8.3: Output generated by the onstat –u command

One of the key pieces of information in the output shown in this listing is the **sessid** number listed in the third major column. These session ID numbers correspond to session identification numbers and can be used as parameters to query for additional information about a specific session and its threads. Obtaining these details requires using the **-g** flag with extra parameters. In this case, because we're interested in session-related information, we would use the flags **-g ses** *sessid*, replacing *sessid* with a valid user session ID as appropriate. For example, to see what the user ID **carlton** is doing in the session 220, we would execute the command **onstat -g ses 220**. This command would produce a result set like that shown in Listing 8.4.

```
IBM Informix Dynamic Server Version 11.50.UC1
-- On-Line -- Up 00:47:45 -- 105120 Kbytes

session              effective                   #RSAM    total    used     dynamic
id       user        user     tty  pid  hostname threads  memory   memory   explain
220      carlton     -        2    3549 nichole  1        73728    67240    off


tid      name      rstcb     flags     curstk    status
60       sqlexec   45e02d98  Y--P---   5680      cond wait  netnorm   -

Memory pools     count 2
name        class addr      totalsize freesize #allocfrag #freefrag
22          V     46e72020  69632     4056     138        3
22*00       V     46e5b020  4096      2432     1          1

name             free      used          name           free       used
overhead         0         3328          scb            0          96
opentable        0         2808          filetable      0          536
blobio           0         5080          log            0          12064
temprec          0         1632          blob           0          488
keys             0         160           ralloc         0          14168
gentcb           0         1208          ostcb          0          2632
sqscb            0         14368         sql            0          40
rdahead          0         832           hashfiletab    0          280
osenv            0         1624          buft_buffer    0          2144
sqtcb            0         2616          fragman        0          1048
sapi             0         40

sqscb info
scb        sqscb     optofc  pdqpriority sqlstats optcompind  directives
46e83018 46ec4018 0         0           0        2           1

Sess      SQL        Current      Iso Lock       SQL  ISAM F.E.
Id        Stmt type  Database     Lvl Mode       ERR  ERR  Vers Explain
220       SELECT     stores       LC  3          0    0    9.24 Off

Current statement name : slctcur

Current SQL statement :
    select * from catalog a, manufact b where a.manu_code = b.manu_code

Last parsed SQL statement :
    select * from catalog a, manufact b where a.manu_code = b.manu_code
```

Listing 8.4: Output generated by the "onstat –g ses 220" command

From the information in these results, we can tell that, among other things, this session is running a **select** statement, most likely from the **dbaccess** utility. I know this because the **F.E. Vers** (Front End Version) column has a valid value that does not match any of the Informix tools or client connectivity drivers. This value does correspond to a valid IDS release number, though, and reflects, to the best of my knowledge, the last time the **dbaccess** utility was revised within IDS.

The isolation level (**Iso Lvl** column) has been set to **last committed**, but you can't tell from this column whether it's in **dirty** or **committed read**. The fact that the lock mode is also set to wait for 3 seconds if necessary implies that the isolation mode is most likely set to **committed read**.

You can also see statistics about the virtual memory the session is using, as well as the type, state, and thread ID of the actual thread handling the request.

Many times, however, you're going to be interested only in the SQL statement being executed by a thread instead of all the statistical information about the session. Perhaps the session is showing a high number of reads or writes, or it's dying unexpectedly. In this case, use the **-g sql** *sessid* flags. The resulting output shows only the SQL-related information, as illustrated in Listing 8.5, which shows the results of running **onstat** with these flags against session number 772. In this case, you can tell that the front-end application is IBM Informix 4GL and that some debugging is occurring because the **set explain on** functionality has been enabled.

```
IBM Informix Dynamic Server Version 11.50.UC1
-- On-Line -- Up 01:07:02 -- 105120 Kbytes

Sess    SQL          Current     Iso Lock    SQL  ISAM F.E.
Id      Stmt type    Database    Lvl Mode    ERR  ERR  Vers  Explain
772     SELECT       system      LC  Not Wait  0    0   7.3    On

Current statement name : i00002180_0102af82

Current SQL statement :
  SELECT aothd.assg_prio, aothd.lhty_id, aothd.rpln_mthd, aothd.wust_id,
aothd.mpp_id, COUNT(*) FROM aothd WHERE aothd.dc_id = 1 AND
aothd.whse_id = 4 AND aothd.rtime_flg = 'Y' AND aothd.wust_id IN
('ASG','ABN','AVL','CMT','BSR','BSY') AND aothd.lhty_id IS NOT NULL
GROUP BY wust_id, lhty_id, rpln_mthd, assg_prio, mpp_id

Last parsed SQL statement :
  SELECT aothd.assg_prio, aothd.lhty_id, aothd.rpln_mthd, aothd.wust_id,
aothd.mpp_id, COUNT(*) FROM aothd WHERE aothd.dc_id = 1 AND
aothd.whse_id = 4 AND aothd.rtime_flg = 'Y' AND aothd.wust_id IN
('ASG','ABN','AVL','CMT','BSR','BSY') AND aothd.lhty_id IS NOT NULL
GROUP BY wust_id, lhty_id, rpln_mthd, assg_prio, mpp_id
```

Listing 8.5: Output generated by the "onstat –g sql 772" command

With the session ID and shared memory address listed in the first column of the result set produced by an **onstat -u** command, you can track locks (**-k**); latches (**-s**, lower case); transactions (**-x**); buffer usage (**-X**); active, ready, and waiting threads (**-g act**, **-g rea**, **-g wai**, respectively); and other items of interest for a specific user thread in the instance.

Disk and Chunk Information

As you learned in Chapter 3, one of the more important tasks when deciding on the physical implementation of the logical database design is to balance disk I/O. You need to fragment or distribute your tables in such a way as to prevent the instance from becoming disk-bound either from the sheer volume of reads or writes or from having too many tables or table fragments located on too few drives, causing waits to occur. To monitor for these types of hot spots, you need to be able to look at disk access statistics.

The **onstat -d** command is handy to use when you want to view the overall disk configuration for the instance. It does not, however, provide the type of information you need to monitor the I/O load within the instance. Three other **onstat** command flags do provide that type of information. The first one is **onstat -D**. Listing 8.6 contains some sample output generated by this command.

```
IBM Informix Dynamic Server Version 11.50.UC1
-- On-Line -- Up 01:17:20 -- 105120 Kbytes

Dbspaces
address   number flags   fchunk  nchunks  pgsize  flags  owner      name
45d757f8  1       0x40001 1       1        2048    N  B   informix   rootdbs
45e3d8c8  2       0x40001 2       1        2048    N  B   informix   data_space_1
45e3da28  3       0x40001 3       1        2048    N  B   informix   queue_space
45e3db88  4       0x42001 4       1        2048    N  TB  informix   work_space
45e3dce8  5       0x48001 5       1        2048    N  SB  informix   smart_space_1
45e3de48  6       0x48001 6       1        2048    N  SB  informix   er_sbspace
  6 active, 2047 maximum

Chunks
address   chunk/dbs     offset      page Rd  page Wr  pathname
45d75958  1     1       0           1203     664      root_space
45e2bc30  2     2       0           238      0        data1
45e2be00  3     3       0           3        0        queuespace
45d75b70  4     4       0           1        4        tmpspace
45d75d40  5     5       0           11       0        slobspace
4676e018  6     6       0           11       0        ersbspace
  6 active, 32766 maximum
```

Listing 8.6: Output generated by the onstat –D command

Unfortunately, nothing exciting was occurring in the instance when I executed command. Although some of the information shown in the figure is the same as that created with the **onstat -d** command, the **-D** flag also displays pages read (**page Rd**) and written (**page Wr**) at a chunk level. This information is particularly helpful when a dbspace has more than one chunk allocated to it. As with all the other instance's statistical counters, you can reset these values to zero by executing an **onstat -z** (lower case) command if necessary.

The second command to use when monitoring disk I/O is **onstat -g iof**. As Listing 8.7 shows, this command displays total disk operations rather than pages read or written. In IDS 11, this command's output is significantly enhanced to provide additional statistical information, including average I/O times, I/Os per second, and more.

```
IBM Informix Dynamic Server Version 11.50.UC1
-- On-Line -- Up 01:19:09 -- 105120 Kbytes

AIO global files:
gfd pathname        bytes read page reads  bytes write  page writes io/s
3   root_space      2463744    1203         1359872      664         223.5
        op type     count      avg. time
        seeks       0          N/A
        reads       0          N/A
        writes      0          N/A
        kaio_reads  923        0.0048
        kaio_writes 166        0.0029

4   data1           487424     238          0            0           592.5
        op type     count      avg. time
        seeks       0          N/A
        reads       0          N/A
        writes      0          N/A
        kaio_reads  221        0.0017
        kaio_writes 0          N/A

5   queuespace      6144       3            0            0           110.4
        op type     count      avg. time
        seeks       0          N/A
        reads       0          N/A
        writes      0          N/A
        kaio_reads  3          0.0091
        kaio_writes 0          N/A

6   tmpspace        2048       1            8192         4           114.0
        op type     count      avg. time
        seeks       0          N/A
        reads       1          0.0239
        writes      3          0.0037
        kaio_reads  0          N/A
        kaio_writes 0          N/A
```

Listing 8.7: Output generated by the "onstat –g iof" command (part 1 of 2)

```
 7    slobspace        22528     11       0        0       132.5
         op type       count    avg. time
         seeks         0        N/A
         reads         0        N/A
         writes        0        N/A
         kaio_reads    11       0.0075
         kaio_writes   0        N/A

 8    ersbspace        22528     11       0        0       160.9
         op type       count    avg. time
         seeks         0        N/A
         reads         0        N/A
         writes        0        N/A
         kaio_reads    11       0.0062
         kaio_writes   0        N/A
```

Listing 8.7: Output generated by the "onstat –g iof" command (part 2 of 2)

Last, you can also monitor the load of the I/O-oriented virtual processors and either add or delete VPs as necessary by using the **onstat -g iov** command. Listing 8.8 shows sample output produced by this command.

```
IBM Informix Dynamic Server Version 11.50.UC1
-- On-Line -- Up 01:22:04 -- 105120 Kbytes

AIO I/O vps:
class/vp s  io/s totalops dskread dskwrite  skcopy wakeups  io/wup errors
   kio  0 i   0.3    1335    1169      166       0    3382     0.4      0        0
   msc  0 i   0.0      17       0        0       0      12     1.4      0       17
   aio  0 i   0.0     133      15       54       0     122     1.1      0        5
   aio  1 i   0.0       2       0        0       0       7     0.3      0        0
   aio  2 i   0.0      16       0       15       0      18     0.9      0       15
   aio  3 i   0.0       1       0        0       0       2     0.5      0        0
   aio  4 i   0.0       1       0        0       0       2     0.5      0        0
   aio  5 i   0.0       1       0        0       0       2     0.5      0        0
   aio  6 i   0.0       1       0        0       0       2     0.5      0        0
   aio  7 i   0.0       1       0        0       0       2     0.5      0        0
   aio  8 i   0.0       1       0        0       0       2     0.5      0        0
   aio  9 i   0.0       1       0        0       0       1     1.0      0        0
   aio 10 i   0.0       0       0        0       0       1     0.0      0        0
   aio 11 i   0.0       0       0        0       0       1     0.0      0        0
   pio  0 i   0.0       0       0        0       0       1     0.0      0        0
   lio  0 i   0.0       0       0        0       0       1     0.0      0        0
```

Listing 8.8: Output generated by the "onstat –g iov" command

In this case, there are a high number of AIO VPs to support MACH-11 functionality and the processing of log records. They aren't very active because the additional instances weren't busy when I executed the command.

Using these three **onstat** commands, you can look at the volume of data reads and writes as well as total disk activity for any given chunk about which you're concerned. Potential disk bottlenecks are pretty easy to spot.

A number of factors can have an impact on these statistics. For example, continued monitoring of chunk activity levels might indicate that most of the activity to the chunk in question occurs during once-a-week data loads, aggregation, and **update statistics** activity. As such, the apparent lopsidedness in the values displayed may not be as serious as originally thought. The best way to know would be to reset the statistical counters and monitor the instance's activity throughout a normal workload. Based on what you see, database reorganization, such as separation of indexes from tables, can take place if warranted.

Another command that could be of interest when monitoring disk activity is **onstat -C** (upper case). As displayed in Listing 8.9, the output from this command shows the number of backlogged index deletions. At the moment in time the output displayed in the figure was generated, all the indexes were clean.

```
IBM Informix Dynamic Server Version 11.50.UC1
-- On-Line -- Up 01:48:25 -- 105120 Kbytes

Btree Cleaner Info
BT scanner profile Information
=================================
Active Threads                          1
Global Commands                   2000000    Building hot list
Number of partition scans              74
Main Block                     0x465d9e58
BTC Admin                      0x45e00a88

BTS info      id   Prio    Partnum      Key    Cmd
0x465e6ac0     0   High    0x00000000    0      40  Yield N
    Number of leaves pages scanned                    0
    Number of leaves with deleted items               0
    Time spent cleaning (sec)                         0
    Number of index compresses                        0
    Number of deleted items                           0
    Number of index range scans                       0
    Number of index leaf scans                        0
    Number of index alice scans                       0
```

Listing 8.9: Output generated by the onstat –C command

General Instance Monitoring

When it comes to monitoring the general health and performance of an instance, it's difficult to draw an imaginary cutoff and say that flags 1, 2, and 7 are important enough to cover in this chapter while others are not. Depending on your situation, any number of flag options could be more important to run than the three I will mention here. That said, the flags explained here are fairly important, and you should use them on some sort of a regular basis for all instances.

The first command, **onstat -g seg**, displays general shared memory statistics. As Listing 8.10 illustrates, this command shows the two portions of shared memory (resident and virtual), the size of each segment, and the number of free blocks for each segment.

```
IBM Informix Dynamic Server Version 11.50.UC1
-- On-Line -- Up 00:10:19 -- 105120 Kbytes

Segment Summary:
id          key        addr       size       ovhd      class blkused  blkfree
65537       52bd4801   44000000   28999680   391964    R     7076     4
98306       52bd4802   45ba8000   78643200   461936    V     4580     14620
Total:      -          -          107642880  -         -     11656    14624

     (* segment locked in memory)
```

Listing 8.10: Output generated by the "onstat –g seg" command

It's important to monitor the number of virtual shared memory segments allocated within an instance. This is the portion used to support end-user threads, and its efficiency decreases with each new segment allocation. If you see two or more segments of virtual shared memory during the normal processing cycle, try to consolidate the segments with the **onmode -F** command. If that doesn't free up the additional segment(s), at the next maintenance period increase the value of **SHMVIRTSIZE** to whatever the total value of the virtual shared memory segments are, and restart the instance. Be sure to check the value of **SHMTOTAL** as well to make sure the new value for **SHMVIRTSIZE** does not cause a conflict.

IDS 11 adds functionality that can make monitoring instance memory somewhat pro-active. In earlier versions, IDS allocated a new portion of memory reactively when the current portions were full. The **SHMVIRT_ALLOCSEG** parameter has two parts to it. The first part triggers when a new portion of virtual memory is allocated and can be either a percentage of allocated memory used (within a range of .40 to .99) or the number of unused kilobytes left in the instance (range 256 to 1,000,000. The second part of the parameter is the alarm raised to the **SYSALARMPROGRAM** when a new allocation is made. The values for this part of the parameter range from *0* (zero) for "not noteworthy" to *5* for "fatal."

The default for this parameter is **0,3**. With a **0** (zero) in the first part, the parameter is disabled and additional virtual memory allocation occurs in legacy mode. You could set **SHMVIRT_ALLOCSEG** to **.85,3**, in which case the instance will make an additional allocation when 85 percent of the existing allocations are being used, and an "attention" alarm will be raised. You could also set the parameter to **512,4** to have the instance allocate a new portion when only 512 KB of free memory remains. An "emergency" alarm will be raised.

For more information about this and other **$ONCONFIG** parameters, see the *IBM Informix Dynamic Server Administrator's Reference* that accompanied your distribution of the software.

The second command you should run on a regular basis is **onstat -R**. As shown in Listing 8.11, this command generates statistics about the use of the LRU queues.

```
Buffer pool page size: 2048

8 buffer LRU queue pairs                    priority levels
# f/m   pair total    % of    length    LOW      HIGH
 0 f      1250        89.0%     1113     1104        9
 1 m                  11.0%      137       79       58
 2 f      1250        90.6%     1132     1119       13
 3 m                   9.4%      118       68       50
 4 f      1250        90.0%     1125     1112       13
 5 m                  10.0%      125       76       49
 6 f      1250        89.8%     1122     1113        9
 7 m                  10.2%      128       75       53
 8 F      1250        90.0%     1125     1108       17
 9 m                  10.0%      125       76       49
10 f      1250        90.0%     1125     1115       10
11 m                  10.0%      125       77       48
12 f      1250        91.3%     1141     1128       13
13 m                   8.7%      109       67       42
14 f      1250        89.8%     1123     1109       14
15 m                  10.2%      127       82       45
994 dirty, 10000 queued, 10000 total, 16384 hash buckets, 2048 buffer size
start clean at  80.000% (of pair total) dirty, or 1000 buffs dirty, stop
at  70.000%
```

Listing 8.11: LRU queue information generated by an onstat –R command

Unfortunately, nothing terribly interesting was occurring in the instance at the time I captured this snapshot, but you can see that LRU queues come in pairs and contain all the shared memory buffers specified by the **BUFFERPOOL** parameter in the **$ONCONFIG** file. In each LRU queue pair, there is a separate line for those buffers classified as "free" and another for those classified as "modified." New or modified data to write out to disk is stored in the modified portion of the LRU queues for processing by the page cleaners. Several conditions can trigger the writing of this data out to disk, including checkpoints and tripping the **LRU_MAX_DIRTY** parameter defined in the **$ONCONFIG** file.

Depending on the condition that triggers the write to disk, the write will be handled more or less efficiently as far as the instance is concerned. Writes caused by the LRU queues filling and triggering the **LRU_MAX_DIRTY** parameter, although not the least efficient, are not the most efficient way to flush data to disk. As a result, you should run this command periodically during heavy database activity to see how full the queues become. You should always expect some LRU writes to occur, but if the percentage of buffers in the "dirty" queues constantly exceeds the "start clean at" percentage (the **LRU_MAX_DIRTY** configuration parameter), you should probably increase the number of LRU queues and/or buffers.

Enhancements to the data server in IDS 11 help make constant monitoring and tuning of the LRU queues a nonissue. I strongly recommend enabling parameters **AUTO_AIOVPS**, **AUTO_CKPTS**, and **AUTO_LRU_TUN-ING** in addition to setting **LRU_MIN_DIRTY** and **LRU_MAX_DIRTY** to **70** and **80**, respectively.

You can monitor the efficiency of disk write operations using the **onstat -F** (upper case) command. This command returns the number of foreground, LRU, and chunk writes that have occurred since the statistics were reset to 0 (zero). If foreground writes (the least-efficient kind of write operation) are occurring on a regular basis, you'll need to do additional monitoring of operations to see what is causing such an overload within the instance. From there, you'll be able to make the necessary configuration or application changes.

The third command I'll cover in this section is **onstat -g glo**. Listing 8.12 shows a portion of the output generated by this command.

```
MT global info:
sessions threads  vps  lngspins
0        34       18   5

          sched calls thread switches yield 0   yield n   yield forever
total:    1702896     38503           1664868   19750     10224
per sec:  36          36              0         33        0
```

Listing 8.12: Output produced by the "onstat –g glo" command (part 1 of 2)

```
Virtual processor summary:
 class      vps      usercpu   syscpu     total
 cpu         1       9.77      0.97       10.74
 aio        12       0.04      0.05        0.09
 lio         1       0.00      0.00        0.00
 pio         1       0.00      0.00        0.00
 adm         1       0.00      0.02        0.02
 soc         1       0.01      0.03        0.04
 msc         1       0.00      0.00        0.00
 total      18       9.82      1.07       10.89

Individual virtual processors:
 vp   pid     class   usercpu  syscpu   total    Thread   Eff
 1    3498    cpu      9.77     0.97     10.74    17.38    61%
 2    3499    adm      0.00     0.02     0.02     0.00     0%
 3    3500    lio      0.00     0.00     0.00     0.00     0%
 .
 .
 .
 18   3515    aio      0.00     0.00     0.00     0.00     0%
              tot      9.82     1.07     10.89
```

Listing 8.12: Output produced by the "onstat –g glo" command (part 2 of 2)

This command displays information about the instance's virtual processors as well as the multithreading counters. From the top section of the sample command output, you can see the number of individual sessions (including administrative and overhead sessions initiated by the data server itself) connected to the instance and the number of spawned threads. In this case, there are 34 active threads, although no end-user sessions are connected. The thread count reflects administrative and other overhead as well as support for the MACH-11 instance connections that were active when the command was executed.

The next section of the output provides a summary of how much physical CPU time each VP class has logged and what amount of that time was spent executing overhead or system functions versus user-oriented tasks. This information is followed by a detailed accounting of the physical CPU time for each VP. As with the other commands, you should monitor the workload of each VP class and tune if appropriate.

Of particular interest is the load on the CPU VPs. If the instance is configured to use multiple CPU VPs, monitor periodically to ensure all are fairly well load-balanced as far as physical processor time is concerned. If, for example, you should see that a CPU VP isn't logging much processor time, it would indicate that perhaps you could drop one CPU VP dropped from the instance without too much of a negative impact on performance.

Database Integrity Reports: The oncheck Utility

Because I think I'm a better database administrator than Dynamic Server Administrator, I have a greater affinity for the **oncheck** utility than for the **onstat** utility. Just as the **onstat** utility enables you to look inside an instance and check its configuration and status, the **oncheck** utility lets you look inside a database or table for configuration and status information. Unlike the **onstat** utility's interaction with the instance, which is read-only, there are options in the **oncheck** utility that let you make changes or repairs to database structures. This repair mechanism is limited to index structures only, however.

As Listing 8.13 shows, there are fewer command flags to the **oncheck** utility. They are grouped into two distinct action categories.

```
USAGE: oncheck {-cCheckOption | -pPrintOption} [ -y | -n ] [ -q ]
               [ { database[:[owner.]table[,fragdbs|#index] ] |
               TBLspace number | Chunk number }
               { rowid | page number } ] [ # pgs ] [ -h ]

FLAG    DESCRIPTION
-c      CheckOption
   r       Reserved pages
   R       Reserved pages including logical and physical logs
   e       Extents
   c       Database catalogs
              [database]
   i       Table indexes
              database[:[owner.]table[#index]]
   I       Table indexes and rowids in index
              database[:[owner.]table[#index]]
   x       Place share lock on table during index check
   d       Tablespace data rows including bitmaps
              database[:[owner.]table[,fragdbs]]
   D       Tablespace data rows including bitmaps, remainder pages & BLOBs
              database[:[owner.]table[,fragdbs]]
   s       SBLOBspace metadata partitions
   S       SBLOBspace metadata partitions and LO extents

-p      PrintOption
   r       Reserved pages (-cr)
   R       Reserved pages including logical and physical logs (-cR)
   e       Extents report (-ce)
   c       Catalog report (-cc) [database]
   k       Keys in index (-ci)
              database[:[owner.]table[#index]]
   K       Keys and rowids in index (-cI)
              database[:[owner.]table[#index]]
   l       Leaf node keys only (-ci)
              database[:[owner.]table[#index]]
```

Listing 8.13: Flag options for the oncheck command (part 1 of 2)

L	Leaf node keys and rowids (-cI)	
	database[:[owner.]table[#index]]	
x	Place share lock on table during index check	
d	Tablespace data rows (-cd)	
	database[:[owner.]table[,fragdbs]] [rowid]	
	or TBLspacenum [logical_pagenum]	
D	Tablespace data rows including bitmaps, remainder pages & BLOBs (-cD)	
	database[:[owner.]table[,fragdbs]] [page number]	
	or TBLspacenum [logical_pagenum]	
t	Tablespace report	
	database[:[owner.]table[,fragdbs]]	
T	Tablespace disk utilization report	
	database[:[owner.]table[,fragdbs]]	
p	Dump page for the given [table[,fragdbs] and rowid |	
	table[%fragpart] and rowid | TBLspace and page number]	
	{[# pgs] [-h]}	
P	Dump page for the given chunk number and page number	
	[chunknum and pagenum] {[# pgs] [-h]}	
B	BLOBspace utilization for given table(s)	
	database[:[owner.]table[,fragdbs]]	
s	SBLOBspace metadata partitions	
S	SBLOBspace metadata partitions and LO extents	
-q	Quiet mode - print only error messages	
-n	Answer NO to all questions	
-y	Answer YES to all questions	

Listing 8.13: Flag options for the oncheck command (part 2 of 2)

Similar to the **onstat** utility, each of **oncheck**'s command flags is explained in detail in the *IBM Informix Dynamic Server Administrator's Reference*, including a description of the multifaceted nature of the utility. By that I mean the ability to check, repair, or simply generate a report. The fact that you can use this utility to perform three different types of functions explains why there are two major category flags: **-c** (lower case) for "check and possibly repair" and **-p** (also lower case) for "print." Both of these categories share a number of identical subflags.

As with the **onstat** utility, it is difficult to arbitrarily decide which flags are more or less important and should be covered here, but given that the focus of this chapter is oriented more toward monitoring than troubleshooting, I'll focus on a couple of flags that best illustrate the reporting functionality of this utility.

Instance Reserved Pages

The first command, **oncheck -pr**, checks and prints out the entire contents of the reserved pages in an instance's rootdbs. Because these pages contain reference information about each physical chunk in the instance, you should run this command for each of your instances and save the output somewhere as part of your disaster recovery plan. Listing 8.14 contains a heavily abridged copy of what is generated.

```
M_Prod: oncheck -pr

Validating IBM Informix Dynamic Server reserved pages

    Validating PAGE_PZERO...

    Identity                        IBM Informix Dynamic Ser
                                    ver Copyright(C) 2001-20
                                    07  IBM Informix Softwar
    Database system state           0
    Database system flags           0x2
    Page Size                       2048 (b)
    Date/Time created               01/16/2008 14:53:49
    Version number of creator       16
    Last modified time stamp        0
    Index Page Logging              ON since 01/16/2008 15:14:17
    HA Disk Owner                   mproduction


    ------------------------------------------------------------------
    Validating PAGE_CONFIG...

    ROOTNAME                        rootdbs
    ROOTPATH                        root_space
    ROOTOFFSET                      0 (k)
    ROOTSIZE                        80000 (k)
    MIRROR                          0
    MIRRORPATH
      .
      .
      .
    PHYSDBS                         rootdbs
    PHYSFILE                        20000 (k)
    LOGFILES                        5
    LOGSIZE                         4000 (k)
    MSGPATH                         /opt/IBM/informix/logs/mproduction.log
    CONSOLE                         /dev/null
    TAPEDEV                         /opt/IBM/informix/backups/
      .
      .
      .
    DBSERVERNAME                    mproduction
    SERVERNUM                       103
    DEADLOCK_TIMEOUT                60 (s)
    RESIDENT                        0
    LOCKS                           50000
    BUFFERPOOL
```

Listing 8.14: Highly abridged output from the oncheck –pr command (part 1 of 4)

```
size=2K,buffers=10000,lrus=8,lru_min_dirty=70.000000,lru_max_dirty=80.000000
```

```
    Validating PAGE_1CKPT & PAGE_2CKPT...
        Using check point page PAGE_2CKPT.

    Time stamp of checkpoint        0x8e1b7
    Time of checkpoint              03/22/2008 22:56:27
    Physical log begin address      1:263
    Physical log size               10000 (p)
    Physical log position at Ckpt   7155
    Logical log unique identifier   13
    Logical log position at Ckpt    0x56f018 (Page 1391, byte 24)
    Checkpoint Interval             332
    DBspace descriptor page         1:5
    Chunk descriptor page           1:6
    Mirror chunk descriptor page    1:8

    Log file number                 1
    Unique identifier               -
    Log file flags                  0x0
    Physical location               1:10263
    Log size                        2000 (p)
    Number pages used               0
    Date/Time file filled           -
    Time stamp                      -

    Log file number                 2
    Unique identifier               12
    Log file flags                  0x5       Log file in use
    &                                         Log file has been backed up
        .
        .
        .
```

```
    Validating PAGE_1DBSP & PAGE_2DBSP...
        Using DBspace page PAGE_2DBSP.

    DBspace number                  1
    DBspace name                    rootdbs
    Flags                           0x40001   No mirror chunks
    Number of chunks                1
    First chunk                     1
    Date/Time created               01/16/2008 14:53:49
    Partition table page number     14
    Pagesize (k)                    2
    Logical Log Unique Id           12
    Logical Log Position            0xc2044
    Oldest Logical Log Unique Id    13
    Last Logical Log Unique Id      -1
```

Listing 8.14: Highly abridged output from the oncheck –pr command (part 2 of 4)

```
        Time of last physical restore  03/03/2008 17:07:12
        DBspace archive status

                Archive Level             0
                Real Time Archive Began   03/04/2008 01:14:17
                Time Stamp Archive Began  479830
                Logical Log Unique Id     12
                Logical Log Position      0x11f018

        DBspace number                    2
        DBspace name                      data_space_1
        Flags                             0x40001    No mirror chunks
        Number of chunks                  1
            .
            .
            .

--------------------------------------------------------------------

        Validating PAGE_1PCHUNK & PAGE_2PCHUNK...
                Using primary chunk page PAGE_1PCHUNK.

        Chunk number                      1
        Flags                             0x30040    Chunk is online
        Chunk path                        root_space
        Chunk offset                      0 (p)
        Chunk size                        40000 (p)
        Number of free pages              12985
        DBspace number                    1

        Chunk number                      2
        Flags                             0x30040    Chunk is online
            .
            .
            .

--------------------------------------------------------------------

        Validating PAGE_1ARCH & PAGE_2ARCH...
                Using archive page PAGE_1ARCH.

        Archive Level                     0
        Real Time Archive Began           03/04/2008 01:14:17
        Time Stamp Archive Began          0x75256
        Logical Log Unique Id             12
        Logical Log Position              0x11f018

        Archive Level                     1
        Real Time Archive Began           01/27/2008 00:34:45
        Time Stamp Archive Began          0x4d6d9
        Logical Log Unique Id             10
        Logical Log Position              0xa3044
```

Listing 8.14: Highly abridged output from the oncheck –pr command (part 3 of 4)

DR Ckpt Logical Log Id	12	
DR Ckpt Logical Log Pos	0xc2044	
DR Last Logical Log Id	12	
DR Last Logical Log Page	194	
DR Last Mode Change	1	Standard to Primary mode

Listing 8.14: Highly abridged output from the oncheck –pr command (part 4 of 4)

There are actually 12 major sections in the output of this command, although several are combined and appear as the seven sections illustrated in the listing. Each section begins with the keyword "Validating" followed by a somewhat cryptic description of the information the section contains. The seven sections of the **oncheck -pr** command can be described as follows.

- *Instance creation information*—The first section of the command output provides the date and time when the instance was created as well as its default page size. Other fields here indicate whether the instance is the "primary" on the disk or is sharing the disk as a Shared Disk Secondary (SDS) instance and other MACH-11 cluster flags.

- *Instance configuration information*—This section contains a copy of almost all the information in the **$ONCONFIG** file. Should your file become corrupted, you can recover the parameter settings from the output of this command.

- *Logical log information*—This section contains checkpoint information and a complete physical description of all the logical logs created in the instance.

- *Dbspace information*—This section contains logical information about each dbspace in the instance. It does not contain any physical information, such as locations of the physical chunks that make up a dbspace; the next section stores that information. Status flags indicate whether the dbspace is mirrored and whether it is a simple or smart BLOBspace. The command also reports date, time, and creator information and the last time the dbspace was backed up.

- *Primary chunk information*—This section contains the physical information for each primary chunk in the instance. Information about chunks defined as "mirror" chunks is not included in this section. A series of status flags indicate, for example, whether the chunk is down or online, whether it is a raw or a cooked device, or whether the chunk is part of a simple or smart BLOBspace.

- *Mirror chunk information*—This section is similar to the primary chunk section, but it contains information only about chunks defined as mirror chunks. The sample output includes no information for this section because I don't have dbspaces mirrored using IDS mirroring.

- *Backup Information*—The last section of the command output contains information generated when an instance backup is created using either the **ontape** or **ON-Bar** utility. Only the backup information required to execute a complete restore to the last fully consistent serial-mode backup is maintained in these reserved pages. Included in this information is the active logical log and checkpoint-related records, as you would expect. In the sample output, the last backup completed in the instance was a level 0 backup. Although it is not required for a restore, information about the last completed level 1 backup, including the logical log information, is also stored and displayed. If a level 2 backup had been created in the instance at some moment in time, its information would be listed as well.

System Catalog Tables

Executing **oncheck -pc** checks the integrity of the system catalog tables and prints out statistical information. The command, if executed as I've just noted, will check all the real catalog tables in the instance, including overhead and regular tables within end-user–created databases. This includes the real tables in the **sysmaster** database as well as all the tables in the other **sys** databases. As I stated in Chapter 4, some tables in the **sysmaster** database are simply pointers into shared memory. As a result, quantifiable information such as number of pages allocated, number of pages used, and physical location is impossible to capture because the information does not exist. The output of the **oncheck -pc** command lists these shared memory tables, but only by table name.

Listing 8.15 reproduces a very small part of the output generated by the **oncheck -pc** command. In this illustration, I've included only the first two tables of the **sysmaster** database.

```
        Database:  sysmaster
        Owner                          informix
        Date created                   01/16/2008 14:53:53

    TBLspace sysmaster:informix.systables
        Physical Address               1:17
        Creation date                  01/16/2008 14:53:53
        TBLspace Flags                 902         Row Locking
                                                   TBLspace contains VARCHARS
                                                   TBLspace use 4 bit bit-maps
        Maximum row size               497
        Number of special columns      3
        Number of keys                 2
        Number of extents              4
        Current serial value           256
```

Listing 8.15: Highly abridged output from the oncheck –pc command (part 1 of 3)

```
        Current SERIAL8 value          1
        Current BIGSERIAL value        1
        Current REFID value            1
        Pagesize (k)                   2
        First extent size              8
        Next extent size               8
        Number of pages allocated      32
        Number of pages used           31
        Number of data pages           19
        Number of rows                 222
        Partition partnum              1048580
        Partition lockid               1048580

    Extents
         Logical Page      Physical Page       Size Physical Pages
                    0         1:20283             8            8
                    8         1:20827             8            8
                   16         1:21933             8            8
                   24         1:22483             8            8

    Index information.
         Number of indexes             2
         Data record size              497
         Index record size             2048
         Number of records             222

TBLspace sysmaster:informix.syscolumns
    Physical Address               1:18
    Creation date                  01/16/2008 14:53:53
    TBLspace Flags                 902       Row Locking
                                             TBLspace contains VARCHARS
                                             TBLspace use 4 bit bit-maps

    Maximum row size               157
    Number of special columns      1
    Number of keys                 2
    Number of extents              10
    Current serial value           1
    Current SERIAL8 value          1
    Current BIGSERIAL value        1
    Current REFID value            1
    Pagesize (k)                   2
    First extent size              8
    Next extent size               8
    Number of pages allocated      104
    Number of pages used           103
    Number of data pages           56
    Number of rows                 2488
    Partition partnum              1048581
    Partition lockid               1048581
```

Listing 8.15: Highly abridged output from the oncheck –pc command (part 2 of 3)

```
Extents
     Logical Page    Physical Page    Size Physical Pages
              0         1:20291          24          24
             24         1:21537           8           8
             32         1:21597           8           8
             40         1:21801           8           8
             48         1:22059           8           8
             56         1:22279           8           8
             64         1:22539           8           8
             72         1:21347          16          16
             88         1:21479           8           8
             96         1:21511           8           8

Index information.
     Number of indexes              2
     Data record size             157
     Index record size           2048
     Number of records           2488
```

Listing 8.15: Highly abridged output from the oncheck -pc command (part 3 of 3)

For tables or indexes that are partitioned, each table and index partition is considered separately, and information for each partition is printed out. As a result, the output from this command looks much like the tablespace report we'll look at next.

Tablespace Report

The **oncheck -pt** and **oncheck -pT** commands are similar in terms of the output they create. Both enable you to examine statistical information on a table-by-table basis within a database as opposed to an entire database (or instance, as with the **oncheck -pc** command). The difference between the two commands is that the **-pT** option includes data page usage and index level information. Another critical difference is that the **-pT** option must be able to lock the table in order to execute all its functionality. Although the lock is held only briefly, this command either blocks table access while it runs or fails if active SQL operations are executing against the table. Listing 8.16 shows the output generated by an **oncheck -pt** command on a table partitioned by expression.

```
M_Prod: oncheck -pt stores:catalog

TBLspace Report for stores:informix.catalog

Table fragment partition data_space_1 in DBspace data_space_1

     Physical Address               2:543
     Creation date                  03/22/2008 23:51:42
```

Listing 8.16: Output from the oncheck –pt command (part 1 of 4)

```
        TBLspace Flags                   d01        Page Locking
                                              TBLspace contains VARCHARS
                                              TBLspace contains TBLspace BLOBs
                                              TBLspace use 4 bit bit-maps
        Maximum row size                 377
        Number of special columns        3
        Number of keys                   0
        Number of extents                1
        Current serial value             10075
        Current SERIAL8 value            1
        Current BIGSERIAL value          1
        Current REFID value              1
        Pagesize (k)                     2
        First extent size                8
        Next extent size                 8
        Number of pages allocated        16
        Number of pages used             9
        Number of data pages             5
        Number of rows                   39
        Partition partnum                2097244
        Partition lockid                 2097244

        Extents
             Logical Page       Physical Page       Size Physical Pages
                     0             2:1864              16          16

Table fragment partition queue_space in DBspace queue_space

        Physical Address                 3:5
        Creation date                    03/22/2008 23:51:42
        TBLspace Flags                   d01        Page Locking
                                            TBLspace contains VARCHARS
                                            TBLspace contains TBLspace BLOBs
                                            TBLspace use 4 bit bit-maps
        Maximum row size                 377
        Number of special columns        3
        Number of keys                   0
        Number of extents                1
        Current serial value             1
        Current SERIAL8 value            1
        Current BIGSERIAL value          1
        Current REFID value              1
        Pagesize (k)                     2
        First extent size                8
        Next extent size                 8
        Number of pages allocated        8
        Number of pages used             7
        Number of data pages             4
        Number of rows                   35
        Partition partnum                3145730
        Partition lockid                 2097244
```

Listing 8.16: Output from the oncheck –pt command (part 2 of 4)

```
        Extents
            Logical Page      Physical Page        Size Physical Pages
                  0               3:53                8         8

Index  108_21 fragment partition data_space_1 in DBspace data_space_1

    Physical Address              2:544
    Creation date                 03/22/2008 23:51:42
    TBLspace Flags                801          Page Locking
                                               TBLspace use 4 bit bit-maps
    Maximum row size              377
    Number of special columns     0
    Number of keys                1
    Number of extents             1
    Current serial value          1
    Current SERIAL8 value         1
    Current BIGSERIAL value       1
    Current REFID value           1
    Pagesize (k)                  2
    First extent size             4
    Next extent size              4
    Number of pages allocated     4
    Number of pages used          3
    Number of data pages          0
    Number of rows                0
    Partition partnum             2097245
    Partition lockid              2097244

        Extents
            Logical Page      Physical Page        Size Physical Pages
                  0               2:1888              4         4

Index  108_22 fragment partition data_space_1 in DBspace data_space_1

    Physical Address              2:545
    Creation date                 03/22/2008 23:51:42
    TBLspace Flags                801          Page Locking
                                               TBLspace use 4 bit bit-maps
    Maximum row size              377
    Number of special columns     0
    Number of keys                1
    Number of extents             1
    Current serial value          1
    Current SERIAL8 value         1
    Current BIGSERIAL value       1
    Current REFID value           1
    Pagesize (k)                  2
    First extent size             4
    Next extent size              4
    Number of pages allocated     4
```

Listing 8.16: Output from the oncheck –pt command (part 3 of 4)

```
Number of pages used          3
Number of data pages          0
Number of rows                0
Partition partnum       2097246
Partition lockid        2097244

Extents
     Logical Page    Physical Page        Size Physical Pages
               0          2:1892              4        4
```

Listing 8.16: Output from the oncheck –pt command (part 4 of 4)

Notice that this output includes information about each of the two indexes on the table. Since IDS 9.4, index pages are no longer stored "in table" but have their own extents of space, even if created in the same dbspace(s) as the table itself. As an aside, you can tell by the index names that these were system-generated indexes created to support constraints, rather than end-user–created objects. The naming convention leaves much to be desired. As you learned in Chapter 6, if you need to create a primary, foreign, or unique constraint, you should always create the index you need first and then "promote" it to enforce the desired constraint.

The **-pT** flag produces the same type of output but includes additional storage efficiency information for each table partition. Information about the depth and breadth of index levels is included for each index as well. This information follows the general tablespace information for each partition of the table. Listing 8.17 shows an example of the table storage efficiency information followed by index-related information generated by the **oncheck -pT** command.

```
[table partition information]

TBLspace Usage Report for stores:informix.catalog

Type              Pages  Empty  Semi-Full  Full  Very-Full
----------------  -----  -----  ---------  ----  ---------
Free                  7
Bit-Map               1
Index                 0
Data (Home)           5
Data (Remainder)      0      0          0     0          0
TBLspace BLOBs        3      0          1     0          2
                  -----
Total Pages          16

Unused Space Summary

     Unused data bytes in Home pages                 2371
```

Listing 8.17: Output from the oncheck –pT command (part 1 of 2)

```
        Unused data bytes in Remainder pages              0
        Unused bytes in TBLspace Blob pages            1303

   Home Data Page Version Summary

              Version                              Count

              0 (oldest)                             4
              1 (current)                            1

[index information]

   Type                 Pages    Empty  Semi-Full  Full  Very-Full
   ----------------     ------- -------- ---------- ----- ----------
   Free                    2
   Bit-Map                 1
   Index                   1
   Data (Home)             0
                        --------
   Total Pages             4

   Unused Space Summary

        Unused data slots                       0
        Unused bytes per data page            115
        Total unused bytes in data pages        0

   Home Data Page Version Summary

              Version                              Count

              0 (current)                            0

Index Usage Report for index  108_21 on stores:informix.catalog

                     Average   Average
   Level     Total No. Keys Free Bytes
   -----   -------- -------- ----------
     1          1       74        762
   -----   -------- -------- ----------
   Total        1       74        762
```

Listing 8.17: Output from the oncheck –pT command (part 2 of 2)

With the advent of the "in-place alter" technology, IBM added another metric to the **oncheck -pT** command. In Chapter 6, I explained that with the in-place alter technology, not all rows in a table would change whenever an **alter table** SQL command was executed. Certain types of changes affect all rows in a table, but other changes affect only rows being added to or updated in the table. There could therefore very well be rows of differing schema structure within the same table, depending on the frequency of table schema changes, the types of changes made, and whether the majority of the table's rows are being updated on a regular basis. This condition is reported in the **Home Data Page Version Summary** section of the **oncheck -pT** command.

As each **alter table** command that does not immediately affect all of a table's rows is executed, this section of the **oncheck** command output will reflect the number of rows at each specific revision of the schema. As you can see from the **Home Data Page Version Summary** portion of the preceding listing (midway through the sample output), the table has, in fact, been altered, and one of the rows in the partition whose information is shown has been modified to reflect the new schema, while the others are still in the original row format.

From the time an in-place alter is executed, whenever an application updates a row, its schema is updated to reflect the most current revision of the table. You can track how quickly rows begin to reflect the new schema version by periodically re-executing the **oncheck -pT** command after having altered a table.

If, over time, you make a series of schema changes, you'd be wise at some point to force all rows in the table to reflect the latest version of the schema by executing a command such as the following:

```
update table_name
set column_name = column_name where 1 = 1
```

This command updates every row in the table, setting the value of the named column to itself. Because this operation affects each row in the table, when the operation is completed, all rows will have the most current schema version.

> Before you upgrade from one version of IDS to another, it is critical that all pages in a table have the same schema. You should execute the **oncheck -pT** to verify that all in-place alters have been fully realized before proceeding with the upgrade.

Chunk Free List and Tablespace Interleaving

The **oncheck -pe** command produces a comprehensive list of page usage in every chunk of the instance. When you use this command in combination with the **oncheck -pt** command, you can see to what degree tablespace interleaving is occurring within chunks and dbspaces. Listing 8.18 contains a small section from the middle of the output generated by the **oncheck -pe** command. The output is generated in the same order in which the chunks were created and allocated to dbspaces. Thus, the output of this command starts with the rootdbs and continues until the last chunk that was added to the instance.

```
DBspace Usage Report: data_space_1  Owner: informix  Created: 01/16/2008

Chunk Pathname                       Pagesize(k)  Size(p)  Used(p)  Free(p)
  2 /opt/IBM/Informix/devices/production/data1  2    75000    55174    19826

Description                                    Offset(p)  Size(p)
RESERVED PAGES                                        0        2
CHUNK FREELIST PAGE                                   2        1
data_space_1:'informix'.TBLSpace                     3       50
stores:'informix'.systables                         53        8
    .
    .
    .
spar:db_a.strpld_info                            15053       73
spar:db_a.afs_tables                             15126        8
spar:db_a.bad_invdts                             15134        8
spar:db_a.cal_ytd_sum                            15142    27000
spar:db_a.fisc_mth_sum                           42142    10000
spar:db_a.strpld_info                            52142        8
spar:db_a.cal_ytd_sum                            52150     1500
afs_acct:db_a.artrans_info                       53650        8
afs_acct:db_a.artrans_err                        53658        8
spar:db_a.strpld_info                            53666        8
spar:db_a.cal_ytd_sum                            53674     1500
    .
    .
    .
```

Listing 8.18: Output from the oncheck –pe command

There are a couple of items of interest in this sample output. First, the dbspace is moderately full, with approximately 20,000 pages free out of the 75,000. Second, some of the tables in the dbspace have more than one extent—specifically, the **strpld_info** and **cal_ytd_sum** tables, with three extents each. This fact is easy to determine because each line in the output of this command represents a table extent. Extents for an individual table can be different sizes depending on the growth that occurred in the table with respect to other tables in the same dbspace. If two or more tables are constantly growing and expanding, you'll see a number of interleaved but smaller-sized extents. If only one table is growing, it will have fewer (maybe only one) additional extents but they/it will be bigger.

Table and index searches occur significantly faster if there is very little or no interleaving of table or index extents in a dbspace. In fact, best practices generally indicate that when a table has more than eight interleaved extents, it should be reorganized and resized to avoid potential performance penalties that can occur as the number of extents increases. This doesn't mean you should panic if you see a table with nine or more extents, I've seen systems working successfully with mid–double-digit table interleaving. It's just not optimal from a performance perspective.

> Proper table sizing is critical to preventing inefficient table extent allocation and is discussed in the Appendix.

In some cases, when reviewing the output from this command, you'll see a table (e.g., **table_a**) with two extents but separated by a block of free pages. This usually indicates that an extent from another table (**table_b**) occupied those pages now listed as "free" when **table_a** needed to allocate another extent. When **table_b** was deleted, the dbspace space taken up by the table remained "free" because the data server does not automatically concatenate adjacent extents of the same table since it would require recalculating all the hidden row IDs stored in all the page headers and index structures.

You can rejoin all the extents of a table into (hopefully) one larger extent either by unloading the table, dropping it, re-creating it with the proper extent sizing to represent the more current projected size of the table, and reloading the data or by altering one of the indexes on the table to "cluster" mode. Altering an index to cluster mode causes a physical rearrangement of the table's rows so that they are ordered similarly to the index order. Because the table is, in effect, being repopulated, the new table extents will be concatenated as much as possible. You can, if you want, change the index back to regular mode after concatenating the extents. Leaving it in cluster mode will not affect the way the index operates or how the data is organized in the table once the cluster process has been completed.

One other option for concatenating extents, available in IDS 10 and later, is to initialize a partitioning scheme on a column but have both partitions in the same dbspace.

Verifying Data and Index Consistency and Integrity

The last two sets of commands I will cover in discussing the **oncheck** utility verify the integrity and consistency of data and index pages. The first pair, **oncheck -ci** and **oncheck -cI** (uppercase letter "I"), verify the general linkage between all nodes in the Btree index structure. The **-cI** option goes one step further and verifies that the key values stored in each index element actually match the values of the row to which the index element refers.

Unlike all the other commands I've covered in this chapter, these two commands not only generate a report but can also effect repairs if they find errors. There are, of course, conditions that must be met before either command will attempt to make these repairs. First, while any user can execute the check functionality on indexes or data discussed next, only the **informix** user account can effect repairs. Second, a shared lock must be placed on the table if it was created with page-level locking. This requirement might have an impact on end-user operations.

In situations in which one or more indexes appear to be corrupted, I tend to err on the side of caution. I've had experiences where the command indicated the index was repaired, but running a query against the index reported errors. I must admit, I have not run into a corrupt index condition for some time. Nevertheless, if one were to occur, rather than use this command I would drop the index and re-create it. This way, if the index builds, I know everything is in order within the index and the data to which it is pointing. If there was a significant amount of "data churn" in the table, the new index(es) might be more compact as well. Besides, this alternative solution takes about the same amount of time as running the repair option.

The second pair of verification commands, **oncheck –cd** and **oncheck –cD**, check the consistency of data pages within a table. The **–cD** command also reads the reference information for any BLOB columns in a table and verifies that the BLOB exists where specified in the reference information.

There are the corresponding **–pd** and **–pD** commands as well, which actually print out the consistency check information. Because of the rather significant amount of output generated, I strongly advise against using these flags if you're redirecting the output to a flat file instead of to a screen display (standard out). If the table has only a few rows, it might be okay to capture the output in a flat file; otherwise, you risk creating a file large enough to fill the file system and possibly cause other system problems. It is not worth the risk.

One additional caveat when using the **–p** flag to print the data as well as check results: You must execute the command as user **informix** or **root** on Linux/Unix/Mac OS X ports or as a member of the **Informix-Admin** group on Windows ports.

Instance and System Monitoring Through OAT

In Chapter 5, I briefly introduced the new graphical administration and reporting tool released with IDS 11, OpenAdmin Tool for IDS. Like the **onstat** and **oncheck** utilities, OAT is a powerful and diverse tool. It is impossible to cover all its functionality in just a couple of pages. You'll have to work with OAT to discover the wealth of information available through the tool.

That said, there are some additional monitoring facilities I'd like to spotlight. The first is a series of physical server and instance reports available under OAT's **System Reports** menu option (Figure 8.1).

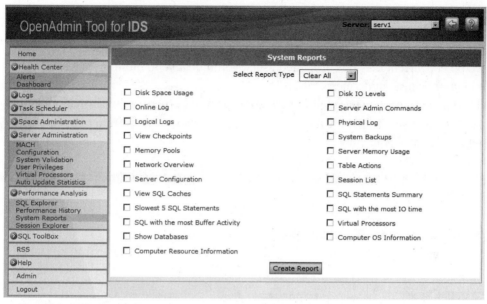

Figure 8.1: OAT's System Reports option

Of particular interest here are the **Computer Resource Information** and the **Computer OS Information** reports. The former report, whose output is illustrated in Figure 8.2, includes some long-sought-after information: the maximum instance load for the week.

Report Run 2008-03-27 01:17:26   **Server Uptime** 02:44:59

1. Computer Resource Information

Computer Resource Information

Resource Summary Report

	Max Connections	Max CPU VPS	MAX VPS	Disk Size	Disk Used	Memory	Memory Used
Average	0.75	1.0	18.0	371 MB	142 MB	102 MB	52.2 MB
Maximum	1.0	1.0	18.0	371 MB	143 MB	102 MB	69.0 MB
Minimum	0.0	1.0	18.0	371 MB	142 MB	102 MB	46.0 MB

Page 1   ALL

Resource Usage Report

For the Week Ending	Max Connections	Max CPU VPS	MAX VPS	Disk Size	Disk Used	Memory	Memory Used
2008-03-25	1	1	18	371 MB	143 MB	102 MB	47.0 MB
2008-03-18	1	1	18	371 MB	142 MB	102 MB	46.0 MB
2008-03-11	1	1	18	371 MB	142 MB	102 MB	69.0 MB
2008-04-01	0	1	18	371 MB	143 MB	102 MB	47.0 MB

Figure 8.2: Spot and rolling system and user connection information from an OAT report

This report gives you a spot session count as well CPU and memory utilization. It also provides a rolling weekly summary that will extend for at least two years. Of particular relevance is the maximum number of user sessions. If you've purchased an IDS license based on concurrent sessions or named users, you'll be able to monitor usage to stay within your license guidelines.

The latter report, illustrated in Figure 8.3, gives you kernel-level information, letting you easily compare against the release notes to see whether you need to tune the operating system for greater efficiency.

Report Run 2008-03-26 23:55:28 · · · · · **Server Uptime** 2 days 05:12:44

1. Computer OS Information

Computer OS Information

Computer Information

Host Name	gama.lenexa.ibm.com
OS Name	Linux
OS Release	2.6.9-34.ELsmp
OS Version	#1 SMP Fri Feb 24 16:56:28 EST 2006
Computer Type	x86_64
Computer Total Memory	3.85 GB
Computer Free Memory	41.0 MB
Processors	4
OS Pagesize	4096
Maximum Open Files per Process 32768	

Shared Memory Informiation

Shmmax	33554432
Shmmin	1
Shmids	4096
Shmnumsegs	2097152

Semaphore Information

Semmap	
Semids	1302004564
Semnum	15621275
Semundo	15621275
Semnumperid	250
Semops	32768
Semundoperproc	0
Semundosize	20
Semmaxvalue	32767

Figure 8.3: Operating system kernel information from an OAT report option

Additional reports of interest from this section of OAT are the five slowest SQL operations, those requiring the most I/O time, and the most active SQL operations from a buffer use perspective. The **Table Actions** report generates activity profile information for all the tables in the instance. This report includes rows processed, inserted, updated, and deleted, as well as the number of sequential scans, number of locks allocated for operations, the read and write cache percentages, and more.

Some of the reports in this section are graphical representations of simple **onstat** commands, such as the **Disk Space Usage** report (**onstat -d**), the **Logical Logs** report (**onstat -l**), the **Disk IO Levels** report (**onstat -g iof**), the **Server Memory Usage** report (**onstat -g seg**), and others.

OAT's **Session Explorer** section, shown in Figure 8.4, lets you obtain information about active sessions in the instance. You can also "kill" a session by clicking one of the lightning bolts on the far-right side of this screen.

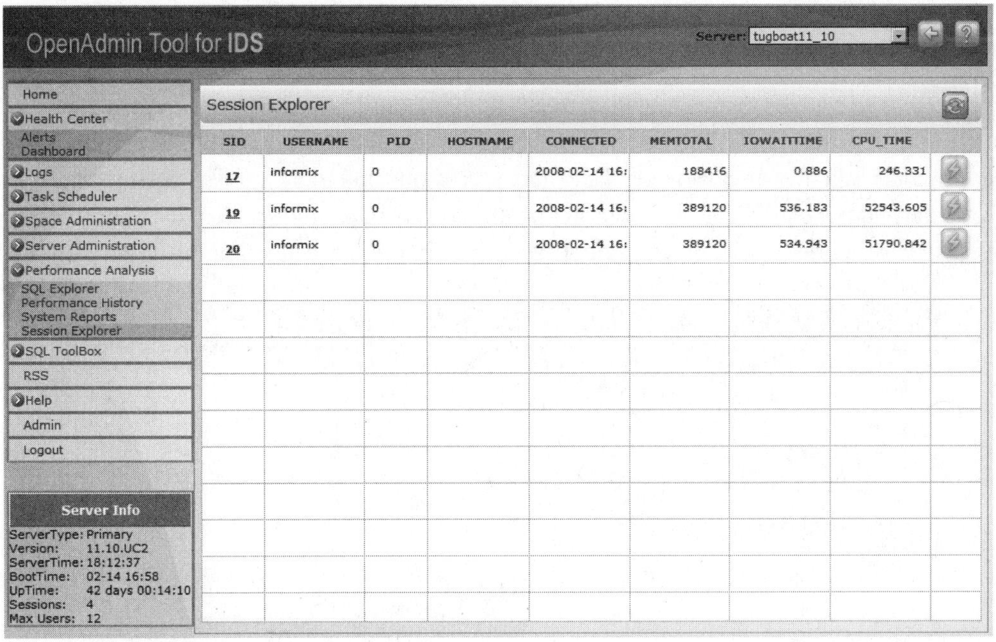

Figure 8.4: Using the Session Explorer in OAT

Click a session number to see a more detailed view of that session's activities, as illustrated in Figure 8.5. For example, you can see the SQL statements executed, locking information, the number and types of threads supporting the session, client environment information (which can, at times, affect how the session's statements are executed), and general session profile information.

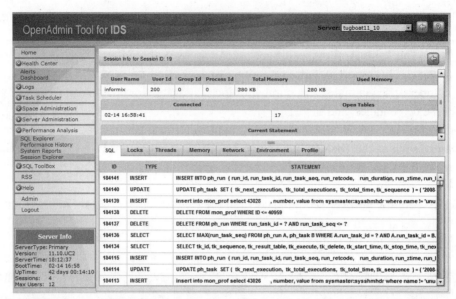

Figure 8.5: Using OAT to look at a session's activities in depth

In OAT's **Performance History** section, you can view about a month's worth of historical performance data over a wide range of categories, as shown in Figure 8.6. The default display shows the entire month's data, but you can drag the red triangles at the bottom to reduce the displayed time period, enabling you to look at more detailed information for the day(s) displayed.

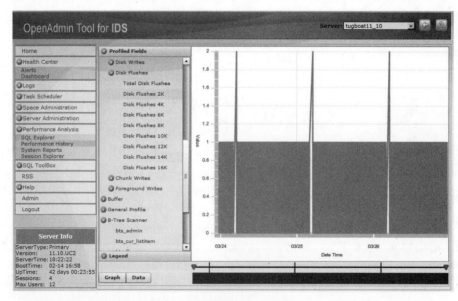

Figure 8.6: Using OAT's Performance History tool

With this brief introduction to this new IDS utility, I hope you can see that OAT is a powerful tool that can make your job easier.

Summary

In this chapter, we reviewed the two major command-line utilities for monitoring instance performance and checking the integrity of instance- and database-level database elements. Although I explained only a few of the many flags and options for each utility, the most important were covered with illustrations of the type of output each flag or option generates. You should understand the difference between the **onstat** and **oncheck** utilities and what each was designed to accomplish. Last, some of the instance monitoring capabilities in OAT were described.

As a final note, you should understand that almost all the information provided by the utilities and tools mentioned in this chapter is gathered by queries to the **sysmaster** and other **sys** databases through an interface simply called the SMI. As you continue to develop your IDS administration and maintenance skills, you'll want to explore how to access this information yourself and use it in your own shell and other homegrown utilities to meet your specific needs.

Appendix

Table Sizing Worksheets

On the Web site supporting this book, *http://www.xmission.com/~dbaresrc/foundation.html*, you'll find two Adobe Acrobat files and two Java methods you can use to determine the first and next extent sizes for tables. The "simple" sizing worksheet/method is for tables with one or more rows on a dbspace page. The "full" sizing worksheet/method is for tables where the row size exceeds the dbspace page size and you need to calculate full and partial remainder pages. Although the obvious best practice would be to move such a table to a dbspace with a larger page size, I realize this might not be possible.

Here, I briefly walk through the steps involved in properly sizing a table using both sheets. I'll start with the simple worksheet followed by the full worksheet. In both cases, you will be calculating using the dbspace page size, in kilobytes (e.g., 2 KB, 4 KB, 10 KB), as well as the actual usable data storage space on the page in bytes. Make sure you pay attention to which number is being asked for.

A couple of notes before you begin. First, calculating the length of a row will be affected by whether the table contains simple BLOB columns and whether the simple BLOBs are stored in a separate simple BLOBspace or left "in table." If the simple BLOBs are stored in a separate simple BLOBspace, all you have to factor in at this stage of the table sizing process is the size of the simple BLOB descriptor. This descriptor, which is largely invisible to you, contains information about where the BLOB is stored. It is 56 bytes in size. Use this value as the field length for any column of type **BINARY** or **TEXT**.

If the simple BLOBs are stored in table, you need to include the disk space they require in the table sizing process. To arrive at the amount of disk space required to store these simple BLOBs, perform the following calculations.

1. Calculate the usable space on the data page using the following formula (remember, the usable page size is the page size in bytes minus 28 bytes for overhead, as the table at the top of each worksheet notes):

   ```
   usable_page_size - 4 additional bytes
   ```

2. Determine the "average" BLOB size for each type of BLOB in the table. For instructions on how to perform this task, see the latter part of the "Creating Spaces" section of Chapter 5.

3. Calculate the number of pages required for the average BLOB by dividing the average BLOB size (determined in step 2) by the usable data page space (step 1) and rounding up:

   ```
   (avg_blob_size / usable_space_on_data_page)
   ```

4. Arrive at the total space required for BLOBs (in kilobytes) by performing the following calculation:

   ```
   (num_of_blobs * num_of_pages_for_avg_blob) * dbspace_size
   ```

Add the result from step 4 to the worksheet total calculated for the other columns to arrive at the total amount of disk space required to store the table's data.

Second, if you are using smart BLOBs, the BLOB descriptor is 72 bytes long. Because smart BLOBs are always stored in a separate space, you will need to calculate the size of that space separately from the rest of the table's data storage requirements.

Using the Simple Worksheet

Begin by entering the initial row count for the table on line 101.

On line 102, enter the number of rows that you anticipate this table will need to hold about six months from now. If you anticipate the table will need to hold a larger number of rows between now and then because of periodic rather than constant data purges, use that number of rows.

On line 103, calculate the size of one data row by summing the size of each column in the table and then adding 4 bytes for row overhead. If you have a column of type **varchar**, use the average length of the **varchar** column when summing column lengths. If the table contains BLOBs, either simple or smart, use the appropriate sizing guidance given at the beginning of this appendix.

On line 104, calculate the number of data rows that will fit on one data page by dividing the usable size of a data page (e.g., 4,068 bytes for a 4 KB page) by the size of a data row (line 103). Round the result down to the next largest whole number. In the event the result exceeds 255, use 255 because no more than 255 rows can be stored on a single data page.

On line 105, you calculate the amount of disk space required, in kilobytes, to store the initial number of rows. Divide the initial row volume (line 101) by the number of rows per data page (line 104). Round this interim result up to the next whole number. It represents the number of data pages you'll require to store the rows. Multiply this result by the dbspace page size (e.g., 2, 4, 10) to generate the storage size in kilobytes.

To generate the next extent size, which allocates an amount of disk space to allow for table growth over a given amount of time, follow the same type of process. Divide the number of rows to be added over time (line 102) by the number of rows per page (line 104), and then multiply by the dbspace page size; finally, divide that result by 7. This formula yields a slightly larger next extent size than is generally recommended, but it gives you a little more room to work with when dealing with a table that is growing faster than you originally anticipated. This size helps reduce the total number of table extents allocated to the table as it approaches the total number of anticipated rows stored.

The worksheet's last calculation, wasted page space, is intended to help you see whether it might be more efficient to store the table's data in a dbspace with a different page size. The idea is to maximize the storage capacity of the page while reducing the total amount of storage required. This calculation might not yield much if the row size is small; going up to a larger dbspace page size may be a moot proposition because you can store only 255 rows on a page. If the number of rows per page is much lower, though, and the amount of wasted space per page is high, try the overall sizing calculations with several different dbspace page sizes to find the best possible combination.

To derive the amount of wasted space per page, multiply the number of rows per page (line 104) by the total row length (line 103) and then subtract that product from the usable page size. This calculation will generate a result in bytes per page.

Using the Full Worksheet

The full worksheet is oriented to those tables where the row size exceeds the page size. In fact, this worksheet prompts you to use the simple worksheet should the initial calculations confirm this case to be true.

If the row length for the table in question is greater than the usable space on a data page, Informix Dynamic Server will create what are called *home* and *remainder* pages for the table within the instance's dbspaces. Any given row of the table will initially fill a home page. The remaining portion will be grouped together with other remaining portions of other rows on a series of remainder pages. To properly size a table with this type of row length, you need to calculate the number of home and remainder pages that will be required.

The first four fields of the worksheet are identical to the simple worksheet. After that, the calculations change to figure out the number of home and remainder pages. Remainder pages don't carry as much overhead as regular data pages, so the usable storage on a remainder page is slightly greater. This difference is important when calculating how many remainder pages will be required to store the rest of a row. On line 105, calculate the amount of additional remainder information to store by taking the length of the data row (line 103) and subtracting from it the value of the usable data page size plus 8 bytes.

If the resulting value is greater than the usable size of a remainder page, the row will not only fill a full home page but will also fill a complete remainder page and still have more data to store on a second remainder page. In this case, you need to calculate how many full remainder pages the table will have (line 106) as well as the number of partial remainder pages. If the value of line 105 is less than the usable space of a remainder page, you need perform only the calculations concerning partial remainder pages.

Remainder Portion Greater Than Remainder Page Size (Line 106)

To calculate the number of full remainder pages that will be required, divide the additional remainder amount (line 105) by the usable storage space of a data page minus an additional 8 bytes for overhead to point to the next remainder page.

Round the result down to a whole number, regardless of the decimal value, and then multiply it by the anticipated number of rows for the table (line 101). Enter this value on line 106, and proceed to calculate the amount of partially filled remainder pages, as explained in the next section.

Remainder Portion Less Than Remainder Page Size

First, calculate a remainder page usage ratio. You obtain this value by dividing the total row length (line 103) by the usable page size minus an additional 8 bytes. What's important here is to use the remainder of this operation—the **mod**—and add 4 bytes to it. Take the resulting value and divide it once again by the usable page size to arrive at the ratio (line 107).

For example, suppose you were calculating the remainder ratio for a row with a total row size of 7,500 bytes on a 2 KB page size dbspace. The answer would be .23:

$$[((7500 \bmod 2012) = 1464) + 4] \; / \; 2020 = .23$$

Depending on the remainder page usage ratio (line 107), calculating the number of partial remainder pages will vary. Based on line 107, use the appropriate equation in the worksheet to calculate a value for line 108.

The total amount of disk space required to store the data for the table in question will be the sum of three values:

- The number of home pages (line 101)
- The number of full remainder pages, if any (line 106)
- The number of partial remainder pages (line 108)

The resulting sum is multiplied by dbspace page size to return the value in kilobytes.

The calculation of next extent size can reuse many of the values you've already calculated. Simply use the growth row count rather than the initial row count to calculate the values for lines 109 and 110. Similar to the first extent size, the next extent size is the sum of the home rows, full remainder rows (if any), and partial remainder rows. You divide this value by 7 for the same reasons explained for the simple worksheet.

The Java methods, also available on the web site supporting this book, allow you to calculate table sizing information for more than one table at a time. There is both a "simple" and "full" Java method that calculates the results based on the same basic table information (row size, number of rows, dbspace size, etc.) you use for the worksheets explained above. For the methods though, you put this information in a flat file and use the file as a parameter when invoking the method. The methods, with their input and output files, are fully documented on the web page.

Index

Note: Boldface numbers indicate illustrations and code; *t* indicates a table.

Note: Boldface numbers indicate illustrations and code; *t* indicates a table.

409

Note: Boldface numbers indicate illustrations and code; *t* indicates a table.

415

Note: Boldface numbers indicate illustrations and code; *t* indicates a table.

Note: Boldface numbers indicate illustrations and code; *t* indicates a table.

423